*International Review of Industrial
and Organizational Psychology
1988*

International Review of Industrial and Organizational Psychology 1988

Edited by

Cary L. Cooper
and
Ivan T. Robertson

*University of Manchester
Institute of Science & Technology UK*

JOHN WILEY & SONS

Chichester · New York · Brisbane · Toronto · Singapore

Copyright © 1988 by John Wiley & Sons Ltd.

The Library of Congress has cataloged this serial publication as follows:

International review of industrial and organizational psychology.
 —1986– —Chichester; New York: Wiley, c1986–
 v.: ill.; 24 cm.
 Annual.
 ISSN 0886-1528 = International review of industrial and organizational psychology

 1.Psychology, Industrial—Periodicals. 2.Personnel management—Periodicals.
 [DNLM: 1.Organization and Administration—periodicals. 2.Psychology,
 Industrial—periodicals. W1IN832U]
 HF5548.7.I57   158.7′05—dc19   86-643874
                                  AACR 2   MARC-S
 Library of Congress   [8709]

British Library Cataloguing in Publication Data:

International Review of Industrial and Organizational Psychology 1986
 1. Psychology, Industrial
 I. Cooper, Cary L.   II. Robertson, Ivan T.
 158.7   HF5548.8

ISBN 0 471 91844 X

Phototypeset by David John Services Ltd, Slough
Printed and bound in Great Britain by
Anchor Brendon Ltd, Essex

CONTRIBUTORS

Cary L. Cooper **Editor**	*Professor of Organizational Psychology, Department of Management Sciences, University of Manchester Institute of Science & Technology, UK.*
Ivan T. Robertson **Editor**	*Senior Lecturer in Organizational Psychology, Department of Management Sciences, University of Manchester Institute of Science & Technology, UK.*
Seymour Adler	*Stevens Institute of Technology, USA.*
Clayton P. Alderfer	*School of Organization and Management, Yale University, USA.*
Michael J. Driver	*Department of Organization Behavior, Graduate School of Business Administration, University of Southern California, USA.*
Fred Fiedler	*Department of Psychology, University of Washington, USA.*
M. Jocelyne Gessner	*Department of Psychology, University of Maryland, USA.*
Irwin L. Goldstein	*Department of Psychology, University of Maryland, USA.*
Robert J. House	*Faculty of Management Studies, University of Toronto, Canada.*
Paul A. Iles	*Department of Management and Administrative Studies, Huddersfield Polytechnic, UK.*
John M. Ivancevich	*College of Business Administration, University of Houston, USA.*
Michael T. Matteson	*College of Business Administration, University of Houston, USA.*
Kevin Murphy	*Department of Psychology, Colorado State University, USA.*
Denise Rousseau	*Department of Organization Behavior, Kellogg Graduate School of Management, Northwestern University, USA.*
William H. Starbuck	*Graduate School of Business Administration, New York University, USA.*
David A. Thomas	*Wharton School, University of Pennsylvania, USA.*

Jane Webster

Howard M. Weiss

Graduate School of Business Administration, New York University, USA.

Department of Psychological Sciences, Purdue University, USA.

CONTENTS

CONTENTS

EDITORIAL FOREWORD

This third volume of the *International Review of Industrial and Organizational Psychology* contains ten chapters on leading-edge issues by outstanding academics and scholars within the industrial, occupational and organizational psychology fields.

We have attempted to extend the range of topics covered from the previous volumes, in an effort to facilitate further research in areas of existing interest and those that will blossom over the next decade. The issues reviewed in this volume are training and development in work organizations, the significance of race and ethnicity for organizational behavior, leadership theory and research, managerial assessment, the construction of climate in organizational research, theory building in industrial and organizational psychology, psychological measurement of abilities and skills, health promotion at work and personality and organizational behavior.

Topics scheduled for inclusion in the 1989 volume are:

Burnout in Work Organizations
Management and Control at Work
Causal Modelling in Industrial and Organizational Psychology
Japanese Management
Retirement: A Psychological Perspective
Cognitive Approaches to Human Behavior in Organizations
Cognitive Style and Complexity: Implications for I/O Psychology
Job Analysis
Quality Circles
Interviewing
Group Behavior at Work

CLC
ITR
August 1987

International Review of Industrial and Organizational Psychology 1988
Edited by C. L. Cooper and I. Robertson
© 1988 John Wiley & Sons Ltd

Chapter 1

THE SIGNIFICANCE OF RACE AND ETHNICITY FOR UNDERSTANDING ORGANIZATIONAL BEHAVIOR

Clayton P. Alderfer
School of Organization and Management
Yale University
USA
and
David A. Thomas
Wharton School
University of Pennsylvania
USA

INTRODUCTION

The research literature on race and ethnicity in relation to organizations exists in a form that poses a number of intriguing questions. To begin, there is a shortage of studies that directly investigate the interdependence between race and ethnicity and organizations. In contrast, the general literature on race and ethnicity is extensive. Since the turn of the century, anthropologists, sociologists and psychologists have focused a very significant proportion of their attention on race and ethnicity—often under the more general heading of intergroup relations (Van den Berghe, 1972). The comparison between the two bodies of work naturally raises the question of why so much attention has been given to race and ethnicity *outside* of organizations and why so little inside. Are race and ethnicity irrelevant to what occurs in the context of organizational behavior? Or are there other reasons why organizational behavior investigators have not devoted a substantial fraction of their time to these questions?

A further characteristic of this work is that whether one examines race and ethnicity studies inside or outside organizations, the overwhelming proportion of studies is about relations between blacks and whites (Lavender and Forsyth, 1976; Flood, 1980). What explains this focus of attention? What might account for the relative inattention to other racial and ethnic relationships?

Faced with a literature showing these characteristics, we decided to frame our review mainly to explain the underlying structure of knowledge in this area. We became less concerned with establishing empirical generalizations than is often the case with surveys of this kind (cf. Pettigrew, 1985; Yinger, 1985) and more attentive to examining key concepts and explanatory mechanisms. We decided to give special attention to the role of methodology in the search for understanding. Of particular importance are researchers' relationships to the material they study. What in the lives of social scientists, as well as in their ideas, might explain their choice of theoretical orientation and methodological procedures? The result of this orientation is a paper with a point of view.

The argument begins with an examination of various conceptions of individuals and groups, because these two concepts and their relationship to one another are central to understanding racial and ethnic dynamics—inside and outside organizations. Next we turn to an examination of the meaning of racial and ethnic identity for individuals. This step applies general terms from the analysis of individuals and groups to the special subject-matter of racial and ethnic relations. The third major step in our analysis takes up questions of groups as entities in relation to one another. The literature we know shows a consistent (and not always conscious) bias in favor of individuals as the primary level of analysis. As a result, we decided that it was necessary to begin where most readers were, in order to convey a complete sense of our understanding. Thus, we give considerable attention in the beginning to working on the topic from an individual perspective and gradually move to a combination of individual and group levels of understanding. The fourth phase directly examines methodological questions, most of which pertain to how investigators individually and collectively relate to the phenomena of race and ethnicity and, in turn, how these relationships influence what they learn about the subject-matter. Finally, we examine a variety of organizational problems in connection with race and ethnicity. This section gets as close as any portion of the review to a search for empirical generalizations. The mode of inquiry, however, is carried out within the perspective developed in the preceding sections.

Any investigation about race and ethnicity is incomplete if it does not, in some way, recognize that emotions are closely associated with the subject-matter. People, including researchers, have strong feelings about racial and ethnic issues—pride, fear, hatred, admiration, disdain. In our view, the research task includes addressing and working with these feelings. This is in contrast to an approach shown by some investigators who chose a perspective that distances themselves and their readers from the richness and complexity intrinsic to the topic. Beware of studies that substitute the emotionally empty terms such as 'individual differences' or 'demographics' for the feeling words of race and ethnicity (e.g. Pfeffer, 1985).

CONCEPTIONS OF INDIVIDUALS IN RELATION TO GROUPS

Much in the language of everyday conversation as well as of social science distinguishes between the individual and the group. Northern European and North American cultures, for example, often make 'the individual' into the focal unit of their political systems. Social scientists who operate within these countries develop theories with premises quite in accord with the prevailing ideologies

(Brown and Turner, 1981). Other cultures and countries, however, place a higher value on the collective. Triandis (1983), for example, analyses the relationship between Hispanic and mainstream United States cultures in terms of the relative value given to individual or group interests. As it turns out, the relationship between individuals and groups defines one of the more central issues in social science. Perhaps because the problem is so important, some investigators solve it by how they define their concepts. Our preference is to declare the two concepts—individual and group—free and independent and then to examine the relationships between the two levels of analysis.

Individual versus Group

Within social psychology, there is a body of research that examines the conditions under which individuals 'conform' to group pressures (Asch, 1958; Sherif, 1958; Hackman, 1976). The Sherif research showed that respondents asked to indicate how much a stationary point of light moved, gradually adjusted their estimates to fit a developing group norm, which always exceeded the zero distance of actual movement. When removed from the group conditions and asked to make their judgements as individuals, respondents maintained their group's estimate. The Asch research showed that a substantial proportion of respondents faced with experimenters who gave clearly incorrect estimates of the length of a line adjusted their own perceptions to match those of the experimental confederates. More over, the number of errors increased monotonically as the number of confederates increased from one to four, decreased when the respondent had a partner who responded accurately, and increased when the support of the partner was withdrawn. Both of these lines of research can be interpreted as demonstrating the effects of group pressure on the individual. They show rather dramatically that group forces can affect how individuals perceive subjective (Sherif) and objective (Asch) phenomena. When individuals give up their own perceptions and accept a group's definition of reality, they are really giving up an aspect of themselves to the group. Findings of this sort understandably are interpreted in terms of the individual versus the group.

Asch also interviewed his people to determine how those who remained independent and how those who conformed to the group forces accounted for their choices. The people who remained independent showed three coping styles: they expressed great confidence in their own judgements; they withdrew from the group pressures; and they focused on their belief in doing the task effectively. The people who yielded to group pressure showed different effects: some were unaware that their judgements had been displaced by the group; others (the largest proportion) came to believe that their own judgements were inaccurate and the group was correct; and a third set simply confessed to being unable to tolerate the appearance of defectiveness in the eyes of the group, even though their own perceptions of reality did not change in the face of group forces. These findings, derived from experimental methodology, show that a combination of individual and group conditions induce individuals to sacrifice their own perceptions of reality to a false group consensus.

On questions of individual versus group, the findings of experimental social psychology and depth psychology are in accord. Explanatory concepts, however, differ somewhat. Writing at the turn of the century, LeBon (1985) and Freud (1922) analysed the effect of crowds on individuals. They observed that emotional forces in groups resulted in the collective inhibition of the intelligence of individuals.

> [I]n general an intensification of emotion [within the group] creates unfavorable conditions for sound intellectual work, and further because the individuals are intimidated by the group and their mental activity is not free, and because there is a lowering in each individual of his sense of responsibility for his own performances. (Freud, 1922, p.29)

According to these investigators, the underlying process in these group effects on the individual was unconscious. People so affected were unaware of what was happening to them. Asch, more than thirty years later, reported similar findings, although he clearly did not place the emphasis on emotional versus intellectual forces that Freud did.

BOUNDARIES AND THE TWIN FEARS OF ENGULFMENT AND ABANDONMENT

To understand the unconscious dynamics of individuals relating to groups, we turn to concepts that have evolved from experiential methods and psychotherapy. The first is the notion of psychological boundary, a term that has relevance for understanding individuals and groups (Rice, 1969; Landis, 1970; Alderfer, 1976). The second is the twin fears of engulfment and abandonment, a pair of constructs that apply to individuals (Storr, 1960). Together, these terms provide the basis for examining the relationship between individuals and groups from the individual's perspective.

A psychological boundary defines a system in relation to its environment and regulates transactions between the system and its environment. The term may also be used in a like manner in order to understand subsystems of a larger system and to analyse a system in relation to the suprasystem of which it is a part. Applied to individuals, the concept of psychological boundary often has the adjectives 'ego' or 'self' preceding it (Landis, 1970). Difficulties arise when the person's boundaries are either too permeable, resulting in a loss of coherent sense of self, or too impermeable, leading to an inability to have productive exchange with others. The twin fears directly follow from these two kinds of threat to optimal boundary permeability. The fear of engulfment arises when the person senses that her or his sense of self is being threatened because others—who could be other individuals or a group—are so overwhelmingly dominant that her or his sense of an independent self is being threatened. The fear of abandonment arises when the person senses that her or his ability to maintain a relationship with others—who could be other individuals or a group—is about to be terminated, and he or she will be left ₐalone. Balancing the two fears is essential to establishing relationships—thus overcoming the fear of abandonment—and at the same time maintaining a secure sense of self—thus preventing the fear of engulfment.

As a consequence, there is a natural tension between the psychological boundaries of the individual and of the group. Unless the person is able to tolerate some boundary permeability, he or she cannot form a psychological relationship with a group. On the other hand, if the group cannot grant some measure of boundary integrity to individuals, it will be unable to retain members. Thus, in general, a dynamic equilibrium between individual and group boundaries unfolds. Individuals adapt to the demands of groups, and groups adjust to the unique qualities of individuals. In any concrete situation, a negotiation occurs between a particular individual and a specific group to determine the degree to which the individual becomes a psychological member and the group establishes a place for the member.

Group Roles and Individual Predispositions

Among a variety of social sciences—including anthropology, psychology and sociology—the concept of role has been employed because it has a double-edged focus toward both the individual and the collective (Levinson, 1959). From the collective side, the notion of role includes a pattern of demands and expectations with associated behaviors that to some degree exist independently of a particular individual who may occupy the role. Roles in social systems contribute to stability and predictability of outcomes (Katz and Kahn, 1978). From the individual side, the notion of role enactment allows for the definition and shaping of a role according to the unique preferences and coping styles of particular persons (Levinson, 1959; Katz and Kahn, 1978).

To this general conception of role, we also recognize the operation of both conscious and unconscious components. At the conscious level, a role may be negotiatied through explicit discussions between an individual and a group or combination of groups, all attempting to define and shape a specific role. A concrete example would be when the personnel committee of a board of directors establishes a job description for the chief executive officer, selects a person to fill the position, and then discusses with that person whether her or his style and results are meeting the directors' expectations. The executive, in turn, talks with directors about whether their behavior is meeting her or his needs (Alderfer, 1986).

At the unconscious level, groups locate naturally occurring emotional tensions with individual members (Whitaker and Lieberman, 1964; Gibbard, Hartman and Mann, 1974), and individuals carry with them personal valences that lead them to be drawn into particular roles within groups (Bion, 1961). The analysis of central figures in experiential groups suggests that a combination of individual predispositions and focal conflicts in the life of a group determine the roles of particular members (Ringwald, 1974; Gibbard, 1974). Experiential groups are temporary educational systems that are particularly well suited for learning about the unconscious components of group life (Rice, 1965; Alderfer and Cooper, 1980; Smith and Berg, 1987). In more permanent organizations, roles have both conscious and unconscious elements. In an unconscious manner, the board of directors described above might select as the new chief executive a person from outside the organization whose style is so incongruous with the existing system that he or she would be unable to function effectively in the role. Understanding and changing roles involves working with both unconscious and conscious elements.

Intragroup and Intergroup Relations

The term 'group-as-a-whole' has been formulated to recognize two major properties of collective life (Wells, 1980). The first is that groups are entities on their own terms—conceptually and empirically separable from the individuals who are members at any particular time. The second is that groups as entities have unconscious components that are different from—although clearly related to—the unconscious of individual members. Taking the group as a unit on its own terms means looking both inside and outside of the group boundary in order to understand the entity. Group dynamics involve both intragroup and intergroup relations.

Accepting the group as an entity has implications for all individuals who are members. From the inward perspective of a group, individuals decide—somewhat consciously and somewhat unconsciously—in what ways they wish to have the group as entity shape their *personal* identities. An especially vivid example of this phenomenon can be found in a memoir by William Sloan Coffin, Jr. In describing his decision to resign from Yale University where he had been chaplain for seventeen years, Coffin (1977, pp. 338–40) wrote:

> I had often noted how in protecting free speech, in protecting professors from other people, tenure could also protect professors from them selves... I wasn't sure what I would do were I not a university chaplain... I thought I needed Yale to tell me who I was. It may be the most frightening thing about institutions of all kinds, that they have this kind of power over so many of us.

Coffin's self-insight is especially powerful about the relationship between group identity and the individual because he was such a forceful person. As university chaplain, he has led social movements for civil rights, against the Vietnam War, and against world hunger. A conventionally thinking person would hardly conceive of him as someone who needed Yale to tell him who he was. Yet according to his own words, he did.

The tendency of groups to influence individuals' identities has an external as well as an internal component. People respond to others, in part, in terms of the groups to which they belong. To continue with the preceding example, people frequently responded to Coffin as if he were a Yale representative. Newspaper accounts of his advocacy work would begin, 'Yale University Chaplain, William Sloan Coffin, Jr, today said...' This grammatical form subordinates his individual identity to group membership. An individual at most has limited control over this phenomenon. Even after Coffin resigned from Yale, he had relationships with people who remembered when he was Yale chaplain and responded to him from that perspective.

Recognizing that group memberships shape the identities of people from both internal and external perspectives is *not* equivalent of asserting that group memberships erase the uniqueness of individuals. Most who know the facts would argue that Coffin shaped the Yale chaplaincy in a unique fashion. In general, individuals as group representatives are shaped by at least three sets of forces: their own unique personalities, the groups with whom they personally identify to a significant degree; and the groups with whom others associate them—whether or not they wish such an association.

This way of thinking about individuals and groups has so far not mentioned ethnicity and race. This has been quite a deliberate choice. The theoretical statements in the preceding paragraphs follow from a particular form of intergroup theory, which makes the *group* the focal unit of analysis (Alderfer, 1986). This theory includes a variety of statements about groups in general and then proceeds to examine specific kinds of groups, including the racial and the ethnic. Because the *individual* has been the focal unit in much of social psychology of intergroup relations, we wanted from the outset to demonstrate how a group-focused theory of intergroup relations deals with the individual. Which unit of analysis a theory takes as focal establishes a position in a lively and important controversy among researchers (Tajfel, 1981; Glazer, 1983). Anyone reading the scholarly literature on this subject should not miss the strongly-held views on this matter.

We suggest that one of the reasons for the force with which social scientists debate this matter relates to the *personal* meaning of the concepts for the investigators. Listening with a kind of 'third ear', one might form the hypothesis that researchers who vigorously take an individual versus group perspective do so from a fear of engulfment by the group. The nature of engulfment may not just be in relation to one's own group on its own terms but may also include forces set off in one's own group because of its relations to other groups. They may argue against group level concepts quite explicit (cf. Turner and Giles, 1981); or they may simply omit explicit treatment of group-level forces in their treatment of open systems (e.g. Katz and Kahn, 1978). In their roles as investigators, some researchers stay away from groups. Recognizing the possibility that unconscious forces might affect researchers as well as the people we study, one might further ask whether groups as concepts are generally as dangerous as some theorists seem to believe.

William Coffin's (1977, p. 340) memoir again is valuable for illustrative purposes. Coffin discovered his own unconscious tie to Yale in the process of listening to himself respond to an angry alumnus who appeared to be upset with the University because of actions by Coffin, and Kingman Brewster Jr, the University President. The Yale chaplain initially speaks to the alumnus:

> ...What I don't understand is why a man like you, a highly successful businessman, an obvious pillar of the community, happily married with splendid children—why a man like you still needs Yale to tell you who you are. I can see why Yale needs you ... but for the life of me I can't see why you need Yale.

Then he reflects upon himself, the person who uttered these words to another, and says, 'As a matter of fact, I was really talking to myself.' That insight was part of the process that ultimately enabled Coffin to resign from the University. We suggest that the process demonstrated by Coffin is more general—that individuals become more conscious in their relationship to group-level forces by recognizing their existence than by denying their presence. Accepting the existence of one's group memberships does not necessary mean one becomes separate or 'independent' from groups. It may or may not be followed by leaving the group, as Coffin did with Yale. It may also mean that one treasures and appreciates one's collective heritage more fully. In fact, our theory argues that it is only organization groups, such as Yale, from which one can formally resign. Membership in identity groups—which include gender, age, family, race and ethnicity—has its basis in biology and, therefore, offers the individual minimal choice about physical membership. People, of course, do have options about how psychologically centrally or peripherally they relate to their identity groups. These statements, if valid, apply no less to social scientists than to the people they study.

The Meaning of Racial and Ethnic Identity for Individuals

The ambivalence about how central theorists decide to make the term group is matched and magnified by how they use the terms racial group and ethnic group. As it turns out, there is a rather extensive literature devoted simply to questions of how to define these terms (e.g. Novak, 1973; Schermerhorn, 1974; Isaacs, 1974; Petersen, 1980). Not far from the issue of definition, of course, is the question of whether the terms should be used at all (Greeley and McCready, 1974). Among a number of social scientists who enter this arena of work, there is open acknowledgement of the personal relevance of their scholarly inquiry (e.g. DuBois, 1968; Novak, 1971; Tajfel, 1981). Others say nothing, and readers are left to wonder whether they believe that their personal lives have nothing to do with their scholarship or whether they are not comfortable in making their self-awareness public.

In the United States, the civil rights revolution of the 1960s marked an important and dramatic change in the nation's attitudes toward race and ethnicity. Black Americans spoke, marched and died in order to change their country's racist practices. To a notable degree, their efforts succeeded (Farley, 1984). From 1981 to the present, however, the country selected a conservative political administration and established a period of distinct regression in race relations (Clark, 1979; Alderfer, 1982). Schermerhorn (1974, p. 3) writes about the change in social science scholarship associated with the civil rights revolution.

> For the purpose of identification, I shall speak of revolt as the 'crisis' or the 'disruption,' synonymously. This will allow us to designate the period of 1900 to the 1960's as the B.C. epoch—before the crisis; in like manner it is possible to call the era after the late 1960's to the present and prospectively to the future as the A.D. era, i.e., after the disruption. A comparison of events and major social trends in the two periods will reveal . . . good reasons why 'ethnicity' as a term in common usage, was hardly ever heard of in the B.C. era, while people are writing articles and books about it in the A.D. epoch.

The change brought on for black Americans as a result of the revolution did not affect their group alone. As blacks became better able to assert and celebrate the favorable aspects of their group identity, other racial and ethnic groups also discovered—or perhaps one should say rediscovered—the benefits of ethnic pride. In the world of scholarship, this change is signified by debate between assimilation and pluralism as overarching principles for regulating relationships between racial and ethnic groups (Hraba and Hoiberg, 1983; Berry, 1984). At heart, the doctrine of assimilation pits the individual against the group, argues for the elimination of ethnic and racial group boundaries, and asserts that this orientation fosters individuality. The philosophy of pluralism, in contrast, respects and affirms the validity of ethnic and racial group boundaries, argues for the preservation of group cultures, and states that in this manner individuals are accepted and valued for a more complete set of their attributes.

The racial and ethnic identification of individuals is not a static condition. It may change as a consequence of intrapersonal development by people, of role changes by individuals in relation to their own groups, and of alterations in the relations among racial and ethnic groups. These three sources of movement are interdependent of one another and follow directly from the conceptions of individuals in relation to groups presented in the preceding section. Cross (1975) analysed the negro-to-black conversion experience, and Jackson (1978) has observed an orderly sequence of stages in the development of black identity. Winter (1974) reported on the kinds of role that emerge for blacks in predominantly white experiential groups and, in a related fashion, Tucker (1980) showed the potential benefits of black human interaction groups. At the societal level, Clark (1966) provided an historical analysis of civil rights organizations in the United States. In complementary fashion, Terry (1970) has explored the ways in which white people can increase their racial awareness; and Alderfer (1982) has analysed sources of resistance within white people (including social scientists) to increasing their racial consciousness. Cateura (1987) brought together a series of biographical essays from Italian men and women, which demonstrate the relationships among individual achievement, family patterns, and the changing position of Italian Americans in the United States.

The other side of asserting one's racial and ethnic identity, of course, is denying it—or at least pretending that it is not important. Novak (1973) examined a variety of reasons why people deny their ethnicity. One view is that people wish to *get over* their ethnicity in order to join the influential mainstream. For them, a reminder of their ethnicity is regressive; it is experienced as taking them away from their path to the influential mainstream. A second kind of rejection of ethnicity comes from individuals who have made it into the influential mainstream and are separated from any ethnic subculture. In recent years, in contrast to the 1930s, there has been a tendency for the intellectual elite to distance themselves from 'the common man', who may be seen as people without conscience (i.e. lacking in concern for those who are less fortunate). A third kind of rejection of ethnicity comes from individuals who are largely unconscious of any ethnicity in their lives at all. These people may be Anglo-Saxons living in a Western European culture for whom it is convenient not to notice their ethnicity, or they may be individuals whose families are veritable melting-pots without anyone having recently traced the pattern of intermarriage. Novak (1973, p. 4) shows at least one American dictionary of the English language which includes the words, 'non-Christian' and 'primitive', as meanings for ethnic. The country that prides itself in welcoming people from all lands and cultures also at times treats ethnicity as a dirty secret.

A fourth reason for individuals to deny their ethnicity, unmentioned by Novak (1973), is that they might be persecuted or discriminated against because of their ethnic or racial group membership (Quinley and Glock, 1979; Simpson, 1987). People who are able to disguise or hide their membership in despised groups escape the harassment directed at those groups. Recognizing the destructive potential of such intergroup hostility leads some to press for the elimination of the public recognition of group differences as a means of preventing unproductive conflict (Glazer, 1983, p. 336).

The terms racial and ethnic are, of course, not identical, although they are not clearly separable either. Often, each appears in the definition of the other (cf. Thermstrom, 1980, pp. 236, 869). Nevertheless, there are differences in meaning. The idea of race places a heavier emphasis on the biological and physiological, while the notion of ethnicity weighs learned behavior patterns and culture more significantly. American writers are known to distinguish between racial groups, such as Blacks and Asians, and ethnic groups, such as Italians and Poles (Petersen, 1980, p. 236). However, whichever term one uses, the connotation of the other is rarely absent. A variety of examples from the literature, however, demonstrate how race and ethnicity can be quite different in their meaning for some people, and how the use of one term by an individual of one race or ethnicity may have implicit (often pejorative) meanings for individuals of a different race or ethnicity (cf. Mead and Baldwin, 1971; or Novak, 1973 versus Jackson, 1973).

Blacks in Relation to Dominant Whites

In the case of black–white racial differences in the United States, the effects of 300 years of white domination and exploitation on black children were shown in research by Clark and Clark (1958). Their study examined racial preferences for 'white' and 'brown' dolls by black children aged 3 to 7 years. Approximately half of their respondents were contacted in racially segregated schools in Arkansas, and the other half from racially mixed schools in Massachusetts. A majority of all children preferred white dolls and rejected brown dolls. Obtained in the early 1940s, these findings were reported more than a decade prior to the *Brown* v. *Board of Education* Supreme Court decision which abolished the separate but equal doctrine of public education in the United States. The research results, in fact, played an important role in influencing the court decision (Cook, 1979).

More than twenty years later, very similar information was reported by Fanon (1967), this time pertaining to the relationship between black people from the Antilles and the predominantly white country of France. Fanon, a psychiatrist, gives his findings in essay form. A key document in his analysis is the autobiographical account of a black Antillian woman, Mayotte Capecia, who wished to be married to a white man. Fanon (1967) describes and explains her account.

She took her inkwell out of the desk and emptied it over his head. This was her own way of turning whites into blacks. But she quite soon recognized the futility of such attempts; and then there were Loulouze and her mother, who told her that life was difficult for a woman of color. So, since she could no longer try to blacken, to negrify the world, she was going to try, in her own body and in her own mind, to bleach it. To start, she would become a laundress. (p. 45)

Later in the book, he talks in more general terms about blacks in relation to whites.

For several years certain laboratories have been trying to produce a serum for 'denegrification'; with all the earnestness in the world, laboratories have sterilized their test tubes, checked their scales, and embarked on researches that might make it possible for the miserable Negro to whiten himself and thus to throw off the burden of that corporeal malediction. (p. 111)

The consequences for blacks living in a land dominated by whites have been severe for more than three centuries (Bennett, 1964). The United States has passed through cycles of regressive and progressive change in race relations, as the country has attempted to come to terms with the contradictions between an ideology that proclaims equality for all citizens and a history noted at best for partial fulfillment of those aims (Myrdal, 1944). The kinds of result reported by the Clarks and by Fanon are caused by white racist practices in the society. During the historical period prior to the civil rights movement, blacks developed doubts about themselves, including the preference to be white, because whites who are in charge used their power to demean black people. When the society acted to reduce its racist practices, the self-perceptions of black people changed as a result. Herbert (1985), in a study of the adult development of black entrepreneurs, found that the lives and self-conceptions of these individuals changed in favorable and often dramatic ways as the United States civil rights movement unfolded.

The relationship between race and ethnicity is perhaps no more sharply recognizable than in dialogue between blacks and whites. As racial and ethnic consciousness has increased in recent years, a new assertiveness among white ethnic groups also emerged. Allen (1975) took on the intellectual task of objecting to WASP (White Anglo-Saxon Protestant) as a sociological concept. His analysis argued that, during the 1960s in the United States, the term shifted from a technical term to an epithet. He charged that stereotyping underlies this process and serves to simplify a more complex reality of significant diversity among European ethnic groups. Tajfel (1970) reported evidence of Scottish children, who 'legally' are British citizens (as black Americans are US citizens), undervaluing themselves in relation to British children in a manner similar to how black children did in relation to white children in the Clarks (1958) and Fanon (1967) studies.

A contrasting perspective is demonstrated by Jackson (1973), who addresses the similarities and differences between racial and ethnic relations in the United States from a black perspective. Her aim is to be clear about the difference between the sorts of struggles that confront all (most) ethnic groups and the special situation of blacks.

Whites have not been able to accept or identify with the totality of human life represented in our society, because they place a false value on a single attribute: skin color, or, more accurately race... To be acknowledged and understood are the *extra* burdens, the *extra* suffering, imposed by racism; else one seems to dismiss casually a basically human claim to justice. (pp. 41–2) [emphasis in the original]

Italians in Relation to Dominant Anglo Culture in the United States

Italians stand as an example of a white ethnic group which migrated to the United States, faced, and continues to face, discrimination in a variety of forms, and assimilated to a considerable degree into the mainstream of the United States culture. Initially, the majority of male Italians who came to the United States had peasant origins and took jobs as laborers (Nelli, 1980). In subsequent years, however, they moved from blue- to white-collar work and eventually into politics, business and the professions.

The period showing the largest Italian migration into the United States was 1900 to 1920, during which more than three million people entered the United States (Nelli, 1980). The Immigration Act of 1924, in part aimed at Italian people, dramatically slowed the rate of immigration. After their arrival, Italians struggled to survive economically and to overcome various forms of discrimination. Of particular importance in these efforts was the formation of mutual benefit societies in the urban communities where many Italians lived. Arising in part from their relatively low economic status, and in part from the prejudice of the wider society, self-doubt and low self-esteem were common among immigrant families. Contemporary scholars write about their experience of struggling between the well-developed sense of their own ethnicity and the pressures of the dominant white Anglo-Saxon Protestant culture. Vecoli (1973, pp. 122–3), for example, describes his experience of living between the two worlds and of the transformation that occurred as he came to terms with this duality:

Being an obedient, ambitious Italian boy, I tried diligently to assimilate. I embraced the liberal creed of progress and enlightenment; I decried the benighted outlook of working-class ethnics; I sought to model myself after the cosmopolitan, sophisticated intellectual. I succeeded in part, and I did learn a great deal in the process. Yet I could never completely forget who I was. I gradually came to realize that much of what I was trying to be and to believe was at odds with my true self, my values, my loyalties. Not only could I never be an authentic WASP; I did not want to be one.

He goes on to say that by accepting and affirming his own ethnicity, he acquired a new prespective on American history that liberated him from the conventional interpretations.

We discuss blacks and Italians as illustrative cases of a racial group and an ethnic group moving progressively away from being in a subordinated position to being in a position of greater power in the wider culture in which they are embedded. There are both common processes and dramatic differences. For American blacks the process has been under way for more than 300 years and has involved war and social revolution. For Italian-Americans, the process has been under way for somewhat over 100 years and has been more evolutionary in character. Threats to individual identity and group survival can be observed for both groups—though much more severely for blacks than for Italians. And in recent years, both groups have participated actively in an era that increasingly affirms their contributions to the rich diversity of the larger culture (Greene, 1978; Farley, 1984; Cateura, 1987). The effect of improved standing for the groups has been a greater sense of wholeness and vitality for individual members, and the accomplishments of individual members have brought greater influence for the respective groups.

None of this change, however, has been easy or simple—or without anguish. And the process is not complete. Even though a variety of indicators show evidence of progressive change for blacks, Italians and other racial and ethnic groups within the United States, the effects of ethnic bias and racism remain present in virtually all sectors of society. To deny these phenomena is either consciously or unconsciously to maintain the pattern. Racial and ethnic dynamics are rooted not only in the relationships between individuals and groups, but also in the relationships among racial and ethnic groups as entities and between identity and organizational groups.

GROUPS IN RELATION TO GROUPS

A key theme in any discussion of racial and ethnic groups is the relative influence of one group in relation to others. Racism is only possible if one racial group has the resources and the motivation to dominate, demean and destroy another racial group. Ethnic or racial conflict, on the other hand, is not necessarily equivalent to racism. Ethnocentrism—the tendency for groups to have a more favorable view of themselves than of other groups—is a common property and may or may not lead one group to pursue a relationship of dominance and destruction in relationship to other groups (Levine and Campbell, 1972). Racial and ethnic groups vary in their experiences, and as a consequence, develop unique ways of understanding their relationship to other groups (Alderfer and Smith, 1982). Differences in perception, in understanding, and in objectives may become the basis for escalating hostility, or these very same differences may become the roots of creative diversity.

Identity Groups and Organization Groups

Physically, people belong to racial and ethnic groups from birth. The ethnic and racial elements of lives are begun by events over which no one has choice. What people do have choice about—although perhaps less than they are consciously aware of—is the nature of their psychological relationship to ethnic and racial groups. Individuals may conceive of themselves as more or less psychological members of their racial and ethnic groups, and as a result, their personal identities may give more or less weight to racial and ethnic group membership. But the process, as we have seen, is more complex than what the individual decides in relation to her or his own identity group. There is also the question how other groups relate to one's own group.

Historically, there are situations when dominant groups wish to heighten the salience of subordinate groups, and there are cases when dominant groups wish to diminish signs of subordinate groups. Perhaps the most extreme case of heightening salience occurred in Nazi Germany when the ruling party required Jews to wear yellow stars of David in order to identify their group membership (Schoenberner, 1969). The purpose of the Nazi rule was to make it possible for the racist group to direct their hatred efficiently. In contrast, immigrants to the United States during the early part of the twentieth century felt pressure from the dominant culture to join the vast melting-pot, that is, to give up their ethnic origins and become 'loyal' Americans (Glazer and Moynihan, 1963). Immigrants did become loyal Americans, as shown by their willingness to fight for their adopted country in two world wars, but they did not give up their ethnic and racial identifications.

The conflict between increasing and decreasing the salience of ethnic and racial group membership is seen no more clearly than in the life of Israel Zangwill, whose play *The Melting Pot*, opened with great success in New York City in 1908. The message of the play was that America was 'God's Crucible', in which all the races of Europe were melting and reforming. As it turned out, Zangwill was also a Zionist, and eight years after the opening, he publicly moved away from the strong message delivered in his play (Glazer and Moynihan, 1963, pp. 289–90). Zangwill's vacillation suggests the operation of both fears of abandonment and of engulfment in his relations to ethnic groups.

In contrast to membership in racial and ethnic groups, organization groups provide individuals with choices about physical as well as psychological membership. When people join organizations, they become members of hierarchical and functional groups. These joint memberships are signified by titles such as Vice-President (giving the person's membership in a hierarchical group) of Sales (giving the person's membership in a functional group). Unlike racial and ethnic ties, organization group memberships last only as long as the person remains an organization member. When a person leaves the system, he or she gives up these memberships. From the institution's perspective, organization groups are created for the purpose of achieving planned objectives, and are eliminated when no longer necessary for those ends.

The relationship between ethnic and racial groups, on the one hand, and organization groups, on the other, is inevitably problematic (Alderfer 1977; 1986). Empirically, there are established relationships between ethnic and racial group membership and organization group membership (e.g. Purcell and Cavanagh, 1972; Greeley and Wells, 1978). These sorts of finding indicate that members of certain racial and ethnic groups are more likely to become members of some functional and hierarchical groups than of others. While a portion of these differences may reflect natural responses to different interests and abilities, others undoubtedly are rooted in covert racial and ethnic struggles. As a result, there are incentives for those in senior positions to ignore or deny the existence of such patterns. Wells and Jennings (1983) have suggested that beneath the various forms of denial is an unconscious (and in some cases conscious) sense of entitlement—the belief that certain racial and ethnic groups *by virtue of their racial group membership* are entitled to exclusive possession of specific organizational group memberships.

Whether consciously or unconsciously, organizations do face the question of whether they choose to recognize the presence of racial and ethnic groups in their systems and, in turn, whether they wish to examine the consequences of those entities for the experiences of organization members. For example, the top management group of a major US firm may consist of individuals all of whom are white and male. As noted above, the history of Italian-Americans includes the formation of ethnically based self-help groups. Black employees in US corporations sometimes consider forming an association within the specific organization to cope with institutional racism. Faced with a request from a racial or ethnic group to be recognized, the corporation's leadership cannot respond neutrally; they either support the strengthening of the group's boundaries, or they do not. Both patterns have been observed in US corporations (Alderfer, *et al.*, 1980; Davis and Watson, 1982).

Embedded Intergroup Relations

The concept of embedded intergroup relations recognizes that from an open-systems perspective, varying-sized entities serve as subsystems, focal systems and suprasystems in relation to one another (Alderfer and Smith, 1982). If, for example, the focal system is a work group, then an individual person would be a subsystem of the work group, and the department would be a suprasystem of the work group. Another example might take the organization as focal unit. Then racial and ethnic groups may be subsystems within the organization, and they may also be elements in the suprasystem of the organization. Whichever level of analysis becomes the focus, one observes the phenomena of interpenetration. Both subsystems and suprasystems influence the focal system. The analysis of embedded intergroup relations examines the nature of these cross level influence processes. It applies to any situation consisting of intergroup relations, including those pertaining to racial and ethnic groups (Alderfer, 1986).

The concept of embedded intergroup relations was developed to explain empirical findings that were inconsistent with the phenomena of ethnocentrism (Alderfer and Smith, 1982). This research found that a set of interdependent groups *both* believed that the other occupied the more favorable position of influence. These effects were observed in a study of organization groups (engineering and marketing) and in an investigation of racial groups (black and white). By examining how the groups were embedded in their systems, otherwise inexplicable patterns of perception became meaningful.

By taking account of patterns of embeddedness, for example, one can understand more fully the supervisory situation facing a racial or ethnic minority manager in a racial or ethnic majority corporation. Such a manager would have mainly majority people as subordinates and as bosses. The effective authority of a person in such a situation is inevitably more problematic than a majority manager in the same organizational position. Because the minority manager's subordinates and boss share a common identity group that is different from that of the manager, the temptation for the two parties to communicate 'around' the minority manager will be greater than if all were members of the same racial or ethnic group. The boundaries of the different identity groups place an unusual strain on the boundaries of the organization groups. Without understanding the different patterns of embeddedness facing majority as compared to minority managers, one might mistakenly assume that because individuals have the same organizational positions (e.g. Manager of Quality Control), they have the same jobs, when the racial or ethnic intergroup dynamics facing majority and minority managers would be quite different. Realistic job descriptions for the two would recognize the differences.

RESEARCH METHODS IN RACIAL AND ETHNIC STUDIES

Along with the conceptual revolution brought on by the United States civil rights movement of the 1960s, which we have noted above, came also a significant reorientation in methodological practice. The impending change involves a variety of dimensions, such as who conducts research and with whom, how racial and ethnic groups are represented in the design and conduct of research, what level of racial and ethnic consciousness investigators demonstrate in their data analysis and interpretation, and how researchers involve themselves in the processes by which their findings are used to influence the condition of the people they study. Concerns about these sorts of issue have never been totally absent among those who studied racial and ethnic subjects, but neither have they been fully incorporated into the norms that determine what the social science establishment legitimizes as competent methodology. With a few notable exceptions, the basic operating pattern is for the methodological sections of research reports *not* to report the relevant information.

The missing material tends to appear in two forms—one quiet and easy to overlook and the other noisy and hard to receive. The first source is available in prefaces, in footnotes, and in appendices. These locations are all peripheral to the main body of research reports, and it takes special interest and attentiveness not to miss what they offer. Recently, a new soft-spoken source has also appeared; it is the growing literature of biographies and autobiographies of social scientists (Alderfer, 1985). At the close of their lives, when distinguished people are somewhat freed from the methodological controls that have shaped their professional work, they are more able to report how their personal lives shaped their professional work or to recount interesting events from research projects that by conventional standards are deemed irrelevant or anomalous.

The second source takes the form of controversy. A group of investigators who are feeling aggrieved band together and demand to be heard. Their medium may be the special issue of an established journal, the publication of a book of readings, or the founding of a new journal. These events are somewhat more likely to receive the explicit attention of 'the field' than their soft-spoken alternatives, but concentration is also likely to be shortlived. The work is outside the mainstream, and among social scientists who are personally conflict-averse the labeling of a phenomenon as 'controversial' is often a code for 'not to be taken seriously'.

The parallels between how social scientists treat methodological issues associated with race and ethnicity are similar to how society as a whole relates to the same topics. The preferred coping method is largely (but not completely) to ignore the problems. When that does not work and an oubreak occurs, then the impulse is to devote resources intensively to short-term efforts at solution. Both approaches leave the conscious and explicit methodological dictates unaffected.

Brewer and Kramer (1985, pp. 236–7), in their literature review on 'The Psychology of Intergroup Attitudes and Behavior', offer a conclusion whose implications for research methods may be more than the writers realize.

There are some common themes, however, that supersede differences in methodological orientation and problem focus... One is the extent to which group membership influences the attributions we make about our own and others' behavior, intentions, and values. This suggests that the knowledge structures or 'subjective culture' that individuals bring *to* an intergroup contact situation may be as important as the structure of the situation in shaping the behavioral and attitudinal outcomes.

Our impression is that Brewer and Kramer (1985) wrote these words thinking about the people psychologists study—their 'subjects'—not about the researchers themselves. The most frequent stance among research social psychologists is not to reflect whether their findings apply to themselves in their roles of investigators. But is not any research transaction an 'intergroup contact situation'? If so, do not investigators bring their own subjective cultures based on their group memberships to those situations? And if so, do not these group memberships importantly shape the behavioral and attitudinal outcomes (otherwise known as results)? Drawing on both historical and contemporary accounts, we examine evidence bearing on these questions.

Personal Experiences of Individual Investigators

Disciplines in the social sciences and subfields within them differ in their attitudes about what to make of the personal experiences of investigators. The more a group of investigators is committed to positivist values, the more the personal experiences of investigators are treated as if they do not exist, represent undesirable error variance, or provide evidence of researchers' incompetence (Stevens, 1939). Investigators who employ clinical methods and theory, in contrast, pay special attention to the personal experiences of investigators and employ them in a disciplined fashion to understand the material under study (Berg and Smith, 1985).

At the close of her career as an anthropologist, Hortense Powdermaker (1967) prepared an autobiography reviewing her personal experiences with four intensive field studies. In this account, she tells of her socioeconomic and ethnic background and reports having undertaken two long psychoanalyses, the second of which she indicates contributed greatly to her growth as an anthropologist. As a child, Powdermaker (1967, p. 21) grew up in an upper middle-class German-Jewish family, and describes 'a definite sense of being Jewish, particularly for my mother'. She also comments on the difference between *studying about* psychoanalysis, which she did early in her career, and *learning about it from direct experience*, which she did later (p. 39). Her reaction to the family's socioeconomic standing and to its sense of superiority in relation to Eastern European Jews was rebellion. We mention briefly these facts from her personal history because they provide a sense of the woman's self-awareness at both personal and ethnic group levels. The particular data we shall cite below from her fieldwork may seem improbable to some readers, and we wanted to show why, in our opinion, Powdermaker was extraordinarily well prepared to make the observations she reported.

In the years 1933 and 1934, Powdermaker carried out a study of race relations in Indianola, Mississippi. The rural town's population was approximately half black and half white. Her experience with the project was challenging, as she indicates:

> I had to find my way and fit into a southern community which, even in the mid-thirties, was characterized by deep fears and anxieties of both Negroes and whites. I had to live and work within the dominant white power structure and at the same time be an accepted part of the Negro community. I had to alternate between seeing and feeling as a Negro and as a white person in Mississippi, and then standing outside, both as myself with a personal value system, and myself as a social scientist. (p. 13).

A number of remarkable things happened to Powdermaker as she negotiated her way between the black and white communities of Indianola. She found herself giving alternative views of what she was studying to whites and to blacks. As she stated it, 'To him [a white man] and to all the whites, I said I was studying Negro life; to the Negroes, I said I was studying the community—Negroes and whites' (p. 146). It is interesting to observe that Wax (1982) asserts that Powdermaker was practising deceit (his words) in giving different versions of what she was doing to the two racial groups. We would not evaluate the situation in the same way. Her differing accounts of what she was doing simply followed the then (and to a large degree still) present cultures of the racial groups. White people, by and large, do not study themselves as a racial group (Alderfer, 1982). Black people, on the other hand, find that they must be aware of both their own and of the other group (Dubois, 1903; Bell, 1986). Whether conscious of it or not, Powdermaker worked with, rather than disturbed, the norms of the race relationship she was studying.

At a later point in her account, she reports that a rumor spread among the blacks that, 'I was really Negro, and passing for white in order to study whites... Probably the most significant point was that I felt comfortable with Negroes... I was amused at the rumor and denied it' (p. 148). The dialogue between Powdermaker and male social scientists, such as Wax (1982), had yet another component. She reports that when she happened to tell a social scientist about the rumor, 'His immediate reaction was "But why didn't you let the rumor stand as it were true?" ' (p. 148). The racial intergroup dynamics *within the research community* included a white male (Wax) perceiving Powdermaker as deceitful to white people and another male (by her account) advising her to be deceitful to black people! Powdermaker's account of her personal experience informs not only about her relationships with the people she studied but also about norms in the white male research world.

Some twelve years after *Street Corner Society* was first published, William F. Whyte (1943; 1955) prepared a second edition, which added a methodological appendix to the book as it initially appeared. Then, 26 years after the second edition, Whyte (1981) prepared a third edition. This edition revised somewhat Whyte's first methodological appendix and added another—this one written by one of his informants. The third edition revealed the actual location of the study and provided real names of the major characters. The third edition also revealed the extent to which some Cornerville men remained significant characters in Whyte's life.

The second appendix, entitled 'The Whyte Impact on an Underdog', was written by Angelo Ralph Orlandella and was first delivered as a speech at a conference honoring Whyte on the occasion of his formal retirement from Cornell University in 1980. Whyte and Orlandella had maintained a relationship for more than 40 years. In the 1955 edition Whyte commented directly on the fact that his study had had a profound effect on 'Sam Franco', Orlandella's fictitious name in the research monograph. Whyte (1955, p. 349) wrote, 'Working with me made Sam Franco, who had only a high-school education, want to be a human relations research man...I was not always sure that the effect would be constructive.' Then Whyte proceeded to describe a number of human relations work assignments Sam had in the military and indicated that his performance had been highly effective. Whyte (p. 353), nevertheless, concluded his first account of Orlandella's life after Cornerville tentatively.

So the story has a happy ending—so far. But it was only by an extraordinary chance that Sam was able to pursue the work he wanted to do. Had the chance not come, his association with me might simply have served to frustrate him with ambitions he could never expect to gratify.

Orlandella's (1981) account of his adult lifetime relationship with Whyte makes clearer both the personal and ethnic dimensions of their tie.

The deeply personal connection is perhaps shown most powerfully when Orlandella (1981, p. 368) reports his fantasies as he faced death during a World War II battle in the Pacific.

The tension inside of me mounted with the intensity of the operation. A new sensation gripped me with a wild, desperate feeling to the depth of my stomach. It was at this very instant that a flashback of my whole world came before my eyes: Rose, my parents and sisters, *and Bill Whyte*. [emphasis added]

The ethnic tie is shown in the beginning of Orlandella's (1981, pp. 361–2) account as he describes with feeling the condition of Italian-Americans at the time Whyte began his study. His account includes five different episodes of politically-motivated assaults on Italians. Some included murder as a direct means to political power.

Whyte's sensitivity to the ethnic tensions involved in his study is shown several times throughout the original research report. From the very beginning of the book, he tells about how the waves of Italian migration to the United States shaped the population of Cornerville. Included with this account is a reflection on how middle- and upper middle-class people, including social scientists, perceive the slum. Whyte is attentive to the blindspots in their vision, and he is careful to let the Cornerville people speak for themselves. The concluding question, which he poses for his readers, is, 'What is the effect upon the individual when he has to subordinate himself to people that he recognizes are different than his own?' (p. 276). This question is answered by Doc, the lead character in Whyte's account, who explains the impact.

In the settlement house, none of the people with authority are Italians... When the Italian boy sees that none of his own people have the good jobs, why should he think he is as good as the Irish or the Yankees? It makes him feel inferior... If I had my way, I would have half the schoolteachers Italians and three quarters of the settlement. Let the other quarter be there just to show we're in America...

As one might expect, Whyte's capacity for empathy with the people of Cornerville is related to an awareness of his own social position. In the first appendix, he describes a little of his own social history and the factors in his own life that drew him to Cornerville:

My home life had been very happy and intellectually stimulating—but without adventure. I had never had to struggle over anything... I knew nothing about life in the factories, fields, or mines—except what I had gotten out of books. So I came to feel that I was a pretty dull fellow. At times the sense of dulness [sic] became...oppressive...I began to feel that, if I were really to write anything worthwhile, I would somehow have to get beyond the narrow social borders of my existence up to that time. (p. 281)

The 1981 edition of *Street Corner Society* expands Whyte's original appendix and tells of his struggles with the academic establishment of his day. In retrospect, two features of that period stand out. First, Whyte had done his study without reviewing the literature. When he eventually got around to reading it, his evaluation was not favorable. 'I become convinced that most of it was worthless and misleading' (p. 356). Second, he had developed a conception of the slum as highly organized with many cohesive social groupings. The established view of that day was that 'social disorganization' was central to any conception of slums. Fortunately for all of us, Whyte got through his contest with certain reigning authorities by compromise and with help from other senior people. In retrospect, it seems that Whyte's difficulties with the establishment occurred in part because he listened first to the people he studied and formed his concepts based on their data, and reflected second on the state what was considered existing knowledge at the time. We can only wonder what would have happened if Whyte had incorporated existing 'findings' and concepts before embarking on his adventure into Cornerville.

Interpersonal and Intergroup Relationships in Data Collection

The literature on race relations is especially noted for the necessity of attending to the race of investigators in relation to respondents. On this topic there is a body of research results that extends across several decades and includes studies inside and outside of organizations. Viewing this work from an historical perspective suggests how changes in the relationships between blacks and whites in the society at large affect methods of data collection.

In the minds of many social scientists, an interview is an interpersonal event. Concepts that are brought to bear in order to understand what occurs in the transaction are terms such as rapport, expectation, warmth, involvement and sociability. As white researchers began to enter the realms of race research, however, the potential for expanding the conceptualization of the research interview to include an intergroup perspective began. Dollard (1957), reporting on his study of *Caste and Class in a Southern Town*, gave extensive attention to the complexities of his relationships with black and white people and to his own biases. Hyman *et al.* (1954) in an extensive series of empirical studies about interviewing developed a point of view that included both interpersonal and intergroup explanations for what occurred between interviewers and respondents. They observe that, 'Since interviewers are a fairly homogeneous group, it seems logical to assume that they will be perceived (and reacted to) in accordance with their homogeneous characteristics (p. 150). They then proceeded to tabulate the group memberships of the interviewing staff of several major survey organizations. These data show that 74 per cent were women, 78 per cent had at least some college education, and about 98 per cent were white. From those observations, they then proceeded to test for interviewer effects and, on matters of race relations, found the effects to be quite marked. A study in 1942 in Memphis, Tennessee randomly assigned black and white interviewers to black respondents. The data showed that blacks were more reluctant to express to white interviewers their resentments over discrimination by employers, labor unions, the army or in public places (Hyman *et al.*, 1954, p. 159). Similar findings were reported by Stouffer *et al.*, (1950, pp. 720–1) for blacks in the US Army during World War II.

Because their original study was conducted in a southern US city where race relations might be expected to be especially strained, Hyman *et al.* (1954, p. 170) replicated their study in New York City, a location where they expected different social norms about race relations. Again they found that the race of the interviewer affected black responses, but the frequency of these effects was lower in New York City than in Memphis. They concluded that there was little doubt that blacks in Memphis were more reluctant to talk freely to white interviewers than were blacks in New York. These results—though not conceptualized in these terms by the original writers—are consistent with the notion of embedded intergroup relations presented above.

Hyman *et al.* (1954, pp. 162–4) also examined the effects of Jewish and Gentile interviewers studying the attitudes of Gentiles about Jews. In two different studies, employing different methodologies, they found that Gentiles were much more likely to express antisemitic attitudes to Gentile interviewers than to Jewish interviewers. The second study showed that the more clearly identified as Jewish the interviewer was, the stronger the interviewer effect appeared.

The studies thus far reported were all conducted prior to the American civil rights movement. Race relations research conducted by predominantly white institutions during and subsequent to the movement changed. In addition to the long-standing concerns about discrimination, new sets of questions to assess black alienation and black militancy were designed (Schuman and Converse, 1971; Schuman and Hatchett, 1974). Following what had by then become a methodological tradition, research was conducted to determine whether race of interviewer affected responses to these questions, and the results were affirmative.

Comparing responses to a large number of questions, Schuman and Converse (1971, p. 52) found that the race-of-interviewer effect was largest on questions that dealt with overt hostility toward whites, suspicion of whites, and identification with black militancy. Furthermore, this study extended further implicit intergroup reasoning in attempting to explain their effects. The writers consider two classes of explanation for the race-of-interviewer effect: (1) that blacks have a tendency to withhold their frank opinions from white interviewers, thus making the white interviewer data less valid; or (2) that blacks attempted to impress black interviewers with their militancy, thus making the black interviewer data less valid. They also entertained the possibility of both kinds of effects operating. Additional analyses suggested that both kinds of effects were operating. In support of black interviewers obtaining more valid data about militancy, they found a higher correlation between militant attitudes and reports of militant behavior from black interviewers than from white interviewers. In support of both racial groups affecting the interview transaction, they found that responses to a question about the respondents' favorite entertainers drew more white responses for white interviewers and more black responses for black interviewers. In a study three years later, Schuman and Hatchett (1974, pp. 51–2) replicated the race-of-interviewer effects on measures of black alienation. In this later study, they also note, 'We have shown...quite large effects on white responses when race-of-interviewer is introduced as a variable' (Schuman and Hatchett, 1974, p. 52).

Consistently finding that data about racial and ethnic relations are affected by the race or ethnicity of interviewers is an anomalous and a disturbing result. On the one hand, it raises questions about conventional notions of 'objectivity', and on the other, it suggests inquiry about how the social science enterprise as a whole relates to the culture in which it is embedded. We observe that a number of white researchers who have had sustained contact with race or ethnic relations research do develop views of objectivity that call for an increased consciousness of one's own values and biases by investigators (cf. Myrdal, 1944; Dollard, 1957; Whyte, 1981; Alderfer, 1986). Writers also cope with the implications of the findings by suggesting that they appropriately maintain the current social equilibrium. Schuman and Converse (1971, p. 60) propose that a type of 'valid insight' is provided by the white effects in survey interviewing: 'If white interviewers serve to depress the "natural" level of militancy of black respondents, we must expect something similar to happen in other white-black interaction outside the survey context, for example, in ordinary integrated social situations.' In drawing this inference, Schuman and Converse (1971) and Schuman and Hatchett (1974, p. 52), who make the statement again four years later, make a connection between research and non-research situations and apparently are able to see some implications of the *methodology* (not just the substantive findings) for understanding race relations in 'integrated' settings. In this sense, Schuman and his collaborators differ from many social scientists who tend to separate methodology from real (i.e. non-research) life. But what Schuman *et al.* apparently do not see, however, is that the research relationship they create is integration based upon white dominance. Do they mean to suggest that suppression of black militancy by white domination is the desirable end-state for improved race relations?

A related argument is also made by Gerard and Miller (1975, pp. 64–5) in their study of school desegregation. In this instance, however, the investigators did not systematically match the race or ethnicity of the investigators with that of the respondents arguing that, 'Attempts to hire Blacks and Mexican-Americans were thwarted by university rules that required a certain minimum educational background for the workers doing such testing.' These investigators were aware of the research consequences for what they did, and they justify the possible effects in terms of their being consistent with the structural patterns of the larger society.

The tester's bias effects thus remain an alternative explanation for ethnic group differences on many of our measures. However, the experience of the minority child in the interview situation was not unlike the situation he constantly had to face in the 'real world.' American culture is dominantly white and middle class. In particular, most teachers and school officials are white. In this sense, the interview situation did not constitute a serious threat to validity.

We add that the interview situation created by Gerard and Miller (1965) did not create a serious threat to validity from a *dominant white Anglo* point of view. One can only wonder what they would have found if they had designed their methods in accord with existing knowledge about the effects of intergroup relations between investigators and respondents. Moreover, one must also question the effects not only on what data are collected but also on what interpretations are made based on the race and ethnicity of the investigators. The fact that Gerard and Miller could operate as they did leads naturally to questions about authority among social scientists.

Institutional Debate and New Organizational Forms

The civil rights revolution in the United States did not bring only new interest in racial and ethnic studies, new topics for investigation, and continued attention to methodological questions. It also brought new forms of debate among social scientists about proper understanding and implementation of authority within the academy. In the arena of teaching, the change was manifested in programs on racial and ethnic studies. In the research world, the challenge took the forms of debates about interpretation, control of resources, and formation of new organizations.

The literature on these issues is extensive—especially if one chooses to look beyond the most established publications. For the purposes of this chapter, we compare two papers selected because they represent a kind of natural experiment. Both written in the early 1970s, they share a common focus: the comparison of 'insider and outsider' knowledge. Phrased in relatively neutral terms, the papers examine the strengths and weaknesses of knowledge obtained by people who are naturally members of the groups studied (insiders) versus by people who are not naturally members of the groups examined (outsiders). Both papers have a special concern with studies of black Americans. Both papers indicate that they favor neither insider nor outsider knowledge exclusively; each is careful to identify assets and liabilities of both kinds of knowledge. There are, of course, differences in the papers as well—thus their value for comparison.

Robert K. Merton (1972), Professor of Sociology at Columbia and a white male, is the author of 'Insiders and Outsiders: A Chapter in the Sociology of Knowledge'. Delmos J. Jones (1970), Assistant Professor of Anthropology at SUNY and a black man, is the author of 'Towards a Native Anthropology'. The authors thus differ by rank, by institution, by field, by age and by race. If asked, both would probably acknowledge that these differences might affect their analyses, although, as we shall see, they would probably do so differently. In examining the differences in how they approach their topic, we shall be concerned primarily with how they seem to relate to themselves and to the subject-matter of their inquiry.

The authors begin their works differently. Merton enters on a highly abstract note. He wants to bring ideas from the sociology of knowledge to bear upon the problems agitating society at a time of great social change, precipitated by acute social conflict. The particular social conflict he has in mind is the civil rights revolution in the United States, and his primary concern is about what he calls insider doctrines advocated by 'spokesmen for certain black social movements' (Merton, 1972, p. 12). He establishes what he calls the 'strong version' of Insiderism, which holds that '*only* black historians can truly understand black history, *only* black ethnologists can understand black culture, *only* black sociologists can understand the social life of blacks...' (Merton, 1972, p. 13). With that sort of beginning, Merton leaves little doubt that he is going to question quite severely the claims that he attributes to black scholars. Jones (1970, p. 251), on the other hand, begins by asserting that field methodology as taught in anthropology means that research is carried out by an 'outsider' or 'stranger' to the people being studied. As a contrast, he proposes the notion of 'native anthropology', which he defines as, 'a set of theories based on non-Western precepts and assumptions in the same sense that modern anthropology is based on and has supported Western beliefs and values....' (p. 251). Jones observes that doctoral students generally are taught not to study their own people because it is generally believed that they cannot achieve adequate objectivity—except for foreign students in American universities. In this connection, he makes special note of Africanists who take degrees at American universities and study their own people. He goes on from this point to note that the pattern of exception has also included women. From the analysis of exceptions to the general pattern of 'outsiderism', Jones suggests that female and native anthropologists are in fact being used as tools by the ' "real", white male anthropologists' (p. 252). Thus, Merton begins his paper by criticizing the insider doctrines of black scholars, and Jones begins his article by exposing the contradictions in the outsider doctrines of white scholars.

The two scholars use their own material in different ways. Merton (1972) makes frequent use of his own published articles, particularly those of a theoretical nature. To the first paragraph of the paper, he adds a footnote stating, 'This passage... has not been written for this occasion' (Merton, 1972, p. 10). The implication of this citation and others like it throughout the paper is that well in advance of what was then occurring between black and white scholars, Merton possessed the theoretical equipment to understand what was happening. This both gives him a sense of having a superior position in the debate and suggests he is learning little from the issues being raised by black scholars. Jones (1970) writes the body of his paper to report an empirical comparison between what happened to him when, as an insider, he studied a lower-income black community in Denver, Colorado and, as an outsider, he studied the Lahu, a hill tribe in northern Thailand. Readers hear about Jones interacting as anthropologist in two quite different settings. We receive his personal experience of being an anthropologist as insider and as outsider. There is a sense of dialogue between the data and the investigator as human being. On balance, Merton argues from theory and principle, Jones reasons from observable data and personal experience.

As might be expected from the relative use of data by the two, we also learn quite a lot more about Jones as a person than we do about Merton. Jones tells the reader directly that he grew up in a poor black community, that he experienced discrimination, and that he can speak and understand the 'dialect'. About Merton, readers learn virtually nothing personal. There is only the citing of his own articles to which the reader may refer in order to get a fuller sense of the man. We identify him as a white male based on information available outside of the article. No information about his ethnicity or ethnic identification is available in the paper.

The two authors differ in their evaluation of the extant scholarship on the dimension of its fairness to non-western people. On this dimension, Jones is quite critical. At the beginning of his article, he quotes another anthropologist, Maquet, to the effect that anthropology reflected a Victorian sense of European superiority and was quite useful for the colonial expansion of that period (Jones, 1970, p. 251). Furthermore, Jones gives his own personal objection to the literature, reporting that blacks have a more negative self-image than whites. He writes, 'When I looked at my own experience of relating to other blacks within a black social context, I could not see the general conclusion of a negative self-image as being consistent with these experiences' (Jones, 1970, p. 253). Merton, in contrast, shows no indication of being bothered by white social science literature's giving an inaccurate or unfair picture of blacks. He does acknowledge racism in society at large, and recognizes what he terms 'white male Insiderism in American sociology during the past generations' (Merton, 1972, p. 13). But the only consequences he sees from this Insiderism is to affect the topics people studied. He does cite black scholars throughout his article—some approvingly and others disapprovingly—depending on whether they seem to agree or disagree with his criticism of Insiderism.

Lastly, there is the issue of integration versus differentiation. On this question, Merton is clearly the integrationist. He closes his paper with a plea: 'Insiders and Outsiders in the domain of knowledge, unite. You have nothing to lose but your claims. You have a world of understanding to win' (Merton, 1972, p. 44). Jones, on the other hand, argues for greater differentiation—for the support of a 'native anthropology'. He closes his article by saying, 'The emergence of a native anthropology is part of an essential decolonization of anthropological knowledge and requires drastic changes in the recruitment and training of anthropologists' (Jones, 1970, p. 258). In the end, Merton argues for the status quo and Jones for significant institutional change.

Through the 1970s, the kinds of issue raised by Jones' and Merton's articles were very much alive in anthropology, sociology and pyschology. The fundamental question was whether these social science disciplines, stimulated and inspired by the political change of that era, were also about to undertake alterations in their methods, theories and structures of governance. Some change has undoubtedly occurred—perhaps in about the same degree and with the same ambivalence as in the larger society. The debate, nevertheless, continues, most recently in a series of articles debating the composition, structure, methods and theory to be used by the Committee on the Status of Black Americans—a major effort to marshall both intellectual and material resources to assess the changing position of blacks in American society since 1940 (Jaynes and Williams, 1987a,b; Duster, 1987; Butler, 1987; Willie, 1987; Chachere, Smith and Walters, 1987; Barker, 1987).

On matters of race and ethnicity, it becomes more and more difficult for professional social scientists to act as if their own identities, their relationships with respondents, and their modes of professional organization are independent from the way knowledge is formed and what the written product turns out to be. The traditional positivist position still rules—witness Jaynes' and Williams' (1987b) integrated response to their challengers. But for the first time in the history of such studies, it is a black (Jaynes) and white (Williams) team who speak for the establishment, and their committee is 50 per cent black and 50 per cent white. Whether acknowledged or not, the white pillars in the temple of western positivist social science are being replaced by more diverse models. How rapidly and how thoroughly this change occurs are more open qustions (Berg, 1984; Berg and Smith, 1985).

RACIAL AND ETHNIC STUDIES WITH ORGANIZATIONS

We began this chapter by observing that there is a relative shortage of studies about race and ethnicity in connection with organizations. A relative deficit, however, is not a total absence. There is some literature exploring racial and ethnic relations within the framework of organizational studies, and we shall discuss that research in this section. Initially, however, we shall examine possible reasons for the overall limitation and then move to a consideration of what has been studied.

Historical Roots of the Inhibitions

As an identifiable field of study, organizational behavior is a young member of the social sciences. Surely, its origins are in the twentieth century—perhaps in the second quarter. In recent years, a growing literature about the history of the field has developed. From it we receive an enriched sense of the people who did the original studies. Data are becoming available to examine the kinds of connection that might exist between the lives of the investigators and their intellectual products.

Few studies have had more influence in shaping the field of organizational behavior than Roethlisberger and Dickson's (1939) *Management and the Worker*. The empirical research from this project was carried out between 1927 and 1932 (p. 3). In terms of United States history, this was a period of increasing restrictions on immigration. The year 1924 saw the passage of the Johnson–Reid Immigration Act, which generally restricted the influx of new people into the United States and most especially those from south-eastern Europe and Asia. The sponsor of this Bill, Senator Johnson, noted, 'The day of unalloyed welcome to all peoples, the day of indiscriminate acceptance of all races, has definitely ended' (Bernard, 1980, p. 493). Living in these times, Roethlisberger and Dickson (1939, p. 6) show an awareness of the racial and ethnic diversity among their respondents.

In 1972, when the studies commenced, the company employed approximately 29,000 workers, representing some 60 nationalities. About 75 per cent...were American born. The Poles and Czechoslovakians were by far the largest foreign groups; there was a fair sprinkling of Germans and Italians.

At various points throughout the book, there are clear suggestions about the effects of racial and ethnic differences on the phenomena being observed by the researchers. One example, taken from the notes of an observer, has the quality of ethnic and racial joking (Roethlisberger and Dickson, 1939, pp. 460–1).

S1 and W1 have been kidding each other this afternoon. S1's family is going to move. He told W1 that they're moving to a neighborhood where no Polacks are allowed.

W1: 'I suppose they won't allow *any* white people there' (emphasis in original)

Despite clear suggestions from their data that racial and ethnic forces were important elements at the Hawthorne Works, the writers did not include these variables in their theoretical analysis. The spirit of those times, as shown by the legislation on immigration, may have taken its toll on what the pioneering researchers decided to employ as explanatory concepts.

Roethlisberger's (1977, pp. 14–15) autobiography suggests that more personal factors may also have been operating. Explaining his relationship to his family, which included a mother and father of differing ethnic backgrounds who were frequently in conflict, the researcher explained his decision to 'disinherit' himself from his family.

I was an American—an isolationist by factors then unknown to me...who was not going to have anything to do with battles fought in Switzerland...or with the Franco-Prussian War. This was America, where race, color, creed, birth, heredity, nationality, family, and so forth, did not count and where individual merit, skill, competence, knowledge, freedom, and so on did. I believed it with all my heart and in a crazy way, *in spite of many subsequent experiences to the contrary, I still do*. [Emphasis added]

Perhaps it is not surprising that Roethlisberger and Dickson (1939) did not include racial and ethnic variables in their analysis, when Roethlisberger showed such a strong desire to keep them out of his life. *Management and the Worker* helped to set the stage for much of what was to become the field of organizational behavior by what was studied, by the range of methods used in the series of studies reported in the book, and by the concepts the authors put forward. Unwittingly, it may have also established what was *not* to be emphasized in subsequent years.

Historical Origins of the Inquiry

But not all early studies of organizations were averse to examining the consequences of race and ethnicity in organizational settings. Stouffer *et al.* (1949), in their study of the *American Soldier*, included a chapter on 'Negro Soldiers'. The findings from this series of studies are unusually thorough and, indeed, show some patterns of behavior and attitudes that persist until today, in civilian as well as in military organizations.

The proportion of blacks of military age who were inducted into the service was lower than for whites, the proportion of blacks who were assigned to staff as opposed to line assignments was greater than for whites, and the proportion of blacks who became officers was lower than for whites. The military as a whole was segregated during World War II. Black units did sometimes have black officers, although there was a limit on how high in the hierarchy black officers could rise. There was a tendency for black non-commissioned officers, however, to reach the same levels as whites who served in comparable units.

On matters of attitude, blacks were quite forceful in their comments about racial discrimination in the military. When matters of concern were ordered by severity, this was their first priority. Whites, on the other hand, had as their first concern job assignments. Whites also remained apparently unaware of the black soldiers' feelings about discrimination. More than two-thirds of Southern white soldiers and over half of Northern white soldiers reported that they thought most blacks were satisfied with their circumstances. Also found was evidence that blacks more than whites tended to explain relative success and failure in racial group terms, while whites showed a more individualistic model of social causality.

The findings pertaining to black soldiers' attitudes about the military were developed by having black soldiers interview and administer questionnaires to other black soldiers. This process recognized some of the racial dynamics of the research transaction and probably partially accounts for the lasting value of the research results. At the close of the war, the research was turned over to an investigating board which reviewed the major points of racial friction experienced by black soldiers (Stouffer *et al.*, 1949, p. 597). In 1948, President Harry S. Truman issued an executive order desegregating the United States armed services.

During this same period, a growing body of social research and public opinion was setting the stage for a legal assault on segregated public schools in the United States. Eventually a brief, written by Isidor Chein, Kenneth Clark and Stuart Cook, and signed by 32 social scientists, was submitted to the US Supreme Court for consideration in the now historic *Brown v. Board of Education* case. In deciding that 'Separate educational facilities are inherently unequal', the Court referred in a footnote to some of the references contained in the social scientists' brief (Clark, 1979). Although not all scholars agree, we conclude that the social scientists' brief exerted a positive influence on the Court's decision and thus helped to stimulate a period of active intervention to desegregate public schools. Although often not conceptualized in this way by the social scientists who helped to guide the intervention attempts and who conducted research on the outcomes, we frame these efforts as *organizational* interventions. Schools, after all, are organizations and, therefore, efforts to desegregate them are aimed at changing organizations.

Historically, then, we see three classes of organization which might have participated in studies of their racial and ethnic dynamics during the first 25 years of organizational behavior research. In the case of business, the historical materials suggest reluctance. The military and the public schools, however, show a different pattern—one of engaging rather than denying the phenomena. Additionally, in the latter cases, a close connection emerged between political and legal change, on the one hand, and opportunities for organizational change, on the other. With the passage of the Civil Rights Act 1964 and the Equal Opportunity Act of the same year, predominantly white business organizations of the United States faced a political environment similar to what had earlier confronted the military and public schools. In the following years, there was a modest increase in research and intervention about racial and ethnic matters in business organizations.

More Recent Business Studies

Whyte (1961, pp. 76–8) drew together a body of literature showing the effects of ethnic influences in organizations. These included a report from the steel plant in which top management were predominantly Yankees, foremen and skilled workers were mainly Irish, and the lower-level positions were primarily held by Italians and other ethnic groups. At one point in this research, an effort to appoint a Yankee who had come up through the ranks to a foreman's position was successfully resisted by workers and union officials. Even though the man belonged to the higher-status ethnic group in that community, his promotion was inhibited. The researchers observed that the data on the effects of ethnicity were not directly acknowledged in public discussions but uncovered in what workers said privately.

Other studies showed the significance of various ethnic group memberships in determining who belonged to highly skilled occupational groups, who held positions of informal leadership, and who voted for particular candidates in union elections (Whyte, 1961, p. 77). Sayles and Strauss (1953) described the effects of contests among members of diverse ethnic groups—including the 'white man', Jews and Italians—for membership in particular occupational groups and for positions in the union hierarchy. Dalton (1959) reported a detailed case that involved connections between an industrial relations manager's business career, his political aspirations, his behavior toward the union, and his relations with the black community in the location where his plant was. These findings did not show that ethnic group membership completed determined these effects. Differences among individuals were observed, and the pressures of particular situations were associated with changes by individuals. However, as Whyte (1958, p. 78) indicates, ethnic and racial dynamics, in general, tended to be officially denied at the same time that they are tacitly acknowledged.

Purcell and Cavanagh (1972), stimulated by the civil rights movement, made a detailed study of minority employment practices in the electrical industry. Included were both statistical analyses of country as a whole and in-depth cases of particular settings. This work was carried out during a period of accelerated change and documented many indications of naturally occurring tensions. Their statistics showed evidence of an increasing black presence in the electrical industry and some tendency for blacks to move into the more highly skilled occupations. The position of the unions often was ideologically to favor the change but not to act rapidly or forcefully to aid movement. In some cases, black employee organizations directed complaints against the union as well as toward the companies. The case studies showed the importance of regional variations in how changes occurred. White women in the South, for example, were especially wary of working side by side with black men due to the severe local sanctions about sexual contacts between black men and white women. Black workers often received less favorable evaluations than white workers from white foremen, and whites tended to have more optimistic feelings about their career prospects than did blacks. At the time of the Purcell and Cavanagh studies, the signs of change that were detected occurred primarily among non-management people. Several of the case studies made a particular point of examining what it meant (or would mean) when blacks entered the ranks of management.

Almquist (1979, pp. 51–3) reviewed the history of the labor movement as a whole in relation to blacks and observed that there has been struggle from the outset. A frequently observed pattern is that local unions undercut anti-discrimination policies espoused at the national level. In the early part of the century blacks were often admitted only to segregated locals, and the CIO faced situations where whole industries or jobs within firms were segregated. Prior to their merger in 1956, the craft-based AFL tended to be more resistant to black members than the industry-based CIO. During the 1960s national labor leaders actively supported civil rights legislation, and some improvement in the relationship between blacks and unions occurred.

Small (1976) reviewed the literature to determine the extent of unionism among black workers and to ascertain the relationship among union membership, unemployment and earnings among black workers. She found that in nearly all industries, except construction and transportation, blacks had penetrated unions in the same or higher proportions as would be expected from their presence in the industry as a whole. In the construction industry, however, where data were available to make the comparison, she also found that blacks were much more likely to have manual rather than craft occupations. As a result of a variety of comparisons between union and non-union members, she also found that employment was more secure, and income was higher for blacks if they belonged to unions than if they did not. These effects were more marked for black men than for black women, and they were more pronounced for lower- than higher-level occupations. Union membership did not eliminate income discrepancies between black and white workers, but blacks who were union members earned more and had more stable employment than blacks who were not.

Starting in the 1980s is yet another development in the study of race and organizations—the study of black managers. Needless to say, it was difficult to form a literature on black managers until there were black managers in sufficient number to study. This change in the intellectual content of the field was also accompanied by a change in methodological style. The new methodology involved alterations in how researchers relate to one another as well as to their respondents.

Fernandez (1981) designed a questionnaire to study the work experiences of Native American, Asian, Black and Hispanic managers in twelve large companies, all of whom had active affirmative action commitments. Prior to administering the instrument, he conducted individual and group interviews in order to develop questions that were responsive to their perceptions of the experience of being a minority manager. He found that there were notable differences by group and by subgroup within the larger groups in how critical the managers were of how they were treated in the predominantly white corporations. Fernandez related these differences to the history of each group's relations to white Anglo society, to the degree of threat posed by the group to the larger culture, to variations in social class within each group, and to the norms for dealing with authority within each culture.

Alderfer et al. (1980) showed the results of diagnosing race relations in a predominantly white organization by working with a race and gender-balanced outside consulting team and, in turn, by developing a Race Relations Advisory Group, also balanced by race and gender. Working with the advisory group, the consultants developed an organic questionnaire that included statements about race relations from both blacks and whites. The diagnostic process produced a picture of race relations which both racial groups accepted as valid from their respective perspectives, set into motion a program of change that has now been underway for more than ten years, and subsequently yielded a method for intervening into the upward mobility system in such a way that black managers were less impeded than previously from reaching senior positions in the corporation (Alderfer et al., 1987). This project also provided detailed analyses of within-group differences among black and white managers in how they understood changing race relations in management (Alderfer et al., 1983). A crucial element in this project was establishing and maintaining an effective dialogue within and between the racial groups during all phases of the intervention process.

This period has also seen increasing attention to the methods by which black managers cope effectively with the special stresses of working in predominantly white organizations. Thomas (1986) examined the psychological and sociological dynamics of cross-racial mentoring processes. He identified the differences between the instrumental effects of sponsorship and the psychosocial consequences of mentorship. He showed evidence that *both* black and whites may pass through developmental phases in their own racial consciousness and that the sponsorship–mentorship relationship tends to reflect the state of consciousness of both parties. He discovered that some blacks establish supportive relationships with both white and black senior managers and find those relationships helpful in dealing with the performance demands and the racial obstacles of their jobs. Bell (1986) examined the life structures of black women by following the research philosophy of co-inquiry. She worked closely with her respondents and collaborators in an attempt to generate sound knowledge that was also responsive to the developmental needs of the people who provided data. The major finding in her study was identifying three primary life structures adopted by black women: career orientation, black community orientation and family orientation. Central to each of the life structures was the necessity for the women to develop a double consciousness—a capacity to live in and relate to both their own black culture and the dominant white culture. While providing important stimuli for growth and development, the phenomena of biculturalism was also a source of significant stress. The women had the task of living in two worlds and, to some degree, periodically being marginal in both. Bell's (1986) findings are consistent with Thomas's (1986) discoveries about the benefits to black managers of having both black and white sponsor–mentors and with the Alderfer and Tucker (1980; 1983; 1987) intervention method that consistently employed the perspectives of both races in the process of changing race relations in management.

More Recent Military Studies

Research about race relations in the military has continued the pattern established by the *American Soldier*. In the years since President Truman's executive order desegregating the armed services, there has been continuing inquiry into the state of relations between black and white military personnel, into the indications of change in these relationships, and more recently, into the race relations training programs that have been developed for military personnel. The net results of these studies are complex. On some indicators, the findings support the suggestions of investigators that the army in particular may be the most progressive of American institutions on matters of race. Other measures, however, show lasting and persistent signs of racism.

Nordlie (1979) developed and analysed a variety of indicators testing for race effects in the US Army. In the period between 1970 and 1973, for example, he found that blacks were highly overrepresented among those receiving dishonorable discharges, and the more undesirable the discharge, the more blacks were likely to receive it (p. 164). He also found that the period from 1962 to 1975 showed a marked increase in black representation among officer and enlisted ranks in the army. The representation of blacks in the military service, however, varied by branch. In 1981, for example, the army had the highest proportion of enlisted personnel (33.2 per cent) and the highest proportion of officers (7.8 per cent) of all branches (Blinkin *et al.*, 1982). However, among black enlisted army personnel, Nordlie (1979) also discovered an *inverse* relationship between their scores and the Armed Forces Qualification Test and speed of promotion, while among white enlisted personnel, exactly the converse relationship—as would be expected—was observed. The question, unanswered by the research, was why the Army would decide to promote black soldiers with lower aptitudes more rapidly than those with higher aptitudes.

Efforts to change the racial structure of the army were also accompanied by educational programs. Social scientists developed and tested a variety of techniques to increase the racial sensitivity of white officers to racial dynamics in the army. Landis *et al.*, (1976) showed that a culture assimilator designed to teach junior white officers how to improve their handling of racial episodes initially showed a higher level of knowledge for black than for white officers and subsequently detected increased understanding by white officers after they had been trained. Landis, Hope and Day (1984) described their efforts to evaluate broad-based army educational efforts to improve race relations. Their results were largely inconclusive—due in no small measure to changes in the management structure of the program and to difficulties in obtaining relevant measures of outcome.

Moskos (1985) brought together a variety of data about blacks in the army and concluded that the overall pattern was one of success—especially when contrasted with the larger society. He observed that instruction on the dynamics of prejudice and black history became part of every soldier's training, that the efficiency reports of officers and non-commissioned officers were modified to include race relations skills, that during the 1970s the army had a black secretary (Clifford Alexander), and that the current secretary, who is white, brings a sensitivity to racial issues that is unusual for this Republican administration. He observes that the army is a more attractive career alternative for black youths than for whites— and especially so for black women—and that blacks today have a lower attrition rate than whites, including when controls for education and aptitude scores are included. He recognizes that blacks in the Army perceive more discrimination than whites, and for the most part he does not question the validity of those perceptions.

A special feature of the black success in the military is the extent to which achievement in the service remains separate from civilian life. Moskos (1985) reports that black army generals and other senior officers who retire do not face the array of attractive career alternatives that greet their white counterparts. He observes that there is decidedly not a supportive relationship between black military leaders and black politicians. Particularly poignant was the absence of any national black political figure at a 1982 dinner honoring Black Flag Officers. This tension he traces to military officers being instrumental in promoting a foreign policy that, due to racist elements in the doctrine, rarely, if ever, receives the support of black political leaders. Moskos (1985, p. 28) concludes his review by saying that blacks in the army confront more racism in the integrated setting than even sympathetic whites comprehend and overcome more racism by individual achievement than black leaders acknowledge.

More Recent Public School Studies

Of the three classes of organization in which racial and ethnic variables have been examined, the research on the desegregation of public schools may be the largest (e.g. Stephan and Feagin, 1980; Amir, Sharan and Ben-Ari, 1984; Prager,

Longshore and Seeman, 1986). Stimulated largely by the efforts to understand and to evaluate the effects of desegregating US public schools, the literature grew rapidly and expansively during the 1960s and 1970s (Prager, Longshore and Seeman, 1986). It also took on an international dimension when investigators began comparing United States and Israeli schools (Miller, 1984). Today, there are a number of literature reviews covering this material, and they reach no consensus about what has been learned. Here we examine this array of research and commentary from the perspective in these pages.

Much of the research on school desegregation is based upon the contact hypothesis in ethnic relations (Cook, 1984). The construction of this hypothesis, whether recognized or not, is more fitted for interpersonal relations between individuals than for more complex social entities, such as schools or school systems. Many of the investigators who work with the contact hypothesis at heart are experimental social psychologists. Their arena of work—the situation they know best and which generates the greatest personal comfort for them—is the laboratory. Generally speaking, their perspective on the laboratory is on the 'subjects' of their study. From an organizational perspective, the experimenters are in charge; they control and predict the conditions under which their subordinates (the subjects) think and act. They do not reflect upon their identity and organizational group memberships.

The problem of application is to take what is learned in the laboratory and to use it in naturally-occuring settings. The literature about desegregated classrooms is least equivocal at the level of the individual classroom. Although not always consistent in exactly which dependent variables detect the effects and whether they occur for all racial and ethnic groups, repeatable studies that do show intervention at the classroom level based on the contact hypothesis has favorable consequences for students (Sharan, 1980). We suggest that the individual classroom is a lot like the social psychology laboratory. Well-trained teachers may have roughly the equivalent control over their students as carefully prepared experimenters do over their subjects.

Results and interpretations, however, become far more problematic as the level of analysis moves from the classroom to higher orders of aggregation—to schools, to school systems, to communities and to nations (Cohen, 1984; Ogbu, 1984). It is far less clear whether there is a consistent pattern of findings, and it is even less clear what the relevant political groups—and here we include social scientists as a relevant political group—believe the desirable goals should be. Concerning both what has happened and why it has occurred, dispute exists among social scientists of varying disciplines, methodologies, political ideologies and national origins (cf. Cook, 1979; Clark, 1979; Gerard, 1983; Amir, Sharan and Ben-Ari, 1984; Willie, 1984).

We suggest that these problems, at least in part, have their origins in the social organization of the research community that has developed this body of research. Their conceptual positions do not consistently distinguish between individual and group levels of analysis. Often they do not take groups and interdependent embedded groups as systems worthy of attention and analysis. They do not identify and examine the racial and ethnic identification of the investigators and how that might shape the research results and their interpretation. They do not have a *theory of changing* intergroup relations to accompany their theory of understanding intergroup relations. They do not have a tradition that calls for a disciplined self-scrutiny by the researchers of their relationships with respondents as the research project unfolds. These limitations may explain why their findings and the implications are far more promising for the individual and interpersonal levels of analysis than for more complex social entities. These comments, of course, bring our own point of view to bear on the research literature about public school desegregation.

CONCLUSION

Underlying the description and interpretation presented in this chapter are two key assumptions. They established the basis on which we examined the significance of race and ethnicity for organizational behavior, and they affected the logic by which we constructed this review. We conclude by making the assumptions explicit and by showing how they affected this article.

First, the work of social research involves an intricate interdependency among theory, method and data (Alderfer and Smith, 1982). The most common dialogue conducted by social scientists is between theory and data: what investigators consider relevant data for a research problem follows from the concepts they hold and, in turn, researchers' confidence in particular theories increases and decreases as a consequence of what data show. We have no argument with these statements as a *partial* explanation for how social research gets done. But without an account of methodology—and in particular of the behavior, feelings and cognitions of the investigators as they do their work—the picture is incomplete. Methodology follows from theory, whether tacitly or consciously, and, in turn, generates data for analysis. Methodology is not simply an appended technology that is theory and data neutral.

Second, for a more complete understanding of what we know about racial and ethnic dynamics in relation to organizations and for significant advances in knowledge to occur, we believe researchers should recognize themselves as individuals, as members of identity and organization groups, and as people with relationships to those whom they study in the methodological equations they report. Throughout this review, we have been consistently impressed with the new orders of understanding and insight—and the increased possibilities for constructive change—that become available when this kind of knowledge becomes conscious. And conversely, the amount of confusion and disorientation are more likely to increase when data about the investigators are not examined.

The first three sections of this review developed a theoretical perspective. Expecting that the majority of our readers to be white people with a Western European positivist perspective, we presented the theory by starting with an individual orientation. That is where we imagined most of our readers would begin. We moved from the individual orientation to take account of group-level and collective phenomena. Having established a conceptual position, we then, in the fourth section, examined a variety of methodological studies in order to show the complex ways in which researchers relate to their material and the likely effects that these relationships have on the data and interpretations produced.

The fifth section described and criticized the empirical research on race and ethnicity for several classes of organizations. The chapter thus reflects the kinds of interdependency among theory, method and data that we propose. The chapter is also the product of a relationship between two people whose identity and organization groups shape what they understand and whose relationship with each other is a significant ingredient in the jointly-produced document. Alderfer is a white male of Pennsylvania Deutsch ancestry. Thomas is a Black American from Kansas City, Missouri. In terms of age and time in the profession, Alderfer is the more senior person, and, for this writing, he is the lead author. There is a related paper in which Thomas is senior author (cf. Thomas and Alderfer, 1988). Our relationship began when Thomas was a student at Yale and remains alive and well at the time of this writing. We assume that our differences in race, ethnicity and age periodically influence how we experience our lives and work. Having worked together on a variety of projects over the years, we have an understanding that each of our identity group differences—and perhaps especially race—may be associated with variations in our perceptions and interpretations. We also recognize that our common maleness may result in our not being aware of another kind of difference that might improve our work. Our relationship includes a willingness by both parties to initiate and to participate in discussions of how these effects occur.

REFERENCES

Alderfer, C. P. (1976) Change processes in organizations.. In M. D. Dunnette (ed.), *Handbook of Industrial and Organizational Psychology*. Chicago: Rand-McNally, 1591–1638.
Alderfer, C. P. (1977) Group and intergroup relations. In J. R. Hackman and J. L. Suttle (eds), *Improving Life at Work*. Santa Monica: Goodyear, 227–296.
Alderfer, C. P. (1982) The problems of changing white males' beliefs and behavior in race relations. In P. Goodman (ed.), *Change in Organizations*. San Francisco: Jossey-Bass, 122–165.
Alderfer, C. P. (1985) Taking our selves seriously as researchers. In D. Berg and K. Smith (eds), *Exploring Clinical Methods for Social Research*. Beverly Hills, CA: Sage, 35–70.
Alderfer, C. P. (1986) An intergroup perspective on group dynamics. In J. Lorsch (ed.), *Handbook of Organizational Behavior*. Englewood Cliffs: Prentice-Hall, 190–222.
Alderfer, C. P., Alderfer, C., Tucker, R. C. and Tucker, L. (1980) Diagnosing race relations in management. *Journal of Applied Behavioral Science*, **16**, 135–166.
Alderfer, C. P. and Cooper, C. L. (1980) (eds), *Advances in Experiential Social Processes*, Volume 2. New York: John Wiley.
Alderfer, C. P. and Smith K. K. (1982) Studying intergroup relations embedded in organizations. *Administrative Science Quarterly*, **27**, 35–65.
Alderfer, C. P., Tucker, R. C., Alderfer, C. and Tucker, L. (1987) In R. W. Woodman and W. A. Passmore (eds) The race relations advisory group. An intergroup intervention. *Research in Organizational Change and Development*, Volume 2. JAI Press, in press.
Alderfer, C. P., Tucker, R. C., Morgan, D. R. and Drasgow, F. (1983) Black and white cognitions of changing race relations. *Journal of Occupational Behavior*, **4**, 105–136.
Allen, I. L. (1975) WASP—from sociological concept to epithet. *Ethnicity*, **2**, 153–162.
Almquist, E. McT. (1979) *Minorities, Gender, and Work*. Lexington, Mass. D.C. Heath.
Amir, Y., Sharan, S. and Ben-Ari, R. (1984) (eds) *School Desegregation*. Hillsdale, N.J.: Lawrence Erlbaum.

Asch, S. E. (1958) Effects of group pressure upon the modification and distortion of judgments. In E. R. Maccoby, T. M. Newcomb and E. ärley (eds), *Readings in Social Psychology*. New York: Holt, Rinehart and Winston, 174–183.

Barber, L. J. (1987) Dialogue on a new dilemma. *Society*, 24 (2), 29–36.

Bell, E. L. (1986) The power within: bicultural life structures and stress among black women. Unpublished Doctoral Dissertation: Case Western Reserve University.

Bennett, L., Jr (1964) *Before the Mayflower: A History of the Negro in America*. Baltimore: Penguin Books.

Berg, D. N. (1964) Objectivity and prejudice. *American Behavioral Scientist*, 27, 387–402.

Berg, D. N. and Smith, K. K. (1985) (eds) *Exploring Clinical Methods for Social Research*. Beverly Hills, CA: Sage.

Bernard, W. S. (1980) Immigration: history of US policy. In S. Thernstrom (ed.) *Harvard Encyclopedia of American Ethnic Groups*. Cambridge, Mass.: Harvard University Press, 486–495.

Berry, J. W. (1984) Cultural relations in plural societies: alternatives to segregation and their sociopsychological implications. In N. Miller and M. B. Brewer (eds) *Groups in Contact: The Psychology of Desegregation*. New York: Academic Press.

Binkin, M., Eitelberg, M., Schexnider, A. and Smith, M. (1982) *Blacks and the Military*. Washington: The Brookings Institution.

Bion, W. R. (1961) *Experiences in Groups*. New York: Basic Books.

Brewer, M. B. and Kramer, R. M. (1985) The psychology of intergroup attitudes and behavior. *Annual Review of Psychology*, 36, 219–244.

Brown, R. J. and Turner, J. C. (1981) Interpersonal and intergroup behavior. In J. C. Turner and H. Giles (eds) *Intergroup Behavior*. Chicago: University of Chicago Press, 33–65.

Butler, J. S. (1987) Social research and scholarly interpretation. *Society*, 24 (2), 13–18.

Cateura, L. B. (1987) *Growing Up Italian*. New York: William Morrow.

Chachere, B., Smith, R. C. and Walters, R. W. (1987) Causes for alarm. *Society*, 24 (2), 22–28.

Clark, K. B. (1966) The civil rights movement: momentum and organization. *Daedalus*, 95, 239–267.

Clark, K. B. (1979) The role of social scientists 25 years after Brown. *Personality and Social Psychology Bulletin*, 5, 477–481.

Clark, K. B. and Clark, M. P. (1958) Racial Identification and preference in negro children. In E. Maccoby, T. M. Newcomb and E. L. Hartley (eds) *Readings in Social Psychology*. New York: Holt, Rinehart and Winston, 602–612.

Coffin, W. S. Jr (1977) *Once to Every Man*. New York: Atheneum.

Cohen, E. (1984) The desegregated school: problems in status power and interethnic climate. In N. Miller and M. B. Brewer (eds) *Groups in Contact: The Psychology of Desegregation*. New York: Academic Press, 77–96.

Cook, S. W. (1979) Social science and school desegregation: did we mislead the Supreme Court? *Personality and Social Psychology Bulletin*, 5, 420–437.

Cook, S. W. (1984) Cooperative interaction in multiethnic contexts. In N. Miller and M. B. Brewer (eds) *Groups in Contact: The Psychology of Desegregation*. New York: Academic Press, 156–185.

Cross, W. (1975) The negro to black conversion experience. In J. Ladner (ed.) *The Death of White Sociology*. New York: Random House.

Dalton, M. (1959) *Men Who Manage*. New York: John Wiley.

Davis, G. and Watson, G. (1982) *Black Life in Corporate America*. New York: Doubleday.

Dollard, J. (1957) *Caste and Class in a Southern Town*. New York: Doubleday.

DuBois, W. E. B. (1903) *The Souls of Black Folk: Essays and Sketches*. New York: Fawcett.

DuBois, W. E. B. (1968) *The autobiography of W. E. B. DuBois*. International Publishers.

Duster, T. (1987) Purpose and bias. *Society*, **24** (2), 8–12.
Fanon, F. (1967) *Black Skin, White Masks*. New York: Grove Press.
Farley, R. (1984) *Blacks and Whites: Narrowing the Gap?* Cambridge, Mass.: Harvard University Press.
Fernandez, J. P. (1981) *Racism and Sexism in Corporate Life*. Lexington, Mass.: D. C. Heath.
Flood, L. G. (1980) Ethnic politics and political science: a survey of leading journals. *Ethnicity*, 7, 96–101.
Freud, S. (1922) *Group Psychology and the Analysis of the Ego*. New York: Liveright.
Gerard, H. B. (1983) School desegregation: the social science role. *American Psychologist*, **38**, 869–877.
Gerard, H. B. and Miller, N. (1975) *School Desegregation: A Long-Term Study*. New York: Plenum.
Gibbard, G. S. (1974) Individuation, fusion, and role specialialization. In G. S. Gibbard, J. S. Hartman and R. D. Mann (eds) *Analysis of Groups*. San Francisco: Jossey-Bass, 247–266.
Gibbard, G. S., Hartman, J. S. and Mann, R. D. (eds) *Analysis of Groups*. San Francisco: Jossey-Bass.
Glazer, N. (1983) *Ethnic Dilemmas: 1964–1982*. Cambridge, Mass.: Harvard University Press.
Glazer, N. and Moynihan, D. P. (1963) *Beyond the Melting Pot: The Negroes, Puerto Ricans, Jews, Italians, and Irish of New York City*. Cambridge, Mass.: MIT Press.
Greeley, A. M. and McCready, W. C. (1974) Does ethnicity matter? *Ethnicity*, 1, 89–108.
Greeley, A. M. and Wells, C. J. (1978) Editorial research note. *Ethnicity*, 5, 1–13.
Greene, V. (1978) Old ethnic stereotypes and the new ethnic studies. *Ethnicity*, 5, 328–350.
Hackman, J. R. (1976) Group influences on individuals. In M. D. Dunnette (ed.) *Handbook of Industrial and Organizational Behavior*. Chicago: Rand-McNally, 1455–1526.
Herbert, J. I. (1985) Adult psychosocial development: the evolution of the individual life structure of black male entrepreneurs. Unpublished Doctoral Dissertation: Yale University.
Hraba, J. and Hoiberg, E. (1983) Ideational origins of modern theories of ethnicity: individual freedom versus organizational growth. *Sociological Quarterly*, 24, 381–391.
Hyman, H., Cobb, W., Feldman, J. J., Hart, C. W. and Stember, C. H. (1954) *Interviewing in Social Research*. Chicago: University of Chicago Press.
Isaacs, H. R. (1974) Basic group identity. *Ethnicity*, 1, 15–42.
Jackson, A. M. (1973) To see the 'Me' in 'Thee': challenge to ALL white americans or, white ethnicity from a black perspective and a sometimes response to Michael Novak. In S. TeSelle (ed.) *The Rediscovery of Ethnicity*. New York: Harper.
Jackson, B. (1978) Stages of black identity development. Unpublished Manuscript. University of Massachusetts School of Education.
Jaynes, G. D. and Williams, R. M. Jr (1987a) Challenges and opportunities. *Society*, 24 (2), 3–7.
Jaynes, G. D. and Williams, R. M. Jr (1987b) Looking before we leap. *Society*, 24 (2), 37–38.
Jones, D. J. (1970) Towards a native anthropology. *Human Organization*, 29, 251–259.
Katz, D. and Kahn, R. L. (1978) *The Social Psychology of Organizations*. New York: John Wiley.
Landis, B. (1970) Ego boundaries. *Psychological Issues*, **6**, Whole Issue.
Landis, D., Day, H. R., McGrew, P. L., Thomas, J. A. and Miller, A. B. (1976) Can a black 'cultural assimilator' increase racial understanding? *Journal of Social Issues*, 32, 169–183.

Landis, D., Hope, R. O. and Day, H. R. (1984) Training for desegregation in the military. In N. Miller and M. B. Brewer (eds) *Groups in Contact: The Psychology of Desegregation.* New York: Academic Press, 258—278.

Lavender, A. D. and Forsythe, J. M. (1976) The sociological study of minority groups as reflected by leading sociological journals. Who gets studied and who gets neglected. *Ethinicity*, **3**, 388–398.

LeBon, G. (1895) *The Crowd.* New York: Viking.

LeVine, R. A. and Campbell, D. T. (1972) *Ethnocentrism.* New York: John Wiley.

Levinson, D. J. (1959) Role, personality, and social structure in the organizational setting. *Journal of Abnormal and Social Psychology*, **58**, 170–180.

Mead, M. and Baldwin, J. (1971) *A Rap on Race.* New York: Dell.

Merton, R. K. (1972) Insiders and outsiders: a chapter in the sociology of knowledge. *American Journal of Sociology*, **78**, 9–47.

Miller, N. (1984) Israel and the United States: comparisons and commonalities in school desegregation. In Y. Amir, S. Sharan and R. Ben-Ari (eds) *School Desegregation.* Hillsdale, NJ.: Lawrence Erlbaum, 237–253.

Moskos, C. C. (1985) Blacks in the army: an American success story. Unpublished Manuscript, United States Army.

Myrdal, G. (1944) *An American Dilemma.* New York: Pantheon.

Nelli, H. S. (1980) Italians. In S. Thernstrom (ed.) *Harvard Encyclopedia of American Ethnic Groups.* Cambridge, Mass.: Harvard University Press, 545—560.

Nordlie, P. G. (1979) Proportion of black and white army officers in command positions. In R. Alvarez, K. G. Lutterman and associates (eds) *Discrimination in Organizations.* San Francisco: Jossey-Bass, 158–171.

Novak, M. (1971) *The Rise of the Unmeltable Ethnics.* New York: Macmillan.

Novak, M. (1973) How American are you if your grandparents came from Serbia in 1888? In S. TeSelle (ed.) *The Rediscovery of Ethnicity.* New York: Harper, 1–20.

Ogbu, J. U. (1984) Development of interracial peer relations. *Contemporary Psychology*, **29**, 373–374.

Orlandella, A. R. (1981) The Whyte impact on an underdog. In W. F. Whyte *Street Corner Society*, 3rd edition. Chicago: University of Chicago Press, 361–375.

Petersen, W. (1980) Concepts of Ethnicity. In S. Thernstrom (ed.) *Harvard Encyclopedia of American Ethnic Groups.* Camgridge, Mass.: Harvard University Press, 234–242.

Pettigrew, T. F. (1985) New black–white patterns: how best to conceptualize them? *Annual Review of Sociology*, **11**, 329–346.

Pfeffer, J. (1985) Organizational demography: implications for management. *California Management Review*, **28**, 67–81.

Powdermaker, H. (1967) *Stranger and Friend: The Way of An Anthropologist.* New York: W. W. Norton.

Prager, J., Longshore, D. and Seeman, M. (eds) (1986) *School Desegregation Research: New Directions in Situational Analysis.* New York: Plenum.

Purcell, T. V. and Cavanagh, G. F. (1972) *Blacks in the Industrial World: Issues for the Manager.* New York: Free Press.

Quinley, H. E. and Glock, C. Y. (1979) *Anti-Semitism in America.* New York: Free Press.

Rice, A. K. (1965) *Learning for Leadership.* London: Tavistock.

Rice, A. K. (1969) Individual, group, and intergroup processes. *Human Relations*, **22**, 565–584.

Ringwald, J. W. (1974) An investigation of group reaction to central figures. In G. S. Gibbard, J. Hartman and R. D. Mann (eds) *Analysis of Groups.* San Francisco: Jossey-Bass, 220·246.

Roethlisberger, F. J. and Dickson, W. J. (1939) *Management and the Worker.* New York: John Wiley.

Sayles, L. and Strauss, G. (1953) *The Local Union.* New York: Harper.
Schermerhorn, R. A. (1974) Ethnicity in the perspective of the sociology of knowledge. *Ethnicity*, **1**, 1–14.
Schoenberner, G. (1969) *The Yellow Star.* New York: Bantam.
Schuman, H. and Converse, J. M. (1971) The effect of black and white interviewers on black responses in 1968. *Public Opinion Quarterly*, **35**, 44–68.
Schuman, H. and Hatchett, S. (1974) *Black Racial Attitudes: Trends and Complexities.* Ann Arbor, Mich.: Institute for Social Research University of Michigan.
Sharan, S. (1980) Cooperative learning in small groups: recent methods and effects on achievement, attitudes, and ethnic relations. *Review of Educational Research*, **50**, 241–271.
Sherif, M. (1958) Group influences upon the formation of norms and attitudes. In E. Maccoby, T. Newcomb and E. Hartley (eds) *Readings in Social Psychology.* New York: Holt, Rinehart and Winston, 219–232.
Simpson, J. C. (1987) Black college students are viewed as victims of a subtle racism. *Wall Street Journal*, 3 April, 1 and 18.
Small, S. (1976) Black workers in labor unions—a little less separate, a little more equal. *Ethnicity*, **3**, 174–196.
Smith, K. K. and Berg, D. N. (1987) *Paradoxes of Group Life.* San Francisco: Jossey-Bass.
Stephen, W. G. and Feagin, J. R. (1980) *School Desegregation: Past, Present, and Future.* New York: Plenum.
Stevens, S. S. (1939) Operationalism and logical positivism. *Psychological Bulletin*, **36**, 221–263.
Storr, A. (1960) *The Integrity of the Personality.* Baltimore, MD: Penguin.
Stouffer, S. A., Suchman, E. A., DeVinney, L. C., Star, S. A. and Williams, R. M., Jr (1950) *The American Soldier*, Volumes 1 and 4. New York: John Wiley.
Tajfel, H., Nemeth, C., Jahoda, G., Campbell, J. D. and Johnson, N. B. (1970) The development of children's preference for their own country. *International Journal of Psychology*, **5**, 245–253.
Tajfel, H. (1981) *Human Groups and Social Categories.* London: Cambridge University Press.
Terry, R. (1970) *For Whites Only.* Grand Rapids: Eerdmans.
Thernstrom, S. (ed.) (1980) *Harvard Encyclopedia of American Ethnic Groups.* Cambridge, Mass.: Harvard University Press.
Thomas, D. A. (1986) An intra-organizational analysis of differences in black and white patterns of sponsorship and the dynamics of cross-racial mentoring. Unpublished Doctoral Dissertation, Yale University.
Thomas, D. A. and Alderfer, C. P. (1988) The influence of race on career dynamics: theory and research on minority career experiences. In Arthur, M., Hall, D. and Lawrence, B. (eds) *Handbook of Career Theory.* London: Cambridge University Press, in press.
Triandis, H. C. (1983) Allocentric versus idiocentric behavior: a major cultural difference between hispanics and the mainstream. *Technical Report* ONR–16. Champaign: University of Illinois Department of Psychology.
Tucker, R. C. (1980) Planning for black human interaction groups. In C. P. Alderfer and C. L. Cooper (eds) *Advances in Experiential Social Processes*, Volume 2. New York: John Wiley, 201–224.
Turner, J. C. and Giles, H. (1981) (eds) *Intergroup Behavior.* Chicago: University of Chicago Press.
Van den Berghe, P. (ed.) (1972) *Intergroup Relations: Sociological Perspectives.* New York: Basic Books.
Vecoli, R. J. (1973) Born Italian: color me red, white, and green. In S. TeSelle (ed.) *The Rediscovery of Ethnicity.* New York: Harper, 117–123.

Wax, M. L. (1982) Research reciprocity rather than informed consent in fieldwork. In J. E. Sieber (ed.) *The Ethics of Social Research: Fieldwork, Regulation, and Publication.* New York: Springer-Verlag, 33–48.

Wells, L., Jr (1980) The group-as-a-whole: a systemic socioanalytic perspective on interpersonal and group relations. In C. P. Alderfer and C. L. Cooper (eds) *Advances in Experiential Social Processes*, Volume 2. New York: John Wiley.

Wells, L., Jr and Jennings, C. L. (1983) Black career advances and white reactions: remnants of Herrenvolk democracy and the scandalous paradox. In D. Vails-Webber and W. N. Potts (eds) *Sunrise Seminars*. Arlington: NTL Institute.

Whitaker, D. S. and Lieberman, M. A. (1964) *Psychotherapy through the Group Process.* New York: Atherton.

Willie, C. V. (1984) *School Desegregation Plans that Work.* Westport: Greenwood Press.

Willie, C. V. (1987) Appearances and sensitivities. *Society*, **24** (2), 19–22.

Winter, S. K. (1974) Interracial dynamics in self-analytic groups. In G. S. Gibbard, J. Hartman and R. Mann (eds) *Analysis of Groups*. San Francisco: Jossey-Bass, 197–219.

Whyte, W. F. (1961) *Men at Work.* Homewood, Ill.: Irwin-Dorsey.

Whyte, W. F. (1943) *Street Corner Society.* Chicago: University of Chicago Press.

Whyte, W. F. (1955) *Street Corner Society*, 2nd edition. Chicago: University of Chicago Press.

Whyte, W. F. (1981) *Street Corner Society*, 3rd edition. Chicago: University of Chicago Press.

Yinger, J. M. (1985) Ethnicity. *Annual Review of Sociology*, **11**, 151–180.

International Review of Industrial and Organizational Psychology 1988
Edited by C. L. Cooper and I. Robertson
© 1988 John Wiley & Sons Ltd

Chapter 2

TRAINING AND DEVELOPMENT IN WORK ORGANIZATIONS

Irwin L. Goldstein
and
M. Jocelyne Gessner
Department of Psychology
University of Maryland
USA

INTRODUCTION

All human beings are exposed to learning opportunities every day of their lives. In most of these cases, these are not planned experiences, and whether the individual learns anything is dependent upon a whole host of factors including whether the experience is at the appropriate level, whether the experience is useful, whether appropriate feedback is given, and a whole list of other factors. When these experiences are systematically planned, they are often called training programs. From this perspective, training is defined as the systematic acquisition of skills, rules, concepts or attitudes that result in improved performance in the work situation. In some of these instances, such as direct on-the-job training, the instructional environment is very similar if not identical to the on-the-job environment. In other instances, the training occurs in a place far removed from the actual worksite, such as a classroom. However, in both situations, effective training stems from a systematically designed learning atmosphere designed to produce changes in the working environment.

Since this is the first review chapter on training to appear in the *International Review of Industrial and Organizational Psychology*, it is worthwhile to describe some of the major reviews and texts that have been previously been published on this topic. Most researchers in the field consider the book by McGehee and Thayer originally published in 1961 to be the first comprehensive and systematic treatment of the subject. Most readers would note that many of the topics discussed in that text are still being examined today. Bass and Vaughan (1966) followed with a text that tended to focus more on the learning issues involved in designing training programs. In 1971, Campbell completed the first *Annual Review of Psychology* chapter that systematically examined the research and evaluation issues involving training systems. In 1974, Goldstein published his text which focused heavily on a systems view of training with particular emphasis on needs assessment and evaluation issues. Goldstein followed that text with the second *Annual Review of Psychology* chapter on that topic in 1980 and a revision of his text in 1986. In the intervening years, Wexley and Latham published their training text in 1981 and Wexley completed the latest annual review chapter in 1984; Latham is preparing one for 1988. For readers who are interested in the history of training and how it has developed in the last 25 years, those articles and books provide a fine perspective. In this chapter, the focus will be on the more recent issues facing training systems. However, since this is the first chapter on this topic for this annual international review where appropriate, we shall refer to important issues which were developed in one of these previous books or chapters.

THE TRAINING SCENE

Almost more than any other intervention, the training scene has been dominated by breast-beating about the faddish nature of training, the design of training systems without appropriate needs assessment and the failure to evaluate the training system. Probably the most pertinent remarks in this regard were originally made by Campbell (1971) when he made the following observation:

> By and large, the training and development literature is voluminous, non-empirical, non-theoretical, poorly written, and dull. As noted elsewhere, it is faddish to an extreme. (p. 565)

That is to some extent true even today, and will probably always be true. From the perspective of the entrepreneur, profits are made by selling an organization a training system such as the films for a behavioral role-modeling program, not by performing needs assessment or training evaluation. However, given all of these problems, the last decade has been witness to some very fine research on needs assessment, evaluation, and training techniques. This led Goldstein (1980) to note that there are now at least several descriptive categories which can be used to describe work in this field.

The first category consists of work that fits Campbell's description. That is, it is non-empirical and non-theoretical and typically consists of a description of a training technique or an article emphasizing the need for training in particular jobs or organizations. Recently, these types of article have expanded to include new topics such as the need for training for women entering the world of management, or the need for training programs for management in Third World countries. In some cases, they might even repeat an important goal such as the need for sound needs assessment procedures; although except for expressing an important goal, they contribute very little else. However, as the reader might expect, these types of non-theoretical and non-empirical article still constitute the largest segment of the training literature.

More recently, a new category of articles is appearing. They describe research involving very thoughtful empirical investigations in organizational environments or important theoretical and conceptual material related to the instructional process. While these articles do not appear as often as those in the first category, they are appearing with more frequency from an increasingly larger number of thoughtful researchers. This review will attempt to focus mainly on the work in this second grouping. However, there is an attempt to include materials that have implications for training which come from diverse literatures including educational psychology, vocational instruction and military systems.

Before exploring these developments, it is important to acknowledge the degree to which training has become very big business all across the world. Thus, the International Labor Office (ILO, 1980) notes that due to labor and population trends, there is an increasing need for the developing world to carry an increasingly heavier training burden. In the United States, a report by the Carnegie Foundation (Eurich, 1985) indicated that education and training has become a booming business with industrial corporations spending more than $40 billion a year on such programs. These range from programs teaching employees basic skills such as reading, to programs for executive development of high-level managers. Given the increases in technology required in the workplace and the need for more sophisticated management required to compete in worldwide markets, future training and development activities will be on the increase. In his review, Wexley (1984) describes the ever-increasing effects of technology on training efforts. Thus, he estimates that the effects of office automation might result in having to retrain office workers five to eight times in their careers and that does not even begin to estimate the effects of automation and robotics on the millions of factory jobs that will disappear by the year 2000. Certainly, the effects of failing to provide adequate training can be devastating, as was sadly demonstrated in the nuclear power accident at Three Mile Island in Pennsylvania, where a major finding was that the maintenance personnel did not have adequate training for their job.

GENERAL SYSTEMS PHILOSOPHY

During the 1970s, a systems philosophy developed which recognized the interrelated components of needs assessment, development and evaluation. Relevant articles focused on educational systems (Cogan, 1971), work organizations (US Civil Service Commission, 1969) and military systems (Montemerlo and Tennyson, 1976). Almost all of the articles have emphasized the specification of instructional goals, the design of learning environments to reach those goals and the design of criteria and evaluation systems to assess the degree to which the goals are achieved. Other aspects stressed by authors are feedback systems to permit the modifications of the training system and a recognition of the complex interactions between training systems and other aspects of the organizations including its selection system and management philosophy. The later points have become particularly important and it is clear that the best training system in the world will not work if the learned behaviors do not fit into the organization when the trainee arrives back on the job. Many of these systems models have become more complex as researchers try to conceptualize the issues involved in the design and evaluation of training systems. Thus, Goldstein (1986) expanded his systems model to include consideration of four different training goals which he named training validity, transfer validity, intra-organizational validity and inter-organizational validity. Training validity refers to whether the trainees learn during training, and transfer validity refers to whether it carries over into the working environment. Intra-organizational validity asks whether the performance of a new group of trainees (following the original trained individuals) in the same organization are also likely to learn. Inter-organizational validity asks whether a training program validated in one organization is likely to work in another organization. In his text, Goldstein notes how different needs assessment questions and different evaluation design questions need to be asked depending upon which type of validity the researcher is trying to achieve. Another type of systems model has been offered by Marx (1982) who presented a cognitive behavioral model of the relapse process which describes how learned behavior gained by managers might tend to collapse in the actual job environment. These types of model have many implications for the needs assessment process, some of which will be discussed below.

Needs Assessment

In their classic text, McGehee and Thayer (1961) described the three basic components of needs assessment as being organizational analysis, task analysis and person analysis. Moore and Dutton (1978) elaborated on these factors by describing the large number of different variables that could be examined by researchers interested in these three components. Unfortunately, there has been no systematic research comparing different needs assessment techniques to determine which have more utility for different types of situations. This is made abundantly clear by an article (Levine *et al.*, 1983) which describes an evaluation of job-analysis methods by experienced job analysts. Essentially, these authors indicate that there was no research available to compare job analysis methods so they had experienced job analysts offer their opinions of the effectiveness of different job analysis methods for different purposes. The best general advice on the use of needs assessment systems has been offered by Steadham (1980) who suggested the following postulates.

> Energy Conservation: Do not use so much time and effort in the assessment process that there is no energy left for the actual educational activity.
> Methods Potpourri or Never Use One When Two Will Do: Select two or more methods in such a way that the advantages of one offset the disadvantages of another...
> Freedom To Respond: Each assessment method exerts a degree of control on its subject (your client). Reduce the control and increase the method's flexibility to allow the client to respond in the way he/she considers important.
> Having Something Happen: Needs assessment efforts that never lead to a relevant response are useless. (p. 58)

Steadham's points make sense, although it is hard to worry much about energy conservation given the typical lack of effort in needs assessment. This lack often results in training programs that either do not teach relevant knowledge or skills or do not ensure that what is learned actually transfers onto the job. Of course, this assumes that the technology for performing relevant needs-assessment techniques are available. While job analysts might agree that some techniques should be more useful for training design than other approaches, the technology for the actual design of training programs remains more of an art than a science. The concern over this point is made clear by McCormick (1976), who has developed a major job-analytic technique in the PAQ but despaired that there was little progress toward the design of a task-analytic system which would make it possible to design specific training procedures. The one bright point on the horizon is that clearly real progress is now being made in a number of areas.

Organizational Analysis

Originally, organizational analysis as conceptualized by McGehee and Thayer focused on factors that provided information about where and when training could be utilized in an organization. Thus, the analysis focused on variables such as manpower and skill inventories. More recently, Goldstein (1986) has reconceptualized organizational analysis into an examination of system-wide components that determine whether the training program can produce behavior which will transfer into the organization. He noted that persons who participate in training are faced with a problem; they are required to learn something in one environment (training situation) and utilize the learning in another environment (on-the-job). Goldstein suggested that this requires an examination of the system-wide components of the organization that may affect a trainee arriving with newly learned skills. He noted that training programs are often judged to be a failure because of organizational constraints that were not originally intended even to be addressed by the instructional program. As an example, he noted that it is difficult to overcome a situation where the trainee arrives with a set of behaviors which are not consistent with the way the manager prefers to have the job performed. Also, training programs are not likely to be successful when managers are forced to maintain production standards while the employee is sent to a training program.

Other authors have also focused on similar concerns. Thus, Michalak (1981) warns us that trainers have put too much effort into the portion of training dealing with the acquisition of skill, and not enough in what happens afterwards. Similarly, Marx (1982) stressed the identification of high-risk situations which the trainee would face and the need for coping skills in those situations. Also, Baumgartel and his associates (Baumgartel and Jeanpierre, 1972; Baumgartel, Sullivan and Dunn, 1978) have found that training is more effective when management provides a supportive climate that encourages trainees to explore new ideas and utilize their training knowledge.

This type of work has exciting possibilities. First, it is likely that it will be possible to design assessment instruments that determine whether an organization is really ready for a training program. Also, it is likely that such information can be used to advise the organization on what it needs to do before embarking on the design of a training program. Finally, it makes it more likely that all of the up front efforts required in training may actually result in transfer into the work organization. Obviously, the degree to which this can be achieved remains to be seen, but the possibilities are one of the more exciting recent happenings in needs assessment technology. However, it is probably wise to have this enthusiasm tempered by a warning from Wexley's (1984) review. In that article he noted the importance of organizational analysis and questioned why 'training researchers have either intentionally or unintentionally chosen to ignore the influence of organizational variables on the training function' (p. 521). That question deserves consideration.

Another interesting issue which is first being conceptualized is related to the issue of future objectives. Thus, Hall (1986) described the importance of establishing a relationship between the future strategic objectives of the organization and the future requirements for their executives. In order to accomplish this, techniques will need to be developed which permit subject-matter experts to describe explicitly future requirements for their organization. This may not be a very easy task, but it is certainly an important one. This is especially the case if future job requirements are likely to change as much as everyone is predicting.

Task and Knowledge, Skill and Ability Analysis

Since the mid-1970s, there has also been several steps forward in the use of task and knowledge, skill and ability (KSA) analysis as inputs for the design of training systems. Some of the important early work was conducted by Ammerman and his colleagues (Ammerman and Pratzner, 1974; 1975; 1977). These authors described rules and procedures for the design of tasks which removed much of the ambiguity concerning the descriptive nature of tasks. They also developed methodology for the collection of information relevant to task dimensions such as importance and frequency. Their findings enabled them to decipher clues which indicated the need for training. Christal (1974) developed similar procedures for the military and in a system named CODAP developed computer routines for analysing job inventory data.

Another group of researchers (Goldstein and Wexley, 1983; Goldstein, 1986; Prien, Goldstein and Macey, in press) joined together to broaden the needs-assessment database for training systems. They essentially argued that while task analysis provides a critical foundation for any training job analysis system, a task-based system could not provide the entire foundation for a training system. Basically, Goldstein was arguing that using task analyses is the same thing as having physical fidelity. It is nice to have perfect physical fidelity, but the reason most training systems exist is that you cannot train an individual on the exact tasks that constitute the job. In some cases, such as flying an airplane, it is simply too dangerous, while in other cases the representation of the exact task is too overwhelming for the trainee to learn. Thus, in almost all situations the task is some physical simulation of the actual job. This includes simulations for learning management techniques such as role-playing or learning to fly an airplane in a simulator. Essentially, even when the task is a perfect simulation, the training investigator is still left with the overall problem of what knowledge, skills and abilities (KSAs) need to be learned. When training does not occur on a perfect simulation, the problem is even more serious. Thus, these investigators have designed work shop procedures to obtain specific knowledge, skills and abilities (KSAs) that needed to be learned to perform specific tasks. They also designed scaling systems to obtain information on the importance of the KSAs, difficulty of learning, where they should be acquired and when they were are needed on the job. In addition, they designed procedures to tie the KSAs back to tasks so that training developers could design programs teaching particular KSAs with certain simulated tasks. While these procedures are still being designed and implemented, there have been some unexpected benefits, one of which is providing the job analytic base for content validation of training programs. This will be discussed further in the section on evaluation.

Another important development in addition to the establishment of procedures for tasks and KSAs is the use of critical incident procedures as a way of establishing the behaviors expected as a result of training. Latham and Wexley, (1981) designed group workshop procedures to develop effective and ineffective behaviors which are tied to the specific KSAs described above, which in turn are tied to specific task statements. As a result, it may now be possible for the training designer to develop training materials focused on particular KSAs tied to simulated tasks for learning purposes. Then, it is possible to use effective and ineffective behaviors as bench marks to determine if the training program is achieving its goals.

Person Analysis

Person analysis asks two questions: who within the organization needs training, and what kind of instruction do they need? Clearly, the development of the type of approach described above provides the foundation for asking what needs to be implemented at what point in time. It also demonstrates the interactive systems nature of all of these type of programs. A job analysis provides the foundation for all sorts of systems besides training programs. Thus, the development of a performance appraisal system based upon the job analysis can provide information about the needs of persons in the organization for various types of training. It might even be possible to ask, from a career development point of view, what KSAs need to be learned at various points in time to reach the next level of the organization and then actually design the appropriate systems. It should even be possible to determine for which KSAs it makes more sense to test in a selection system as versus designing training systems. While there may be such systems in place, it is not very obvious from the literature. An exception is a study by Klimoski (1982) which examined self-assessments, as well as assessments by subordinates and peers of managers for a personalized training development program for managers in city government.

Most of the questions of assessment for person analysis purposes requires consideration of all of the issues facing organizations in the use of performance appraisal systems. Thus, problems such as whether supervisors are willing to provide accurate ratings turn out to be more formidable issues than technical concerns such as the format of the performance appraisal system. Some observers might think there might be less resistance to this type of appraisal because it is going to be used as a basis to provide learning experiences which will be helpful to the employee, but that is likely to be dependent upon how the whole process is viewed and managed by the organization. Another way of approaching the problem is to have the employee perform self-assessment of their abilities for training purposes. Unfortunately, a review of 55 studies (Mabe and West, 1982) in which self-evaluation of ability was compared with measures of performance, found a low mean validity coefficient of 0.29 with very high variability of SD = 0.25. Interestingly enough, Mabe and West did find some conditions that maximize the validity. They include conditions when employees expected the self-evaluations to be compared with other evaluations, when the employee had previous experience performing self-evaluation, and when there were guarantees of anonymity.

A recent study (Noe and Schmitt, 1986), involving educators participating in an assessment center for high school principals, adds some very important information to the consideration of assessment of training skills. In their study, one variable of interest was employee acceptance of assessment of their skill. They found that trainees who reacted positively to the needs-assessment procedure indicating their skill needs were more likely to be satisfied with the training program content. This type of consideration is important because it not only asks whether we can assess trainee skills in order to determine appropriate training placement, but also asks whether it is possible to determine which variables affect the trainees' willingness to participate and learn from training. In this regard, Noe and Schmitt also found that trainees who had the strongest commitment to job involvement were also the persons who were more likely to acquire the key behaviors in the training program. In addition, those employees committed to career planning were the individuals who were more likely to apply training content to their work behavior resulting in actual on the job improvement.

A clear warning on the difficulties researchers are likely to encounter in the use of self assessments is provided by the work of McEnery and McEnery (1987). They found that self and supervisory needs assessment performed by hospital employees were not related. They also discovered that supervisors tended to project their own needs when they were asked to identify the needs for their subordinates. Clearly, more work in these areas is needed.

EVALUATION

The word evaluation tends to result in anxiety because researchers have failed to treat the evaluation process as a problem-solving approach to help the organization. Perhaps remarks published earlier (Goldstein, 1980) deserve to be repeated here.

Evaluation is the systematic collection of descriptive and judgmental information necessary to make effective training decisions related to the selection, adoption, value and modification of various instructional activities. The objectives of instructional programs reflect numerous goals ranging from trainee progress to organizational goals. From this perspective, evaluation is an information-gathering technique that cannot possibly result in decisions that categorize programs as good or bad. Rather evaluation should capture the dynamic flavor of the training program. Then the necessary information will be available to revise instructional programs to achieve multiple instructional objectives. (p. 237)

Evaluation methodology is clearly evolving through a series of stages. In the earliest stages, methodology was ignored and decisions were based on anecdotal evidence such as trainee reactions. Fortunately, in recent years, there have been fewer of these types of effort. The next stage is the imposition of experimental designs from the academic laboratories which do not recognize the constraints imposed by the environment. Because the design is not matched to the environment, these efforts often do not answer the questions being asked. Finally, there is the creative design of evaluation methodologies matched to the constraints of the environment such that threats to validity are minimized and the data-sets collected are likely to answer the questions being asked by the investigators. Over the last ten years, there have been some very thoughtful efforts which have significantly improved the tools available for training researchers interested in assessing their products. The most comprehensive text devoted to a discussion of experimental and quasi-experimental designs is Cook and Campbell's (1979) volume. This text is an update of Campbell and Stanley's (1963) text. It includes some important sections on conducting research in organizations including obstacles to conducting evaluations and situations conducive to field experiments. This book should sit in a prominent place on everyone's bookshelf. Other investigators, such as Komaki (1977) and Armenakis and Smith (1978), have added to our understanding by describing the use of time-series designs as an alternative to traditional experimental pre- and post-comparisons.

In addition to these efforts, there has also been a series of articles on other factors and approaches to the evaluation process. Thus, Arvey *et al.* (1985), in a very important article, analysed the sample size requirements needed to achieve various levels of statistical power dependent upon the design being utilized. They present research indicating that the power to detect true effects differs based upon the type of design, the correlation between the pre- and post-test and the size of the effect due to the training program.

Program evaluation efforts have also begun to focus on other questions including the utility of the training effort. Cascio (1982) has described some of the issues involved in utility efforts for a variety of personnel issues including training. Thus, he presents the concept of cost-benefit analysis which refers to the examination of 'training costs in monetary units as compared to benefits derived from training in nonmonetary terms' (p. 208). Some examples of the nonmonetary terms include trainee attitudes, health and safety. Cascio distinguishes cost-benefit analysis from the concept of cost-effectiveness which is the examination of training costs in monetary units as compared to the benefits of training also in monetary units. Cullen *et al.* (1978) have actually outlined the costs for structured versus unstructured training for a production worker. Some of the costs that are included in their model include training development, training materials, training time and production losses. Each of these variables is then carefully detailed.

In broader terms, the use of utility analysis is a good sign in the sense that researchers are beginning to recognize that there are many different types of evaluation model which can provide important information concerning the impact of training programs. Thus, Simpson (1984) describes an econometric model examining issues affecting training policy in Canada. Some of his results indicate that turnover discourages specific training but does encourage general training, and that unionization in Canada does not appear to have a significant impact on training decisions in industry. In addition to econometric analysis, Goldstein (1986) describes a number of different types of evaluation model that could be useful in various situations, including qualitative models, adversarial models based on legal considerations, and content-validity models.

The later model—content validity—deserves some further comment. For some time now, there has been considerable interest in the development of methods which would permit an analysis of the degree to which training programs reflect the important knowledge, skills and abilities as determined by a job analysis. This work has also been stimulated by issues in fair employment practices concerns in the United States. In this situation, professional standards have maintained that in order for a selection test to be validated against a training program, there needs to be evidence that the training program is either content-valid or that performance in training is related to performance on the job. The problem is that the methodology for establishing content validity for training programs has been lacking. Recently, two lines of investigation have showed some promise. One approach advocated by Ford and his colleagues (Ford and Wroten, 1984) advocates the use of Lawshe's content validity ratio to determine whether a Knowledge, Skill and Ability (KSA) covered in training is also rated as an important KSA for the job. In this type of analysis, the data provide an analysis on each individual KSA as to whether a KSA which is covered in training is rated as important for the job. Another approach being developed by Goldstein and his colleagues (Newman, 1985; Goldstein, 1986) collects data from a set of Subject-Matter Experts (SMEs) scaling KSAs as to degree of criticality or importance for the job. Then, an independent set of SMEs scale the KSAs on the degree to which they are emphasized or the time spent in training. Typically the SMEs on the degree of emphasis in training are both trainees who have just completed the program and trainers who teach in the program. These researchers then correlate the set of ratings on job importance and training emphasis. In addition, this method produces comparative information on the degree of criticality on the job versus emphasis in training which can be used in a qualitative way to revise the training program. Thus, when KSAs are determined to be not important for the job but emphasized in training, it is possible to consider whether the KSA should have such a prominent place in the training program. Similarly, if a KSA is critical for the job but not present in training, it is possible to ask whether persons are selected to have that KSA or whether it might be obtained in another way such as on the job instruction. If it is not, then it is necessary to consider where that KSA fits into the organization's plans.

Two other approaches which are variants of the above methods for examining content validity have recently been published. In one effort (Bownas, Bosshardt and Donnelly, 1985), the authors developed an approach to test the degree of fit between training curriculum content and job task performance requirements. In another study, Faley and Sundstrom (1985) presented a procedure used the Position Analysis Questionnaire to compare a training program and its profile match with the job. While it is clear that these methods do not all produce the same information, it is interesting that after twenty years of discussion, researchers are finally beginning to focus on the problem. While there is considerable research to be done on these content-validity schemes, it is one of the more interesting applications of evaluation models now being developed.

Finally, one other topic concerning evaluation deserves to be mentioned. That is, it has become increasing clear that both the implementation of a training program and certainly any attempt to evaluate it, need to be treated as an intervention within the organization. Thus, it is important to recognize that there are a whole set of values and attitudes which belong to the evaluator, the trainees, the decision-makers in the organization, and the trainers, which affect the decisions concerning the intervention. Further, there is a growing recognition that all of our decisions in conducting the training or the evaluation or the needs assessment have an affect on the study itself. One example is a study by Pfister (1975) in which the assignment of 24 of 78 police officer volunteers to a control condition resulted in the officers becoming angry and making unpublishable comments regarding the research investigation. One could easily imagine managers who were assigned to control conditions being upset because they assume that since they are not being trained, they are being passed over for promotion.

Clearly, there are many types of intervention effect and understanding those issues are important in the design of interventions. This is amply demonstrated by research conducted by Eden and Shani (1982) on the Pygmalion effect. This study, conducted with members of the Israeli defense forces, inoculated instructors to expect better performance because the trainees were selected on the basis of their test scores, previous course performance, etc. The outcomes of this study indicated that the trainees outperformed appropriate control groups on objective measures of performance. Eden's explanation of this phenomenon is that instructor expectancies were changed, which in turn influenced trainee performance. Research studying these types of effects and how to understand and utilize intervention is a worthwhile topic for further attention.

TRAINING METHODS AND TECHNIQUES

Many of the recent efforts in the development of techniques have focused on management training. Thus, this review will also tend toward more emphasis on programs and research related to management development. However, the reader should remember that although a technique is validated for managers, it does not mean that it could not be used for other populations. Thus, behavioral role-modeling is potentially useful for many types of personal interactions ranging from teaching a store clerk how to respond to customer complaints or teaching a member of the hard-core unemployed how to respond in a job interview. Unfortunately, research on these types of use is rather limited.

As noted above, the use of management training and development programs has become a fact of life for most major organizations. The purpose of these programs has been to teach and develop managerial skills that would increase managerial effectiveness. Perhaps one of the most severe problems in manage-ment development programs, and one that is not often explicitly addressed in the training literature, is conceptual in nature. Within the field of management there appears to be little agreement about the nature of the construct itself, much less a consensus about which skills are necessary or relevant. This lack of consensus make the task of developing effective training programs a problem and creating programs that would be generalizeable across organizations even more difficult.

Techniques associated with management training and development include achievement motivation training, behavioral role-modeling, business games, case studies, encounter groups, problem-solving/decision-making training, and self-awareness programs, to name but a few (Burke and Day, 1986). Wexley (1984) reached the conclusion that most of the literature was neither empirical nor theoretical, but rather was prone to anecdotal reports. Any review of the literature would be hard-pressed to reach any other conclusion. However, it is important to be aware of the fact that there are a series of studies that have been conducted on a number of these techniques such as, achievement motivation, behavioral role-modeling, Fiedler's Leader Match, and rater training.

A meta-analysis of some of these techniques has been conducted by Burke and Day (1986). They examined 70 managerial training studies, both published and unpublished, including six training content areas, seven training methods, and four types of criteria (subjective learning, objective learning, subjective behavior and objective results). In general, management training, as measured by objective criteria, was found to be effective in improving performance. However, in many instances the meta-analysis was based on a small number of studies and the authors warn the readers that more research is necessary in order to reach firmer conclusions. They also note that the number of studies utilizing objective-results criteria are few, thus further limiting interpretations. Finally, they indicate that a more thorough reporting of methodology and analysis is crucial when describing evaluations of training techniques, in order to facilitate further efforts at comparison. While Burke and Day's analyses include research conducted over a period of years, an examination of the most recent literature indicates some other interesting trends. The following section describes some of these developments.

Leader Match

One of the managerial training methods included in Burke and Day's meta-analysis was Fiedler's Leader Match training (Fiedler, 1967), which has been the focus of several studies in recent years. Leader Match training is a self-instructional programmed text (Fiedler, Chemers and Mohar, 1976) based on Fiedler's (1967) contingency theoy of leadership. This model of leadership asserts that managerial effectiveness is dependent on the match between two factors: the leadership style of the individual and the leadership situation. Once the individuals determine their style of leadership, the situation is then evaluated to determine situational favorableness. In the event that the situation is not optimal for the individual's leadership style, instructions are given to change the situation to match the style.

Empirical evidence has been presented by Fiedler and his associates to evaluate the effectiveness of this technique (e.g. Fiedler and Chemers, 1984). However, there is still controversy concerning the outcomes of the studies and the evaluation designs. Kabanoff (1981) has criticized several studies for using inappropriate criterion measures and other possible biases, as well as attacking the design of the training program itself. Jago and Ragan (1986a) explored one of these criticisms in a computer simulation concerning the scaling procedure used in Leader Match to determine situational favorableness. Their results indicate that the instruments used in the training program would classify almost a quarter of the trainees in a manner inconsistent with the contingency model. This study spurred a rejoinder by Chemers and Fiedler (1986) attacking the assumptions used in the simulation, to which Jago and Ragan (1986b) replied by testing the additional assumptions suggested by Chemers and Fiedler. They concluded that they had underestimated the inappropriate matching, which they found to be closer to 60 per cent than the 25 per cent originally suggested.

The issues concerning these controversies are very complex. It is true that Fiedler and his associates have conducted considerable research on their technique. It is also true that the results of the studies have been somewhat mixed and that some of their results are open to multiple interpretations. On the other hand, they are conducting research in complex environments where rigid controls are not easily achieved. Thus, it will take considerable work over a long period of time to determine the efficacy of the technique but the degree of effort must be applauded.

Behavioral Role-Modeling

One particular technique which has been evaluated with increasing frequency in the last several years is behavioral role-modeling. This popular technique stems from a book by Goldstein and Sorcher (1974) who build on the vicarious learning and social learning theory and research by Bandura (1977). Modeling, as defined by Bandura (1977), is 'the tendency for a person to match the behavior or attitudes as exhibited by actual or symbolized models'. Most behavioral role-modeling in training environments utilize video tapes of the modeled behaviors, role-playing, rehearsal, feedback and social reinforcement. The underlying philosophy of Goldstein and Sorcher's development of the behavioral-modeling technique as a training method is two-fold. First, they maintain that it is easier to change behaviors than it is to change attitudes in a training program. Secondly, the focus of a training program should be concrete, behavioral goals. In their opinion, too many training programs fail because they over emphasize theoretical information without giving enough 'how-to's'.

The use of behavior role-modeling in industrial settings was pioneered by Sorcher (1971) in a study at General Electric, and a number of pilot studies were reported in the 1970s (e.g. Burnaska, 1976; Byham, Adams and Kiggins, 1976; Moses and Ritchie, 1976; Smith, 1976). These studies were preliminary with little confirmed information available concerning effective changes in the work setting. After several years passed and no further studies were conducted, McGehee and Tullar (1978) published an article comending the original researchers but noting the lack of further work. They cautioned against taking the reported results as iron-clad evidence as to the effectiveness of behavioral modeling.

Shortly thereafter, the effectiveness of this technique was demonstrated in an excellent study by Latham and Saari (1979). They evaluated the training of 40 first-line supervisors randomly assigned to either a control group or a training group. They obtained significant results employing multiple criteria including job performance. More recently, Meyer and Raich (1983) evaluated the technique in terms of actual changes in performance (behavior) using sales records as a means of tracking performance changes in a six-month period following the training of the experimental group. An unpredicted consequence of the training was that turnover decreased significantly for the trainees as compared to the control group. Another study by Russell, Wexley and Hunter (1984) found less favorable results. The results of the study indicate that although the modeling elicited favorable reactions and showed an increase in learning, it did not appear to produce changes in behavior on the job, or improved performance results. The authors suggest that social learning theory may not be as adequate a means of predicting performance change as other theories such as self-perception theory or psycho-cybernetics (Maltz, 1960). However, they do suggest that modeling may be successful if combined with other techniques. These issues remain to be explored but two reviews have since been written that may aid in illuminating these processes (Manz and Sims, 1981; Gioia and Manz, 1985).

In addition to the evaluation research, some recent research on behavioral role-modeling has been concerned with issues exploring questions as to what components of the program make it effective. A series of studies by Decker (1980; 1982; 1983; 1984) are particularly noteworthy in their efforts to explore various means of enhancing the behavioral rehearsal and social reinforcement components of behavioral modeling training. For example, Decker (1983) also explored two issues affecting learning in a typical role-modeling workshop. His results indicate that small groups of observers (one or two) should be present during a behavioral rehearsal, and that video-taped feedback presented with the trainer's critique is more effective than the trainer's critique without the videotape.

Other studies have focused on issues of symbolic coding. Thus, a field study by Hogan, Hakel and Decker (1986) compared trainee-generated coding to trainer-provided coding for generalization purposes. The underlying rationale was that allowing individuals to generate their own codes would facilitate the integration of the information in each one's cognitive framework. Trainee-generated codes were found to result in significantly superior performance. Hogan et al. make the caveat, however, that all subjects may not be competent to generate their own rules, and some care must be taken to ensure reasonable competence.

It is refreshing to see these lines of research develop and to speculate on the direction which they will take. Readers who are interested in a complete overview of research and action ideas concerning behavioral role-modeling should consult the recent text by Decker and Nathan (1985).

Rater Training

Rater training refers to the instructional programs designed to teach managers how to appraise employees. As such, the training programs for these programs are intertwined with the research on the development of appropriate performance appraisal instruments. Research in the area of training and to some extent the development of appraisal instruments are marked by considerable controversy. In part, these controversies are marked by a growing frustration among organizational psychologists that they have been unable to design research which captures the flavor of the dynamic interactions involved in performance appraisal situations.

The seriousness of this issue is reflected by the fact that researchers cannot even agree on the criterion measure which should be used to judge the effectiveness of training programs. An excellent review of this problem is provided by Zedeck and Cascio (1984) who note that 'we have developed procedures and conducted comparative studies of appraisal methods using indices as criteria that are unclear, ambiguous, and in part, wrong' (p. 471). Some of these comments are related to the idea of having true scores where truth is defined as expert raters who typically are just a sample from the population who are eventually asked to complete the rating. Zedeck and Cascio question how viewers of such tapes can be experts when they have not typically ever performed the job in question. After reviewing 34 rater training studies, Bernardin and Villanova (1986) make the same points concerning true scores and then wonder why our research has focused almost exclusively on psychometric characteristics such as halo, leniency and accuracy, while ignoring the idea that the true goal is accuracy in observing. Bernardin and Beatty (1984) further argue that training programs which focus on minimizing rating errors such as halo or leniency error simply exchange one response set for another and thus may substitute one set of errors for another without improving the accuracy of observations.

Another serious problem noted by a number of authors (e.g. Bernardin and Villanova, 1986; Goldstein and Musicante, 1986) is that the vast majority of rater training studies involve student raters in an experimental context often rating paper people. As noted by Goldstein and Musicante, even the few field studies often involve managers rating hypothetical persons. Also, very few studies examine the effects of rater training over any reasonable time period such that it is possible to determine whether training has any lasting effects. Essentially, all of these issues make generalizing to real work situations tenuous at best. The dangers here are amply noted by Murphy et al. (1986) who evaluated research involving the performance of paper people and found that results for that type of study led to systematically different outcomes from studies in which ratings are based on direct or indirect (such as a video tape) observations of behavior. Basically, the point is that we have failed to understand the dynamics of organizations and thus our research does not seem to be focusing on the issues that makes a difference. This issue is made particularly well by Ilgen and Favaro (1985) who note, for example, that a rater's behavior is likely to be influenced by the fact that in an organization the appraisal of the ratee will affect their future relationship. As near as we are able to determine, there are no training efforts that have even begun to explore these type of intervention issues. It is somewhat ironic to have a situation where research is being conducted but it is being questioned in terms of relevance. We hope the research will continue, but will begin to explore more relevant issues.

Computer-based Training

As mentioned earlier, training techniques often appear to be faddish in nature (Campbell, 1970), and sometimes come and go rather quickly. One area in which a technique seems to have suffered from much unfilfilled promise is computer-assisted instruction (CAI), more recently referred to as computer-based training (CBT), (Wexley, 1984). CAI was hailed as one of the hot techniques of the 1970s (Goldstein, 1974; Wexley and Latham, 1981). Yet, Wexley, in his (1984) Annual Review, cites only six references to recent research, four of which are technical reports, primarily of military origin. These reviewers had about the same luck in locating research using CAI in the published training literature. None the less, these few studies are worth mentioning.

Dossett and Hulvershorn (1984) conducted two studies of peer training using CAI in technical training of electronics in a military setting. In the first study, they compared three groups: a peer-trained CAI group, an individually-trained CAI group, and a conventionally-trained group. No differences in mean level of achievement were found; however, significant differences in training time were found between all three groups. Peer-trained CAI groups were trained in less time than the individually-trained CAI groups, who in turn were trained faster than the conventionally-trained group. This study has important implications for the use of CAI as a cost-effective training technique. Two people can be trained using a single terminal more quickly than one person can be trained. In other words, more people can be trained in less time using fewer terminals, which greatly increases the training capabilities of facilities with limited resources.

A more technical application of computer-based training (CBT) was conducted with aviation maintenance trainees using computer-simulation programs to teach and test troubleshooting skills (Johnson and Rouse, 1982). The conclusion of the study was that an appropriate combination of low to moderate fidelity in the computer simulations can provide enough problem-solving experience to be competitive with more traditional lecture/demonstration forms of instruction, with the added advantage of possibly lowering training costs because of decreased demands for qualified instructors.

Hassett and Dukes (1986) assert that CBT software is becoming increasingly popular in both private industry and government. They discuss programs currently in use teaching a diverse range of topics from managerial skills to medical diagnosis. Unfortunately, they present virtually no data on research ascertaining effectiveness. Perhaps, future research should concentrate on how to use the technique most appropriately, efficiently and creatively. As Wexley (1984) states, it has probably been sufficiently demonstrated that this technique is quicker than more conventional methods, and research efforts should now focus on more applied uses.

Simulations

The use of complex simulations involving role-playing and assessment elements appears to have become more widespread in industry although there are no actual statistics concerning their use. One of the more recent efforts is an exercise known as Looking Glass, Inc. (McCall and Lombardo, 1982). The specific purpose of this simulation is the development of both a management team and the individuals on it. It is a six-hour program in which the participants are assigned management roles in a fictitious glass manufacturing company. On the basis of the information they receive in an in-basket form, they are asked to interact with each other in a typical working day. Their behavior and interactions in the recognition and solution of complex problems involving the daily running of this organization are carefully assessed. The participants then receive intensive feedback for their performances both as a group and as individuals. Research has been conducted to demonstrate the content validity of this simulation (McCall and Lombardo, 1979). In another study, Kaplan, Lombardo and Mazique (1983) describe the use of this program with a 17-member management team from a public service agency. Several follow-up studies were conducted examining at both qualitative interview data and survey questionnaires of the managers. The originally positive results showed some decay over time, but were still reasonably stable given various shifts in the organization. Their evaluation support the use of Looking Glass, Inc. as a valuable learning device for organizational interaction processes, although more evaluations should be encouraged.

Case Studies

While research studies involving case studies are not nearly as voluminous, controversies concerning its usefulness has also arisen. Argyris (1980) maintains that the espoused theory of the goals of the case method does not coincide with the outcomes of the ways in which the method is used to train managers. He makes a distinction between two types of learning—single-loop and double-loop. In single-loop learning, one learns to detect error and correct it, without necessarily questioning the underlying assumptions, policies, or goals which may have created the original error. In double-loop learning, these underlying issues are questioned and reviewed, so as to understand why something occurs, in addition to finding it and correcting it. Argyris believes that double-loop learning is the responsibility of upper-level management, and that the current system of using case methodology does not facilitate the development of double-loop learning. He discusses problems with case methodology in respect to a three-week training program which he observed and analysed. In addition to his findings, he also presents some cogent arguments concerning paradigms of learning and their implications for managers. Berger (1983) presents a thoughtful rebuttal to Argyris in defence of the case method. He critiques Argyris's methodology, and suggests that a more rigorous evaluation of the method would demonstrate its merit in a less limited capacity than that suggested by Argyris. It is fascinating how the conclusion on more research is needed keeps being noted. However, at least there is research to discuss. That point could not have been made twenty years ago.

Other Training Studies

In addition to the more traditional managerial training literature, there have been several articles on managerial training of a more international flavor. Safavi (1981) describes a model of management education in Africa based on extensive field research. He proposes a dynamic model based on a four-year study of management education programs and management development programs in the 57 African countries and territories. His model shows a number of conflicts between classroom and culture for the African students, as well as conflicts between 'Western theory and African reality'. Safavi concludes with a plea for more commitment on the part of Western countries to solving African's management problems through improved education.

Eden (in press) describes recent research on managerial training in Israel. One of the most interesting is work by Mailick (1985) who has introduced intensive on-the-job training to senior management personnel in public and governmental bureaucracy. In addition, a recent study by Bottger and Yetton (in press) studied team processes in problem-solving among Australian managers and management students. Building on a body of work on group problem solving (Yetton and Bottger, 1982; 1983; Bottger and Yetton, 1984; Bottger, 1984), the authors used a management exercise known as 'Moon Survival' to investigate the effects of an intervention in which individuals receive task-specific training to aid in-group problem-solving. Their results suggest that task training for individuals helps teams to solve problems more effectively. In terms of managerial training programs, the implication is that problem-solving performance might be as readily improved by an intervention which improves individual contributions to the group, as by process consultation.

Finally, there are a number of other isolated pockets of research that are interesting and important to mention. First, there is a continuation of Robertson and Downs (1979) earlier work on the development of trainability exercises as selection tests. Readers will enjoy Down's book (1985) which describes her work in England on how trainability tests are developed and designed for a variety of vocational occupations. Goldstein (1986) also describes in his text the use of training measures as tests and predictors of job performance. One topic which seems to have disappeared from the literature is training for the hard-core unemployed (HCU) although unfortunately, the problems of the HCU in the United States do not seem to have disappeared. An exception is an interesting report by Johnson (1982) on the state of the art in job-search training. Most of the report is negative in tone concerning our ability to be able to deal with training issues for the hard core unemployed. Perhaps, the most important article in the HCU area is a newspaper editorial in the *Washington Post* (1983) describing all the characteristics of HCU training programs which make no sense in training any type of worker. They include problems like creating unrealistic expectations and stress in the trainees, not helping trainees in finding a job, etc. It does not appear that work in this area has advanced at all in the last twenty years.

A few interesting articles related to safety issues have also appeared. In one article (Spettell and Liebert, 1986), the authors discuss learning principles for safety training for automated machine systems. The nuclear power industry's concern for safety, resulting from the Three Mile Island accident, has also been a focus of attention. One interesting article (Davis, Gaddy and Turney, 1985) discussed our present state of knowledge concerning team-skills training for nuclear power plant crews.

Finally, it is important to describe an excellent research study on self-monitoring and regulation by Frayne and Latham (in press). They trained unionized employees to increase their attendance at work with a program combining goal-setting, behavioral contracts, self-monitoring, and the self-selection of rewards and punishments. Their results indicated that as compared to a control condition, training in these self-regulation activities taught the participants how to control many of the obstacles to attendance at work. As a result, work attendance was significantly higher in the trained group. To our knowledge, this is the first demonstration of the use of behavioral approaches to self-regulation as applied to behavior in work organizations. We suspect it will not be the last such study, and we hope that future research will be conducted as well as this first effort.

TRAINING ISSUES

There is a number of topics such as training and careers, training and fair employment practices, and cross-cultural training which are not related to particular techniques or methods but instead are broader issues that deserve separate attention. Those issues are treated in this section.

Cross-Cultural Training

Wexley, in his (1984) Annual Review chapter, remarks on the dearth of recent research on cross-cultural training issues. He cites a survey of 105 American companies with overseas branches in which 68 per cent have no training programs to prepare individuals for work abroad, due, at least in part, to skepticism concerning the effectiveness of such programs (Tung, 1981). The absence of such programs has been suggested as one possible explanation for the relatively high failure rate (approximately 30 per cent) of Americans abroad (Hays, 1971). While empirical studies remain scarce, a few sources in the literature have begun to address some of the cross-cultural issues with most frequently encountered articles concerned with international sales training programs (e.g. Kallett, 1981; Mitchell, 1981).

One of the major issues in this area concerns where the training should be focused. Eden (in press) cites a study by the International Labour Office (ILO, 1980) indicating that the bulk of training in the future should be carried by developing countries, especially Asia, due to population and labor force trends. Yet, most current training programs and innovations arise from research in the more industrialized countries of Europe and the United States. An even more salient cross-cultural issue stems from an ILO multinational enterprises. The conclusion was that most of the multinational enterprises created training programs in the host countries that were modeled after the training programs of the parent organization, a practice that may be dysfunctional (Eden, in press). Mitchell (1981) points out that American organizations often automatically use their domestic-training programs overseas without consideration of their appropriateness to the needs of the international setting. As discussed above, organizational analysis would probably greatly aid the transition of the training program across countries with specific attention to the cultural aspects of the new geographic location as well as the changes in organization structure that may occur (e.g. hierarchical levels, subunits).

Some direction in how to create a more effective training program in foreign countries was offered by a group of international experts who met in Tanzania under UN support (United Nations, 1982). Two of their more cogent suggestions concerning the role of indigenous research were summarized by Eden (in press). One suggestion was that training designs be tied to the national development plan, a much more macro-approach than is usually taken, but one which makes intuitive sense. The second suggestion concerned the necessity of allowing the training programs and techniques to grow out of experimentation within the relevant culture. 'Technology can be imported effectively; training cannot' (Eden, in press).

This idea is supported by the early work of Triandis and his colleagues (Triandis et al., 1975) on ecosystem distrust. These authors note that members of different cultures often have less trust for persons of other cultures and more suspicions of motives. This leads to distrustful interpretations of events that may even be intended to be friendly. These authors have developed training programs called cultural assimilators to inform individuals about differences in cultures and how events are interpreted. O'Brien and Plooij (1977) used such a program for nurses being trained to work with Aborigines in Australia. In this case the training program, consisting of a programmed instructional manual, was effective but the trained group became much more cautious about wanting to undertake their assignment. Thus, the training program provided a realistic job preview which had a sobering effect about working with persons from other cultures. This supports the idea that training persons from one culture to work in another culture will not be easy. On the other hand, performing in another culture without relevant training can not be the recommended solution. Thus, in a particularly bold piece of research, Sorcher and Spence (1982) used behavior-modeling techniques to improve inter-racial harmony among white supervisors and black employees in a pharmaceutical company in South Africa. Although questionnaires were unable to detect noticeable changes, improvements in inter-racial attitudes were revealed through structured interviews.

One of the most direct approach to the issues of cross-cultural or international training was presented by Alromaithy and Reynolds (1981). They suggested a model for international training which they call the SUCCESS model. SUCCESS is an acronym for their basic philosophy: Systematic understanding contributes to comprehensive, effective, and successful strategies. Their model focuses on the human dimension, the program content and the human resource development activities. Their attention to the entire experience of shifting cultures, such as a concern for the attitudes and training of the non-employees such as spouses and families is important. They also remind the reader that one of the critical responsibilities of the HRD professional is to treat everyone, regardless of culture, with simple human dignity, a point they claim is sometimes overlooked by American trainers, but rarely by their foreign co-workers.

One final note which may be particularly relevant here is a warning by Kaplan (1979) about 'the perils of intensive management training'. He points out that management training which seeks to help the manager develop insight and new perspectives can also be potentially harmful by creating situations in which the manager can be attacked or rejected. Several sources of harm are outlined and discussed, including the power relationship between trainer and participants, the make-up of the trainer, and the vulnerable characteristics of the participants. Kaplan then recommends practices which will help trainers keep risks to a minimum by overdetermining the conditions for safety, and allocating responsibility to both trainers and participants to avoid potentials for harm.

A future look at jobs and organizations cannot help but note the increasingly fluid world market arrangements. It also makes it obvious that cross-cultural aspects of training programs are a topic which we shall hear more about in the future. Needs-assessment issues are likely to be of great concern and it may be that researchers will have to rethink some aspects of organizational analyses in order for our training procedures to be useful.

Fair Employment Practices

An issue which has had a major impact on human resources research in the United States is fair employment practices. Title VII of the Civil Rights Act makes it illegal to discriminate on the basis of race, color, religion, sex or national origin. The categories of the aged and handicapped were not part of this Act but were added later on the basis of other legislative action. Early court decisions were almost entirely related to charges of unfair discrimination in selection and hiring. However, as individuals entered the workplace, questions concerning promotion and opportunities for other jobs have become increasingly a focus of litigation. Often this brings training issues into the process. Thus, the use of training as a job prerequisite, or the use of test instruments to select persons for training or the use of training performance as a criterion for a job have all been questioned. Basically, addressing these type of concerns require that the use of training data for decision purposes must be validated. Thus, for example, if training scores are used as a criteria for selection into the next job, it is necessary to show that training performance is actually related to job performance. Of course, the validation of training measures and programs should always be required anyway but the threat of litigation has increasingly focused on the necessity for validation. It is unfortunate that all of this has occurred in this way because certainly the adversarial aspects of court trials are not necessarily the best arena for progress in scientific work. On the other hand, more than one investigator has noted that some interesting work in areas such as the content validation of training programs have increasingly been emphasized because researchers are focusing more closely on developing sound evaluation strategies. An excellent overall review of training and fair employment practices is offered by Russell (1984). In addition, Goldstein (1986) presents materials related to the impact of fair employment practices on training issues such as needs assessment and evaluation.

Changing Careers and Training Issues

There are a number of very interesting areas related to training and changing careers. One issue is related to the point that there are large numbers of individuals who for one reason or another find themselves seeking retraining for new jobs or careers. The reasons for this are rather varied and complex. In some cases, individuals have lost jobs because of rapidly changing technologies. Thus, the rapid changes in automated and computerized systems have made some jobs obsolete. In other cases, individuals have reached a point in their career where there is a formal or informal age limit (for example, athletes or airline pilots or firefighters). In other cases, there is recognition that the first career offers little opportunity for advancement or the individual is interested in seeking other interests.

These kinds of concerns involve a whole set of individual, organizational and societal issues. One set of issues relate to the questions of the needs of the future labor force. Thus, Vobejda (1987) describes the executives of the new Madza plant in Michigan as having very clear future objectives for their workforce. 'They want their new employees to be able to work in teams, to rotate through various jobs, to understand how their tasks fit into the entire process, to spot problems in production, to trouble shoot, articulate the problems to others, suggest improvements and write detail charts and memos that serve as a road map in the assembly of the car' (p. A14). Adding to this issue is rapid technical obsolescence of individuals who previously had very advanced training. Thus, the estimate is that the engineer's education has a half-life of five years. That is, half of what has been learned in school is obsolete five years after graduation. An important article by Fossum et al. (1986) presents a model of the skills obsolescence process and describes factors contributing to job and personal changes. It also considers job and organizational influences associated with obsolescence. These kinds of issues and the direction of the future and what it will consist of present quite a menu of challenges for training. Some predict that the declining number of persons in the population of a number of industrialized societies will make every worker a very valuable resource and training and retraining will become increasingly important.

Odiorne (1980) suggests that strategic planning should be an integral part of the jobs of industrial trainers. He feels that trainers must assume part of the responsibility of determining the needs of future labor forces and start developing programs now to meet those needs. It is worth noting that this type of planning is not just necessary for jobs that are being changed because of technology. Thus, Zenger (1981) points out career planning is an overlooked skill in the management training area. In his view, one of the responsibilities of the organization should be to ensure that employees have qualified people with whom to discuss their future career goals and how to attain them. One of the serious issues involved in the entire area of training and retraining is that the individuals involved are often entering careers which are not traditional such as women entering management. In other cases, the individuals changing careers are older than persons traditionally entering the workplace. As indicated above, both groups have been subjected to discrimination in employment situations and the issues involved in these situations are quite emotional. In the case of the older worker, most discrimination cases are based upon the premise that older workers can not perform as well on the job and can not acquire new skills.

Rhodes' (1983) review of studies conducted over the last 30 years does not support such a premise. Basically, while a few of the studies found relationships between age and performance, they tend to disappear when effects of experience are partialled out. Also, those few studies where effects remain tend to be where there is high demand for speed and accuracy of movement. However for the most part, the jobs were not extreme enough for these differences to show up and in those cases where there were high-demand jobs, the older persons remaining in that situation were individuals who could perform the job. These issues become even more complicated when measures other than turnover are used. Thus, Rhodes's analysis found evidence for a negative relationship, that is the higher the age the less the turnover. Unfortunately, the entire literature is marked by problems including failing to conduct longitudinal rather than cross sectional studies. Also, there is a tendency to make unjustified linear assumptions such as if 30 to 40 year olds have lower morale than 20 to 30 year olds, then 40 to 50 year olds must have even lower morale. An additional problem is the lack of literature regarding analysis of training and retraining data to help us understand those issues. An excellent article by Sterns (1986) summarizes what we presently know about training for older adult workers.

There are also a number of training issues concerning individuals entering careers that at one time were not considered traditional for those people. Women entering work organizations as managers is one example where there has been considerable controversy. An article by White, Crino and DeSanctis (1981) discusses many of these issues, including the problem of barriers to women entering such careers. One serious concern has been the judgement of a woman's performance on the basis of male stereotypes such as dominance. Of course, this is a performance appraisal issue, and all the comments made concerning rater training are relevant here. The other issue is whether persons entering new fields require some sort of special training program. Basically, we have not seen any evidence from needs assessment that indicates that the job of a manager for a woman is different from the job of manager for a man. Also, there is no clear-cut evidence from person analysis that women need special training on particular KSAs that are not needed by men. Thus, at this time it is difficult to support the need for special training programs. As noted by White *et al.*, that has not prevented the development of thousands of special training programs for women. However, also as noted by White *et al.*, data supporting any accomplishments by these programs is virtually non-existent. Our conclusion about these efforts is similar to the thoughts that we have offered about programs like those for the hard core unemployed. That is, it probably makes more sense to train people in the organization on how to work with new groups of individuals rather than only placing such emphasis on the reverse.

CONCLUSIONS

There has been a definite improvement in the quantity and quality of the research on training issues. There is a number of excellent attempts to both explore new techniques and examine more established programs. We would not want to be carried away by all of this, and it is clear that in some areas, any empirical research at all would be an improvement over the present state of affairs. However, it is refreshing to note some of the developments on needs assessment and evaluation models as well as work on techniques such as behavioral role-modeling. More specifically, we would like to offer the following thoughts and conclusions:

1. Further work on the needs assessment and evaluation process is critical. Research on needs assessment models specifically related to the training process is a very recent accomplishment and data concerning these models are still very limited. Similar comments concerning evaluation models could also be made. It is important to note that the development of evaluation models using base-line methods now permit the assessment of training even when sample sizes are small. Also, the emerging development of content-validity models provides another useful evaluation tool. More of these kinds of development are very important for field researchers who wish to explore the development and evaluation of new training strategies.

2. Even where research is being conducted, more sophisticated and systematic research efforts are badly needed. A good example of the possibilities is offered by the work of Decker exploring how and why behavioral role-modeling works. We need more of this systematic type of work. One-shot evaluations are useful but they are not enough. We need research that explores why techniques work, how the technique relates to specific populations and situations, and most of all, determinations of the functional utility of the procedure.

3. We have to remember that training research has as its home the work organization. Thus, while laboratory research is useful in exploring many theoretical and conceptual issues, it cannot stand by itself. A perfect example of these problems is the research on rater training where there is a failure to understand the critical intersections of performance appraisal and work organizations. Thus, as noted in this review, laboratory studies on rater training has failed to explore the critical psychological issues. People studying such issues should look carefully at the philosophy of interventions which stem from the evaluation literature.

4. It is important to begin exploring what the future will bring to work organizations and what that means for training systems. There is already some indication that future workers will need to be more flexible in their ability to learn new skills as jobs continually evolve. Undoubtedly, this will have serious implications for career development and planning. Organizations will have to take a more direct interest in the career paths and necessary training of their employees to ensure maximum utilization of their actual and potential human resources. There is also some indication that training will have to consider more cross cultural issues. In addition, we already know that organizations will have to concern themselves with more of an aging population as well as specific focal groups such as women in management. Unfortunately, this entire field of endeavor is characterized by continual discussion but accompanied by very little research.

We hope that the next set of reviewers will be fortunate to also find more empirical and theoretical developments in these crucial areas.

REFERENCES

Alromaithy, A. and Reynolds, A. (1981) A new model for international training. *Training and Development Journal*, **35** (10), 63–69.

Ammerman, H. L. and Pratzner, F. C. (1974) Occupational survey report on business data programmers: Task data from workers and supervisors indicating job relevance and training criticalness. *R & D Ser. 108, Cent. Vocat. Educ.* Columbus, OH.

Ammerman, H. L. and Pratzner, F. C. (1975) Occupational survey report on automotive mechanics: Task data from workers and supervisors indicating job relevance and training criticalness. *R & D Ser. 110, Cent. Vocat. Educ.* Columbus, OH.

Ammerman, H. L. and Pratzner, F. C. (1977) Performance content for job training. *R & D Ser. 121–125, Vols 1–5. Cent. Vocat. Educ.* Columbus, OH.

Argyris, C. (1980) Some limitations of the case method: Experiences in a management development program. *Academy of Management Review*, 5, 291–286.

Armenakis, A. and Smith, L. (1978) A practical alternative to comparison group designs in OD evaluations: The abbreviated time series design. *Academy of Management Journal*, 21, 499—507.

Arvey, R. D., Cole, D. A., Hazucha, J. F. and Hartanto, F. M. (1985) Statistical power of training evaluation designs. *Personnel Psychology*, 38, 493–508.

Bandura, A. (1977) *Social Learning Theory.* Englewood Cliffs, NJ: Prentice-Hall.

Bass, B. M. and Vaughan, J. A. (1966) *Training in Industry: The management of learning.* Belmont, CA: Wadsworth.

Baumgartel, H. and Jeanpierre, F. (1972) Applying new knowledge in the back-home setting: A study of Indian managers' adaptive efforts. *Journal of Applied Behavioral Science*, 8, 674–694.

Baumgartel, H., Sullivan, G. J. and Dunn, L. E. (1978) How organizational climate and personality affect the pay-off from advanced management training sessions. *Kansas Business Review*, 5, 1–10.

Berger, M. A. (1983) In defense of the case method: A reply to Argyris, *Academy of Management Review*, 8, 329–333.

Bernardin, H. J. and Beatty, R. W. (1984) *Performance Appraisal: Assessing human behavior at work.* Boston: Kent.

Bernardin, H. J. and Villanova, P. (1986) Performance appraisal. In E. A. Locke (ed.) *Generalizing from laboratory to Field Settings.* Lexington, Ma.: Lexington Books.

Bottger, P. C. (1984) Expertise and airtime as bases of actual and perceived influence in problem solving groups. *Journal of Applied Psychology*, 69, 214–221.

Bottger, P. C. and Yetton, P. W. (1984) Group problem solving: Roles of resources, strategy, and creativity. *AGSM Working Paper Series*, 84–20.

Bottger, P. C. and Yetton, P. W. (in press) Improving group performance by training in individual problem solving. *Journal of Applied Psychology.*

Bownas, D. A., Bosshardt, M. J. and Donnelly, L. F. (1985) A quantitative approach to evaluating training curriculum content sampling adequacy. *Personnel Psychology*, 38, 117–131.

Burke, M. J. and Day, R. R. (1986) A cumulative study of the effectiveness of managerial training. *Journal of Applied Psychology*, 71, 232–245.

Burnaska, R. F. (1976) The effects of behavior modeling training upon managers' behaviors and employees' perceptions. *Personnel Psychology*, 29, 325–328.

Byham, W. C., Adams, D. and Kiggins, A. (1976) Transfer of modeling training to the job. *Personnel Psychology*, 29, 345–349.

Campbell, D. and Stanley, J. (1963) *Experimental and Quasi-experimental Designs for Research.* Chicago: Rand-McNally.

Campbell, J. P. (1971) Personnel training and development. In *Annual Review of Psychology.* Palo Alto, CA: Annual Reviews.

Campbell, J. P., Dunnette, M. D., Lawler, E. E. and Weick, K. E. Jr (1970) *Managerial Behavior, Performance and Effectiveness.* New York: McGraw-Hill.

Cascio, W. F. (1982) *Costing Human Resources: The Financial Impact of Behavior in Organizations.* Boston, MA.: Kent.

Chemers, M. M. and Fiedler, F. E. (1986) The trouble with assumptions: A reply to Jago and Ragan. *Journal of Applied Psychology*, **71**, 560–563.

Christal, R. E. (1974) The United States Air Force occupational research project. *AFHRL Technical Report 77–34*. Brooks Air Force Base, Texas.

Cogan, E. A. (1971) Systems analysis and the introduction of educational technology in schools. *HumRRO Prof Paper 14–71*. Alexandria, VA.

Cook, T. D. and Campbell, D. T. (1976) The design and conduct of quasi experiments and true experiments in field settings. In M. D. Dunnette (ed.) *Handbook of Industrial and Organizational Psychology*. Chicago: Rand-McNally, 223–415.

Cook, T. D. and Campbell, D. T. (1979) *Quasi-Experimentation: Design and Analysis Issues for Field Settings*. Chicago: Rand-McNally.

Cullen, J. G., Sawzin, S. A., Sisson, G. R. and Swanson, R. A. (1978) Cost effectiveness: a model for assessing training investment. *Training and Development Journal*, **32**, 24–29.

Davis, L. T., Gaddy, C. D. and Turney, J. R. (1985) *An Approach to Team Skills Training of Nuclear Power Plant Control Crews*. Washington, D.C.: US Nuclear Regulatory Commission.

Decker, P. J. (1980) Effects of symbolic coding and rehersal in behaviour modeling training. *Journal of Applied Psychology*, **65**, 627–634.

Decker, P. J. (1982) The enhancement of behavior modeling training of supervisory skills by the inclusion of retention processes. *Personnel Psychology*, **35**, 323–335.

Decker, P. J. (1983) The effects of rehearsal group size and video feedback in behavior modeling training. *Personnel Psychology*, **36**, 763–773.

Decker, P. J. (1984) Effects of different symbolic coding stimuli in behavior modeling training. *Personnel Psychology*, **37**, 711–720.

Decker, P. J. and Nathan, B. R. (1985) *Behavior Modeling Training*. New York: Praeger.

Dossett, D. L. and Hulvershorn, P. (1984) Increasing technical training efficiency: peer training via computer-assisted instruction. *Journal of Applied Psychology*, **68**, 552–558.

Downs, S. (1985) *Testing Trainability*. Windsor, England: NFER-Nelson.

Eden, D. (in press) Training. In B. Bass, P. Drenth, and P. Weissenberg (eds) *Advances in Organizational Psychology: An International Review*. Beverly Hills, CA: Sage.

Eden, D. and Shani, A. B. (1982) Pygmalion goes to boot camp: Expectancy, leadership, and trainee performance. *Journal of Applied Psychology*, **67**, 194–199.

Eurich, N. P. (1985) *Corporate Classrooms*. Princeton, N. J.: Carnegie Foundation.

Faley, R. H. and Sundstrom, E. (1985) Content representativeness: An empirical method of evaluation. *Journal of Applied Psychology*, **70**, 567–571.

Fiedler, F. E. (1967) *A Theory of Leadership Effectiveness*. New York: McGraw-Hill.

Fiedler, F. E. and Chemers, M. M. (1984) *Improving Leadership Effectiveness: the Leader Match Concept*, rev. edn. New York: John Wiley.

Fiedler, F. E., Chemers, M. M. and Mahar, L. (1976) *Improving Leadership Effectiveness: The Leader Match Concept*. New York: John Wiley.

Ford, J. K. and Wroten, S. P. (1984) Introducing new methods for conducting training evaluation and for linking training evaluation to program redesign. *Personnel Psychology*, **37**, 651–666.

Fossum, J. A., Arvey, R. D., Paradise, C. A. and Robbins, N. E. (1986) Modeling the skills/obsolescence process: A psychological/economic integration. *Academy of Management Review*, **11**, 362–374

Frayne, C. A. and Latham, G. P. (in press) The application of social learning theory to employee self-management of attendance. *Journal of Applied Psychology*.

Gioia, D. A. and Manz, C. C. (1985) Linking cognition and behavior: A script processing interpretation of vicarious learning. *Academy of Management Review*, **10**, 527–539.

Goldstein, A. P. and Sorcher, M. (1974) *Changing Supervisor Behavior*. New York: Pergamon Press.

Goldstein, I. L. (1974) *Training: Program Development and Evaluation.* Monterey, CA: Brooks/Cole.

Goldstein, I. L. (1980) Training in work organizations. In *Annual Review of Psychology.* Palo Alto, CA.: Annual Reviews.

Goldstein, I. L. (1986) *Training in Organizations: Needs Assessment, Development, and Evaluation,* 2nd edition. Monterey, CA: Brooks/Cole.

Goldstein, I. L. and Musicante, G. R. (1986) The applicability of a training transfer model to issues concerning rater training. In E. A. Locke (ed.) *Generalizing from Laboratory to Field Settings.* Lexington, Mass.: Lexington Books.

Goldstein, I. L. and Wexley, K. N. (1983) *Needs Assessment Approaches in the Design of Training Systems.* Workshop presented at the American Psychological Association, Los Angeles, CA.

Gray, J. L. (1979) The myths of the myths about behavior modification in organizations: A reply to Locke's criticisms of behavior modification. *Academy of Management Review,* **4,** 121–129.

Hall, D. T. (1986) Dilemmas in linking succession planning to individual executive learning. *Human Resource Management,* **25,** 235–65.

Hassett, J. and Dukes, S. (1986) The new employee trainer: A floppy disk. *Psychology Today,* **20** (9), 30–36.

Hays, R. D. (1971) Ascribed behavioral determinants of success–failure among US expatriate managers. *Journal of International Business Studies,* **2,** 40–46.

Hogan, P. M., Hakel, M. D. and Decker, P. J. (1986) Effects of trainee-generated versus trainer-provided rule codes on generalization in behavior-modeling training. *Journal of Applied Psychology,* **71,** 469–473.

Ilgen, D. R. and Favero, J. L. (1985) Limits in generalizing from psychological research to performance appraisal processes. *Academy of Management Review,* **10,** 311–321.

International Labor Office (1980) *Training: Challenge of the 1980s.* Geneva: Author.

International Labor Office (1981) *Multinationals' Training Practices and Development.* Geneva: Author.

Jago, A. G. and Ragan, J. W. (1986a) The trouble with LEADER MATCH is that it doesn't match Fiedler's contingency model. *Journal of Applied Psychology,* **71,** 555–559.

Jago, A. G. and Ragan, J. W. (1986b) Some assumptions are more troubling than others: Rejoinder to Chemers and Fiedler. *Journal of Applied Psychology,* **71,** 564–565.

Johnson, M. (1982) *The State of the Art in Job Search Training.* Washington, D.C.: US Dept of Labor.

Johnson, W. B. and Rouse, W. B. (1982) Training maintenance technicians for troubleshooting: Two experiments with computer simulations. *Human Factors,* **24** (3), 271–276.

Kabanoff, B. (1981) The critique of LEADER MATCH and its implications for leadership research. *Personnel Psychology,* **34,** 749–764.

Kallett, M. W. (1981) Conducting international sales training. *Training and Development Journal,* **35,** 30–33.

Kaplan, R. E. (1979) The perils of intensive management training and how to avoid them. (Technical Report 19). Greensboro, N.C.: Center for Creative Leadership.

Kaplan, R. E., Lombardo, M. M. and Mazique, M. S. (1983) A mirror for managers: Using simulation to develop management teams. (Technical Report 13). Greensboro, N.C.: Center for Creative Leadership.

Kirkpatrick, D. (1959; 1960) Techniques for evaluating training programs. *Journal of the American society for Training Directors,* **13,** 3–9; **14,** 13–18, 28–32.

Klimoski, R. J. (1982) *Needs Assessment for Management Development.* Presented at Ann. Meet. Am. Psychol. Assoc., 90th, Washington, D.C.

Komaki, J. (1977) Alternative evaluation strategies in work settings. *Journal of Organizational Behavior Management*, **1** (1), 53–77.

Latham, G. P. and Saari, L. M. (1979) Application of social learning theory to training supervisors through behavior modeling. *Journal of Applied Psychology*, **64**, 239–246.

Latham, G. P. and Wexley, K. N. (1981) *Increasing Productivity Through Performance Appraisal*. Reading, Mass.: Addison-Wesley.

Latham, G. P. (in press). Human resource training and development. In *Annual Review of Psychology*. Palo Alto, CA: Annual Reviews.

Levine, E. L., Ash, R. A., Hall, H. and Sistrunk, F. (1983) Evaluation of job analysis methods by experienced job analysts. *Academy of Management Journal*, **26**, 339–348.

Locke, E. (1977) The myths of behavior modification in organizations. *Academy of Management Review*, **2**, 543–555.

Locke, E. (1979) Myths in 'The myths of the myths about behavior modification in organizations'. *Academy of Management Review*, **4**, 131–136.

Mabe, P. A. III and West, S. G. (1982) Validity of self-evaluation of ability: A review and meta-analysis. *Journal of Applied Psychology*, **67**, 280–296.

Maltz, M. (1960) *Psycho-cybernetics*. Englewood Cliffs, N.J.: Prentice-Hall, 256.

Manz, C. C. and Sims, H. P. (1981) Vicarious learning: The influence of modeling on organizational behavior. *Academy of Management Review*, **6**, 105–113.

Marx, R. D. (1982) Relapse prevention for managerial training: A model for maintenance of behavior change. *Academy of Management Review*, **7**, 433–441.

McCall, Jr M. W. and Lombardo, M. M. (1979) Looking Glass, Inc: The first three years. *Technical Report* 13. Greensboro, N.C.: Center for Creative Leadership.

McCall, Jr M. W. and Lombardo, M. M. (1982) Using simulation for leadership and management research: Through the Looking Glass. *Management Science*, **28**, 533–549.

McCormick, E. J. (1976) Job and task analysis. In M. Dunnette (ed.), *Handbook of Industrial and Organizational Psychology*. Chicago: Rand-McNally, 651–696.

McEnery, J. and McEnery, J. M. (1987) Self-rating in management training need assessment: A neglected opportunity. *Journal of Occupational Psychology*, **60**, 49–60.

McGehee, W. and Thayer, P. W. (1961) *Training in Business and Industry*. New York: John Wiley.

McGehee, W. and Tullar, W. L. (1978) A note on evaluating behavior modification and behavior modeling as industrial training techniques. *Personnel Psychology*, **31**, 477–484.

Meyer, H. H. and Raich, M. S. (1983) An objective evaluation of a behavior modeling training program. *Personnel Psychology*, **36**, 755–761.

Michalak, D. F. (1981) The neglected half of training. *Training and Development Journal*, **35**, 22–28.

Miner, J. B. and Crane, D. P. (1981) Motivation to management and the manifestation of a managerial orientation in career planning. *Academy of Management Journal*, **24**, 626–633.

Mitchell, F. G. (1981) Developing an international marketing training approach. *Training and Development Journal*, **35** (11), 48–51.

Montemerlo, M. D. and Tennyson, M. E. (1976) *NAVTRAEQUIPCEN Tech Report IH–257*. Orlando, FL.

Moore, M. L. and Dutton, P. (1978) Training needs analysis: Review and critique. *Academy of Management Review*, **3**, 532–545.

Moses, J. L. and Ritchie, R. J. (1976) Supervisory relationships training: a behavioral evaluation of a behavior modeling program. *Personnel Psychology*, **29**, 337–343.

Murphy, K. R., Herr, B. M., Lockhart, M. C. and Maguire, E. (1986) Evaluating the performance of paper people. *Journal of Applied Psychology*, **71**, 654–661.

Newman, D. (1985) The pursuit of validity in training: An application. PhD Dissertation, University of Maryland, College Park.

Noe, R. A. and Schmitt, N. (1986) The influence of trainee attitudes on training effectiveness: Test of a model. *Personnel Psychology*, **39**, 497–523.

O'Brien, G. E. and Plooij, D. (1977) Comparison of programmed and prose culture training upon attitudes and knowledge. *Journal of Applied Psychology*, **62**, 499–505.

Odiorne, G. S. (1980) Training to be ready for the 90's. *Training and Development Journal*, **34**, 12–20.

Pfister, G. (1975) Outcomes of laboratory training for police officers. *Journal of Social Issues*, **31**, 115–121.

Prien, E. P., Goldstein, I. L. and Macey, W. H. (in press) Multi-domain job analysis: Procedures and applications in human resource management and development. *Training and Development Journal*.

Ramos, R. A. (1982) *The Use of Job Analysis Data for Career Identification and Development*. Presented at the 42nd Annual Meeting of the Academy of Management Association, New York.

Rhodes, S. (1983) Age-related differences in work attitudes and behavior: A review and conceptual analysis. *Psychological Bulletin*, **93**, 328–367.

Robertson, I. and Downs, S. (1979) Learning and the prediction of performance: development of trainability tests in the United Kingdom. *Journal of Applied Psychology*, **64**, 42–50.

Russell, J. S. (1984) A review of fair employment cases in the field of training. *Personnel Psychology*, **37**, 261–276.

Russell, J. S., Wexley, K. N. and Hunter, J. E. (1984) Questioning the effectiveness of behavior modeling training in an industrial setting. *Personnel Psychology*, **37**, 465–481.

Simpson, W. (1984) An econometric analysis of industrial training in Canada. *Journal of Human Resources*, **19**, 435–51.

Smith, P. (1976) Management modeling training to improve morale and customer satisfaction. *Personnel Psychology*, **29**, 351–359.

Sorcher, M. (1971) A behavior modification approach to supervisory training. *Professional Psychology*, **2**, 401–402.

Sorcher, M. and Spence, R. (1982) The InterFace Project: Behavior modeling as social technology in South Africa. *Personnel Psychology*, **35**, 557–581.

Spettell, C. M. and Liebert, R. M. (1986) Training for safety in automated person–machine systems. *American Psychologist*, **41**, 545–550.

Steadham, S. V. (1980) Learning to select a needs assessment strategy. *Training and Development Journal*, **34**, 55–61.

Sterns, H. L. (1986) Training and retraining adult and older adult workers. In J. E. Birren, P. K. Robinson and J. E. Livingston (eds) *Age, Health, and Employment*. Englewood Cliffs, N.J.: Prentice-Hall.

Triandis, H. C., Feldman, J. M., Weldon, D. E. and Harvey, W. M. (1975) Ecosystem distrust and the hard to employ. *Journal of Applied Psychology*, **60**, 44–56.

Tung, R. L. (1981) Selection and training of personnel for overseas assignments. *Columbia Journal of World Business*, **1668**–78.

United Nations (1982) Curricula design for management development. *UN Publication No. E.82.II.A.18*. New York: United Nations Department of Technical Cooperation for Development.

US Civil Service Commission (1969) Instructional systems and technology: an introduction to the field and its use in federal training. *Train. Syst. Technol. Ser. No. 1, Bur. Train.*, Washington, D.C.

Vobejda, B. (1987) *The New Cutting Edge in Factories*, p. A14. Washington, D.C.: Washington Post Company, 14 April.

Washington Post (1983) *How not to Retrain Workers*, p. A18. Washington, D.C.: Washington Post Company, 12 November.

Weick, K. E. (1979) *The Social Psychology of Organizing*, 2nd edition. Reading, Mass.: Addison-Wesley.

Wexley, K. N. (1984) Personnel training. *Annual Review of Psychology*, **35**, 519–551.

Wexley, K. N. and Latham, G. P. (1981) *Developing and Training Human Resources in Organizations*. Glenview, Ill.: Scott, Foresman.

White, M. C., Crino, M. D. and DeSanctis, G. L. (1981) A critical review of female performance, performance training and organizational initiatives designed to aid women in the work-role environment. *Personnel Psychology*, **34**, 227–248.

Yetton, P. W. and Bottger, P. C. (1982) Individual versus group problem solving: An empirical test of a best member strategy. *Organizational Behavior and Human Performance*, **29**, 307–321.

Yetton, P. W. and Bottger, P. C. (1983) Relationships amongst group size, member ability, decision schemes and performance. *Organizational Behavior and Human Performance*, **32**, 145–159.

Zedeck, S. and Cascio, W. F. (1984) Psychological issues in personnel decisions. In *Annual Review of Psychology*. Palo Alto, CA: Annual Reviews.

Zenger, J. H. (1981) Career planning: Coming in from the cold. *Training and Development Journal*, **35** (7), 47–52.

International Review of Industrial and Organizational Psychology 1988
Edited by C. L. Cooper and I. Robertson
© 1988 John Wiley & Sons Ltd

Chapter 3

LEADERSHIP THEORY AND RESEARCH: A REPORT OF PROGRESS

Fred E. Fiedler
Department of Psychology
University of Washington
USA
and
Robert J. House
Faculty of Management Studies
University of Toronto
Canada

INTRODUCTION

This chapter discusses selected research and theories in two areas of the literature which are, in many respects, at opposite poles of the rational–emotional continuum in our conceptions of leadership: those which deal with cognitive aspects and those which deal with the affective and motivational aspects of leadership, that is, the highly affect-laden and motivational variables inherent in charismatic and transformational leadership.

We do not intend to duplicate the inclusive treatments of the field represented in the *Annual Review* series and similar works, but present a more extended discussion of certain recent developments in the two leadership topics mentioned above, and conclude with some general comments about the current status of the field.

DOMINANT TOPICS IN LEADERSHIP RESEARCH: 1970–1987

The topics that dominated the leadership field in the decades from 1950 to 1970 have been transactional theories and contingency theories. The transactional models of that era in large part dealt with the exchange and social contract between leader and group members, and the leader behaviors that enable group members to gain satisfaction and reward by performing the tasks mandated by the organization. The primary examples of this genre are: Hollander's (1978) work on idiosyncracy credits; Path Goal theory (House, 1971); the Normative Decision Model (Vroom and Yetton, 1973); Vertical Dyad Theory (Graen and Scandura,

1987); and the work of the University of Michigan group (e.g. Bowers and Seashore, 1966; Katz and Kahn, 1978). The contingency theories specify the situations in which certain leadership styles or behaviors will be most successful (e.g. Fiedler, 1964; 1967; House and Mitchell, 1974). These also imply that group members perform their jobs as part of the social contract. The interest in transactional approaches to leadership remains strong and is expected to continue to be so in the foreseeable future.

It is perhaps somewhat ironic that two concerns of the earliest years of empirical leadership (Terman, 1904) and the nature of charismatic leadership (Carlyle, 1910; 1917; Weber, 1946)—are now reemerging after many years of relative neglect. Since the late 1970s, leadership researchers have increasingly turned their attention to the role of such cognitive variables as the leader's judgement, perceptions, intelligence, competence, and experience, in determining leader–member relations and performance. In this respect they are in tune with the direction in which many other areas of psychology have turned in the last two decades (e.g. Jones, 1985). However, as we noted, researchers also returned to another early concern in leadership, namely, the nature of charismatic and the closely-related transformational leadership, and the effects of these phenomena on the cognitions and performance of followers.

COGNITIVE VARIABLES AND LEADERSHIP PERFORMANCE

A growing number of researchers have been asking how leaders perceive, think and judge, and how they make use of these cognitive processes (e.g. Calder, 1977). This is exemplified by the excellent collection of papers in Sims and Gioia's (1986) book, *The Thinking Organization*. Likewise, motivation theories have moved in the cognitive direction, following the early seminal work by Vroom (1964) on expectancy theory, and more recently the work by Locke and Latham (1984) on goal-setting. The present section deals mainly with developments related to cognitive approaches to leadership during the past decade.

Attribution Theory and Leadership

A number of studies have applied the principles of attribution theory to problems in the leadership area. One good example of this type, based on attribution theory, is by Mitchell, Green and Wood (1981). Their study showed that a leader's judgement of the followers' competence depends on the consequences of the subordinate's actions. This is true even when the behavior causing undesirables outcomes is identical to that not causing undesirable outcomes. Thus, Mitchell *et al.* found lower performance ratings for a nurse whose patient fell out of bed and sustained an injury because of her failure to raise a bed rail than for a nurse in the same situation whose behavior did not result in an injury to the patient.

A series of studies by Lord has shown that cognitive schemes and labeling strongly affect perceptions of leaders. Thus, Foti, Fraser and Lord (1982) found marked changes over time and across candidates in the percentage of respondents who believed that strong leadership qualities were possessed by the person whom they rated. The authors hypothesized that as these leadership perceptions changed, so would the perceptions of other characteristics that were strongly associated with leadership. Consistent with this expectation, correlational results clearly showed a greater change for more prototypical items when the leadership ratings given to the same person (e.g. President Carter) were compared at earlier and later times in his term of office, or when comparisons were made of leadership ratings given to different politicians (President Carter versus Senator Kennedy).

In another study, Phillips and Lord (1981) showed that the individual's focus affects the attributions made to the individual. The investigators had subjects view video tapes of the same group discussion with the TV camera focused either on the leader or on others in the group. The results showed that the saliency of the leader (as manipulated by focusing the camera on different persons) srongly affected leadership ratings.

Such findings as those by Mitchell, Green and Wood, as well as by Phillips and Lord, and Foti, Fraser and Lord, are of considerable importance in interpreting leader behavior and performance ratings. It is clear that the frame of reference of the rater and the nature of the outcomes play a significant role in how leaders are evaluated, and in turn, how they evaluate the behavior and performance of subordinates. On the other hand, we must not lose sight of the fact that the effects obtained by these studies do not account for more than a relatively small portion of the variance. That the single, one-shot rating of leader behavior or follower behavior has its problems has been apparent for some time (Epstein, 1975). The above studies based on attribution theory tell us more specifically what the causes of the distortions are, and perhaps, how to correct for them in the future.

Cognitive Resource Theory

A quite different direction has been taken in a 15-year research program by Fiedler and his associates (Blades, 1976; Blades and Fiedler, 1976; Fiedler, 1978; 1986; Fiedler et al., 1979; Potter and Fiedler, 1981; Fiedler and Garcia, 1987). The research has led to the development of 'Cognitive Resource Theory' (CRT). This theory provides an integration of the roles played by intellectual abilities, competence and experience, as well as leader behavior and stress, in determining leadership and group performance. CRT addresses the long-standing question of why the leader's intellectual abilities and experience correlate so poorly (.20 – .30) with performance (e.g. Bass, 1981). The question is of theoretical importance since such critical leadership functions as decision-making, planning or evaluating are intellectual in nature, and should, therefore, be related to leader intelligence.

There also is no consistent evidence that leader experience generally contributes to performance (e.g. Fiedler, 1970). In fact, there is so little research on the effects of leader experience that the term is not even listed in the index of Stogdill's Handbook of Leadership (Bass, 1981). The problem is of practical importance in organizational psychology since ability and experience probably are among the most important factors in determining managerial hiring and promotion decisions.

One component of cognitive resource theory deals with the effects of stress. It is based on the assumption that leader intelligence and technical knowledge determine the quality of the leader's plans, decisions and action strategies, and that these, in turn, are affected by interpersonal stress. In contrast to job stress, which often focuses the individual's intellectual abilities on the task, interpersonal stress with a boss or subordinates cannot be dealt with intellectually. It distracts the leader from the task and, like examination anxiety (Sarason, 1984), channels his or her thinking into worry, concerns about self-efficacy, or how to evade the boss or the stress-producing situation. Under these stressful conditions, intellectual ability will not contribute to the task, and the leader will fall back on previously learned behavior. Hence, experience rather than intellectual abilities will correlate with performance. In other words, under low stress, leaders use their intelligence but not their experience; under high stress they use their experience but not their intelligence.

A second aspect of this problem was pointed out by Blades (1986; Blades and Fiedler, 1976). Namely, leader plans, decisions and action strategies are communicated principally in the form of directive behavior, and are implemented only if the group is supportive. On the other hand, member abilities contribute to the task primarily if the leader is nondirective and the group is supportive.

Support for the theory comes from studies of military and nonmilitary line and staff personnel at various levels of the organizational hierarchy, volunteer public health teams, and college students in laboratory experiments (Fiedler et al., 1979; Potter and Fiedler, 1981; Fiedler and Garcia, 1987). These show that correlations between leader intelligence and group performance are near zero for the entire sample. However, the correlations for army mess stewards, squad leaders, volunteer public health workers and leaders in two sets of experiments, averaged 0.58 for supportive groups with directive leaders, but .19, .14 and −.18 for nonsupportive groups or those which had nondirective leaders. In groups divided on the basis of stress rather than group support, the corresponding mean correlations showed a similar pattern (.57, .07, .00, .03).

As one would expect, mean performance scores showed that the directive leaders of supportive groups performed substantially better if they were relatively bright; they performed poorly if they were relatively less intelligent. However, the nondirective leaders who were relatively bright performed considerably *less well* than did nondirective leaders who were relatively dull, especially in nonsupportive groups. In other words, bright leaders should be directive and tell group members what to do; the relatively less bright leaders should be participative and listen to others.

The interesting question is, of course, why the more intelligent leaders should perform less well than do those with lower intelligence under the given conditions (e.g. high stress, low group support, or being nondirective). This is an important problem since it means that the individual, selected for his or her intellectual abilities, in fact performs much less well than one who lacks these abilities.

Several alternative explanations appear plausible. First, the more intelligent leaders probably have higher expectations of themselves which might lead them to seek exotic and more risky solutions than would their less able and less imaginative counterparts. Second, the more intelligent leaders might be more conscious of the consequences of failure and hence also more anxious than those of less intelligence. Third, the bright leaders might well introduce many new and original ideas into the discussion but provide no direction for integrating the ideas and arriving at an acceptable solution.

The question also arises of why leaders use their experience but not their intelligence in stressful situations. Fiedler bases the interpretation on social faciliation theory (Zajonc, 1965) which predicts that a critical audience leads to better performance of overlearned and simple tasks but to poorer performance on new and complex tasks. The results make sense if we equate the stressful boss with a critical audience and experience with overlearned behavior.

Several recent laboratory experiments extend the theory. One dissertation by Blyth (1987) examined the conditions in which technical training of leaders and group members is effectively utilized. The task consisted of ranking various objects in order of their survival value to a crew that supposedly crashed in the desert. The rankings were then compared with those of experts.

In one study, Blyth randomly assigned leaders to four conditions: leaders were either trained or untrained in the potential use of various survival gear, and they were instructed either to be directive or nondirective in the management of their groups. As predicted, only the directive leaders with training had groups that performed well. Nondirective leaders with training performed no better than those without training. In a second study, Blyth (1987) trained only the group members, and instructed leaders to be directive or nondirective. In this experiment, the groups with nondirective leaders performed better than those with directive leaders.

McGuire (Fiedler and McGuire, 1987) used an in-basket exercise to study the effect of stress on the responses of leaders with high or low 'fluid' or 'crystallized' intelligence. Horn (1968) defined fluid intelligence as the ability to deal with new and unusual problems, and crystallized intelligence as the ability to solve problems on the basis of information previously learned or acquired through knowledge of the culture.

The in-basket exercise was performed either under relatively relaxed or under stressful conditions. The results showed that fluid intelligence correlated highly with responses indicating good judgement, effective problem analysis, and decisiveness when stress was low. However, under high stress, fluid intelligence correlated *negatively* with frequency and effectiveness of these leader behaviors.

Finally, the theory suggests a partial explanation for the Contingency Model of Leadership Effectiveness (Fiedler, 1964), since this model predicts not only performance but also directive leader behavior. The prediction is complex: Relationship-motivated leaders are directive if they have high situational control; task-motivated leaders are directive if they have moderate or low situational control (Sample and Wilson, 1965; Fiedler, 1970; Larson and Rowland, 1974; Shirakashi, 1980; Fiedler and Garcia, 1987). These interactions are quite strong in some cases, and have been found in a broad variety of group and organizational settings (see Fiedler and Garcia, 1987). The contingency model thus seems to predict when the leader is directive; cognitive resource theory specifies the conditions under which the leader's cognitive abilities will be most effectively used.

CRT has major implications for leader selection which should be of particular interest to industrial and organizational psychologists. Selection procedures typically are based on the assumption that a person will be effective in direct proportion to his or her job-relevant abilities and competence. Cognitive resource theory demonstrates that this assumption holds true only under limited conditions. Thus, selection will be substantially improved if the conditions obtain under which intelligence or experience is effectively utilized. CRT specifies these conditions. There have been many calls for leadership theories that combine situational and personality variables. Contingency theory and CRT provide one such combination, as well as preliminary supporting evidence.

The findings related to the effect of boss stress also are of significance to the practice of leadership since stress management, relaxation exercises and cognitive self-instruction methods provide means for alleviating stress. Thus, through the management of stress it is possible to increase the effective use of intelligence by leaders and, in Simon's (1976) terms, to relax one of the major 'limits to bounded rationality' in organizations.

Concluding Comments

Cognitive theories are becoming increasingly dominant in the leadership area as in psychology in general. Research based on attribution theory has contributed important new insights about factors that partly determine leader behavior and performance ratings. Cognitive resource theory provides a more general framework for integrating previous theories. It suggests the underlying basis for the predictions made by the contingency model, it identifies the role of such cognitive attributes as intellectual ability, experience, technical knowledge and training in determining organizational performance.

CHARISMATIC AND TRANSFORMATIONAL LEADERSHIP THEORIES

The theories reviewed in the first part of this chapter focus on the leader: how his or her cognitions affect behavior and performance. Charismatic and transformational leadership theories focus on the followers: their emotional responses to the leader. They ask how the leader affects the followers' work-related stimuli—their self-esteem, trust, values and confidence in the leaders, and their motivation to perform above and beyond the call of duty. These theories describe leaders in terms of articulating a vision and mission, and creating and maintaining a positive image in the minds of followers and superiors. At least in theory, these leaders challenge their followers and provide a personal example by behaving in a manner that reinforces the vision and the mission of the leader (see Berlew, 1974; House, 1977; Burns, 1978; Bennis and Nanus, 1985; Sashkin and Fulmer, 1985; and Bass 1985). Charismatic leaders have their major effect on the emotions and the self-esteem of followers, that is, on the followers' affective motivational responses rather than their cognitions and abilities.

At the risk of some oversimplification, transactional theories describe how leaders make work behavior more instrumental for the followers to reach their own *existing* goals while concurrently contributing to the goals of the organization. Charismatic or transformational theories primarily address the actions of leaders that cause subordinates to *change* their values, goals, needs and aspirations.

Smith (1982) showed, for example, that reputedly charismatic leaders have significantly different effects on followers than successful but non-charismatic leaders. Followers of charismatic leaders were more self-assured, saw more meaning in their work, reported more back-up from their leaders and saw them as more dynamic, reported working longer hours, and had higher performance ratings than the followers of the non-charismatic but effective leaders.

Howell (1985) compared the effects of charismatic leader behavior on followers with the effects of directive and considerate leader behavior under experimentally induced high and low productivity-norm conditions. The findings showed that charismatic leader behavior specified by prior theory (House, 1977) had a stronger and more positive influence on the performance, satisfaction and adjustment of followers than did directive and considerate leader behavior.

It is perhaps most interesting that only the charismatic leader behavior was able to overcome the negative effects of the low productivity norm condition. That is, regardless of whether the subjects were in the high or low productivity-norm condition, those working under charismatic leaders had higher general satisfaction, higher specific task satisfaction and less role conflict than individuals working under structuring or considerate leaders. Under the latter the negative effects of the low productivity norm treatment persisted.

House, Woycke and Fodor (1985) examined the behavior and motivation of US presidents. They asked nine political historians to classify US presidents as charismatic or non-charismatic with respect to their cabinet members. A charismatic leader was defined as one who induces a high degree of loyalty, commitment and devotion to the leader; identification with the leader and his mission, emulation of his values, goals and behavior; a sense of self-esteem from relationships with the leader and his mission; and an exceptionally high degree of trust in the leader and the correctness of his beliefs.

At least seven of the nine historians agreed on classifying six presidents as charismatic (Jefferson, Jackson, Lincoln, Theodore Roosevelt, Franklin D. Roosevelt and Kennedy) and six as non-charismatic (Tyler, Pierce, Buchanan, Arthur, Harding and Coolidge). Inaugural addresses of these presidents were coded for achievement, power and affiliation motives, using the major theme statements developed by Donley and Winter (1970).

All six charismatic presidents were either re-elected, or assassinated during their first term. Only one of the six non-charismatic presidents was re-elected. Content-analysed biographies of their cabinet members showed twice as many expressions of positive affect toward the charismatic than non-charismatic presidents ($p < .006$).

Political historians viewed charismatic presidents (Maranell, 1970) as engaging in significantly stronger actions, being more prestigious, active, flexible and having accomplished more in their administrations. Further, content-analysis of the inaugural addresses clearly demonstrated that charismatic presidents, as a group, were rated significantly higher on *both* the need for achievement and the need for power ($p < .03$). This finding is consistent with longitudinal field research by McClelland and Boyatzis (1982), and laboratory research by Fodor (personal communication, 1987). (President Reagan also has the same motive pattern as the charismatic presidents identified by the expert panel but was not categorized by the expert panel as he had just gained office at the time of the study.)

McClelland and Boyatzis (1982) found that managers with a combination of high need for achievement and high need for power had significantly higher levels of advancement eight and sixteen years later. Fodor (personal communication, 1987) found this same motive pattern on the part of group leaders to be predictive of group decision quality in an experimental decision-making simulation in which college students were subjects. Thus, the high achievement/high power motive pattern appears to have wide generalizability across such diverse samples as US presidents (House *et al.*, 1986), middle managers (McClelland and Boyatzis, 1984) and college undergraduate students (Fodor, personal communication). Correlational studies, as well as predictive studies, have yielded results consistent with the above findings (Cummin, 1967; Wainer and Rubin, 1969; Varga, 1975; McClelland and Burnham, 1976).

Another empirical study relevant to charismatic theory is presented by Yukl and Van Fleet (1982). These authors found in four separate military samples that 'inspirational leadership' was significantly related to leader effectiveness and high levels of follower motivation. These findings held under combat, noncombat and similated combat conditions. Thus, studies of charismatic (or inspirational) leaders demonstrated that the behaviors specified by prior theory (House, 1977) rather consistently have the effects predicted by that theory.

A second theory of the same genre is the transformational leadership theory advanced by James MacGregor Burns (1978). Burns defines transactional leadership as based on a bargain, struck by both parties to the transaction. Transactional leaders induce followers to behave in ways desired by the leader, in exchange for some good desired by the follower. Such relationships usually endure only as long as the mutual need of the leader and follower can be satisfied by continuing exchanges of goods for services. This exchange of goods is usually specific, tangible and calculable. Hollander's (1958) concept of idiosyncracy points; Vertical Dyadic Linkage Theory (Graen and Scandura, 1984) and Path–Goal Theory of Leadership (House and Mitchell, 1974) fit the Burns' definition of transactional theories of leadership.

Bass (1985) and Avolio and Bass (1985) argue that transactional skills are necessary but not sufficient for transformational leadership. According to Burns (1978), transformational leadership occurs 'when one or more persons *engage* with others in such a way that leaders and followers raise one another to higher levels of motivation and morality' (p. 20; emphasis original). Accordingly, transformational leaders address themselves to their followers' 'wants, needs, and other motivations, as well as their own and, thus, they serve as an independent force in changing the make-up of followers' motive base through gratifying their motives' (ibid.).

Burns (1978) argues that transformational leadership in its most effective form appeals to the higher, more general, and more comprehensive values that express the followers' fundamental and enduring needs: equality, freedom, a world of beauty, and the instrumental value of self-control. Bass and his associates have conducted a substantial amount of research testing hypotheses devised from Burns' theory of transformational leadership.

Bass (1985) found that managers who were seen by their followers as transformational could be characterized by three behavioral dimensions. The first dimension or factor, accounting for 66 per cent of the response variance, reflects the behaviors and effects as hypothesized by House's (1977) theory of charismatic leadership. This factor is concerned with faith in the leader, respect for the leader, and inspiration and encouragement provided by his or her presence. The remaining two dimensions were individualized consideration and intellectual stimulation, accounting for 6.0 per cent and 6.3 per cent of the response variance respectively. Two other factors consistently associated with transactional leadership were management by exception and contingent reward, accounting for 3.1 per cent and 7.2 per cent of the response variance respectively. These scales developed by Bass are collectively referred to as the Multifactor Leadership Questionnaire.

A number of studies have been conducted by Bass and his associates using the Multifactor Leadership Questionnaire. Managers who are rated by subordinates as high on the three transformational scales were compared to random samples of managers who are low on these three scales, and to those who are rated high on the transactional scales but low on the transformational scales. Those rated as transformational received higher ratings by superiors for performance, promotability, and ability to manage (Bass, 1985; Hater and Bass, 1986). Transformational leaders are more frequently classified as 'great or world class leaders' (Bass, 1985) by biographers and historians (although there is some question about the cause–effect relationship). Transformational leaders also have higher performing teams in a management simulation exercies. Furthermore, these leaders take greater strategic risks in the same management simulation (Avolio and Bass, 1985) and their subordinates report greater satisfaction and more or 'extra' work effort (Bass, 1985; Hater and Bass, 1986; Pereira, 1986), as well as having subordinates who, themselves, demonstrate transformational leader behaviors (Bass et al., 1986).

These findings are impressive because they have occurred in India as well as in the United States (Pereira, 1986), and because the correlations between transformational leader behavior, followers' peformance and satisfaction are significantly higher under transformational than transactional leaders. Finally, the correlations between transformational leader behaviors and ratings by followers and superiors are consistently above .5 and often as high as .7.

Conclusions: Charismatic and Transformational Leadership

Empirical studies lend support to the charismatic and transformational theories. Leaders who manifest charismatic or transformational behaviors produce the predicted charismatic effects and are viewed as more effective by their superiors and followers than transactional leaders. Further, the correlations between follower satisfaction and performance are consistently high compared with prior field study findings concerning leader behavior.

SOME REFLECTIONS ON THE STATE OF LEADERSHIP THEORY

It seems fashionable in some quarters to assert that the term 'leadership' has lost its meaning and that leadership research is all just so much dross. Thus, Calder (1977) doubts that 'the accumulation of research is really leading anywhere' and proposes that 'leadership is not a viable scientific construct'—a sentiment previously also voiced by Miner (1975) and Perrow (1972). And in the first chapter of the leadership symposia edited by Hunt *et al.* (1984), Quinn, (1984, p. 10) laments that 'Despite an immense investment in the enterprise, researchers have become increasingly disenchanted with the field [of leadership]'.

What is the basis for all this gloom? *Stogdill's Handbook of Leadership* (Bass, 1981) referenced about 5000 items in the bibliography, and Bass (personal communication, 1987) estimates that about 7000–10 000 bibliographic reference items might legitimately be included in the forthcoming version of the *Handbook*. And while not all of these items are world-shakers, a substantial number will be more than respectable. This volume of research does not indicate disenchantment with the field nor does it represent compelling evidence that we should stop talking about leadership.

The more specific critiques are equally unconvincing. To take but one example, Tsui (1984, pp. 28–9) prounounces that the 'literature on managerial effectiveness is as much in a state of dismay as the literature on leadership effectiveness' because:

> Existing theories and research have concentrated on the personal characteristics of the managers.... The lack of attention to these environmental determinants is a major problem that has retarded progress in both leadership and managerial effectiveness research.

What has Tsui been reading? According to Kerr's (1984) survey of management texts, the most frequently cited theories are: the contingency model, Path–Goal Theory, Normative Decision Theory, Vertical Dyad Linkage Theory and Substitutes for Leadership. Not one of these ignores environmental determinants.

Another example of this kind is McCall and Lombardo's (1978, p. 3) scathing criticism of the field which states at one point that:

> Students of leadership—academics and practitioners alike—have no doubt discovered three things: (1) the number of unintegrated theories, prescriptions, and conceptual schemes of leadership is mind-boggling; (2) much of the leadership literature is fragmentary and trivial, unrealistic and dull; and (3) the research results are characterized by Type III errors (solving the wrong problems precisely) and by contradictions.

We have not discovered these supposed verities. There are today less than a dozen empirically-based theories that are taken seriously (e.g. Kerr, 1984), and we doubt that the area of leadership has a corner on trivial studies. Whether one considers other people's papers dull obviously is a matter of taste.

We share McCall and Lombardo's concern for realism, but have some reservations about the realism to be found in the six-hour management game on which McCall and Lombardo base most of their conclusions. This management simulation, called, Looking Glass, has twenty participating executives play at running a simulated glass manufacturing company. Is this real life? At this point we do not even know the reliability of management games. We know even less about how well behavior and performance in a management game would predict behavior and performance of a manager two or three years down the road.

In trying to support their claim that bottom-line criteria of leadership effectiveness are mostly worthless, McCall and Lombardo cite Pfeffer and Salancik's (1978) finding that individual mayors accounted for less than 10 per cent of the variance in leadership performance, and Simonton's (1979) statement that Napoleon accounted for 'only 15 per cent of the variance in French military success' (p. 85).

First of all, most generals and managers (not to mention football coaches) would give their eye teeth for this extra 10 or 15 per cent of the variance. More to the point, there is considerable evidence from other studies that the leader contributes a great deal to the success or failure of an organization. One recent example comes from a carefully conducted study of the 200 trawlers in the Icelandic fishing fleet (Thorlindsson, 1987). These ships, which are 100–200 feet in length and typically carry a crew of eleven men, operate under almost identical conditions in a highly competitive environment. An analysis of a three-year period showed that the skipper accounted for 35–49 per cent of the variation in the catch. The best skippers remained at the top of this highly competitive occupation year after year, and that the correlation of catch by skipper were substantial over a three-year period (.59, .66 and .70), controlling for such variables as size of boat and number of days spent in fishing during the season. This and similar studies of leadership provide convincing empirical evidence that the leader represents a major factor in an organization's success.

Based on our reading of the field we cannot agree with the authors who describe most leadership research (save their own) as meaningless drivel. We also find many of the harsh condemnations hard to reconcile with much that we see in current books and journals. Could it be that the more vocal critics have been too disenchanted to read the literature? Bernard Bass, who certainly has read the leadership literature, strongly shares our opinion that these blanket criticisms are more hypberbole than sound scholarly evaluations of the field (personal communication, 1987).

Several viable and empirically supported theories have emerged, and there has been a notable complementarity and convergence among theories in recent years (e.g. Yukl, 1981). Contrary to Rauch and Behling (1984) and others, we believe that leadership research and theory have had a significant impact on leadership development and managerial selection although the research does not provide one-minute answers to the many complex problems the field presents.

Several theories and research programs (e.g. on assessment centers, trans-formational leadership, goal-setting, behavior modeling) show that the field is far from facing imminent death. Moreover, two sets of meta-analyses have been reported which deal with the validity of leadership theories (happily our own!), and we briefly report their results as further evidence that obituaries of leadership theory are premature.

The Contingency Model

This theory postulates two main types of personality attributes important to leadership performance. These attributes are the primary motivation to accomplish assigned tasks or the motivation to develop and maintain close relations with others. The situational component of the theory is the degree to which the leadership situation provides control, power and influence. The theory states that the effectiveness of a leader or an organization is contingent on the match between the leader's task or relationship motivation and the degree to which the situation gives the leader control and influence. Task-motivated (low LPC) leaders perform best in situations of very high or relatively low control; relationship-motivated leaders (high LPC) perform best in situations of moderate control. (For a recent summary see Fiedler and Garcia, 1987).

Based on a review of the literature, *Psychological Abstracts* and the *Social Science Citation Index*, Strube and Garcia (1981) located 33 tests on which the model was based, and 145 subsequent tests of the validity of the model. They defined a test as a statistical analysis within any of the eight octants (i.e. degrees of situational control). A meta-analysis of these data, using Rosenthal's (1978; 1979) technique, overwhelmingly supported the validity of the basic hypothesis. Strube and Garcia report a combined probability of all octant-bound studies of 1.71×10^{-23}. For studies which could only be classified as having high, moderate or low situational control, they reported a combined probability of 1.58×10^{-6}.

A less extensive meta-analysis by Peters, Hartke and Pohlman (1985), using the Schmidt and Hunter method (1977), presents a more guarded endorsement, again noting (as did Strube and Garcia) that the theory does not predict results for Octant II. However, the authors concur with Strube and Garcia 'in concluding that considerable evidence exists in support of the Contingency Theory'.

Path–Goal Theory

This theory, based on early work by Evans (1970), was developed by House (1971) and extended by House and Mitchell (1974). It postulates that effective leader behavior facilitates the attainment of the followers' desires, contingent on effective performance. The leader's role is 'instrumental' in enabling followers to achieve their desires. The leader does this by (a) identifying the personal goals of each follower, (b) establishing a reward system that makes such goals contingent on effective performance, and (c) assisting followers in achieving effective performance. Thus, according to this theory, followers and leaders enter into a transaction of performance for rewards.

Some of the specific leader behaviors that are instrumental to follower's goal attainment are (a) providing support for followers, (b) alleviating boredom and frustration with work, especially in time of stress, (c) providing direction, and

(d) fostering follower expectations that effort will lead to successful task accomplishment. The leader uses rewards and punishment contingent on the followers' compliance with the leaders' directions and the followers' level of performance.

According to the theory, it is the role of the leader to complement that which 'is missing' to enhance follower motivation, satisfaction and performance. What is 'missing' is determined by the environment, the task, the competence and the motivation of followers. It is also the role of the leader to enhance follower competence by coaching and support.

A recent meta-analysis of 48 studies designed to test Path–Goal Theory has yielded very promising results. Indvik (1986) tested for the theoretically predicted moderator effects of situational variables on relationships between leader behavior, leader directiveness, participation and supportiveness, and followers' role clarity, satisfaction and performance.

The situational moderators tested were task structure, job level and organizational size. These three variables were considered sources of psychological structure for followers. The results supported most of the hypotheses proposed by the theory. Following is a brief summary of Indvik's findings.

Path-goal theory predicts that directive leader behavior positively influences the subordinate's affect level to the degree that structure is absent from the work environment. That is, when followers have ambiguous task demands and little policy and procedural guidance, directive leader behavior will provide guidance and reduce role ambiguity. This hypothesis was supported with respect to intrinsic and overall satisfaction, and with satisfaction with the superior, but not with role clarity. A related path–goal hypothesis predicts that directive leader behavior improves performance regardless of the level of work environment (when environmental structure is low, directive leader behavior enhances performance by increasing role clarity; when environmental structure is high, directive leader behavior prevents low motivation from decreasing performance). Although as predicted, performance was enhanced by directive leader behavior when task structure was high, the effect was minimal when task structure was low, contrary to the hypothesis.

The path–goal hypothesis for supportive leader behavior predicts that leader support enhances subordinate affect and behavior to the degree that the work environment is structured. This hypothesis was supported for intrinsic, extrinsic and overall satisfaction, performance and role clarity.

Path–goal theory also predicts that participative leader behavior will be most effective under conditions where the followers' tasks are unstructured and when subordinates have a preference for internal structure. When both of these variables are high, it is hypothesized that participative leader behavior will enhance subordinate affect and behavior. The only test of the moderating effect of task structure on the relationship between participative leader behavior and criterion variables that could be made concerned overall satisfaction. As predicted, task structure negatively moderated this relationship as predicted.

Indvik considered job level as a surrogate for task structure, and organizational size as a surrogate for organizational formalization. Consistent with the theory, the relationship between leader behaviors and criterion variables were moderated by organizational level and organizational size. Further, in the moderated groups which were predicted to show positive relationships between leader behaviors and criteria, the correlations were generally in the .3 to .5 range. While the direction and statistical significance of relationships were largely as predicted, the number of studies considered to test any specific prediction was small, ranging from 2 to 11, depending upon the specific predictions tested. We are not aware of any other meta-analyses of leadership theories at this time. We confidently expect, however, that meta-analyses supporting other theories will begin to appear in the course of the next few years.

Management Training

How seriously should we take Argyris's pronouncement (cited in Rauch and Behling, 1984) that 'the additivity of the findings [on leadership] is limited and... their implications for the central problems of leaders are minimal'? In other words, to what extent has work in the leadership area produced tangible results in managerial training and selection?

A meta-analysis of management training programs by Burke and Day (1986) speaks to this point. First, most of the 64 studies included in the Burke and Day meta-analyses indicated changes in ratings by self or others of leader behaviors or attitudes, or interpersonal values. Only 15 of the reported studies used performance ratings by supervisors or advancement in the company as criteria. On the basis of the latter, the authors conclude that lecture training methods have been effective, as well as singling out two management training methods, both based on leadership theory. They go on to say:

> The results [of the meta-analyses] suggest that the Leader Match training method [Fiedler and Chemers, 1984] with respect to subjective behavior criteria [i.e. superiors' ratings] generalizes across situations. On the basis of these results as well as cost-effectiveness of Leader Match training compared with that of other leadership training programs, this method of leadership training is encouraged... "The effectiveness of managerial behavioral modeling training with respect to subjective behavior criteria was also shown to generalize across settings. This finding is consistent with the impressive empirical support for social learning theory obtained from well-controlled studies in experimental situations (cf. Bandura, 1977), as well as previous findings in organizational settings (cf. Burnaska, 1976; Byham, Adams and Kiggins, 1976; Latham and Saari, 1979; Smith, 1979). The magnitude of the estimated true mean effect for behavioral modeling provides an indication of how useful this method of managerial training is likely to be in improving managerial behaviors.

The conclusions by Burke and Day speak for themselves. In addition, we point to the work on motivation by Locke and Latham (1984), McClelland (1985) and Miner (1978) which provides not only a contribution to our understanding of leadership phenomena, but also to the practice of leadership training. Several other applications of leadership research to management (e.g. on assessment centers, goal-setting) also have been extensively validated.

There is little doubt that leadership research has resulted in an accumulation of substantial knowledge and that we are well beyond the slough of despair in which some of our colleagues seem to wallow with such gusto. Moreover, a wholesale condemnation of all research that preceded the author's own particular study raises a natural expectation that the remainder of the chapter will now resolve the dire problems that beset the field. These expectations are rarely fulfilled. We therefore urge our disenchanted colleagues to moderate their sweeping denunciations unless they are prepared either to document their claims that the leadership field is a disaster area, or to provide an empirically supported remedy for the problems that lead to their utter despair. For the sake of the record, we list some well-established conclusions about leadership which have come to light since 1936 and constitute important contributions to our knowledge.

Some Solid Contributions of Leadership Research

1.   The field has identified two major categories of leader behavior, one concerned with interpersonal relations (e.g. consideration), the other with task-accomplishment (e.g. structuring). While there are questions about substructures of the various scales, questions of halo effect and attribution, there is solid evidence that leaders are judged on these two aspects of behavior by their subordinates, (Misumi, 1985).

2.   There is no one ideal leader personality. However, effective leaders tend to have a high need to influence others, to achieve, and they tend to be bright, competent and socially adept, rather than stupid, incompetent and social disasters.

3.   Leader–follower relations affect the performance, satisfaction, motivation, self-esteem and well-being of followers. Therefore, the study of leadership is of substantial social, as well as organizational significance.

4.   We know that different situations require different leader behaviors. These are the behaviors required to compensate for deficiencies in the followers' environment and abilities. Whether these behaviors can be called out at will is a question in dispute. There are no behaviors exclusively manifested by leaders. For example, Megargee, Bogart and Anderson (1966) showed that pro-social assertiveness is aroused by salient factors related to the leader's control and influence; McClelland (1985) and his associates have consistently shown that social cues arouse needs for achievement and power. Fiedler's (1987) research shows that intellectual abilities are effectively used only if the leader is not under stress, is directive, and has the support of group members.

5.   Attributions play a substantial part in the leadership process. As in any other human interaction, the motivations attributed by leaders to group members in judging their behavior and performance determine in large part how leaders behave toward them (Mitchell and Wood, 1980).

6.   Intellectual abilities and experience contribute highly to performance only under selected conditions. Research is very clear in showing that experience correlates with performance only under conditions of stress while intelligence tends to correlate with performance only when stress experienced by the leader is relatively low. Whether leader intelligence or experience is required is determined by the task and the environment.

7.   Charismatic or transformational leadership is not a mysterious process,

but the result of such clearly identifiable behaviors as the articulation of transcendent goals, demonstration of strong self-confidence and confidence in others, setting a personal example for followers, showing high expectations for followers' performance, and the ability to communicate one's faith in one's goals.

8. We have considerable evidence in support of several leadership theories. While the details and specific interpretations of measures may be in dispute, and some of the initial theoretical propositions have been rejected, there can be little question that many of their principles are supported empirically. We would consider among the more prominent to be, roughly in order of date of publication, Fiedler's contingency model (1964), McClelland's need-achievement theory (1961), House's (1971) path–goal theory, Vroom and Yetton's (1973) theory of leader decision-making, Graen's (Graen and Cashman, 1975) vertical dyad linkage theory, Misumi's (1985) PM theory, as well as the more recent charismatic and transformational theories of leadership (House, 1977; Bass, 1985).

9. Several leadership training methods have been subjected to a rigorous evaluations. These include behavior modeling (Goldstein and Sorcher, 1974), leader match training (Fiedler and Chemers, 1984), motivation training (McClelland, 1985; Miner, 1978), and goal-setting (Locke, 1968; Latham and Saari, 1979).

The above list is illustrative rather than inclusive. We do not yet have a single overarching theory of leadership, and we are not likely to achieve one for some years. The same can, of course, also be said of theories of depression, motivation, schizophrenia, microbiology, tectonic plates, and the origin of the common cold, to mention but a few.

All this is to be expected in a field which is complex and challenging. It is not a place for those who are impatient to have quick solutions and final answers. Our current theories are not what they are likely to be in another 50 or 100 years; but 50 or 100 years ago our theories were not what they are today. The nine contributions to our knowledge of leadership we listed are ample evidence that our understanding of leadership phenomena continues to progress at a respectable rate. A considerable amount of work still remains to be done, and we hope that this happy state of affairs will continue.

ACKNOWLEDGMENTS

We would wish to express our thanks to Sarah Lehman for critically reading the manuscript as well as for her editorial assistance.

REFERENCES

Avolio, B. and Bass, B. M. (1985) Charisma and beyond. Paper presented at the Academy of Management, San Diego.
Bandura, A. (1977) *Social Learning Theory*. Englewood Cliffs, N.J.: Prentice-Hall.
Bass, B. M. (1981) *Stogdill's Handbook of Leadership*. New York: The Free Press.
Bass, B. M. (1985) *Leadership and Performance: Beyond Expectations*. New York: The Free Press.

Bass, B. M., Waldman, D. A., Avolio, B. J. and Bebb, M. (1987) Transformational leadership and the falling dominoes effect. *Group and Organization Studies*, **12** (1), 73–87.

Bennis, W. and Nanus, B. (1985) *Leaders: The Strategies for Taking Charge*. New York: Harper and Row.

Berlew, D. E. (1974) Leadership and organizational excitement. In D. A. Kolb, I. M. Rubin and J. M. Mcintyre (eds), *Organizational Psychology*, Englewood Cliffs, N.J.: Prentice-Hall.

Blades, J. W. (1976) The influence of intelligence, task ability, and motivation on group performance. Unpublished doctoral dissertation, University of Washington, Seattle.

Blades, J. W. (1986) *Rules for Leadership*. Washington, D.C.: National Defense University Press.

Blades, J. W. and Fiedler, F. E. (1976) *The Influence of Intelligence, Task Ability, and Motivation on Group Performance*, (Organizational Research Tech. Rep. No. 76–78) University of Washington, Seattle.

Blyth, D. E. (1987) Leader and subordinate expertise as moderators of the relationship between directive leader behavior and performance. Unpublished doctoral dissertation, University of Washington, Seattle.

Bowers, D. G. and Seashore, S. E. (1966) Predicting organizational effectiveness with a four-factor theory of leadership. *Administrative Science Quarterly*, **11**, 238–263.

Burke, M. J. and Day, R. R. (1986) A cumulative study of the effectiveness of managerial training. *Journal of Applied Psychology*, **71**, 232–245.

Burns, J. M. (1978) *Leadership*. New York: Harper and Row.

Byham, W. C., Adams, D. and Kiggins, A. (1976) Transfer of modeling training to the job. *Personnel Psychology*, **29**, 345–349.

Calder, B. (1977) An attribution theory of leadership. In B. H. Staw and G. R. Salancik (eds), *New Directions in Organizational Behavior*. Chicago: St Clair Press.

Carlyle, T. Lecture on heroes, hero worship and the heroic in history. P. C. Parr (ed.) (1910) Clarendon Press, Oxford. [Weber, M. (1917), *Gesammelte Aufsätze der Religionssoziologie*, Vol. 3, J. C. B. Mohr, Tübingen.]

Cummin, P. (1967) TAT correlates of executive performance, *Journal of Applied Psychology*, **51**, 78–81.

Donley, R. E. and Winter, D. G. (1970) Measuring the motives of public officials at a distance; an exploratory study. *Behavioral Science*, **15**, 227–236.

Epstein, S. (1975) Stability of behavior: On predicting most of the people much of the time. *Journal of Personality and Social Psychology*, **37**, 1097–1126.

Evans, M. G. (1970) The effects of supervisory behavior on the path–goal relationship. *Organizational Behavior and Human Performance*, **5**, 277–298.

Fiedler, F. E. (1964) A contingency model of leadership effectiveness. In L. Berkowitz (ed.) *Advances in Experimental Social Psychology*, Vol. 1, New York: Academic Press.

Fiedler, F. E. (1967) *A Theory of Leadership Effectiveness*. New York: McGraw-Hill.

Fiedler, F. E. (1970) Leadership experience and leader performance – another hypothesis shot to hell. *Organizational Behavior and Human Performance*, **5**, 1–14.

Fiedler, F. E. (1978) The contingency model and the dynamice of the leadership process. In L. Berkowitz (ed.) *Advances in Experimental Social Psychology*, **11**, New York: Academic Press.

Fiedler, F. E. (1986) The contribution of cognitive resources and behavior to organizational performance. *Journal of Applied Social Psychology*, **16** (6), 532–548.

Fiedler, F. E. (1987) The contribution of cognitive resources to organizational performance. In C. F. Graumann and S. Moscovici (eds), *Changing Conceptions of Leadership*. New York: Springer-Verlag.

Fiedler, F. E. and Chemers, M. M. (1984) *Improving Leadership Effectiveness: The Leader Match Concept*, 2nd edition. New York: John Wiley.

Fiedler, F. E. and Garcia, J. E. (1987) *New Approaches to Effective Leadership: Cognitive Resources and Organizational Performance.* New York: John Wiley.

Fiedler, F. E. and McGuire, M. A. (1987) *Proceedings of the Third Army Leadership Conference.* Kansas City.

Fiedler, F. E., Potter, E. H. III, Zais, M. M. and Knowlton, W. A. Jr (1979) Organizational stress and the use and misuse of managerial intelligence and experience, *Journal of Applied Psychology,* **64**, 635–647.

Foti, R. J., Fraser, S. L. and Lord, R. G. (1982) Effects of leadership labels and prototypes on perceptions of political leaders. *Journal of Applied Psychology,* **67**, 326–333.

Goldstein, A. P. and Sorcher, M. (1974) *Changing Supervisory Behavior.* New York: Pergamon.

Graen, G. and Cashman, J. F. (1975) A role-making model of leadership in formal organizations: A developmental approach. In J. G. Hunt and L. L. Larson (eds) *Leadership Frontiers.* Carbondale: Southern Illinois University Press.

Graen, G. B. and Scandura, T. A. (1986) Toward a psychology of dyadic organizing. In B. M. Staw and L. L. Cummings (eds) *Research in Organizational Behavior.* Greenwich, CT: JAI Press.

Hater, J. J. and Bass, B. M. (1986) Superiors' evaluations of subordinates' perceptions of transformational and transactional leadership. Working paper, State University of New York: Binghamton.

Hollander, E. P. (1958) Conformity, status and idiosyncrasy credit. *Psychological Review,* **65**, 117–127.

Hollander, E. P. (1978) *Leadership Dynamics: A Practical Guide to Effective Relationships.* New York: The Free Press.

Horn, J. L. (1968) Organization of abilities and the development of intelligence. *Psychological Review,* **75**, 242–259.

House, R. J. (1971) Path–goal theory of leader effectiveness. *Administrative Science Quarterly,* **16**, 321–338.

House, R. J. (1977) A 1976 theory of charismatic leadership. In J. G. Hunt and L. L. Larson (eds) *Leadership: The Cutting Edge.* Carbondale, Ill.: Southern Illinois University Press.

House, R. J. and Mitchell, T. R. (1974) Path–goal theory of leadership. *Journal of Contemporary Business.* **3**, 81–97.

House, R. J., Woyke, J. and Fodor, E. (1986) Research contrasting the motives and effects of reputed charismatic versus reputed non-charismatic U.S. Presidents. Presented at the Academy of Management, San Diego.

Howell, J. M. (1985) A laboratory study of charismatic leadership. Working paper, the University of Western Ontario.

Hunt, J. G. and Larson, L. L. (1984) *Leadership: The Cutting Edge.* Carbondale, Ill.: Southern Illinois University Press.

Hunt, J. G., Sekaran, U. and Schriesheim, C. A. (eds) (1981) *Leadership: Beyond Establishment Views.* Carbondale, Ill.: Southern Illinois University Press.

Indvik, J. (1986) Path–goal theory of leadership: A meta-analyses. *Proceedings.* Academy of Management, Chicago.

Jones, E. E. (1985) Major developments in social psychology during the past five decades. In G. Lindzey and E. Aronson (eds) *Handbook of Social Psychology.* New York: Random House, 47–108.

Katz, D. and Kahn, R. L. (1966) *The Social Psychology of Organizations.* New York: John Wiley.

Kerr, S. (1984) Leadership and participation. In A. Brief (ed.) *Research on Productivity.* New York: Praeger.

Larson, L. L. and Rowland, K. M. (1973) Leadership style, stress, and behavior in task performance. *Organizational Behavior and Human Performance,* **9**, 407–420.

Latham, G. P. and Saari, L.M. (1979) Application of social learning theory to training supervisors through behavioral modeling. *Journal of Applied Psychology*, **64**, 239–246.

Locke, E. A. (1968) Toward a theory of task motivation and incentives. *Organizational Behavior and Human Performance*, **3** 157–189.

Locke, E. A. and Latham, G. P. (1984) *Goal Setting: A Motivational Technique that Works!* Englewood Cliffs, N.J.: Prentice-Hall.

Lord, R. G. (1985) An information processing approach to social perceptions, leadership, and behavioral measurement in organizations. In L. L. Cummings and B. M. Staw (eds) *Research in Organizational Behavior*, **7**. Greenwich, CT.: JAI Press.

Maranell, G. M. (1970) The evaluation of presidents: An extension of the Schlesinger Polls. *Journal of American History*, **57**, 104–113.

McCall, M. W. Jr and Lombardo, M. (eds) (1978) *Leadership: Where Else Can We Go?* Durham, N.C.: Duke University Press.

McClelland, D. (1961) *The Achieving Society*. Princeton, N.J.: Van Nostrand.

McClelland, D. (1985) *Human Motivation*. Glenview, Il: Scott, Foresman.

McClelland, D. C. and Boyatzis, R. E. (1982) Leadership motive pattern and long term success in management. *Journal of Applied Psychology*, **67**, 737–43.

McClelland, D. C. and Burnham, D. H. (1976) Power is the great motivator. *Harvard Business Review*, **54** (2), 100–110.

Megargee, E. I., Bogart, P. and Anderson, B. J. (1966) Prediction of leadership in a simulated industrial task. *Journal of Applied Psychology*, **50**, 292–295.

Miner, J. B. (1975) *The Uncertain Future of the Leadership Concept: An overview. Third Leadership Symposium*, at Southern Illinois University. Carbondale, Ill.: Southern Illinois University Press.

Miner, J. B. (1978) Twenty years of research on role-motivation theory of managerial effectiveness. *Personnel Psychology*, **31**, 739–760.

Misumi, J. (1985) *The Behavioral Science of Leadership: An Interdisciplinary Japanese Research Program*. Ann Arbor: University of Michigan Press.

Mitchell, T. R. and Wood, R. E. (1980) Supervisors' responses to subordinates' poor performance: A test of the attributional model. *Organizational Behavior and Human Performance*, **25**, 123–138.

Mitchell, T. R., Green, S. G. and Wood, R. E. (1981) An attributional model of leadership and the poor-performing subordinate: development and validation. In B. Shaw and L. Cummings. (eds) *Research in Organizational Behavior*, **3**. Greenwich, CT.: JAI Press.

Pereira, D. F. (1987) *Factors Associated with Transformational Leadership in an Indian Engineering Firm*. Administrative Sciences Association of Canada, Toronto.

Perrow, C. (1972) *Complex organizations: A critical essay*. Glenview, Ill.: Scott, Foresman.

Peters, L. H., Hartke, D. D. and Pohlmann, J. T. (1985) Fiedler's contingency theory of leadership: An application of the meta-analysis procedures of Schmidt and Hunter. *Psychological Bulltein*, **97**, 274–285.

Pfeffer, J. and Salancik, G. R. (1978) *The External Control of Organizations*. New York: Harper and Row.

Phillips, J. S. and Lord, R. G. (1981) Causal attributions and perceptions of leadership. *Organizational Behavior and Human Performance*, **28**, 143–163.

Potter, E. H. and Fiedler, F. E. (1981) The utilization of staff member intelligence and experience under high and low stress. *Academy of Management Journal*, **24** (2), 361–376.

Quinn, R. E. (1984) Applying the competing values approach to leadership: Toward an integrative framework. In J. G. Hunt, D. Hosking, C. A. Schrieshiem and R. Stewart (eds) *Leaders and Managers: International Perspectives on Managerial Behavior and Leadership*. New York: Pergamon Press.

Rauch, C. F., Jr and Behling, O. (1984) Functionalism: Basis for an alternate approach to the study of leadership. In J. G. Hunt, D. Hosking, C. A. Schriesheim and R. Stewart (eds) *Leaders and Managers: International Perspectives on Managerial Behavior and Leadership*. New York: Pergamon Press.

Rosenthal, R. (1978) Combining results of independent studies. *Psychological Bulletin*, 85 (1), 185–193.

Sample, J. A. and Wilson, T. R. (1965) Leader behavior, group productivity, and ratings of least-preferred co-worker. *Journal of Personality and Social Psychology*, 266–270.

Sarason, I. (1984) Stress, anxiety, and cognitive interference: reactions to tests. *Journal of Personality and Social Psychology*, 46, 929–938.

Sashkin, M. and Fulmer, R. M. (1985) A new framework for leadership: Vision, charisma, and culture creation. Paper presented at Biennial Leadership Symposium at Texas Tech University.

Schmidt, F. L. and Hunter, J. E. (1977) Development of a general solution to the problem of validity generalization. *Journal of Applied Psychology*, 62, 529–540.

Shirakashi, S. (1980) The interaction effects for behavior of least preferred coworker (LPC) score and group-task situations: a reanalysis. *The Commercial Review of Seinan Gakuin University*, 27 (2).

Simon, H. A. (1976) *Administrative Behavior*, 3rd edition. New York: The Free Press.

Simonton, D. K. (1979) Was Napolean a military genius? Score: Carlyle 1, Tolstoy 1. *Psychological Reports*, 44, 21–22.

Sims, H. P., Jr and Gioia, D. A. (1986) *The Thinking Organization*. San Francisco: Jossey-Bass.

Smith, B. J. (1979) Management, modeling, training to improve morale and customer satisfaction. *Personnel Psychology*, 29, 351–359.

Smith, B. J. (1982) An initial test to a theory of charismatic leadership based on the responses of subordinates.

Strube, M. J. and Garcia, J. E. (1981) A meta-analytical investigation of Fiedler's contingency model of leadership effectiveness. *Psychological Bulletin*, 90, 307–321.

Terman, L. (1904) A preliminary study of the psychology and pedagogy of leadership. *Pedagogical Seminary*, 11, 413–451.

Thorlindsson, T. (1987) *The skipper effect in the Icelandic herring fishing Reykavik*. University of Iceland.

Tsui, A. S. (1984) Multiple-constituency framework of managerial reputational effectiveness. In J. G. Hunt, D. Hosking, C. A. Schrieshiem and R. Stewart (eds) *Leaders and Managers: International Perspectives on Managerial Behavior and Leadership*. New York: Pergamon Press.

Varga, K. (1975) N achievement, n power and effectiveness of research development. *Human Relations*, 23, 571–590.

Vroom, V. H. (1964) *Work and Motivation*. New York: McGraw-Hill.

Vroom, V. H. and Yetton, E. W. (1973) *Leadership and Decision Making*. Pittsburgh: University of Pittsburgh Press.

Wainer, H. A. and Rubin, I. M. (1969) Motivation of research and development entrepreneurs: Determinants of company success. *Journal of Applied Psychology*, 53 178–184.

Weber, M. (1946) The sociology of charismatic authority. In H. H. Mills and C. W. Mills (eds and trans.) fr. Max Weber, *Essays in Sociology*. New York: Oxford University Press.

Yukl, G. A. (1981) *Leadership in Organizations*. Englewood Cliffs, N.J.: Prentice-Hall.

Yukl, G. A. and Van Fleet, D. D. (1982) Cross-situational multi-method research on military leader effectiveness. *Organizational Behavior and Human Performance*, 30, 87–108.

Zajonc, R. B. (1965) Social facilitation. *Science*, 149 (3681), 269–274.

International Review of Industrial and Organizational Psychology 1988
Edited by C. L. Cooper and I. Robertson
© 1988 John Wiley & Sons Ltd

Chapter 4

THEORY BUILDING IN INDUSTRIAL AND ORGANIZATIONAL PSYCHOLOGY

Jane Webster
and
William H. Starbuck
Graduate School of Business Administration
New York University
USA

SUMMARY

I/O psychology has been progressing slowly. This slowness arises partly from a three-way imbalance: a lack of substantive consensus, insufficient use of theory to explain observations, and excessive confidence in induction from empirical evidence. I/O psychologists could accelerate progress by adopting and enforcing a substantive paradigm.

Staw (1984: 658) observed:

> The micro side of organizational behavior historically has not been strong on theory. Organizational psychologists have been more concerned with research methodology, perhaps because of the emphasis upon measurement issues in personnel selection and evaluation. As an example of this methodological bent, the I/O Psychology division of the American Psychological Association, when confronted recently with the task of improving the field's research, formulated the problem as one of deficiency in methodology rather than theory construction. . . . It is now time to provide equal consideration to theory formulation.

This chapter explores the state of theory in I/O psychology and micro-Organizational Behavior (OB).[1] The chapter argues that these fields have progressed very slowly, and that progress has occurred so slowly partly because of a three-way imbalance: a lack of theoretical consensus, inadequate attention to using theory to explain observations, coupled with excessive confidence in induction from empirical evidence. As a physicist, J. W. N. Sullivan (1928;

---

1. We thank Jane Dutton, Steve Kerr and Terry Mitchell for their substantive contributions.

quoted by Weber, 1982, p. 54), remarked: 'It is much easier to make measurements than to know exactly what you are measuring.'

Well-informed people hold widely divergent opinions about the centrality and influence of theory. Consider Dubin's (1976, p. 23) observation that managers use theories as moral justifications, that managers may endorse job enlargement, for example, because it permits more complete delegation of responsibilities, raises morale and commitment, induces greater effort, and implies a moral imperative to seek enlarged jobs and increased responsibilities. Have these consequences anything to do with theory? Job enlargement is not a theory, but a category of action. Not only do these actions produce diverse consequences, but the value of any single consequence is frequently debatable. Is it exploitative to elicit greater effort, because workers contribute more but receive no more pay? Or is it efficient, because workers contribute more but receive no more pay? Or is it humane, because workers enjoy their jobs more? Or is it uplifting, because work is virtuous and laziness despicable? Nothing compels managers to use job enlargement; they adopt it voluntarily. Theory only describes the probable consequences if they do use it. Furthermore, there are numerous theories about work redesigns such as job enlargement and job enrichment, so managers can choose the theories they prefer to espouse. Some theories emphasize the consequences of work redesign for job satisfaction, others highlight its consequences for efficiency, and still others its effects on accident rates or workers' health (Campion and Thayer, 1985).

We hold that theories do make a difference, to non-scientists as well as to scientists, and that theories often have powerful effects. Theories are not neutral descriptions of facts. Both prospective and retrospective theories shape facts. Indeed, the consequences of actions may depend more strongly on the actors' theories than on the overt actions. King's (1974) field experiment illustrates this point. On the surface, the study aimed at comparing two types of job redesign: a company enlarged jobs in two plants, and began rotating jobs in two similar plants. But the study had a 2 × 2 design. Their boss told two of the plant managers that the redesigns ought to raise productivity but have no effects on industrial relations; and he told the other two plant managers that the redesigns ought to improve industrial relations and have no effects on productivity. The observed changes in productivity and absenteeism matched these predictions: productivity rose significantly while absenteeism remained stable in those two plants, and absenteeism dropped while productivity remained constant in the other two plants. Job rotation and job enlargement, however, yielded the same levels of productivity and absenteeism. Thus, the differences in actual ways of working produced no differences in productivity or absenteeism, but the different rationales did induce different outcomes.

Theories shape facts by guiding thinking. They tell people what to expect, where to look, what to ignore, what actions are feasible, what values to hold. These expectations and beliefs then influence actions and retrospective interpretations, perhaps unconsciously (Rosenthal, 1966). Kuhn (1970) argued that scientific collectivities develop consensus around coherent theoretical positions— paradigms. Because paradigms serve as frameworks for interpreting evidence, for legitimating findings, and for deciding what studies to conduct, they steer research into paradigm-confirming channels, and so they reinforce themselves and remain stable for long periods. For instance, in 1909, Finkelstein reported in his doctoral dissertation that he had synthesized benzocyclobutene (Jones, 1966). Finkelstein's dissertation was rejected for publication because chemists believed, at that time, such chemicals could not exist, and so his finding had to be erroneous. Theorists elaborated the reasons for the impossibility of these chemicals for another 46 years, until Finkelstein's thesis was accidentally discovered in 1955.

Although various observers have argued that the physical sciences have stronger consensus about paradigms than do the social sciences, the social science findings may be even more strongly influenced by expectations and beliefs. Because these expectations and beliefs do not win consensus, they may amplify the inconsistencies across studies. Among others, Chapman and Chapman (1969), Mahoney and DeMonbreun (1977) and Snyder (1981) have presented evidence that people holding prior beliefs emphasize confirmatory strategies of investigation, they rarely use disconfirmatory strategies, and they discount disconfirming observations: these confirmatory strategies turn theories into self-fulfilling prophecies in situations where investigators' behaviors can elicit diverse responses or where investigators can interpret their observations in many ways (Tweney et al., 1981). Mahoney (1977) demonstrated that journal reviewers tend strongly to recommend publication of manuscripts that confirm their beliefs and to give these manuscripts high ratings for methodology, whereas reviewers tend strongly to recommend rejection of manuscripts that contradict their beliefs and to give these manuscripts low ratings for methodology. Faust (1984) extrapolated these ideas to theory evaluation and to review articles, such as those in this volume, but he did not take the obvious next step of gathering data to confirm his hypotheses.

Thus, theories may have negative consequences. Ineffective theories sustain themselves and tend to stabilize a science in a state of incompetence, just as effective theories may suggest insightful experiments that make a science more powerful. Theories about which scientists disagree foster divergent findings and incomparable studies that claim to be comparable. So scientists could be better off with no theories at all than with theories that lead them nowhere or in incompatible directions. On the other hand, scientists may have to reach consensus on some base-line theoretical propositions in order to evaluate adequately the effectiveness of these base-line propositions and the effectiveness of newer theories that build on these propositions. Consensus on base-line theoretical propositions, even ones that are somewhat erroneous, may also be an essential prerequisite to the accumulation of knowledge because such consensus leads scientists to view their studies in a communal frame of reference (Kuhn, 1970). Thus, it is an interesting question whether the existing theories or the existing degrees of theoretical consensus have been aiding or impeding scientific progress in I/O psychology.

Consequently and paradoxically, this chapter addresses theory building empirically, and the chapter's outline matches the sequence in which we pose questions and seek answers for them.

First we ask: How much progress has occurred in I/O psychology? If theories are becoming more and more effective over time, they should explain higher and higher percentages of variance. Observing the effect sizes for some major variables, we surmise that I/O theories have not been improving.

Second, hunting an explanation for no progress or negative progress, we examine indicators of paradigm consensus. To our surprise, I/O psychology does not look so different from chemistry and physics, fields that are perceived as having high paradigm consensus and as making rapid progress. However, physical science paradigms embrace both substance and methodology, whereas I/O psychology paradigms strongly emphasize methodology and pay little attention to substance.

Third, we hypothesize that I/O psychology's methodological emphasis is a response to a real problem, the problem of detecting meaningful research findings against a background of small, theoretically meaningless, but statistically significant relationships. Correlations published in the *Journal of Applied Psychology* seem to support this conjecture. Thus, I/O psychologists may be de-emphasizing substance because they do not trust their inferences from empirical evidence.

In the final section, we propose that I/O psychologists accelerate the field's progress by adopting and enforcing a substantive paradigm. We believe that I/O psychologists could embrace some base-line theoretical propositions that are as sound as Newton's laws, and using base-line propositions would project findings into shared perceptual frameworks that would reinforce the collective nature of research.

PROGRESS IN EXPLAINING VARIANCE

Theories may be evaluated in many ways. Webb (1961) said good theories exhibit knowledge, skepticism and generalizability. Lave and March (1975) said good theories are metaphors that embody truth, beauty and justice; whereas unattractive theories are inaccurate, immoral or unaesthetic. Daft and Wiginton (1979) said that influential theories provide metaphors, images and concepts that shape scientists' definitions of their worlds. McGuire (1983) noted that people may appraise theories according to internal criteria, such as their logical consistency, or according to external criteria, such as the statuses of their authors. Miner (1984) tried to rate theories' scientific validity and usefulness in application. Landy and Vasey (1984) pointed out tradeoffs between parsimony and elegance and between literal and figurative modeling.

Effect sizes measure theories' effectiveness in explaining empirical observations or predicting them. Nelson *et al.* (1986) found that psychologists' confidence in research depends primarily on significance levels and secondarily on effect sizes. But investigators can directly control significance levels by making more or fewer observations, so effect sizes afford more robust measures of effectiveness.

According to the usual assumptions about empirical research, theoretical progress should produce rising effect sizes—for example, correlations should get larger and larger over time. Kaplan (1963: 351–5) identified eight ways in which explanations may be open to further development; his arguments imply that theories can be improved by:

1. taking account of more determining factors,
2. spelling out the conditions under which theories should be true,
3. making theories more accurate by refining measures or by specifying more precisely the relations among variables,
4. decomposing general categories into more precise subclasses, or aggregating complementary subclasses into general categories,
5. extending theories to more instances,
6. building up evidence for or against theories' assumptions or predictions,
7. embedding theories in theoretical hierarchies, and
8. augmenting theories with explanations for other variables or situations.

The first four of these actions should increase effect sizes if the theories are fundamentally correct, but not if the theories are incorrect. Unless it is combined with the first four actions, action (5) might decrease effect sizes even for approximately correct theories. Action (6) could produce low effect sizes if theories are incorrect.

Social scientists commonly use coefficients of determination, r^2, to measure effect sizes. Some methodologists have been advocating that the absolute value of r affords a more dependable metric than r^2 in some instances (Ozer, 1985; Nelson et al., 1986). For the purposes of this chapter, these distinctions make no difference because r^2 and the absolute value of r increase and decrease together. We do, however, want to recognize the differences between positive and negative relationships, so we use r.

Of the nine effect measures we use, six are bivariate correlations. One can argue that, to capture the total import of a stream of research, one has to examine the simultaneous effects of several independent variables. Various researchers have advocated multivariate research as a solution to low correlations (Tinsley and Heesacker, 1984; Hackett and Guion, 1985). However, in practice, multivariate research in I/O psychology has not fulfilled these expectations, and the articles reviewing I/O research have not noted any dramatic results from the use of multivariate analyses. For instance, McEvoy and Cascio (1985) observed that the effect sizes for turnover models have remained small despite research incorporating many more variables. One reason is that investigators deal with simultaneous effects in more than one way: they can observe several independent variables that are varying freely; they can control for moderating variables statistically; and they can control for contingency variables by selecting sites or subjects or situations. It is far from obvious that multivariate correlations obtained in uncontrolled situations should be higher than bivariate correlations obtained in controlled situations. Indeed, the rather small gains yielded by multivariate analyses suggest that careful selection and control of sites or subjects or situations may be much more important than we have generally recognized.

Scientists' own characteristics afford another reason for measuring progress with bivariate correlations. To be useful, scientific explanations have to be understandable by scientists; and scientists nearly always describe their findings in bivariate terms, or occasionally trivariate terms. Even those scientists who advocate multivariate analyses most fervently fall back upon bivariate and trivariate interpretations when they try to explain what their analyses really mean. This brings to mind a practical lesson that Box and Draper (1969) extracted from their efforts to use experiments to discover more effective ways to run factories: Box and Draper concluded that practical experiments should manipulate only two or three variables at a time because the people who interpret the experimental findings have too much difficulty making sense of interactions among four or more variables. Speaking directly of the inferences drawn during scientific research, Faust (1984) too pointed out the difficulties that scientists have in understanding four-way interactions (Meehl, 1954; Goldberg, 1970). He noted that the great theoretical contributions to the physical sciences have been distinguished by their parsimony and simplicity rather than by their articulation of complexity. Thus, creating theories that psychologists themselves will find satisfying probably requires the finding of strong relationships among two or three variables.

To track progress in I/O theory building, we gathered data on effect sizes for five variables that I/O psychologists have often studied. Staw (1984) identified four heavily researched variables: job satisfaction, absenteeism, turnover and job performance. I/O psychologists also regard leadership as an important topic: three of the five annual reviews of organizational behavior have included it (Mitchell, 1979; Schneider, 1985; House and Singh, 1987).

Other evidence supports the centrality of these five variables for I/O psychologists. De Meuse (1986) made a census of dependent variables in I/O psychology, and identified job satisfaction as one of the most frequently used measures; it had been the focus of over 3000 studies by 1976 (Locke, 1976). Psychologists have correlated job satisfaction with numerous variables: Here, we examine its correlations with job performance and with absenteeism. Researchers have made job performance I/O psychology's most important dependent variable, and absenteeism has attracted research attention because of its costs (Hackett and Guion, 1985). We look at correlations of job satisfaction with absenteeism because researchers have viewed absenteeism as a consequence of employees' negative attitudes (Staw, 1984).

Investigators have produced over 1000 studies on turnover (Steers and Mowday, 1981). Recent research falls into one of two categories: turnover as the dependent variable when assessing a new work procedure, and correlations between turnover and stated intentions to quit (Staw, 1984).

Although researchers have correlated job performance with job satisfaction for over fifty years, more consistent performance differences have emerged in studies of behavior modification and goal setting (Staw, 1984). Miner (1984) surveyed organizational scientists, who nominated behavior modification and goal setting as the two of the most respected theories in the field. Although these two theories overlap (Locke, 1977; Miner, 1980), they do have somewhat different traditions, and so we present them separately here.

Next to job performance, investigators have studied leadership most often (Mitchell, 1979; De Meuse, 1986). Leadership research may be divided roughly into two groups: theories about the causes of leaders' behaviors, and theories about contingencies influencing the effectiveness of leadership styles. Research outside these two groups has generated too few studies for us to trace effect sizes over time (Van Fleet and Yukl, 1986).

Many years ago, psychologists seeking ways to identify effective leaders focused their research on inherent traits. This work, however, turned up very weak relationships, and no set of traits correlated consistently with leaders' effectiveness. Traits also offended Americans' ideology espousing equality of opportunity (Van Fleet and Yukl, 1986). Criticisms of trait approaches directed research towards contingency theories (Lord *et al.*, 1986). But these studies too turned up very weak relationships, so renewed interest in traits has surfaced (Kenny and Zaccaro, 1983; Schneider, 1985). As an example of the trait theories, we examine the correlations of intelligence with perceptions of leadership, because these have demonstrated the highest and most consistent relationships.

It is impossible to summarize the effect sizes of contingency theories of leadership in general. First, even though leadership theorists have proposed many contingency theories, little research has resulted (Schriesheim and Kerr, 1977), possibly because some of the contingency theories may be too unclear to suggest definitive empirical studies (Van Fleet and Yukl, 1986). Second, different theories emphasize different dependent variables (Campbell, 1977; Schriesheim and Kerr, 1977; Bass, 1981). Therefore, one must focus on a particular contingency theory. We examine Fiedler's (1967) theory because Miner (1984) reported that organizational scientists respect it highly.

Sources

A manual search of thirteen journals[1] turned up recent review articles concerning the five variables of interest; Borgen *et al.* (1985) identified several of these review articles as exemplary works. We took data from articles that reported both the effect sizes and the publication dates of individual studies. Since recent review articles did not cover older studies well, we supplemented these data by examining older reviews, in books as well as journals. In all, data came from the twelve sources listed in Table 1; these articles reviewed 261 studies.

Measures

Each research study is represented by a single measure of effect: for a study that measured the concepts in more than one way, we averaged the reported effect sizes.

To trace changes in effect sizes over time, we divided time into three equal periods. For instance, for studies from 1944 to 1983, we compare the effect sizes for 1944–57, 1958–70 and 1971–83.

Results

Figures 1–4 present the minimum, maximum and average effect sizes for the five variables of interest. Three figures (1(a), 3(b) and 4) seem to show that no

---

1. We searched the *Academy of Management Journal, Academy of Management Review, American Psychologist, Journal of Applied Behavioral Science, Journal of Applied Psychology, Journal of Occupational Behavior, Journal of Occupational Psychology, Journal of Vocational Behavior, Personnel Psychology, Pyschological Bulletin*, and *Organizational Behavior and Human Performance* for 1984–86, and the *Journal of Organizational Behavior Management* for 1983–85.

Table 1—Review Article Sources

Job satisfaction	Iaffaldano and Muchinsky (1985) Vroom (1964) Brayfield and Crockett (1955)
Absenteeism	Hackett and Guion (1985) Vroom (1964) Brayfield and Crockett (1955)
Turnover	McEvoy and Cascio (1985) Steel and Ovalle (1984)
Job Performance	Hopkins and Sears (1982) Locke *et al.* (1980)
Leadership	Lord *et al.* (1986) Peters *et al.* (1985) Mann (1959) Stogdill (1948)

progress has occurred over time; and four figures (1(b), 2(a), 2(b) and 3(a)) seem to indicate that effect sizes have gradually declined toward zero over time. The largest of these correlations is only .22 in the most recent time period, so all of these effects account for less than five per cent of the variance.

Moreover, four of these relationships (2(a), 2(b), 3(a) and 3(b)) probably incorporate Hawthorne effects: They measure the effects of interventions. Because all interventions should yield some effects, the differential impacts of specific interventions would be less than these effect measures suggest. That is, the effects of behavior modification, for example, should not be compared with inaction, but compared with those of an alternative intervention, such as goal setting.

Figure 2(c) is the only one suggesting significant progress. Almost all of this progress, however, occurred between the first two time periods: Because only one study was conducted during the first of these periods, the apparent progress might be no more than a statement about the characteristics of that single study. This relationship is also stronger than the others, although not strong enough to suggest a close causal relationship: The average correlation in the most recent time period is .40. What this correlation says is that some of the people who say in private that they intend to quit actually do quit.

Progress with respect to Fiedler's contingency theory of leadership is not graphed. Peters *et al.* (1985) computed the average correlations (corrected for sampling error) of leadership effectiveness with the predictions of this theory. The absolute values of the correlations averaged .38 for the studies from which Fiedler derived this theory (approximately 1954–65); but for the studies conducted to validate this theory (approximately 1966–78), the absolute values of the correlations averaged .26. Thus, these correlations too have declined toward zero over time.

I/O psychologists have often argued that effects do not have to be absolutely large in order to produce meaningful economic consequences (Zedeck and

Figure 1   Job Satisfaction.
(a)   Correlations of Job Satisfaction and Job Performance

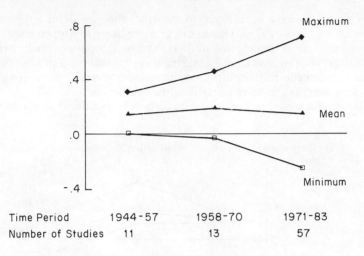

Time Period	1944-57	1958-70	1971-83
Number of Studies	11	13	57

(b)   Correlations of Job Satisfaction and Absenteeism

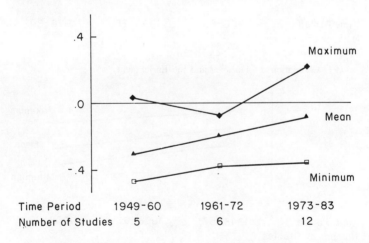

Time Period	1949-60	1961-72	1973-83
Number of Studies	5	6	12

Cascio, 1984; Schneider, 1985). For example, goal setting produced an average performance improvement of 21.6 per cent in the seventeen studies conducted from 1969 to 1979. If performance has a high economic value and goal setting costs very little, then goal setting would be well worth doing on the average. And because the smallest performance improvement was 2 per cent, the risk that goal setting would actually reduce performance seems very low.

This chapter, however, concerns theoretical development; and so the economic benefits of relations take secondary positions to identifying controllable moderators, to clarifying causal links, and to increasing effect sizes. In terms of theoretical development, it is striking that none of these effect sizes rose noticeably after the first years. This may have happened for any of five reasons, or more likely a combination of them:

(a) Researchers may be clinging to incorrect theories despite disconfirming evidence (Staw, 1976). This would be more likely to happen where studies' findings can be interpreted in diverse ways. Absolutely small correlations nurture such equivocality, by making it appear that random noise dominates any systematic relationships and that undiscovered or uninteresting influences exert much more effect than the known ones.

(b) Researchers may be continuing to elaborate traditional methods of infor-

Figure 2 Turnover.
(a) Correlations of Turnover and Realistic Job Previews

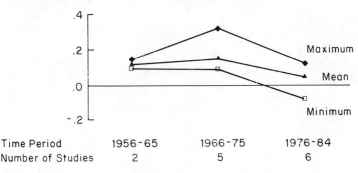

(b) Correlations of Turnover and Job Enrichment

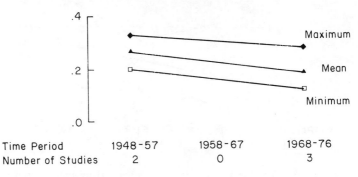

(c) Correlations of Turnover and Intentions to Quit

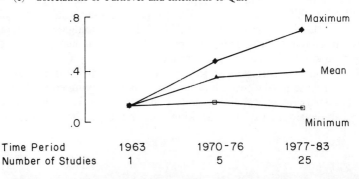

mation gathering after these stop generating additional knowledge. For example, researchers developed very good leadership questionnaires during the early 1950s. Perhaps these early questionnaires picked up all the information about leadership that can be gathered via questionnaires. Thus, subsequent questionnaires may not have represented robust improvements; they may merely have mistaken sampling variations for generalities.

(c) Most studies may fail to take advantage of the knowledge produced by the very best studies. As a sole explanation, this would be unlikely even in a world that does not reward exact replication, because research journals receive wide distribution and researchers can easily read reports of others' projects. However, retrospective interpretations of random variations may obscure real knowledge in clouds of ad hoc rationalizations, so the consumers of research may have difficulty distinguishing real knowledge from false.

Figure 3   Performance Improvements.
(a)   Improvement Percentages with Behaviour Modification

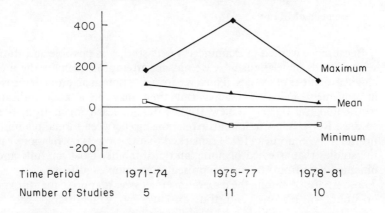

(b)   Improvement Percentages with Goal Setting

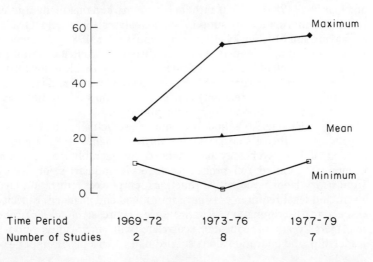

Figure 4 Leadership Traits.
Correlations of Intelligence and Leadership Perceptions

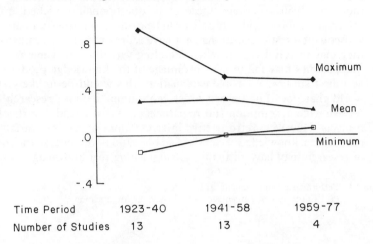

Because we wanted to examine as many studies as possible and studies of several kinds of relationships, we did not attempt to evaluate the methodological qualities of studies. Thus, we are using time as an implicit measure of improvement in methodology. But time may be a poor indicator of methodological quality if new studies do not learn much from the best studies. Reviewing studies of the relationship between formal planning and profitability, Starbuck (1985) remarked that the lowest correlations came in the studies that assessed planning and profitability most carefully and that obtained data from the most representative samples of firms.

(d) Those studies obtaining the maximum effect sizes may do so for idiosyncratic or unknown reasons, and thus produce no generalizable knowledge. Researchers who provide too little information about studied sites, subjects, or situations make it difficult for others to build upon their findings (Orwin and Cordray, 1985); several authors have remarked that many studies report too little information to support meta-analyses (Steel and Ovalle, 1984; Iaffaldano and Muchinsky, 1985; Scott and Taylor, 1985). The tendencies of people, including scientists, to use confirmatory strategies mean that they attribute as much of the observed phenomena as possible to the relationships they expect to see (Snyder, 1981; Faust, 1984; Klayman and Ha, 1987). Very few studies report correlations above .5, so almost all studies leave much scope for misattribution and misinterpretation.

(e) Humans' characteristics and behaviors may actually change faster than psychologists' theories or measures improve. Stagner (1982) argued that the context of I/O psychology has changed considerably over the years: the economy has shifted from production to service industries, jobs have evolved from heavy labor to cognitive functions, employees' education levels have risen, and legal requirements have multiplied and changed, especially with respect to discrimination. For instance, Haire *et al.* (1966) found that managers' years of education correlate with their ideas about proper leadership, and education alters subordinates' concepts of proper leadership

(Dreeben, 1968; Kunda, 1987). In the US, median educational levels have risen considerably, from 9.3 years in 1950 to 12.6 years in 1985 (Bureau of the Census, 1987). Haire *et al.* also attributed 25 per cent of the variance in managers' leadership beliefs to national differences: so, as people move around, either between countries or within a large country, they break down the differences between regions and create new beliefs that intermingle beliefs that used to be distinct. Cummings and Schmidt (1972) conjectured plausibly that beliefs about proper leadership vary with industrialization; thus, the ongoing industrialization of the American south-east and south-west and the concomitant deindustrialization of the north-east are altering Americans' responses to leadership questionnaires.

Whatever the reasons, the theories of I/O psychology explain very small fractions of observed phenomena, I/O psychology is making little positive progress, and it may actually be making some negative progress. Are these the kinds of results that science is supposed to produce?

PARADIGM CONSENSUS

Kuhn (1970) characterized scientific progress as a sequence of cycles, in which occasional brief spurts of innovation disrupt long periods of gradual incremental development. During the periods of incremental development, researchers employ generally accepted methods to explore the implications of widely accepted theories. The researchers supposedly see themselves as contributing small but lasting increments to accumulated stores of well-founded knowledge; they choose their fields because they accept the existing methods, substantive beliefs and values, and consequently they find satisfaction in incremental development within the existing frames of reference. Kuhn used the term paradigm to denote one of the models that guide such incremental developments. Paradigms, he (1970, p. 10) said, provide 'models from which spring particular coherent traditions of scientific research'.

Thus, Kuhn defined paradigms, not by their common properties, but by their common effects. His book actually talks about 22 different kinds of paradigm (Masterman, 1970), which Kuhn placed into two broad categories: (a) a constellation of beliefs, values and techniques shared by a specific scientific community; and (b) an example of effective problem-solving that becomes an object of imitation by a specific scientific community.

I/O psychologists have traditionally focused on a particular set of variables: the nucleus of this set would be those examined in the previous section—job satisfaction, absenteeism, turnover, job performance and leadership. Also, we believe that substantial majorities of I/O pyschologists would agree with some base-line propositions about human behavior. However, Campbell *et al.* (1982) found a lack of consensus among American I/O psychologists concerning substantive research goals. They asked them to suggest 'the major *research needs* that should occupy us during the next 10–15 years' (p. 155): 105 respondents contributed 146 suggestions, of which 106 were unique. Campbell *et al.* (1982, p. 71) inferred: 'The field does not have very well worked out ideas about what it wants to do. There was relatively little consensus about the relative importance of substantive issues.'

Shared Beliefs, Values and Techniques

I/O psychologists do seem to have a paradigm of type (a)—shared beliefs, values, and techniques, but it would seem to be a methodological paradigm rather than a substantive one. For instance, Watkins *et al.*'s (1986) analysis of the 1984–85 citations in three I/O journals revealed that a methodologist, Frank L. Schmidt, has been by far the most cited author. In this methodological orientation, I/O psychology fits a general pattern: numerous authors have remarked on psychology's methodological emphasis (Deese, 1972; Koch, 1981; Sanford, 1982). For instance, Brackbill and Korten (1970, p. 939) observed that psychological 'reviewers tend to accept studies that are methodologically sound but uninteresting, while rejecting research problems that are of significance for science or society but for which faultless methodology can only be approximated.' Bakan (1974) called psychology 'methodolatrous'. Contrasting psychology's development with that of physics, Kendler (1984, p. 9) argued that 'Psychological revolutions have been primarily methodological in nature.' Shames (1987, p. 264) characterized psychology as 'the most fastidiously committed, among the scientific disciplines, to a socially dominated disciplinary matrix which is almost exclusively centred on method.'

I/O psychologists not only emphasize methodology, they exhibit strong consensus about methodology. Specifically, I/O psychologists speak and act as if they believe they should use questionnaires, emphasize statistical hypothesis tests, and raise the validity and reliability of measures. Among others, Campbell (1982, p. 699) expressed the opinion that I/O psychologists have been relying too much on 'the self-report questionnaire, statistical hypothesis testing, and multivariate analytic methods at the expense of problem generation and sound measurement'. As Campbell implied, talk about reliability and especially validity tends to be lip-service: almost always, measurements of reliability are self-reflexive facades and no direct means even exist to assess validity. I/O psychologists are so enamored of statistical hypothesis tests that they often make them when they are inappropriate, for instance when the data are not samples but entire sub-populations, such as all the employees of one firm, or all of the members of two departments. Webb *et al.* (1966) deplored an overdependence on interviews and questionnaires, but I/O psychologists use interviews much less often than questionnaires (Stone, 1978).

An emphasis on methodology also characterizes the social sciences at large. Garvey *et al.* (1970) discovered that editorial processes in the social sciences place greater emphasis on statistical procedures and on methodology in general than do those in the physical sciences; and Lindsey and Lindsey (1978) factor analysed social science editors' criteria for evaluating manuscripts and found that a quantitative-methodological orientation arose as the first factor. Yet, other social sciences may place somewhat less emphasis on methodology than does I/O psychology. For instance, Kerr *et al.* (1977) found little evidence that methodological criteria strongly influence the editorial decisions by management and social science journals. According to Kerr *et al.*, the most influential methodological criterion is statistical insignificance, and the editors of three psychological journals express much stronger negative reactions to insignificant findings than do editors of other journals.

Mitchell *et al.* (1985) surveyed 139 members of the editorial boards of five journals that publish work related to organizational behavior, and received responses from 99 editors. Table 2 summarizes some of these editors' responses.[1]

Table 2—Criteria Espoused by the Average Members of Editorial Boards

Relative weights among four general criteria

	All five journals	JAP and OBHDP	AMJ, AMR, and ASQ
'Importance'	35	38	34
Methodology	26	25	27
Logic	24	24	24
Presentation	15	13	16

Relative weights among three aspects of 'importance'

	All five journals	JAP and OBHDP	AMJ, AMR, and ASQ
Scientific contribution	53	54	53
Practical utility	28	31	26
Readers' interest in topic	19	14	21

Relative weights among three aspects of methodology

	All five journals	JAP and OBHDP	AMJ, AMR, and ASQ
Design	38	39	37
Measurement	31	30	32
Analysis	31	31	31

The average editor said that 'importance' received more weight than other criteria; that methodology and logic were given nearly equal weights, and that presentation carried much less weight. When asked to assign weights among three aspects of 'importance', most editors said that scientific contribution received much more weight than practical utility or readers' probable interest in the topic. Also, they assigned nearly equal weights among three aspects of methodology, but gave somewhat more weight to design.

Table 2 compares the editors of two specialized I/O journals—*Journal of Applied Psychology* (JAP) and *Organizational Behavior and Human Decision Processes* (OBHDP)—with the editors of three more general management journals—*Academy of Management Journal* (AMJ), *Academy of Management Review* (AMR) and *Administrative Science Quarterly* (ASQ). Contrary to our expectations, the average editor of the two I/O journals said that he or she allotted more weight to 'importance' and less weight to methodology than did the average editor of the three management journals. It did not surprise us that the average editor of the I/O journals gave less weight to presentation than did the average

1. Mitchell *et al.* did not make comparisons among the five journals, but they generously sent us their raw data. Table 2 gives equal weight to each journal rather than to each respondent.

editor of the management journals. Among aspects of methodology, the average I/O editor placed slightly more weight on design and less on measurement than did the average management editor. When assessing 'importance', the average I/O editor said that he or she gave distinctly less weight to readers' probable interest in a topic and more weight to practical utility than did the average management editor. Thus, the editors of I/O journals may be using practical utility to make up for I/O psychologists' lack of consensus concerning substantive research goals: if readers disagree about what is interesting, it makes no sense to take account of their preferences (Campbell *et al.*, 1982).

Editors' stated priority of 'importance' over methodology contrasts with the widespread perception that psychology journals emphasize methodology at the expense of substantive importance. Does this contrast imply that the actual behaviors of journal editors diverge from their espoused values? Not necessarily. If nearly all of the manuscripts submitted to journals use accepted methods, editors would have little need to emphasize methodology. And if, like I/O psychologists in general, editors disagree about the substantive goals of I/O research, editors' efforts to emphasize 'importance' would work at cross-purposes and have little net effect. Furthermore, editors would have restricted opportunities to express their opinions about what constitutes scientific contribution or practical utility if most of the submitted manuscripts pursue traditional topics and few manuscripts actually address 'research problems that are of significance for science or society'.

Objects of Imitation

I/O psychology may also have a few methodological and substantive paradigms of type (b) examples that become objects of imitation. For instance, Griffin (1987, pp. 82–3) observed:

> The [Hackman and Oldham] job characteristics theory was one of the most widely studied and debated models in the entire field during the late 1970s. Perhaps the reasons behind its widespread popularity are that it provided an academically sound model, a packaged and easily used diagnostic instrument, a set of practitioner-oriented implementation guidelines, and an initial body of empirical support, all within a relatively narrow span of time. Interpretations of the empirical research pertaining to the theory have ranged from inferring positive to mixed to little support for its validity. (References omitted.)

Watkins *et al.* (1986) too found evidence of interest in Hackman and Oldham's (1980) job-characteristics theory: five of the twelve articles that were most frequently cited by I/O psychologists during 1984–85 were writings about this theory, including Roberts and Glick's (1981) critique of its validity. Although its validity evokes controversy, Hackman and Oldham's theory seems to be the most prominent current model for imitation. As well, the citation frequencies obtained by Watkins *et al.* (1986), together with nominations of important theories collected by Miner (1984), suggest that two additional theories attract considerable admiration: Katz and Kahn's (1978) open-systems theory and Locke's (1968) goal-setting theory. It is hard to see what is common among these three theories that would explain their roles as paradigms; open-systems theory, in particular, is much less operational than job-characteristics theory, and it is more a point of view than a set of propositions that could be confirmed or disconfirmed.

To evaluate more concretely the paradigm consensus among I/O psychologists, we obtained several indicators that others have claimed relate to paradigm consensus.

Measures

As indicators of paradigm consensus, investigators have used: the ages of references, the percentages of references to the same journal, the numbers of references per article, and the rejection rates of journals.

Kuhn proposed that paradigm consensus can be evaluated through literature references. He hypothesized that during normal-science periods, references focus upon older, seminal works; and so the numbers and types of references indicate connectedness to previous research (Moravcsik and Murgesan, 1975). First, in a field with high paradigm consensus, writers should cite the key works forming the basis for that field (Small, 1980). Alternatively, a field with a high proportion of recent references exhibits a high degree of updating, and so has little paradigm consensus. One measure of this concept is the Citing Half-Life, which shows the median age of the references in a journal. Second, referencing to the same journal should reflect an interaction with research in the same domain, so higher referencing to the same journal should imply higher paradigm consensus. Third, since references reflect awareness of previous research, a field with high paradigm consensus should have a high average number of references per article (Summers, 1979).

Journals constitute the accepted communication networks for transmitting knowledge in psychology (Price, 1970; Pinski and Narin, 1979), and high paradigm consensus means agreement about what research deserves publication. Zuckerman and Merton (1971) said that the humanities demonstrate their pre-paradigm states through very high rejection rates by journals, whereas the social sciences exhibit their low paradigm consensus through high rejection rates, and the physical sciences show their high paradigm consensus through low rejection rates. That is, paradigm consensus supposedly enables physical scientists to predict reliably whether their manuscripts are likely to be accepted for publication, and so they simply do not submit manuscripts that have little chance of publication.

Results

Based partly on work by Sharplin and Mabry (1985), Salancik (1986) identified 24 'organizational social science journals'. He divided these into five groups that cite one another frequently; the group that Salancik labeled Applied corresponds closely to I/O psychology.[1] Figure 5 compares these groups with respect to citing half-lives, references to the same journal, and numbers of references per article. The SSCI Journal Citation Reports (Social Science Citation Index, Garfield, 1981–84b) provided these three measures, although a few data were missing. We use four-year averages in order to smooth the effects of changing editorial policies and of the publication of seminal works (Blackburn and Mitchell, 1981). Figure 5 also includes comparable data for three fields that do not qualify as 'organizational social science'—chemistry, physics, and management information systems (MIS).[2] Data concerning chemistry, physics and MIS hold special interest because they are generally believed to be making rapid progress; MIS may indeed be in a pre-paradigm state.

Seven of the eight groups of journals have average citing half-lives longer than five years, the figure that Line and Sandison (1974) proposed as signaling a high degree of updating. Only MIS journals have a citing half-life below five years; this field is both quite new and changing with extreme rapidity. I/O psychologists update references at the same pace as chemists and physicists, and only slightly faster than other psychologists and OB researchers.

Garfield (1972) found that referencing to the same journal averages around 20 per cent across diverse fields, and chemists and physicists match this average. All five groups of 'organizational social science' journals average below 20 per cent references to the same journal, so these social scientists do not focus publications in specific journals to the same degree as physical scientists, although the OB researchers come close to the physical-science pattern. The I/O psychologists, however, average less than 10 per cent references to the same journal, so they focus publications even less than most social scientists. MIS again has a much lower percentage than the other fields.

Years ago, Price (1965) and Line and Sandison (1974) said 15–20 references per article indicated strong interaction with previous research. Because the numbers of references have been increasing in all fields (Summers, 1979), strong interaction probably implies 25–35 references per article today. I/O psychologists use numbers of references that fall within this range, and that look much like the numbers for chemists, physicists and other psychologists.

We could not find rejection rates for management, organizations and sociology journals, but Jackson (1986) and the American Psychological Association (1986) published rejection rates for psychology journals during 1985. In that year, I/O

---

1. Salancik's organizations group consisted of Administrative Science Quarterly, Academy of Management Journal, Academy of Management Review, Human Relations, and Administration and Society; the sociology group consisted of the American Sociological Review and American Journal of Sociology; the management group consisted of the Harvard Business Review, Management Science, Organizational Dynamics, California Management Review, and Journal of Management Studies; the applied (I/O) group consisted of the Journal of Applied Psychology, Organizational Behavior and Human Performance, Personnel Psychology, Journal of Occupational Behavior, and Journal of Applied Behavioral Science; and the psychology group consisted of the Journal of Personality and Social Psychology, Psychological Bulletin, American Psychologist, Psychological Review, and Psychological Reports.
2. The graphed data for chemistry and physics come from the Social Science Citation Index (Garfield, 1981–84a), and the data describe the Journal of the American Chemical Society and Physical Review, Series A. Beyer (1978) reported that these are the most highly regarded journals in their fields. Ives and Hamilton (1982) published the data for MIS, covering 1970–79.

Figure 5   Indicators of Paradigm Consensus in the Organizational Sciences.
(a)   Citing Half-Lives in Years

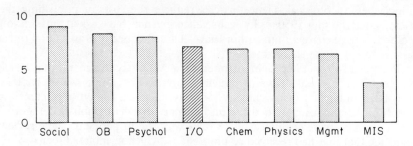

(b)   Percentages of References to the Same Journal

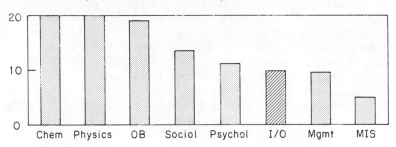

(c)   Numbers of References per Article

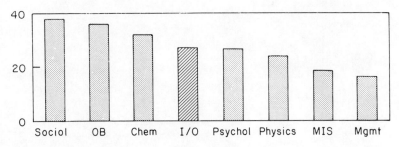

psychology journals rejected 82.5 per cent of the manuscripts, which is near the 84.3 per cent average for other psychology journals. By contrast, Zuckerman and Merton (1971) reported that the rejection rates for chemistry and physics journals were 31 and 24 per cent respectively. Similarly, Garvey *et al.* (1970) observed higher rejection rates and higher rates of multiple rejections in the social sciences than in the physical sciences. However, these differences in rejection rates may reflect the funding and organization of research more than its quality or substance: American physical scientists receive much more financial support than do social scientists, most grants for physical science research go to rather large teams, and physical scientists normally replicate each others' findings. Thus, most physical science research is evaluated in the process of awarding grants as well as in the editorial process, teams evaluate and revise their research reports internally before submitting them to journals, and researchers have incentives to replicate their own findings before they publish them. The conciseness of physical science articles reduces the costs of publishing them. Also, since the mid-1950s, physical science journals have asked authors to pay voluntary page charges, and authors have characteristically drawn upon research grants to pay these charges.

Peters and Ceci (1982) demonstrated for psychology in general that a lack of substantive consensus shows up in review criteria. They chose twelve articles that had been published in psychology journals, changed the authors names, and resubmitted the articles to the same journals that had published them: The resubmissions were evaluated by 38 reviewers. Eight per cent of the reviewers detected that they had received resubmissions, which terminated review of three of the articles. The remaining nine articles completed the review process, and eight of these were rejected. The reviewers stated mainly methodological reasons rather than substantive ones for rejecting articles, but Mahoney's (1977) study suggests that reviewers use methodological reasons to justify rejection of manuscripts that violate the reviewers' substantive beliefs.

Figure 6 graphs changes in four indicators from 1957 to 1984 for the *Journal of Applied Psychology* and, where possible, for other I/O psychology journals.[1] Two of the indicators in Figure 6 have remained quite constant; one indicator has risen noticeably; and one has dropped noticeably. According to the writers on

Figure 6   Changes in Paradigm Consensus in I/O Psychology.

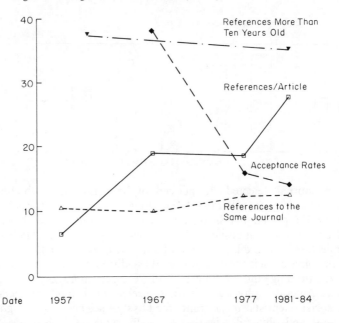

1. These data were published by the *American Psychological Association* (1968, 1978, 1982–85), Blackburn and Mitchell (1981), Garfield (1981–84b), and Xhignesse and Osgood (1967).

paradigm consensus, all four of these indicators should rise as consensus increases. If these indicators actually do measure paradigm consensus, I/O psychology has not been developing distinctly more paradigm consensus over the last three decades.

Overall, the foregoing indicators imply that I/O psychology looks much like management, sociology, and other areas of psychology. In two dimensions— citing half-lives and references per article—I/O psychology also resembles chemistry and physics, fields that are usually upheld as examples of paradigm consensus (Lodahl and Gordon, 1972). I/O psychology differs from chemistry and physics in references to the same journal and in rejection rates, but the latter difference is partly, perhaps mainly, a result of government policy. Hedges (1987) found no substantial differences between physics and psychology in the consistency of results across studies, and Knorr-Cetina's (1981) study suggests that research in chemistry incorporates the same kinds of uncertainties, arbitrary decisions and interpretations, social influences, and unproductive tangents that mark research in psychology.

Certainly, these indicators do not reveal dramatic differences between I/O psychology and chemistry or physics. However, these indicators make no distinctions between substantive and methodological paradigms. The writings on paradigms cite examples from the physical sciences that are substantive at least as often as they are methodological; that is, the examples focus upon Newton's laws or phlogiston or evolution, as well as on titration or dropping objects from the Tower of Pisa. Though far from a representative sample, this suggests that physical scientists place more emphasis on substantive paradigms than I/O psychologists do; but since I/O psychology seems to be roughly as paradigmatic as chemistry and physics, this in turn suggests that I/O psychologists place more emphasis on methodological paradigms than physical scientists do.

Perhaps I/O psychologists tend to deemphasize substantive paradigms and to emphasize methodological ones because they put strong emphasis on trying to discover relationships by induction. But can analyses of empirical evidence produce substantive paradigms where no such paradigms already exist?

INDUCING RELATIONSHIPS FROM OBSERVATIONS

Our colleague Art Brief has been heard to proclaim, 'Everything correlates .1 with everything else.' Suppose, for the sake of argument, that this were so. Then all observed correlations would deviate from the null hypothesis of a correlation less than zero, and a sample of 272 or more would produce statistical significance at the .05 level with a one-tailed test. If researchers would make sure that their sample sizes exceed 272, all observed correlations would be significantly greater than zero. Psychologists would be inundated with small, but statistically significant, correlations.

In fact, psychologists could inundate themselves with small, statistically significant correlations even if Art Brief is wrong. By making enough observations, researchers can be certain of rejecting any point null hypothesis that defines an infinitesimal point on a continuum, such as the hypothesis that two sample means are exactly equal, as well as the hypothesis that a correlation is exactly zero. If a point hypothesis is not immediately rejected, the researcher need only gather more data. If an observed correlation is .04, a researcher would have to make 2402 observations to achieve significance at the .05 level with a two-tailed test; and if the observed correlation is .2, the researcher will need just 97 observations.

Induction requires distinguishing meaningful relationships (signals) against an obscuring background of confounding relationships (noise). The background of weak and meaningless or substantively secondary correlations may not have an average value of zero and may have a variance greater than that assumed by statistical tests. Indeed, we hypothesize that the distributions of correlation coefficients that researchers actually encounter diverge quite a bit from the distributions assumed by statistical tests, and that the background relationships have roughly the same order of magnitude as the meaningful ones, partly because researchers' nonrandom behaviors construct meaningless background relationships. These meaningless relationships make induction untrustworthy.

In many tasks, people can distinguish weak signals against rather strong background noise. The reason is that both the signals and the background noise match familiar patterns. People have trouble making such distinctions where signals and noise look much alike or where signals and noise have unfamiliar characteristics. Psychological research has the latter characteristics. The activity is called research because its outputs are unknown; and the signals and noise look a lot alike in that both have systematic components and both contain components that vary erratically. Therefore, researchers rely upon statistical techniques to make these distinctions. But these techniques assume: (a) that the so-called random errors really do cancel each other out so that their average values are close to zero; and (b) that the so-called random errors in different variables are uncorrelated. These are very strong assumptions because they presume that the researchers' hypotheses encompass absolutely all of the systematic effects in the data, including effects that the researchers have not foreseen or measured. When these assumptions are not met, the statistical techniques tend to mistake noise for signal, and to attribute more importance to the researchers' hypotheses than they deserve. It requires very little in the way of systematic 'errors' to distort or confound correlations as small as those I/O psychologists usually study.

One reason to expect confounding background relationships is that a few broad characteristics of people and social systems pervade psychological data. One such characteristic is intelligence: Intelligence correlates with many other characteristics and behaviors, such as leadership, job satisfaction, job performance, social class, income, education and geographic location during childhood. These correlates of intelligence tend to correlate with each other, independently of any direct causal relations among them, because of their common relation to intelligence. Other broad characteristics that correlate with many variables include sex, age, social class, education, group or organizational size, and geographic location.

A group of related organization-theory studies illustrates how broad characteristics may mislead researchers. In 1965, Woodward hypothesized that organizations employing different technologies adopt different structures, and she presented some data supporting this view. There followed many studies that found correlations between various measures of organization-level technology and measures of organizational structure. Researchers devoted considerable effort to refining the measures of technology and structure and to exploring variations on this general theme. After some fifteen years of research, Gerwin (1981) pulled together all the diverse findings: Although a variety of significant correlations had been observed, virtually all of them differed insignificantly from zero when viewed as partial correlations with organizational size controlled.

Researchers' control is a second reason to expect confounding background relationships. Researchers often aggregate numerous items into composite variables; and the researchers themselves decide (possibly indirectly via a technique such as factor analysis) which items to include in a specific variable and what weights to give to different items. By including in two composite variables the same items or items that differ quite superficially from each other, researchers generate controllable but substantively meaningless correlations between the composites. Obviously, if two composite variables incorporate many very similar items, the two composites will be highly correlated. In a very real sense, the correlations between composite variables lie entirely within the researchers control; researchers can construct these composites such that they correlate strongly or weakly, and so the 'observed' correlations convey more information about the researchers' beliefs than about the situations that the researchers claim to have observed.

The renowned Aston studies show how researchers' decisions may determine their findings (Starbuck, 1981). The Aston researchers made 1000–2000 measurements of each organization, and then aggregated these into about 50 composite variables. One of the studies' main findings was that four of these composite variables—functional specialization, role specialization, standardization and formalization—correlate strongly: The first Aston study found correlations ranging from .57 to .87 among these variables. However, these variables look a lot alike when one looks into their compositions: Functional specialization and role specialization were defined so that they had to correlate positively, and so that a high correlation between them indicated that the researchers observed organizations having different numbers of specialities. Standardization measured the presence of these same specialities, but did so by noting the existence of documents; and formalization too was measured by the presence of documents, frequently the same documents that determined standardization. Thus, the strong positive correlations were direct consequences of the researchers' decisions about how to construct the variables.

Focused sampling is a third reason to anticipate confounding background relationships. So-called samples are frequently not random, and many of them are complete sub-populations. If, for example, a study obtains data from every employee in a single firm, the number of employees should not be a sample size for the purposes of statistical tests: For comparisons among these employees, complete sub-populations have been observed, the allocations of specific employees to these sub-populations are not random but systematic, and statistical tests are inappropriate. For extrapolation of findings about these employees to those in other firms, the sample size is one firm. This firm, however, is unlikely to have been selected by a random process from a clearly defined sampling frame, and it may possess various distinctive characteristics that make it a poor basis for generalization—such as its willingness to allow psychologists entry, or its geographic location, or its unique history.

These are not unimportant quibbles about the niceties of sampling. Study after study has turned up evidence that people who live close together, who work together, or who socialize together tend to have more attitudes, beliefs, and behaviors in common than do people who are far apart physically and socially. That is, socialization and interaction create distinctive sub-populations. Findings about any one of these sub-populations probably do not extrapolate to others that lie far away or that have quite dissimilar histories or that live during different ages. It would be surprising if the blue-collar workers in a steel mill in Pittsburgh were to answer a questionnaire in the same way as the first-level supervisors in a steel mill in Essen, and even more surprising if the same answers were to come from executives in an insurance company in Calcutta. The blue-collar workers in one steel mill in Pittsburgh might not even answer the questionnaire in the same way as the blue-collar workers in another steel mill in Pittsburgh if the two mills had distinctly different histories and work cultures.

Subjective data obtained from individual respondents at one time and through one method provide a fourth reason to watch for confounding background relationships. By including items in a single questionnaire or an single interview, researchers suggest to respondents that they ought to see relationships among these items; and by presenting the items in a logical sequence, the researchers suggest how the items ought to relate. Only an insensitive respondent would ignore such strong hints. Moreover, respondents have almost certainly made sense of their worlds, even if they do not understand these worlds in some objective sense. For instance, Lawrence and Lorsch (1967) asked managers to describe the structures and environments of their organizations; they then drew inferences about the relationships of organizations' structures to their environments. These inferences might be correct statements about relationships that one could assess with objective measures; or they might be correct statements about relationships that managers perceive, but managers' perceptions might diverge considerably from objective measures (Starbuck, 1985). Would anyone be surprised if it turned out that managers perceive what makes sense because it meshes into their beliefs? In fact, two studies (Tosi et al., 1973; Downey et al., 1975) have attempted to compare managers' perceptions of their environments with other measures of those environments: both studies found no consistent correlations between the perceived and objective measures. Furthermore, Downey et al. (1977) found that managers' perceptions of their firms' environments correlate more strongly with the managers' personal characteristics than with the measurable characteristics of the environments. As to perceptions of organization structure, Payne and Pugh (1976) compared people's perceptions with objective measures: they surmised (a) that the subjective and objective measures correlate weakly; and (b) that people often have such different perceptions of their organization that it makes no sense to talk about shared perceptions.

Foresight is a fifth and possibly the most important reason to anticipate confounding background relationships. Researchers are intelligent, observant people who have considerable life experience and who are achieving success in life. They are likely to have sound intuitive understanding of people and of social systems; they are many times more likely to formulate hypotheses that are consistent with their intuitive understanding than ones that violate it; they are quite likely to investigate correlations and differences that deviate from zero; and they are less likely than chance would imply to observe correlations and differences near zero. This does not mean that researchers can correctly attribute causation or understand complex interdependencies, for these seem to be difficult, and researchers make the same kinds of judgement, interpretation, and attribution errors that other people make (Faust, 1984). But prediction does not require real understanding. Foresight does suggest that psychological differences and correlations have statistical distributions very different from the distributions assumed in hypothesis tests. Hypothesis tests assume no foresight.

If the differences and correlations that psychologists test have distributions quite different from those assumed in hypothesis tests, psychologists are using tests that assign statistical significance to confounding background relationships. If psychologists then equate statistical significance with meaningful relationships, which they often do, they are mistaking confounding background relationships for theoretically important information. One result is that psychological research may be creating a cloud of statistically significant differences and correlations that not only have no real meaning but that impede scientific progress by obscuring the truly meaningful ones.

Measures

To get an estimate of the population distribution of correlations that I/O psychologists study, we tabulated every complete matrix of correlations that appeared in the *Journal of Applied Psychology* during 1983–86. This amounts to 6574 correlations from 95 articles.

We tabulated only complete matrices of correlations in order to observe the relations among all of the variables that I/O psychologists perceive when drawing inductive inferences, not only those variables that psychologists actually include in hypotheses. Of course, some studies probably gathered and analysed data on additional variables beyond those published, and then omitted these additional variables because they correlated very weakly with the dependent variables. It seems well established that the variables in hypotheses are filtered by biases against publishing insignificant results (Sterling, 1959; Greenwald, 1975; Kerr *et al.*, 1977). These biases partly explain why some authors revise or create their hypotheses after they compute correlations, and we know from personal experiences that editors sometimes improperly ask authors to restate their hypotheses to make them fit the data. None the less, many correlation matrices include correlations about which no hypotheses have been stated, and some authors make it a practice to publish the intercorrelation matrices for all of the variables they observed, including variables having expected correlations of zero.

To estimate the percentage of correlations in hypotheses, we examined a stratified random sample of 21 articles. We found it quite difficult to decide whether some relations were or were not included in hypotheses. Nevertheless, it appeared to us that four of these 21 intercorrelation matrices included no hypothesized relations, that seven matrices included 29–70 per cent hypothesized relations, and that ten matrices were made up of more than 80 per cent hypothesized relations. Based on this sample, we estimate that 64 per cent of the correlations in our data represented hypotheses.

Results

Figure 7 shows the observed distribution of correlations. This distribution looks much like the comparable ones for *Administrative Science Quarterly* and the *Academy of Management Journal*, for which we also have data, so the general pattern is not peculiar to I/O psychology.

Figure 7 Correlations Reported in the *Journal of Applied Psychology*.

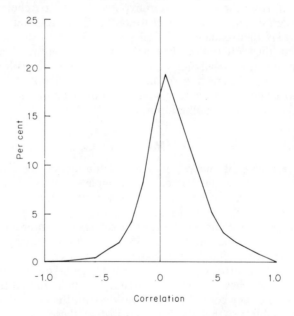

It turns out that Art Brief was nearly right on average, for the mean correlation is .0895 and the median correlation is .0956. The distribution seems to reflect a strong bias against negative correlations: 69 per cent of the correlations are positive and 31 per cent are negative, so the odds are better than 2 to 1 that an observed correlation will be positive. This strong positive bias provides quite striking evidence that many researchers prefer positive relationships, possibly because they find these easier to understand. To express this preference, researchers must either be inverting scales retrospectively or be anticipating the signs of hypothesized relationships prospectively, either of which would imply that these studies should not use statistical tests that assume a mean correlation of zero.

Studies with large numbers of observations exhibit slightly less positive bias.

Table 3 compares studies having less than 70 observations, those with 70 to 180 observations, and those with more than 180 observations. Studies with over 180 observations report 67 per cent positive correlations and 33 per cent negative ones, making the odds of a positive correlation almost exactly 2 to 1. The mean correlation found in studies with over 180 observations is .064, whereas the mean correlation in studies with fewer than 70 observations in .140.

Table 3—Differences Associated with Numbers of Observations

	N<70	70≤N≤180	N>180
Mean numbers of observations	40	120	542
Mean correlations	.140	.117	.064
Numbers of correlations	1195	1457	3922
Percentage of correlations that are:			
Positive	71%	71%	67%
Negative	29%	29%	33%
Percentage of correlations that are statistically significant at .05 using two tails:			
Positive correlations	34%	64%	72%
Negative correlations	18%	41%	56%

Figure 8 compares the observed distributions of correlations with the distributions assumed by a typical hypothesis test. The test distributions in Figure 8 assume random samples equal to the mean numbers of observations for each category. Compared to the observed distributions, the test distributions assume much higher percentages of correlations near zero, so roughly 65 per cent of the reported correlations are statistically significant at the 5 per cent level. The percentages of statistically significant correlations change considerably with numbers of observations because of the different positive biases and because of different test distributions. For studies with more than 180 observations, 72 per cent of the positive correlations and 56 per cent of the negative correlations are statistically significant; whereas for studies with less than 70 observations, 34 per cent of the positive correlations and only 18 per cent of the negative correlations are statistically significant (Table 3). Thus, positive correlations are noticeably more likely than negative ones to be judged statistically significant.

Figure 9a shows that large-N studies and small-N studies obtain rather similar distributions of correlations. The small-N studies do produce more correlations above +.5, and the large-N studies report more correlations between −.2 and +.2. Both differences fit the rationale that researchers make more observations when they are observing correlations near zero. Some researchers undoubtedly anticipate the magnitudes of hypothesized relationships and set out to make numbers of observations that should produce statistical significance (Cohen, 1977); other researchers keep adding observations until they achieve statistical significance for some relationships; and still other researchers stop making observations when they obtain large positive correlations. Again, graphs for *Administrative Science Quarterly* and the *Academy of Management Journal* strongly resemble these for the *Journal of Applied Psychology*.

Figure 9b graphs the test distributions corresponding to Figure 9a. These

Figure 8   Actual Correlations Compared with Test Distributions.
(a)   Correlations with N < 70 compared to Rho = 0 and N = 40

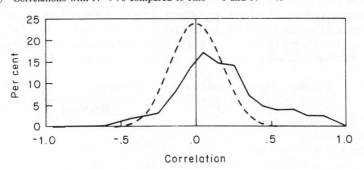

(b)   Correlations with 70 < N < 180 compared to Rho = 0 and N = 120

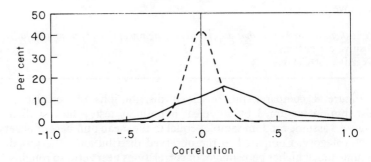

(c)   Correlations with N > 180 compared to Rho = 0 and N = 542

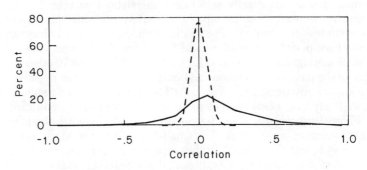

graphs provide a reminder that large-N studies and small-N studies differ more in the criteria used to evaluate statistical significance than in the data they produce, and Figures 9a and b imply that an emphasis on statistical significance amounts to an emphasis on absolutely small correlations.

The pervasive correlations among variables make induction undependable: starting with almost any variable, an I/O psychologist finds it extremely easy to discover a second variable that correlates with the first at least .1 in absolute value. In fact, if the psychologist were to choose the second variable utterly at random,

Figure 9 Small–N Distributions Compared with Large–N Distributions.
(a) Actual correlations: N < 70 compared with N > 180

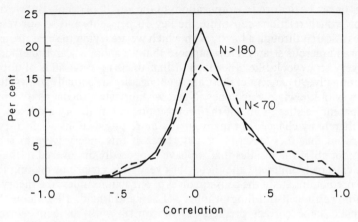

(b) Test correlations: N = 40 compared with N = 542

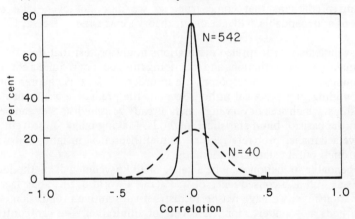

the psychologist's odds would be 2 to 1 of coming up with such a variable on the first try, and the odds would be 24 to 1 of discovering such a variable within three tries. This is a cross-sectional parallel to a finding by Ames and Reiter (1961) relating to the analyses of historical economic statistics: Starting with one time series and choosing a second series at random, an economist would need only three trials on average to discover a correlation of .71 or more; even if the economist would correct each series for linear trend, finding a correlation of .71 or more would require only five trials on average.

Induction becomes even less dependable if a psychologist uses hypothesis tests to decide what correlations deserve attention, and especially so if the psychologist tries to make enough observations to guarantee statistical significance. If the psychologist also defines or redefines variables so as to make positive correlations more likely than negative correlations, hypothesis tests based on the null hypothesis of zero correlation become deceptive rituals.

Suppose that roughly 10 per cent of all observable relations could be theoretically meaningful and that the remaining 90 per cent either have no meanings or can be deduced as implications of the key 10 per cent. But we do not now know which relations constitute the key 10 per cent, and so our research resembles a search through a haystack in which we are trying to separate needles from more numerous straws. Now suppose that we adopt a search method that makes every straw look like a needle and that turns up thousands of apparent needles annually; 90 per cent of these apparent needles are actually straws, but we have no way of knowing which ones. Next, we fabricate a theory that 'explains' these apparent needles. Some of the propositions in our theory are likely to be correct, merely by chance; but many, many more propositions are incorrect or misleading in that they describe straws. Even if this theory were to account rationally for all of the needles that we have supposedly discovered in the past, which is extremely unlikely, the theory has very little chance of making highly accurate predictions about the consequences of our actions unless the theory itself acts as a powerful self-fulfilling prophecy (Eden and Ravid, 1982). Our theory would make some correct predictions, of course; with so many correlated variables, even a completely false theory would have a reasonable chance of generating predictions that come true, so we dare not even take correct predictions as dependable evidence of our theory's correctness (Deese, 1972, pp. 61-7).

I/O psychologists with applied orientations might protest that they primarily need to make correct predictions and that doing this does not require a correct and parsimonious theory. Two responses are in order. First, this chapter concerns theory building, not practical utility. Second, the predictive accuracies of I/O relationships, which are not very high, may already be as high as they can be made solely on the basis of blind statistical methods. Making major improvements in predictive accuracies probably requires actual theoretical insights that will not come through purely statistical methods.

Undependable induction may be a cause of I/O psychology's methodological emphasis as well as a consequence of it. Facing a world of unstable 'facts' and weak relationships, we have reason to distrust substantive propositions and to view methods as sounder, more deserving of admiration. We can control our methods better than substance, so emphasizing methods reduces our risks; and because we evaluate our methods ritualistically, we find it much easier to meet methodological standards than to demonstrate the theoretical significance of our findings. Indeed, if our world changes rapidly, 'facts' are ephemeral and theoretical significance becomes very elusive.

Because we doubt that methodological improvements are what I/O psychology needs most, we do this with reluctance, but we cannot resist pointing out some of the methodological opportunities that exist:

(a)   Statistical significance is a very dangerous criterion. It probably causes more harm than good, by inducing researchers who have few observations to discount strong relationships and encouraging those who have many observations to highlight weak relationships. Moreover, a researcher can be certain of rejecting any point null hypothesis, and point null hypotheses usually look quite implausible if one treats them as genuine descriptions of phenomena (Gilpin and

Diamond, 1984; Shames, 1987). Deese (1972, pp. 56–9), among others, has advocated that researchers replace hypothesis tests with statements about confidence limits. But confidence limits too exaggerate the significance of numbers of observations. In I/O psychology, and in social science research more generally, the numbers of observations are rarely equivalent to the sample sizes assumed in statistical theories, both because truly random sampling is rare and because statistical theories assume that sample sizes are basically the only observable characteristics by which to judge data's dependability, generality, or representativeness. Real life offers researchers many characteristics by which to evaluate data, and carefully chosen observations may be more informative than random samples. Thus, researchers could improve their analyses by using statistical procedures that allow them to assign different weights to observations reflecting their dependability, generality or representativeness; more dependable or more representative observations would receive more weight. As much as from the weights' arithmetic effects, the improvements in induction would come from researchers' efforts to analyse data's dependability or representativeness and from the researchers' efforts to communicate rationales for these weights. Researchers could also improve their analyses by paying more attention to percentage differences between categories: Are males 1 per cent different from females, or 30 per cent? And yet more improvement could come from less use of averages to represent heterogeneous groups and more use of distributions (Brandt, 1982). What fraction of males are 30 per cent different from what fraction of females? Speaking of measures of organizational climate, Payne and Pugh (1976) remarked that respondents' opinions generally vary so greatly that it makes no sense to use averages to characterize groups or organizations.

(b)   Statistical analyses would have greater credibility and greater theoretical significance if researchers would base their analyses on naive hypotheses or realistic hypotheses instead of null hypotheses (Fombrun and Starbuck, 1987). Virtually the entire apparatus of classical statistics was created when high-speed computers did not yet exist and statisticians had to manipulate distributions algebraically. Thus, statisticians built an analytic rationale around distributions that are algebraically pliant even though these distributions make incredible assumptions such as point null hypotheses. With modern computers, however, researchers can generate statistical distributions that reflect either realistic assumptions or naive ones, even if these distributions cannot be manipulated algebraically. For example, computer simulations could generate the distributions of observed correlations in samples of size N from a hypothetical bivariate Normal population with a correlation of .1. To assess the plausibility of alternative theories where several influences interact, some biologists (Connor and Simberloff, 1986) have begun to compare data with computer-generated multinomial distributions that incorporate combinations of several probable influences; such distributions reduce the need for simplifying assumptions such as normality and linearity, and they make it more practical to examine entire distributions of data.

A key value judgement, however, is how challenging should a researcher make the naive or credible hypothesis? How high should the jumper place the crossbar? In science, the crossbar's height has implications for the research community as a whole as well as for an individual researcher: Low crossbars make it easier to claim that the researcher has learned something of significance, but they also lead to building scientific theories on random errors.

(c) Even traditional hypothesis tests and confidence limits could support better induction than they do, but no statistical procedure can surmount inappropriate assumptions, biased samples, overgeneralization, or misrepresentation. Researchers should either eschew the appearance of statistical methods or try to approximate the assumptions underlying these methods.

(d) Researchers should often attempt to replicate others' studies, basing these replications solely on the published reports. Frequent replication would encourage researchers to describe their work completely and to characterize its generality modestly. Replication failures and successes would clarify the reasons for exceptional findings, and thus provide grounds on which to design better studies and to discard inexplicably deviant ones.

(e) I/O psychology has been bounded by two data-acquisition methods: questionnaires and interviews. Although cheap and easy, these methods emphasize subjective perceptions that people recognize and understand well enough to express verbally. These are a part of life. But verbal behavior is bounded by socialization and social constraints that make I/O psychology prone to observe clichés and stereotypes, and it is altogether too easy to find observable behaviors that people do not recognize that they exhibit or that they describe in misleading terms. Thus, researchers should remain skeptical about the validity of subjective data, and they should supplement questionnaires and interviews with their personal observations of behavior, with documents such as letters, memoranda and grievances, and with quantitative data such as costs, turnover statistics, and production volumes (Campbell and Fiske, 1959; Phillips, 1971; Denzin, 1978). Jick (1979) has discussed the advantages and problems of reconciling different kinds of data. However, the greatest payoffs may come from discovering that different kinds of data simply cannot be reconciled.

(f) New sciences tend to begin timidly by gathering data through passive observation and then constructing retrospective explanations for these data (Starbuck, 1976). Unfortunately, most spontaneous events are uninteresting; the more interesting objects of study are unusual, complex, dynamic and reactive; and postdiction makes weak discriminations between alternative theories. Consequently, as sciences gain confidence, they gradually move from the passive, postdictive mode toward a more active and predictive mode: They make more and more efforts to anticipate future events and to manipulate them. Interventions enable scientists to create interesting situations and dynamic reactions. Predictions tend to highlight differences between alternative theories, and trying to make predictions come true may be the only practical way to find out what would happen if. Giving theories visible consequences puts scientists under pressure to attempt innovations (Gordon and Marquis, 1966; Starbuck and Nystrom, 1981).

Thus, potential advantages inhere in I/O psychology's applied orientation and in the numerous I/O psychologists holding non-academic jobs. Compared to academic areas of psychology and to most social sciences, I/O psychology could be more innovative, quicker to discard ineffective theories, more interested in dynamic theories, and more strongly oriented toward prediction and inter- vention. I/O psychology probably does pay more attention than most social sciences to prediction and intervention, but prediction seems to be associated mainly with personnel selection, interventions have focused on goal-setting and behavior modification, and it is doubtful that I/O psychology is exploiting its other potential advantages. We examined several studies of goal-setting and behavior modification published during 1986, and we turned up only static before-and-after comparisons and no analyses that were truly dynamic.

SUMMARY

We started by asking: How much has I/O psychology progressed? Partly because a number of I/O psychologists have been expressing dissatisfaction with the field's progress and asking for more innovation (Hackman, 1982; Nord, 1982), we had an initial impression that progress has been quite slow since the early 1950s. We had also seen a sequence of business-strategy studies that had achieved negative progress, in the sense that relationships became less and less clear as the studies accumulated, and we wondered whether this might have happened in some areas of I/O psychology. We appraised progress by observing the historical changes in effect sizes for some of I/O's major variables. If theories are becoming more and more effective, they should explain higher and higher percentages of variance over time. We found that I/O theories have not been improving by this measure. For the reasons just stated, this did not surprise us, but we were surprised to find such small percentages of variance explained and such consistent changes in variance explained.

Seeking an explanation for no progress or negative progress, we turned to the literature on paradigm development. These writings led us to hypothesize that I/O psychology might be inconsistent with itself: various reviews have suggested that I/O psychologists disagree with each other about the substance of theories. Perhaps I/O psychologists have low paradigm consensus but employ quantitative, large-sample research methods that presume high paradigm consensus. So we assembled various indicators of paradigm consensus. According to these indica- tors, I/O psychology looks much like Organizational Behavior and psychology in general. This is no surprise, of course. I/O psychology also looks different from Management Information Systems (MIS), which appears to be a field that both lacks paradigm consensus and makes rapid progress. But, to our astonishment, I/O psychology does not look so very different from chemistry and physics, two fields that are widely perceived as having high paradigm consensus and as making rapid progress. I/O psychology may, however, differ significantly from the physical sciences in the content of paradigms. Physical science paradigms evidently embrace both substance and methodology, whereas I/O psychology paradigms strongly emphasize methodology and pay little attention to substance. I/O psychologists act as if they do not agree with each other concerning the substance of human behavior, although we believe that this lack of substantive consensus is unnecessary and probably superficial.

Why might the paradigms of I/O psychologists deemphasize substance? We hypothesized that this orientation is probably an intelligent response to a real problem. This real problem, we conjectured, is that I/O psychologists find it difficult to detect meaningful research findings against a background of small, theoretically meaningless, but statistically significant relationships. Thus, I/O psychologists dare not trust their inferences from empirical evidence. To assess the plausibility of this conjecture, we tabulated all of the correlation matrices reported in the *Journal of Applied Psychology* over four years. We found that two-thirds of the reported correlations are statistically significant at the 5 per cent level, and a strong bias makes positive correlations more likely to be reported and to be judged statistically significant than negative ones.

Thus, I/O psychology faces a Catch-22. A distrust of undependable substantive findings may be leading I/O psychologists to emphasize methodology. This strategy, however, assumes that induction works, whereas it is induction that is producing the undependable substantive findings.

CONSTRUCTING A SUBSTANTIVE PARADIGM

Our survey of effect sizes seems to say that I/O theories are not very effective and they are not improving significantly over time. We psychologists seem to have achieved very little agreement among ourselves concerning the substantive products of our research; and it is easy to see why this might be the case, for almost everything in our worlds appears to be somewhat related to everything else, and we use criteria that say almost every relationship is important.

We could make this situation a springboard for despair. People are simple creatures seeking to comprehend worlds more complex than themselves. Scientists attempt to construct rational explanations; but rationality is a human characteristic, not an intrinsic characteristic of nature, so scientists have no guarantee that science will prove adequate to the demands they place on it. Psychological research itself details the cognitive limitations that confine and warp human perceptions (Faust, 1984). The complexity of people's worlds may also be a human characteristic, for people who think they comprehend some aspects of their worlds tend to react by complicating their worlds until they no longer understand them. Thus, social scientists have reason to doubt the adequacy of rational explanations to encompass most phenomena (Starbuck, 1988). Within our limitations, we psychologists may find it impossible to achieve complete explanations without reducing actions and measures to trivial tautologies. For example, we can decide that we will only teach in school what we can measure with an aptitude test, or that we will select and promote leaders solely on the basis of leadership questionnaires.

We need not despair, however. Studies of progress in the physical sciences emphasize the strong effects of social construction (Sullivan, 1928; Knorr-Cetina, 1981; Latour, 1987). Although it is true that physical scientists discard theories that do not work, the scientists themselves exercise a good deal of choice about what aspects of phenomena they try to explain and how they measure theories' efficacies. Newton's laws are one of the best known substantive paradigms. Physicists came to accept these laws because they enabled better predictions concerning certain phenomena, but the laws say nothing whatever about some properties of physical systems, and the laws fail to explain some of the phenomena that physicists expected them to explain, such as light or sub-atomic interactions. In no sense are Newton's laws absolute truths. Rather they are statements that physicists use as base lines for explanation: physicists attempt to build explanations upon Newton's laws first. If these explanations work, the physicists are satisfied, and their confidence in Newton's laws has been reaffirmed. If these base-line explanations do not work, physicists try to explain the deviations from Newton's laws. Are there, for instance, exogenous influences that had not previously been noticed? Finally, if some inexplicable deviations from Newton's laws recur systematically, but only in this extreme circumstance, physicists contemplate alternative theories.

The contrast to I/O psychology is striking... and suggestive. The difference between physics and psychology may be more in the minds of physicists and psychologists than in the phenomena they study (Landy and Vasey, 1984). After arguing that psychological facts are approximately as stable over time as physical ones, Hedges (1987, pp. 453–4) observed:

> New physical theories are *not* sought on every occasion in which there is a modest failure of experimental consistency. Instead, reasons for the inconsistency are likely to be sought in the methodology of the research studies. At least tentative confidence in theory stabilizes the situation so that a rather extended series of inconsistent results would be required to force a major reconceptualization. In social sciences, theory does not often play this stabilizing role.

Campbell (1982, p. 697) characterized the theories of I/O psychology as 'collections of statements that are so general that asserting them to be true conveys very little information.' But, of course, the same could be said of the major propositions of the physical sciences such as Newton's laws: any truly general proposition can convey no information about where it applies because it applies everywhere (Smedslund, 1984). General theoretical propositions are necessarily heuristic guidelines rather than formulae with obvious applications in specific instances, and it is up to scientists to apply these heuristics in specific instances. But general theoretical propositions are more than heuristics because they serve social functions as well.

Scientific progress is a perception by scientists, and theories need not be completely correct in order to support scientific progress. As much as correctness, theories need the backing of consensus and consistency. When scientists agree among themselves to explain phenomena in terms of base-line theories, they project their findings into shared perceptual frameworks that reinforce the collective nature of research by facilitating communication and comparison and by defining what is important or irrelevant. Indeed, in so far as science is a collective enterprise, abstractions do not become theoretical propositions until they win widespread social support. A lack of substantive consensus is equivalent to a lack of theory, and scientists must agree to share a theory in order to build on each others' work. Making progress depends upon scientists' agreeing to make progress.

The absence of a strong substantive paradigm may be more a cause of slow progress than a consequence of it, and I/O psychologists could dramatically accelerate the field's progress by adopting and enforcing a substantive paradigm. Of course, conformity to a seriously erroneous paradigm might delay progress until dissatisfaction builds up to a high state and one of Kuhn's revolutions takes place; but so little progress is occurring at present that the prospect of non-progress hardly seems threatening.

Moreover, I/O psychology could embrace some theoretical propositions that are roughly as sound as Newton's laws. At least, these propositions are dependable enough to serve as base lines: they describe many phenomena, and deviations from them point to contingencies. For example, we believe that almost all I/O psychologists could accept the following propositions as base lines:

Pervasive Characteristics. Almost all characteristics of individual people correlate with age, education, intelligence, sex, and social class; and almost all characteristics of groups and organizations correlate with age, size, and wealth. (Implication: every study should measure these variables and take them into account.)

Cognitive Consonance. Simultaneously evoked cognitions (attitudes, beliefs, perceptions and values) tend to become logically consistent (Festinger, 1957; Heider, 1958; Abelson et al., 1968). Corollary 1: Retrospection makes what has happened appear highly probable (Fischhoff, 1980). Corollary 2: Social status, competence, control, and organizational attitudes tend toward congruence (Sampson, 1969; Payne and Pugh, 1976). Corollary 3: Dissonant cognitions elicit subjective sensations such as feelings of inequity, and strong dissonance may trigger behaviors such as change initiatives or reduced participation (Walster et al., 1973). Corollary 4: Simultaneously evoked cognitions tend to polarize into one of two opposing clusters (Cartwright and Harary, 1956). Corollary 5: People and social systems tend to resist change (Marx, 1859; Lewin, 1943).

Social Propositions:
Activities, interactions, and sentiments reinforce each other (Homans, 1950). Corollary 1: People come to resemble their neighbors (Coleman et al., 1966; Industrial Democracy in Europe International Research Group, 1981). Corollary 2: Collectivities develop distinctive norms and shared beliefs (Roethlisberger and Dickson, 1939; Seashore, 1954; Beyer, 1981). (These propositions too can be viewed as a corollaries of cognitive consonance.) Idea evaluation inhibits idea generation (Maier, 1963). Participation in the implementation of new ideas makes them more acceptable (Lewin, 1943; Kelley and Thibaut, 1954). Corollary 1: Participation in goal setting fosters the acceptance of goals (Maier, 1963; Locke, 1968; Vroom and Yetton, 1973; Latham and Yukl, 1975). Corollary 2: Participation in the design of changes reduces resistance to change (Coch and French, 1948; Marrow et al., 1967; Lawler and Hackman, 1969). Corollary 3: Opportunities to voice dissent make exit less likely (Hirschman, 1970).

Reinforcement Propositions:
Rewards make behaviors more likely, punishments make behaviors less likely

(Thorndike, 1911; Skinner, 1953). (This is a tautology, of course [Smedslund, 1984], but so is Newton's F = ma. A proposition need not convey information in order to facilitate consensus.)
The more immediate a reinforcement the stronger is its impact (Hull, 1943). Continuous reinforcements produce faster learning that is more quickly unlearned, whereas intermittent reinforcements produce slower learning that is more slowly unlearned (Hull, 1943; Estes, 1957).

Other propositions doubtless could be added to the list, but these illustrate what we mean. We would be exceedingly happy to have some august body take responsibility for formulating dogma.

I/O psychologists are quite unlikely to adopt and use a set of base-line propositions voluntarily. Many I/O psychologists hold vested interests in specific propositions that do not qualify for base-line status or that would become redundant. I/O psychologists are not accustomed to projecting everything they do onto a shared framework, so they would have to learn new ways of thinking and speaking. Some I/O psychologists have expressed doubts about the validity of theoretical propositions in the field. Thus, we surmise that constructing a consensus requires explicit actions by the key journals that act as professional gatekeepers. Specifically, to promote progress in I/O psychology, the key journals could adhere to three policies:

1. Journals should refuse to publish studies that purport to contradict the base-line propositions.[1] Since the propositions are known laws of nature, valid evidence cannot contradict them. Apparent discrepancies from these laws point to exogenous influences, to interactions among influences, or to observational errors.
2. Journals should refuse to publish studies that do no more than reaffirm the base-line propositions. Known laws of nature need no more documentation. However, there may be need to explain the implications of these laws in circumstances where those implications are not self-evident.
3. Journals should insist that all published studies refer to any of the base-line propositions that are relevant. There is no need for new theoretical propositions where the existing laws are already adequate, so any phenomena that can be explained in terms of these laws must be so explained.

Will base-line propositions such as those we have listed prove to be adequate psychological laws in the long run? No, unquestionably not. First, because we are simple creatures trying to comprehend complex worlds, it behooves us to expect our theories to prove somewhat wrong; and because we are hopeful creatures, we intend to do better. Secondly, in order to integrate multiple propositions, I/O psychology will have to move from qualitative propositions to quantitative ones. Attempts to apply base-line propositions would likely produce demands for standardized measures, and then more specific propositions. How rapidly do cognitions become consistent, and how can one judge whether they have attained consistency? Thirdly, processes that tend to alter some characteristics of a social system also tend to evoke antithetical processes that affect these characteristics

1. Kerr's Law.

oppositely (Fombrun and Starbuck, 1987). Stability creates pressures for change, consensus arouses dissent, constraint stirs up rebellion, conformity brings out independence, and conviction evokes skepticism. Thus, the very existence of a scientific paradigm would call forth efforts to overthrow that paradigm.

But we believe I/O psychology should try using a consistent paradigm for a few decades before overthrowing it. Moreover, history suggests that I/O psychologists do not actually overthrow theoretical propositions. Instead, they react to unsatisfactory propositions by integrating them with their antitheses.

For example, during the early part of the twentieth century, many writers and managers held that successful organizations require firm leaders and obedient subordinates (Starbuck and Nystrom, 1981, pp. xvii–xviii). Leadership was viewed as a stable characteristic of individuals: some fortunate people have leadership traits, and other unlucky souls do not. This orthodoxy attracted challenges during the 1920s and 1930s: Weber (1947) noted that some organizations depersonalize leadership and that subordinates sometimes judge leaders illegitimate. The Hawthorne studies argued that friendly supervision increases subordinates' productivity (Roethlisberger and Dickson, 1939; Mayo, 1946). Barnard (1938) asserted that authority originates in subordinates rather than superiors. By the early 1950s, various syntheses were being proposed. Bales (1953), Cartwright and Zander (1953), and Gibb (1954) analysed leadership as an activity shared among group members. Coch and French (1948) and Lewin (1953) spoke of democratic leadership, and Bales (1953) distinguished leaders' social roles from their task roles. Cattell and Stice (1954) and Stogdill (1948) considered the distinctive personality attributes of different kinds of leaders. By the late 1950s, the Ohio State studies had factored leadership into two dimensions: initiating structure and consideration (Fleishman et al., 1955; Stogdill and Coons, 1957). Initiating structure corresponds closely to the leadership concepts of 1910, and consideration corresponds to the challenges to those concepts. Thus, views that had originally been seen as antithetical had eventually been synthesized into independent dimensions of multiple, complex phenomena.

REFERENCES

Abelson, R. P., Aronson, E., McGuire, W. J., Newcomb, T. M., Rosenberg, M. J. and Tannenbaum, P. H. (1968) *Theories of Cognitive Consistency*. Chicago: Rand-McNally.
American Psychological Association (1968) Summary report of journal operations: 1967, *American Psychologist*, **23**, 872.
American Psychological Association (1978) Summary report of journal operations for 1977, *American Psychologist*, **33**, 608.
American Psychological Association (1982) Summary report of journal operations: 1981, *American Psychologist*, **37**, 709.
American Psychological Association (1983) Summary report of journal operations: 1982, *American Psychologist*, **38**, 739.
American Psychological Association (1984) Summary report of journal operations, *American Psychologist*, **39**, 689.
American Psychological Association (1985) Summary report of journal operations, *American Psychologist*, **40**, 707.

American Psychological Association (1986) Summary report of journal operations: 1985, *American Psychologist*, **41**, 701.

Ames, E. and Reiter, S. (1961) Distributions of correlation coefficients in economic time series. *Journal of the American Statistical Association*, **56**, 637–656.

Bakan, D. (1974) *On Method: Toward a Reconstruction of Psychological Investigation*. San Francisco: Jossey-Bass.

Bales, R. F. (1953) The equilibrium problem in small groups. In T. Parsons, R. F. Bales and E. A. Shils (eds) *Working Papers in the Theory of Action*. Glencoe, Ill.: Free Press, 111–161.

Barnard, C. I. (1938) *The Functions of the Executive*. Cambridge, Mass.: Harvard University Press.

Bass, B. M. (1981) *Stogdill's Handbook of Leadership*. New York: The Free Press.

Beyer, J. M. (1978) Editorial policies and practices among leading journals in four scientific fields. *The Sociological Quarterly*, **19**, 68–88.

Beyer, J. M. (1981) Ideologies, values, and decision-making in organizations. In P. C. Nystrom and W. H. Starbuck (eds) *Handbook of Organizational Design*. Oxford: Oxford University Press, 166–202.

Blackburn, R. S. and Mitchell, M. (1981) Citation analysis in the organizational sciences. *Journal of Applied Psychology*, **66**, 337–342.

Borgen, F. H., Layton, W. L., Veenhuizen, D. L. and Johnson, D. J. (1985) Vocational behavior and career development, 1984: A review. *Journal of Vocational Behavior*, **27**, 218–269.

Box, G. E. P. and Draper, N. R. (1969) *Evolutionary Operation*. New York: John Wiley.

Brackbill, Y. and Korten, F. (1970) Journal reviewing practices: Authors' and APA members' suggestions for revision. *American Psychologist*, **25**, 937–940.

Brandt, L. W. (1982) *Psychologists Caught: A psycho-logic of psychology*. Toronto: University of Toronto Press.

Brayfield, A. H. and Crockett, W. H. (1955) Employee attitudes and employee performance. *Psychological Bulletin*, **52**, 396–424.

Bureau of the Census (1987) *Statistical Abstract of the United States 1987*. Washington, DC: US Department of Commerce.

Campbell, D. T. and Fiske, D. W. (1959) Convergent and discriminant validation by the multitrait-multimethod matrix. *Psychological Bulletin*, **56**, 81–105.

Campbell, J. P. (1977) The cutting edge of leadership: An overview. In J. G. Hunt and L. L. Larson (eds) *Leadership: The cutting edge*. Carbondale, Ill.: Southern Illinois University Press.

Campbell, J. P. (1982) Editorial: Some remarks from the outgoing editor. *Journal of Applied Psychology*, **67**, 691–700.

Campbell, J. P., Daft, R. L. and Hulin, C. L. (1982) *What to Study: Generating and developing research questions*. New York: Sage.

Campion, M. A. and Thayer, P. W. (1985) Development and field evaluation of an interdisciplinary measure of job design. *Journal of Applied Psychology*, **62**, 29–43.

Cartwright, D. and Harary, F. (1956) Structural balance: A generalization of Heider's theory. *Psychological Review*, **63**, 277–293.

Cartwright, D. and Zander, A. (1953) Leadership: Introduction. In D. Cartwright and A. Zander (eds) *Group Dynamics*. Evanston, Ill.: Row, Peterson, 535–550.

Cattell, R. B. and Stice, G. F. (1954) Four formulae for selecting leaders on the basis of personality. *Human Relations*, **7**, 493–507.

Chapman, L. J. and Chapman, J. P. (1969) Illusory correlation as an obstacle to the use of valid psychodiagnostic signs. *Journal of Abnormal Psychology*, **74**, 271–280.

Coch, L. and French, J. R. P. Jr (1948) Overcoming resistance to change. *Human Relations*, **1**, 512–532.

Cohen, J. (1977) *Statistical Power Analysis for the Behavioral Sciences*. New York: Academic Press.

Coleman, J. S., Katz, E. and Menzel, H. (1966) *Medical Innovation*. Indianapolis: Bobbs-Merrill.

Connor, E. F. and Simberloff, D. (1986) Competition, scientific method, and null models in ecology. *American Scientist*, **74**, 155–162.

Cummings, L. L. and Schmidt, S. M. (1972) Managerial attitudes of Greeks: The roles of culture and industrialization. *Administrative Science Quarterly*, **17**, 265–272.

Daft, R. L. and Wiginton, J. (1979) Language and organization. *Academy of Management Review*, **4**, 179–191.

De Meuse, K. P. (1986) A compendium of frequently used measures in industrial/ organizational psychology. *The Industrial-Organizational Psychologist*, **23** (2), 53–59.

Deese, J. (1972) *Psychology as Science and Art*. New York: Harcourt.

Denzin, N. K. (1978) *The Research Act*. New York: McGraw-Hill.

Downey, H. K., Hellriegel, G. and Slocum, J. W., Jr (1975) Environmental uncertainty: The construct and its application. *Administrative Science Quarterly*, **20**, 613–629.

Downey, H. K., Hellriegel, G. and Slocum, J. W., Jr (1977) Individual characteristics as sources of perceived uncertainty. *Human Relations*, **30**, 161–174.

Dreeben, R. (1968) *On What is Learned in School*. Reading, Mass.: Addison-Wesley.

Dubin, R. (1976) Theory building in applied areas. In M. D. Dunnette (ed.), *Handbook of Industrial and Organizational Psychology*. Chicago: Rand-McNally, 17–39.

Eden, D. and Ravid, G. (1982) Pygmalion versus self-expectancy: Effects of instructor- and self-expectancy on trainee performance. *Organizational Behavior and Human Performance*, **30**, 351–364.

Estes, W. K. (1957) Theory of learning with constant, variable, or contingent probabilities of reinforcement. *Psychometrika*, **22**, 113–132.

Faust, D. (1984) *The Limits of Scientific Reasoning*. Minneapolis, MN: University of Minnesota Press.

Festinger, L. (1957) *A Theory of Cognitive Dissonance*. Evanston, Ill.: Row, Peterson.

Fiedler, F. E. (1967) *A Theory of Leadership Effectiveness*. New York: McGraw-Hill.

Fischhoff, B. (1980) For those condemned to study the past: Reflections on historical judgment. In R. A. Shweder and D. W. Fiste (eds) *New Directions for Methodology of Behavioral Science*. San Francisco: Jossey-Bass, 79–93.

Fleishman, E. A., Harris, E. F. and Burtt, H. E. (1955) *Leadership and Supervision in Industry*. Columbus, Ohio: Ohio State University, Bureau of Educational Research.

Fombrun, C. J. and Starbuck, W. H. (1987) *Variations in the Evolution of Organizational Ecology*. Working paper, New York University.

Garfield, E. (1972) Citation analysis as a tool in journal evaluation. *Science*, **178**, 471–479.

Garfield, E. (1981–84a) *SSCI Journal Citation Reports*. Philadelphia, Penn.: Institute for Scientific Information.

Garfield, E. (1981–84b) *SSCI Journal Citation Reports*. Philadelphia, Penn.: Institute for Scientific Information.

Garvey, W. D., Lin, N. and Nelson, C. E. (1970) Some comparisons of communication activities in the physical and social sciences. In C. E. Nelson and D. K. Pollock (eds) *Communication among Scientists and Engineers*. Lexington, Mass.: Heath Lexington, 61–84.

Gerwin, D. (1981) Relationships between structure and technology. In P. C. Nystrom and W. H. Starbuck (eds) *Handbook of Organizational Design*. New York: Oxford University Press, 3–38.

Gibb, C. A. (1954) Leadership. In G. Lindzey (ed.), *Handbook of Social Psychology*. Cambridge, Mass.: Addison-Wesley.

Gilpin, M. E. and Diamond, J. M. (1984) Are serious co-occurrences on islands non-random, and are null hypotheses useful in community ecology? In D. R. Strong and others (eds) *Ecological Communities: Conceptual issues and the evidence*. Princeton, N.J.: Princeton University Press, 297–315.

Goldberg, L. R. (1970) Man versus model of man: A rationale, plus some evidence, for a method of improving on clinical inferences. *Psychological Bulletin*, **73**, 422–432.

Gordon, G. and Marquis, S. (1966) Freedom, visibility of consequences, and scientific innovation. *American Journal of Sociology*, **72**, 195–202.

Greenwald, A. G. (1975) Consequences of prejudice against the null hypothesis. *Psychological Bulletin*, **82**, 1–20.

Griffin, R. W. (1987) Toward an integrated theory of task design. In L. L. Cummings and B. M. Staw (eds) *Research in Organizational Behavior* (pp. 79–120). Greenwich, Conn.: JAI Press.

Hackett, R. D. and Guion, R. M. (1985) A reevaluation of the absenteeism – job satisfaction relationship. *Organizational Behavior and Human Decision Processes*, **35**, 340–381.

Hackman, J. R. (1982) Preface. In Campbell, J. T., Daft, R. L. and Hulin, C. L. (eds) *What to Study: Generating and developing research questions*. New York: Sage.

Hackman, J. R. and Oldham, G. R. (1980) *Work Redesign*. Reading, Mass.: Addison-Wesley.

Haire, M., Ghiselli, E. E. and Porter, L. W. (1966) *Managerial Thinking*. New York: John Wiley.

Hedges, L. V. (1987) How hard is hard science, how soft is soft science? *American Psychologist*, **42**, 443–455.

Heider, F. (1958) *The Psychology of Interpersonal Relations*. New York: John Wiley.

Hirschman, A. O. (1970) *Exit, Voice, and Loyalty*. Cambridge, Mass.: Harvard University Press.

Homans, G. C. (1950) *The Human Group*. New York: Harcourt, Brace.

Hopkins, B. L. and Sears, J. (1982) Managing behavior for productivity. In L. W. Frederiksen (ed.) *Handbook of Organizational Behavior Management*. New York: John Wiley, 393–425.

House, R. J. and Singh, J. V. (1987) Organizational behavior: Some new directions for I/O psychology. *Annual Review of Psychology*, **38**.

Hull, C. L. (1943) *Principles of Behavior*. New York: D. Appleton Century.

Iaffaldano, M. T. and Muchinsky, P. M. (1985) Job satisfaction and job performance: A meta-analysis. *Psychological Bulletin*, **97**, 251–273.

Industrial Democracy in Europe International Research Group (1981) *Industrial Democracy in Europe*. Oxford: Oxford University Press.

Ives, B. and Hamilton, S. (1982) Knowledge utilization among MIS researchers. *MIS Quarterly*, **6** (4), 61–77.

Jackson, S. E. (1986) Workshop: Results from a survey of editors. Paper presented at the Washington, DC meeting of the APA Annual Convention.

Jick, T. J. (1979) Mixing qualitative and quantitative methods: Triangulation in action. *Administrative Science Quarterly*, **24**, 602–611.

Jones, D. E. H. (1966) On being blinded with science – being a ruthless enquiry into scientific methods, complete with 29 genuine references and a learned footnote. *New Scientist*, 24 November, 465–467.

Kaplan, A. (1963) *The Conduct of Inquiry: Methodology for behavioral science*. San Francisco: Chandler.

Katz, D. and Kahn, R. L. (1978) *The Social Psychology of Organizations*. New York: John Wiley.

Kelley, H. H. and Thibaut, J. W. (1954) Experimental studies of group problem solving and process. In G. Lindzey (ed.), *Handbook of Social Psychology*. Cambridge, Mass.: Addison-Wesley, 735–786.

Kendler, H. H. (1984) Evolutions or revolutions? In K. M. J. Lagerspetz and P. Niemi (eds) *Psychology in the 1990's*. Amsterdam: North-Holland.

Kenny, D. A. and Zaccaro, S. J. (1983) An estimate of variance due to traits in leadership. *Journal of Applied Psychology*, **68**, 678–685.

Kerr, S., Tolliver, J. and Petree, D. (1977) Manuscript characteristics which influence acceptance for management and social science journals. *Academy of Management Journal*, **20**, 132–141.

King, A. S. (1974) Expectation effects in organizational change. *Administrative Science Quarterly*, **19**, 221–230.

Klayman, J. and Ha, Y.-W. (1987) Confirmation, disconfirmation, and information in hypothesis testing. *Psychological Review*, **94**, 211–228.

Knorr-Cetina, K. D. (1981) *The Manufacture of Knowledge: An essay on the constructivist and contextual nature of science*. Oxford: Pergamon.

Koch, S. (1981) The nature and limits of psychological knowledge. *American Psychologist*, **36**, 257–269.

Kuhn, T. S. (1970) *The Structure of Scientific Revolutions*. Chicago: The University of Chicago Press.

Kunda, G. (1987) *Engineering Culture: Culture and control in a high-tech organization*. PhD thesis, Alfred P. Sloan School of Management, MIT.

Landy, F. J. and Vasey, J. (1984) Theory and logic in human resources research. In K. M. Rowland and G. R. Ferris (eds) *Research in Personnel and Human Resources Management*. Greenwich, Conn.: JAI Press, 1–34.

Latham, G. P. and Yukl, G. A. (1975) A review of research on the application of goal setting in organizations. *Academy of Management Journal*, **18**, 824–845.

Latour, B. (1987) *Science in Action*. Cambridge, Mass.: Harvard University Press.

Lave, C. and March, J. (1975) *An Introduction to Models in the Social Sciences*. New York: Harper and Row.

Lawler, E. E. III and Hackman, J. (1969) Impact of employee participation in the development of pay incentive plans: A field experiment. *Journal of Applied Psychology*, **53**, 467–471.

Lawrence, P. R. and Lorsch, J. W. (1967) *Organization and Environment*. Boston, Mass.: Harvard Business School.

Lewin, K. (1943) Forces behind food habits and methods of change. *National Research Council, Bulletin*, **108**, 35–65.

Lewin, K. (1953) Studies in group decision. In D. Cartwright and A. Zander (eds) *Group Dynamics*. Evanston, Ill.: Row, Peterson, 287–301.

Lindsey, D. and Lindsey, T. (1978) The outlook of journal editors and referees on the normative criteria of scientific craftsmanship. *Quality and Quantity*, **12**, 45–62.

Line, M. B. and Sandison, A. (1974) 'Obsolescence' and changes in the use of literature with time. *Journal of Documentation*, **30**, 283–350.

Locke, E. A. (1968) Toward a theory of task motivation and incentives. *Organizational Behavior and Human Performance*, **3**, 157–189.

Locke, E. (1976) The nature and causes of job satisfaction. In M. D. Dunnette (ed.), *Handbook of Industrial and Organizational Psychology*. New York: John Wiley, 1297–1349.

Locke, E. A. (1977) The myths of behavior mod in organizations. *Academy of Management Review*, **4**, 543–553.

Locke, E. A., Feren, D. B., McCaleb, V. M., Shaw, K. N. and Denny, A. T. (1980) The relative effectiveness of four methods of motivating employee performance. In K. D. Duncan, M. M. Gruneberg and D. Wallis (eds) *Changes in Working Life*. New York: John Wiley, 363–388.

Lodahl, J. B. and Gordon, G. (1972) The structure of scientific fields and the functioning of university graduate departments. *American Sociological Review*, **37**, 57–72.

Lord, R. G., De Vader, C. L. and Alliger, G. M. (1986) A meta-analysis of the relation between personality traits and leadership perceptions: An application of validity generalization procedures. *Journal of Applied Psychology*, 71, 402–410.

Mahoney, M. J. (1977) Publication prejudices: An experimental study of confirmatory bias in the peer review system. *Cognitive Therapy and Research*, 1, 161–175.

Mahoney, M. J. and DeMonbreun, B. G. (1977) Psychology of the scientist: An analysis of problem-solving bias. *Cognitive Therapy and Research*, 1, 229–238.

Maier, N. R. F. (1963) *Problem-solving Discussions and Conferences: Leadership methods and skills*. New York: McGraw-Hill.

Mann, R. D. (1959) A review of the relationships between personality and performance in small groups. *Psychological Bulletin*, 56, 241–270.

Marrow, A. J., Bowers, D. G. and Seashore, S. E. (1967) *Management by Participation*. New York: Harper and Row.

Marx, K. (1859) *A Contribution to the Critique of Political Economy*. Chicago: Kerr.

Masterman, M. (1970) The nature of a paradigm. In I. Lakatos and A. Musgrave (eds) *Criticism and the Growth of Knowledge*. London: Cambridge University Press.

Mayo, E. (1946) *The Human Problems of an Industrial Civilization*. Boston, Mass.: Harvard University Press, Graduate School of Business Administration.

McEvoy, G. M. and Cascio, W. F. (1985) Strategies for reducing employee turnover: A meta-analysis. *Journal of Applied Psychology*, 70, 342–353.

McGuire, W. J. (1983) A contextualist theory of knowledge: Its implications for innovation and reform in psychological research. In L. Berkowitz (ed.), *Advances in Experimental Social Psychology*. Orlando: Academic Press, 1–47.

Meehl, P. E. (1954) *Clinical versus Statistical Prediction: A theoretical analysis and review of the evidence*. Minneapolis, Minn.: University of Minnesota Press.

Miner, J. B. (1980) *Theories of Organizational Behavior*. Hinsdale, Ill.: Dryden.

Miner, J. B. (1984) The validity and usefulness of theories in an emerging organizational science. *Academy of Management Review*, 9, 296–306.

Mitchell, T. R. (1979) Organizational behavior. *Annual Review of Psychology*, 30, 243–281.

Mitchell, T. R., Beach, L. R. and Smith, K. G. (1985) Some data on publishing from the authors' and reviewers' perspectives. In L. L. Cummings and P. J. Frost (eds) *Publishing in the Organizational Sciences*. Homewood, Ill.: Richard D. Irwin, 248–264.

Moravcsik, M. J. and Murgesan, P. (1975) Some results on the function and quality of citations. *Social Studies of Science*, 5, 86–92.

Nelson, N., Rosenthal, R. and Rosnow, R. L. (1986) Interpretation of significance levels and effect sizes by psychological researchers. *American Psychologist*, 41, 1299–1301.

Nord, W. R. (1982) Continuity and change in Industrial/Organizational psychology: Learning from previous mistakes. *Professional Psychology*, 13, 942–952.

Orwin, R. G. and Cordray, D. S. (1985) Effects of deficient reporting on meta-analysis: A conceptual framework and reanalysis. *Psychological Bulletin*, 97, 134–147.

Ozer, D. J. (1985) Correlation and the coefficient of determination. *Psychological Bulletin*, 97, 307–315.

Payne, R. L. and Pugh, D. S. (1976) Organizational structure and climate. In M. D. Dunnette (ed.) *Handbook of Industrial and Organizational Psychology*. Chicago: Rand-McNally, 1125–1173.

Peters, D. P. and Ceci, S. J. (1982) Peer-review practices of psychological journals: The fate of published articles, submitted again. *The Behavioural and Brain Sciences*, 5, 187–195.

Peters, L. H., Hartke, D. D. and Pohlmann, J. T. (1985) Fiedler's contingency theory of leadership: An application of the meta-analysis procedures of Schmidt and Hunter. *Psychological Bulletin*, 97, 274–285.

Phillips, D. L. (1971) *Knowledge from What?: Theories and methods in social research.* Chicago: Rand-McNally.

Pinski, G. and Narin, F. (1979) Structure of the psychological literature. *Journal of the American Society for Information Science*, **30**, 161–168.

Price, D. J. de S. (1965) Networks of scientific papers. *Science*, **149**, 510–515.

Price, D. J. de S. (1970) Citation measures of hard science, soft science, technology, and nonscience. In C. E. Nelson and D. K. Pollock (eds) *Communication among Scientists and Engineers.* Lexington, Mass.: Heath Lexington, 3–22.

Roberts, K. H. and Glick, W. (1981) The job characteristics approach to task design: A critical review. *Journal of Applied Psychology*, **66**, 193–217.

Roethlisberger, F. J. and Dickson, W. J. (1939) *Management and the Worker.* Cambridge, Mass.: Harvard University Press.

Rosenthal, R. (1966) *Experimenter Effects in Behavioral Research.* New York: Appleton-Century-Crofts.

Salancik, G. R. (1986) An index of subgroup influence in dependency networks. *Administrative Science Quarterly*, **31**, 194–211.

Sampson, E. E. (1969) Studies in status congruence. In L. Berkowitz (ed.), *Advances in Experimental Social Psychology.* New York: Academic Press, 225–270.

Sanford, N. (1982) Social psychology: Its place in personology. *American Psychologist*, **37**, 896–903.

Schneider, B. (1985) Organizational behavior. *Annual Review of Psychology*, **36**, 573–611.

Schriesheim, C. A. and Kerr, S. (1977) Theories and measures of leadership: A critical appraisal of current and future directions. In J. G. Hunt and L. L. Larson (eds) *Leadership: The cutting edge.* Carbondale, Ill.: Southern Illinois University Press, 9–45.

Scott, K. D. and Taylor, G. S. (1985) An examination of conflicting findings on the relationship between job satisfaction and absenteeism: A meta-analysis. *Academy of Management Journal*, **28**, 599–612.

Seashore, S. E. (1954) *Group Cohesiveness in the Indusrial Work Group.* Ann Arbor, Mich.: Institute for Social Research.

Shames, M. L. (1987) Methodocentricity, theoretical sterility, and the socio-behavioral sciences. In W. J. Baker, M. E. Hyland, H. Van Rappard, and A. W. Staats (eds) *Current Issues in Theoretical Psychology.* Amsterdam: North-Holland.

Sharplin, A. D. and Mabry, R. H. (1985) The relative importance of journals used in management research: An alternative ranking. *Human Relations*, **38**, 139–149.

Skinner, B. F. (1953) *Science and Human Behavior.* New York: Macmillan.

Small, H. (1980) Co-citation context analysis and the structure of paradigms. *Journal of Documentation*, **36**, 183–196.

Smedslund, J. (1984) What is necessarily true in psychology? In J. R. Royce and L. P. Mos (eds) *Annals of Theoretical Psychology.* New York: Plenum Press, 241–272.

Snyder, M. (1981) Seek, and ye shall find: Testing hypotheses about other people. In E. T. Higgins, C. P. Herman and M. P. Zanna (eds) *Social Cognition, The Ontario Symposium.* Hillsdale, N.J.: Lawrence Erlbaum, 277–303.

Stagner, R. (1982) Past and Future of Industrial/Organizational Psychology. *Professional Psychology*, **13**, 892–902.

Starbuck, W. H. (1976) Organizations and their environments. In M. D. Dunnette (ed.) *Handbook of Industrial and Organizational Psychology.* Chicago: Rand-McNally, 1069–1123.

Starbuck, W. H. (1981) A trip to view the elephants and rattlesnakes in the garden of Aston. In A. H. Van de Ven and W. F. Joyce (eds) *Perspectives on Organization Design and Behavior.* New York: Wiley-Interscience, 167–198.

Starbuck, W. H. (1985) Acting first and thinking later: Theory versus reality in strategic change. In J. M. Pennings and Associates, *Organizational Strategy Decision and Change*. San Francisco: Jossey-Bass, 336–372.

Starbuck, W. H. (1988) Surmounting our human limitations. In R. Quinn and K. Cameron (eds) *Paradox and Transformation: Toward a theory of change in organization and management*. Cambridge, Mass.: Ballinger.

Starbuck, W. H. and Nystrom, P. C. (1981) Designing and understanding organizations. In P. C. Nystrom and W. H. Starbuck, (eds) *Handbook of Organizational Design*. Oxford: Oxford University Press, ix–xxii.

Staw, B. M. (1976) Knee deep in the Big Muddy: A study of escalating commitment to a chosen course of action. *Organizational Behavior and Human Performance*, 16, 27–44.

Staw, B. M. (1984) Organizational behavior: A review and reformulation of the field's outcome variables. *Annual Review of Psychology*, 35, 627–666.

Steel, R. P. and Ovalle, N. K. II (1984) A review and meta-analysis of research on the relationship between behavioral intentions and employee turnover. *Journal of Applied Psychology*, 69, 673–686.

Steers, R. M. and Mowday, R. T. (1981) Employee turnover and post-decision accomodation process. In B. M. Staw and L. L. Cummings (eds) *Research in Organizational Behavior*. Greenwich, CN: JAI Press, 235–282.

Sterling, T. D. (1959) Publication decisions and their possible effects on inferences drawn from tests of significance – or vice versa. *Journal of the American Statistical Association*, 54, 30–34.

Stogdill, R. M. (1948) Personal factors associated with leadership: A survey of the literature. *The Journal of Psychology*, 25, 35–71.

Stogdill, R. M. and Coons, A. E. (1957) *Leader Behavior*. Columbus, Ohio: Ohio State University, Bureau of Business Research.

Stone, E. F. (1978) *Research Methods in Organizational Behavior*. Glenview, Ill.: Scott, Foresman.

Sullivan, J. W. N. (1928) *The Bases of Modern Science*. London: Benn.

Summers, E. G. (1979) Information characteristics of the 'Journal of Reading' (1957–1977). *Journal of Reading*, 23, 39–49.

Thorndike, E. L. (1911) *Animal Intelligence*. New York: Macmillan.

Tinsley, H. E. A. and Heesacker, M. (1984) Vocational behavior and career development, 1983: A review. *Journal of Vocational Behavior*, 25, 139–190.

Tosi, H., Aldag, R. and Storey, R. (1973) On the measurement of the environment: An assessment of the Lawrence and Lorsch environmental uncertainty subscale. *Administrative Science Quarterly*, 18, 27–36.

Tweney, R. D., Doherty, M. E. and Mynatt, C. R. (1981) *On Scientific Thinking*. New York: Columbia University Press.

Van Fleet, D. D. and Yukl, G. A. (1986) A century of leadership research. In D. A. Wren and J. A. Pearce (eds) *Papers Dedicated to the Development of Modern Management*. Academy of Management, 12–23.

Vroom, V. H. (1964) *Work and Motivation*. New York: John Wiley.

Vroom, V. H. and Yetton, P. W. (1973) *Leadership and Decision-making*. Pittsburgh: University of Pittsburgh Press.

Walster, E., Berscheid, E. and Walster, G. W. (1973) New directions in equity research. *Journal of Personality and Social Psychology*, 25, 151–176.

Watkins, C. E., Jr., Bradford, B. D., Mitchell, B., Christiansen, T. J., Marsh, G., Blumentritt, J. and Pierce, C. (1986) Major contributors and major contributions to the industrial/organizational literature. *The Industrial-Organizational Psychologist*, 24 (1), 10–12.

Webb, E. J., Campbell, D. T., Schwartz, R. D. and Sechrest, L. (1966) *Unobtrusive Measures*. Skokie, Ill.: Rand McNally.

Webb, W. B. (1961) The choice of the problem. *American Psychologist*, **16**, 223–227.
Weber, R. L. (1982) *More Random Walks in Science*. London: The Institute of Physics.
Weber, M. (1947) *The Theory of Social and Economic Organization*. London: Collier-Macmillan.
Woodward, J. (1965) *Industrial Organization: Theory and practice*. London: Oxford University Press.
Xhignesse, L. V. and Osgood, C. E. (1967) Bibliographical citation characteristics of the psychological journal network in 1950 and 1960. *American Psychologist*, **22**, 778–791.
Zedeck, S. and Cascio, W. F. (1984) Psychological issues in personnel decisions. *Annual Review of Psychology*, **35**, 461–518.
Zuckerman, H. and Merton, R. K. (1971) Patterns of evaluation in science: Institutionalisation, structure and functions of the referee system. *Minerva*, **IX**, 66–100.

International Review of Industrial and Organizational Psychology 1988
Edited by C. L. Cooper and I. Robertson

Chapter 5

THE CONSTRUCTION OF CLIMATE IN ORGANIZATIONAL RESEARCH

Denise M. Rousseau
Kellogg Graduate School of Management
Northwestern University
Evanston, Illinois
USA

The concept of climate is prominent in organizational research. Well over a dozen reviews of the climate literature have appeared since the mid-1960s (e.g. Campbell *et al.*, 1970; Joyce and Slocum, 1979; Schneider and Reichers, 1983), making climate a mature concept in organizational science. This chapter attempts to articulate the current status of the climate construct and critiques its specifications and boundaries.

Since its early use by Argyris (1958) and Forehand and Gilmer (1964) to characterize employee perceptions of their organizations, climate has been a central concept in organizational research. It focuses on perceptions which are critical to virtually all models in Organizational Behaviour (OB) that seek to explain behavior (e.g. motivation, leadership, influence). It is inextricably linked to the predominant data-gathering method in OB—the questionnaire or structured interview administered to individual organization members. These methods yield a variety of perceptions, many of which can be construed to reflect what researchers consider to be climate.

Reliance upon self-report methods has led to the labelling of organizational research as a 'science of perceptions' (Roberts, Hulin and Rousseau, 1978). Though that epithet bears more than a taint of criticism, perceptions are undeniably necessary to understanding both the behavior of individuals and the processes characteristic of their organizations. A large body of evidence exists to argue that the impact of organizational and other contextual characteristics on individual responses (e.g. structure's impact on attitudes, technology's affect on performance) is mediated by individual perceptions of the situation (e.g. Rousseau, 1978; Brass, 1981). There has been less explication of the origins and meaning of these perceptions, except perhaps in climate research.

As the subject of empirical research, climate in organizations has played many roles—(1) an intervening variable in situation-response studies; (2) a surrogate for 'objective' indicators of setting characteristics; and (3) as an indicator in its own right of how individuals experience the workplace. In a sense, both researchers and organization members have constructed the concept of climate, the first to serve their own methodological and conceptual needs and the second to make sense of their experience of the work setting. Regardless of the role climate might play in organizational research, the perceptions it constitutes are more than a convenient source of data—they are important factors in theory, research and practice as well.

Specification of climate, the nature of the perceptions that comprise it, and the processes that underly it are essential to many organizational research issues. Although significant conceptual and methodological progress has been made (Schneider and Reichers, 1983; Glick, 1985), there persist many conflicting definitions of climate, inconsistencies in operationalizations, and little theoretical integration. Moreover, Schneider (1985) has expressed concern that the knowledge climate research has contributed to our understanding of organizations is being neglected now due to the attention given the currently popular concept of organizational culture. The present chapter attempts to provide insights into the construction of climate by researchers and by organization members. It details the meaning of climate, the perceptions it constitutes and the relations between climate and culture. Moreover, it reviews recent literature to highlight trends and developments in the study of climate.

CLIMATE: WHAT IS IT?

Essentially, climate is individual descriptions of the social setting or context of which the person is a part. What the individual describes, whether it is the organization's decision-making processes, relations with superiors, or interactions with co-workers, is neither specified nor constrained by the climate construct. Climate is a content-free concept, denoting in a sense generic perceptions of the context in which an individual behaves and responds. Climate has been assessed in contexts as far-ranging as university dorms (Moos, 1978), US navy ships (James and Jones, 1977), Catholic dioceses (Schneider and Hall, 1972) as well as business organizations and government agencies (e.g. Schneider, 1975; Schneider and Snyder, 1975; Schanke, 1983; Solomon, 1986). The content of climate perceptions has varied widely to include, though not limited to, communication characteristics such as boss/subordinate information (Bass *et al.*, 1975) and flow (Drexler, 1977), leadership style (Payne and Mansfield, 1973; Gavin and Howe, 1975; Jones and James, 1979), and organizational effectiveness (Schneider, Parkington and Buxton, 1980). As Glick (1985) points out, even an abbreviated listing of climate dimensions demonstrates overlap with most major constructs in Organization Behavior.

A chronology of definitions researchers have offered for climate (Table 1) indicates the elaboration of the concept from the perceived organizational properties or characteristics discussed by Forehand and Gilmer (1964) and Friedlander and Margulies (1969), and the cognitive representations and interpretations of James and Jones (1974), James and Sells (1981) and Schneider (1975) to the molar or summary perceptions of Schneider and Reichers (1983). We have gone from organizational characteristics assessed through perceptions (where organizational or situational factors are presumed to dominate), to cognitive schemata (where individual factors are primary determinants), to summary perceptions (where person and situation interact). There is, however, virtually no research that addresses whether any of these conceptualizations are more strongly supported empirically.

Table 1—Climate Definition Chronology

Forehand and Gilmer (1964)	Characteristics that (1) distinguish one organization from another, (2) endure over time, and (3) influence the behavior of people in organizations. The personality of the organization.
Friedlander and Margulies (1969)	Perceived organizational properties intervening between organizational characteristics and behavior.
Campbell *et al.* (1970)	A set of attitudes and expectancies describing the organization's static characteristics, and behavior-outcome and outcome-outcome contingencies.
Schneider and Hall (1972)	Individual perceptions of their organizations affected by characteristics of the organization and the individual.
James and Jones (1974)	Psychologically meaningful cognitive representations of the situation; perceptions.
Schneider (1975)	Perceptions or interpretations of meaning which help individuals make sense of the world and know how to behave.
Payne, Fineman and Wall (1976)	Consensus of individual's descriptions of the organization.
James *et al.* (1978)	Sum of members' perceptions about the organization.
Litwin and Stringer (1978)	A psychological process intervening between organizational characteristics and behavior.
Joyce and Slocum (1979)	Climates are (1) perceptual (2) psychological, (3) abstract, (4) descriptive, (5) not evaluative, and (6) not actions.
James and Sell (1981)	Individuals' cognitive representations of proximal environments...expressed in terms of psychological meaning and significance to the individual...an attribute of the individual, which is learned, historical and resistant to change.
Schneider and Reichers (1983)	An assessed molar perception or an inference researchers make based on more particular perceptions.
Glick (1985)	('Organizational Climate') A generic term for a broad class of organizational, rather than psychological, variables that describe the context for individual's actions.

The treatment of climate as a generic perception of situations has had the advantage of allowing summary assessments of context in research that is otherwise largely individual-level in focus. However, the lack of boundaries differentiating what climate is from it is not is troublesome (Glick, 1985)—and may in fact be 'suppressing' research on climate by causing researchers to focus on either specific perceptions of context exclusively (eschewing any mention of the climate concept as in the case of motivation and leadership research) or to reject its relevance to the study of organizations (a concern addressed by Schneider, 1985).

None the less, climate as a concept clearly does have specific boundaries that differentiate it from both other characteristics and other perceptions. Two consistent defining attributes of climate persist through its various conceptualizations: it is a perception and it is descriptive. Perceptions are sensations or realizations experienced by an individual. Descriptions are a person's reports of these sensations. Whether individual differences or situational factors explain large or minute amounts of variance in these descriptions varies from one notion of climate to the next, and is more an empirical issue than a definitional one.

Descriptions of a behavioral context reported by the individual actor are consistent with what Sproull (1981) has called phenomenological or descriptive beliefs. It is in the distinctions between different types of *beliefs* where the nature and operation of climate can perhaps be best understood. Beliefs are the result of an individual's attempt to make sense of a set of stimuli, a situation, or patterns of interactions between people. They are cognitions, the result of information processing, but beliefs are more than perceptions *per se* (such as sights and sounds). In a sense, perceptions are simply informational cues that are registered or received. Beliefs are the result of active cognitive processing, consistent with the treatment of higher-order schemata by James and Sells (1981, p. 277). Initiated by perceptions, beliefs result from the interpretation and organization of perceptions into an understanding of the relationships between objects, properties and/or ideas (Colby, 1973). Self-report measures of molar constructs such as climate involve interpretation.

Sproull (1981) organizes beliefs into three broad categories: descriptive (phenomological), causal and normative. Phenomological beliefs are descriptive of the attributes and events associated with objects or entities found in nature or in social units: X occurs; I am X; people like X. These beliefs specify what has, does or will occur from the believer's perspective. 'Hard workers are well paid.' 'Customers are a nuisance.' 'Management cannot be trusted.' All these statements are examples of descriptive beliefs an organization member might report. Conceptualizing climate as descriptive beliefs is consistent with Lewin's concept of 'life space' employed by Joyce and Slocum (1979, p. 320) to describe the person/environment interaction specified in their climate model. According to Lewin (1936), the environment experienced by an individual is characterized by 'quasi'-physical and social factors all based upon an individual's interpretation. The concept of life space links to the higher-order schemata described by James and Sells, who argue that these 'descriptively-oriented perceptions' (p. 277) reflect only abstract generalizations about situations, and need not be directly tied to situational attributes and events, but do reflect individual manipulations or interpretations of information.

In addition to descriptive beliefs, individuals also espouse causal and normative beliefs. Causal beliefs express why particular events or states of nature, self or society occur: X happened because of Y; if X occurs Y will occur. Such beliefs specify operational relations between a state or events and objects or entities. 'I make my boss happy by coming to work on time.' 'Help others and they will help you.' Such beliefs result from and promote predictable interactions with others (work-group members, customers and organizations) since causal relations also specify how desired outcomes can be attained and undesirable ones avoided.

Normative beliefs specify preferred states of nature or being: X should be Y. X should be Z. For example, 'You have to win approval from others to get ahead.' 'To fit into this organization, you must appear to work long hours and never make a mistake.' Normative beliefs reflect processes associated with social units (e.g. families, work-groups, firms).

Descriptive beliefs constitute what we define as climate. Causal and normative beliefs are major components in our notions of culture. Beliefs have been used before as the basis for a distinction between climate and culture (e.g. Lammers and Hickson, 1979; Ashforth, 1985). Although descriptive, causal and normative beliefs are related, their content, organization and underlying processes differ. Comparisons of climate and culture presented below suggest both similarities, as well as differences, in these constructs.

CLIMATE AS DESCRIPTION: DESCRIPTIONS OF WHAT?

Specifications of climate requires identification of what is to be described. Situational perceptions can be parsed in three ways: level, type and facet.

Descriptive Level

When perceptions are reported by individuals, each statement made has a level about which the person reports, just as sentences have objects (e.g. 'I trust my boss'). Individuals can describe their work-unit or members of it such as superiors and co-workers (e.g. Joyce and Slocum, 1984), their organization, or a firm with which they do business (Schneider, Parkington and Buxton, 1980). From the object of their descriptions we derive the labels of 'work group' or 'organizational' climate. Researchers have asked respondents to describe the organization that employs them, firms of which they are customers, their subunits, work-groups (bosses and co-workers) and positions within the organization. The level of climate assessed reflects the unit about which the individual provides descriptions (the target or *descriptive level*). However, the individual is always the level of measurement. Lack of strong consensus among unit members regarding descriptions of organizations or work groups has led researchers to infer that climate is an individual attribute (James and Sells, 1981). However, climate measurement has often poorly specified the descriptive level about which individuals were to provide information. In some cases, it has explicitly included many different descriptive levels (e.g. department and organization). Ambiguity in the frame of reference of perceptual reports can readily lead two respondents to relay perceptions about very different parts of the organization (their own job, their workgroup, or the organization as a whole). Moreover, in some cases respondents specifically asked to describe their organization can find it difficult to differentiate a phenomenon at one level from that of another. For example, the openness of communication within the organization can be difficult to distinguish from the quality of communication employees experience with their boss; employees might not be in a position accurately to attribute open or poor communication to organizational practices or to an individual manager's predilictions. None the less, they will answer the questions researchers put to them— potentially a case of what Nisbett and Wilson (1977) have termed 'Telling more than you can know'.

Types of Climate

Debates over the meaning of perceptual differences and various degrees of dispersion in climate scores within organizational units have led to the proliferation of climate 'types': psychological, aggregate, collective and organizational. Some researchers argue that organizational climate cannot exist without consensus (Drexler, 1977; Joyce and Slocum, 1979), while others have interpreted lack of consensus to mean that climate is an individual attribute (James and Sells, 1981). In response to empirically observed differences in consensus among individuals purportedly describing the same descriptive level, four types or conceptualizations of climate have emerged in the literature.

Psychological climate is essentially unaggregated individual perceptions of their environments. Psychological and abstract in nature, these perceptions are not treated as organizational descriptions but rather as reports reflecting how individuals organize their experience of the environment. Individual differences are postulated to play a substantial role in creating these perceptions as do the immediate or proximal environments in which the individual is an active agent. Psychological climate is shaped by factors including individual thinking styles, personality, cognitive processes, culture and social interactions, consistent with Lewin's notion of life space. These perceptions need not agree with those of other individuals in the same environment to be meaningful since: (1) an individual's proximal environment may be unique (e.g. when only one person does a particular job); and (2) individual differences play a substantial role in these perceptions (James and Sells, 1981).

While the concept of psychological climate helps explain the lack of observed agreement in many climate studies, the little research that exists to test the relative contribution of situational and individual factors to such perceptions does not strongly support the aforementioned specification of it. Joyce and Slocum (1984) examined clusters of individuals with similar climate scores and found that personal factors are less important than contextual ones in explaining these perceptions—though personal factors do account for some clusters that contextual factors do not. Regardless of the origins of situation-based descriptive beliefs, they appear to function as intervening variables in the connection between situational characteristics and individual responses (e.g. Newman, 1975)— consistent with the general role of perceptions in cross-level effects on individuals (Rousseau, 1978).

The basic *conceptual* problem posed by the concept of individual-level psychological climate is the weak differentiation of it from the individual's cognitive style. Defined as the characteristic ways in which individuals conceptually organize the environment (Goldstein and Blackman, 1978, p. 1), cognitive style is a construct cognitive psychologists developed to explain the process mediating between stimuli and responses. This conceptualization of cognitive style is virtually identical to what James and Jones (1974) offer for climate. One distinction may lie in the emphasis cognitive psychologists place on the structure rather than the content of thought (Goldstein and Blackman, 1978, p. 2) and the concern in organizational research with particular classes of situational factors. Nevertheless, as a generic model of perception, (where content is downplayed), psychological climate overlaps greatly with cognitive style.

Aggregate climate is individual perceptions averaged at some formal hierarchical level (e.g. workgroup, department, division, plant, ship, organization). Note that the level of aggregation need not conform to the descriptive level of the perceptions. Jones and James (1979) aggregated data to subunit and ship levels, though neither was explicitly the object of all the climate reports naval personnel provided. Aggregated climates are constructed based on membership of individuals in some identifiable unit of the formal organization and within-unit agreement or consensus in perceptions. The rationale behind aggregating individual data to a unit level is the *a priori* assumption that certain organizational groups or collectivities have a climate and that these can be identified through tests of significant difference between units (Joyce and Slocum, 1979). One might also infer that this aggregation of individual perceptions is justified because perceptual agreement implies a shared meaning (James, 1982). However, no research to date has justified this assumed connection between aggregated perceptions and interpretation.

Aggregated climates are established based on empirically observed between-unit differences. These differences are attributed to real situational differences that lead members within a unit to agree more with each other regarding their perceptions than they do with members of other units. The construction of aggregate climate by organizational researchers is a form of operationism where a concept is induced from statistical manipulations of data. Like psychological climate, aggregated climates are believed to intervene between (objective) situational factors and individual responses (Joyce and Slocum, 1979). Although aggregate climate derives from individual-level data reflecting within-unit agreement, the meaning of the construct at a collective level is not well established.

Some questions persist: (1) Does aggregate climate explain responses that psychological climate does not? (2) Does it have surplus meaning beyond individual perceptions? (3) Are its relations with other variables different from those of other climate types? If aggregated climate is a real unit-level phenomenon, individuals should have fewer disconfirming experiences and their interactions with other members should serve to shape and reinforce a common set of descriptors comparable to a social construction of reality (Joyce and Slocum, 1979). But since interaction among unit members is not considered a requirement for consensus, there need be no social or group dynamics underlying that consensus. Thus the etiology and meaning of aggregate climate is not well specified. As a methods-driven concept, its theoretical status and value is not yet well established.

Collective climates emerge from agreement between individuals regarding their perception of behavioral contexts. However, in contrast to aggregated climate, collective climates need not overlap formal units. Collective climates are composites of individuals for whom situations have common stimulus values (Joyce and Slocum, 1984). Essentially, collective climates are identified by taking the individual perceptions of situational factors and combining these (independently of unit membership) into clusters reflecting similar climate scores. Personal and situational factors have been considered as predictors of cluster membership, but findings indicate that personal factors such as management and work experience, time in position and age account for some clusters, while situational factors such as functional area, location and shift account for others (Joyce and Slocum, 1984). In the case of collective (statistical cluster) climate, interactions are postulated to play a substantial role in determining shared perceptions (Joyce and Slocum, 1979; 1984)—though their role has not been empirically assessed.

The potential importance of interaction to climate consensus (for both aggregated and collective climate) and its effect on behavior is perhaps best evident in the diffusion of the unusual phenomenon of mass psychogenic illness— outbreaks of mysterious ailments among large numbers of employees where no physical basis could be found for such symptoms as nausea, headaches and chills. Researchers have established a link between situational characteristics, employee perceptions and attitudes, and mass psychogenic illness (Colligan and Murphy, 1982). In an outbreak of such a condition at a university keypunch department, Stahl and Lebedun (1974) probed to determine why some workers remain unaffected while many of their peers fell victim to a mysterious ailment. One difference between healthy and ill workers was language. A healthy worker who could not speak English had little social interaction on the job with English-speaking employees. Mass psychogenic illness appears linked to the diffusion of dissatisfaction and anxieties among workers who interact while on the job. Here, interactions mean shared negative perceptions of the workplace, dissatisfaction, and a resultant psychogenic illness. Lack of interaction means little group influence on perceptions and an apparent 'inoculation' from psychogenic sickness. The comparable role of social processes in the creation of shared climate perceptions remains suggestive, but largely unexplored.

Organizational climate and its definition seems to reflect two schemes of thought. The interactional view of organizational climate is essentially as individual perceptions of organizational practices and characteristics that meet statistical criteria for aggregating to that level (e.g. James and Jones, 1974). In contrast, Glick (1985) argues that organizational climate is a real organizational attribute (as for instance is technology or structure) as opposed to something 'psychological'. Treating climate as a real thing to be encountered and experienced means that individuals report on climate not as subjects or respondents, but as *informants*. Research has come a long way from the early days where an employee's perceptions of the organization were automatically treated as organizational climate. Glick (1985) argues that individual-level perceptions may have a different dimensionality than the organization's actual climate. For individual-level reports to be an accurate portrayal of organizational factors, individuals must have a clear, consistent, common frame of reference (the organization). Moreover, researchers seeking to establish that information from individuals can be combined into a reliable organization-level score must themselves hold to a consistent frame of reference. Glick (1985, pp. 610–12) details the role of the fallacy of the wrong level in statistical assessments of climate wherein individual-level consensus rather than organization-level reliability of climate scores has been used to justify treating aggregated climate as organizational climate.

The nature and etiology of organizational climate is not specified by Glick (1985). If we view it as an accurate indicator of something *organizational*, it is no longer a perception *per se*, but an attribute of the organization expressed nonetheless in psychologically meaningful terms (e.g. trustworthy, friendly). Removing the cognitive component from organizational climate creates a discontinuity with the climate tradition. At present, it is unclear how Glick's notion of organizational climate fits in with cognition-oriented climate models.

The distinction current climate research seems to make between what is organization-level climate as opposed to organizational structure or other such constructs measurable through individual perceptions is that climate reflects an insider's orientation, as opposed to an outsider's analytic categories. Climate and structure constructs thus respectively appear comparable to the emic (insider) and etic (outsider) orientations discussed in Morey and Luthans' (1984) treatment of cultures. Many constructs researchers use to characterize organizations reflect etic (outsider) orientation, e.g. structures (such as centralization and hierarchy) or processes (such as problem-solving mechanisms, maintenance and strain amelioration); originating in theoretical frameworks rather than in the cognitive organization of individuals. For example, it is doubtful whether any individual ever wondered about the organization's processes 'for ameliorating strain' (see Cooke and Rousseau, 1981) in those terms until he or she was asked about them. However, organizational climate can be construed as a descriptor of organizational attributes expressed in terms characterizing individual experiences (emic orientation) with the organization. This distribution means that climate assessments employ less abstracted descriptors of organizations from the informants' perspective. The great advantage of climate assessments over more discrete topical measures (e.g. leadership, rewards) is their summary quality. It is general descriptions of contexts which climate researchers often seek to obtain (Glick, 1985). The summary quality does not mean that descriptions become more abstract, but rather that they are representations of how organizations feel to the people within them or to those who must deal with them as vendors or customers.

Facets of Climate

As psychologically meaningful descriptions of situations, the perceptions that comprise climate occur in clusters of psychologically related events and meanings. This implies that climates in work settings have numerous facets. As

Schneider and Reichers (1983, p. 21) express it, 'climates are for *something*'. Schneider (Schneider, Parkington and Buxton, 1980; Schneider and Reichers, 1983) has argued for specification of a reference term when the concept of climate is used to tap psychologically meaningful descriptions. Thus, a particular descriptive level might have a climate for service (Schneider, Parkington and Buxton, 1980) or a climate for safety (Zohar, 1980). This shift to facet-specific climate is a movement away from the tradition of climate as undifferentiated summary perceptions. Ironically, specification of climate facets can blur the distinction between research on climate *per se* and studies of specific topics such as leadership or safety. None the less, the movement toward facet-specific climate reflects the trend toward conceptual vigor, methodological sophistication, and precision in the use of perceptual data.

In contrast, researchers often have discussed climates as being 'more positive' or 'less negative' without specifying this directionality with respect to some referent (as in more safety-oriented or less employee-oriented). To speak of climate without a referent has been described as 'meaningless' (Schneider and Reichers, 1983); then to attach an evaluation to it is probably nonsensical.

The increased precision obtained in specifying climate facets is consistent with the notion of linking climate to schemata. Neisser (1976, p. 64) defines a schema as that portion of the perceptual cycle which is modifiable by experience and specific to what is perceived. Schemata development is 'from the general to the particular, from undifferentiated to precise' (p. 65).

New facet-specific climates

The increasing importance of facet-specific climate is evident when new topical research is reviewed. Specific types of climate are often employed as a correlate or predictor when new lines of research are instituted. Marketing channels studies have recently employed the climate concept (Schul, Little and Pride, 1985) and traditional dimensions of climate such as trust (Anderson and Narus, 1986) to explain channel members' satisfaction with the distribution relationship and the relationship's quality. Elements in the relationship, such as well-defined policies and performance-based rewards, contribute to channel member satisfaction (Schul *et al.*, 1985). Channels research on climate indicates that the importance of trust to relationship quality is enhanced by uncertainty in decision-making, as in the case of technologically-complex products in a dynamic market (Anderson and Narus, 1986). Emergence of the concept of channel climate suggests that understanding inter-unit relations of many types (e.g. interorganizational, interdepartmental) can benefit from use of the climate construct.

The use of climate to characterize a relationship is evident in Angle and Perry's (1986) study of the connection of dual commitment to labor–management relationship climate. In a study of unionized municipal bus companies, dual commitment (to both company and union) was higher in cooperative climates than in less cooperative ones. Again, climate appears to be a useful indicator of how parties experience a relationship.

Miceli and Near (1985) investigated the role of the aggregated 'climate of protection from retaliation', finding it negatively related to the organizational incidence of wrongdoing and positively related to organizational size, amount of disseminated information and the number of communication methods used by the organization. They suggest that the 'organizational climate for whistle-blowing' could be empirically separated into at least two dimensions: (1) tolerance for or dependence on wrong-doing, including the degree to which members sensed retaliation would follow whistleblowing; and (2) the extent to which the organization encouraged whistleblowing through formal and informal communication (p. 539). These subdimensions appear themselves to be multifaceted and require further explication.

In a study of the role of climate's relationship with innovation in research and development units, Abbey and Dickson (1983) used Pritchard and Karasick's (1973) ten dimensions of work climate to characterize R & D subunits. Aggregated to the subunit level, the climate dimensions of performance-reward dependence, flexibility, and perceived innovativeness were significantly related to initiation, adoption, and implementation of R & D innovations by the organization. Abbey and Dickson argue that it is the climate of the R & D subunit that influences the organization to adopt and implement innovations, since that unit is typically responsible for initiating innovations. Thus, this study suggests a type of 'reverse' cross-level effect, where the climate of a lower-level unit influences the (higher-level) organization. In all, the trend is toward greater specificity in the facets climate research addresses as well as a broadening of the application of the climate concept to new substantive research areas.

Summary

The use of climate as a general descriptor of organization-based experience raises numerous issues regarding the target to be described, its facets, and the factors underlying the emergence of consensus in individuals' situational perceptions. The need for precision in specification and operationalization is evident. New research areas employing facet-specific climate concepts suggest ways in which this precision might be achieved. The next issue is the need for boundaries differentiating climate from other forms of beliefs in organizational settings.

CULTURE: THE ROLE OF NORMATIVE BELIEFS

There is growing concern regarding climate's distinctiveness from the concept of culture in organizations. Ashforth (1985) and Cooke and Rousseau (in press) argue for a distinction between the two based on the fundamental role of social unit norms in culture and individual descriptive beliefs in climate. As Glick (1985, p. 612) has argued, the disciplinary bases for climate and culture differ. Climate developed primarily from the Lewinian social psychology of person/situation interaction while culture emerged from symbolic interactionism. Interactionism requires a social unit and shared experience and thus an individual alone cannot possess a culture, though his or her work group or organization can. A key element of culture is consensus or shared values and beliefs (Becker and Geer, 1970; Louis, 1983). Not all social units have a culture. Organizations that are new, in transition, or that have conflicting structures and role conflict, might lack common beliefs and values among members. Moreover, the intensity or strength of a culture is reflected in member consensus; some organizations have strong cultures, which shape behavior, and others have weak cultures which have less impact on member actions (Cooke and Rousseau, in press). Although individuals might not experience a culture in their organization, all individuals experience a climate, that is, a behavioral context which they can describe. Normative beliefs are by-products of group membership; climate, however, can be highly idiosyncratic, with as many climates as there are individuals in distinct contexts (James and Sells, 1981).

Normative beliefs specify what individuals think are appropriate behaviors for themselves and others in a particular social context. They are created through social interactions and group dynamics which inform individuals regarding what it takes to fit in and be accepted as a group member. Normative beliefs are individual interpretations of the behavioral norms that characterize interacting social groups.

Normative beliefs shared by members of a social unit are a major feature in the construct of culture (Table 2). Key features in definitions of culture are terms such as 'common'/'shared'; 'members'/'group'/'organization'; and 'communication'/'transmission'/'expression'. Culture, therefore, exists at unit levels, requires sharing or mutuality and vehicles for transmission. Individuals, of course, enact and transmit culture but do so in a social context that patterns their intentions and shapes individual interpretations of behavior (as in Barley's [1983] example of how funeral directors manipulate symbols of sleep and peace in dealing with the bereaved).

Any culture in an organizational context has two features pertinent to its assessment: direction and intensity. Direction refers to the actual content or substance of the culture, exemplified by (though not limited to) the values, behavioral norms, and thinking styles it emphasizes (Trice and Beyer, 1984). Values attached to achievement, failure, and risk can reflect the direction of behavioral norms. Intensity is the strength of this emphasis. Cultures that vary in direction support different behavioral norms. Cultures varying in intensity have different degrees of influence on organizational members. Intensity is a function of consensus regarding appropriate and inappropriate behavior, as well as the consistency between behavioral norms and formal structures such as reward systems and hierarchies.

There are striking similarities between climate and culture in the organizational literature:

1. Consistency or consensus is required to characterize a unit as having a climate or a culture (Payne *et al.*, 1976; Joyce and Slocum, 1979; Louis, 1983).
2. Belief or individual cognitions and interpretations are primary elements in each (Schneider, 1975; James and Sells, 1981; van Maanen and Schein, 1979).
3. Each is historical, enduring, and resistant to change (James and Sells, 1981; Louis, 1983).
4. Each has a tendency toward differentiation with members in different units of a larger organization demonstrating distinctive sets of beliefs (James and Sells, 1981; Louis, 1983).

Table 2—Culture Definitions

Kroeber and Kluckhohn (1952)	Transmitted patterns of values, ideas, and other symbolic systems that shape behavior.
Becker and Geer (1970)	Set of common understandings expressed in language.
Van Maanen and Schein (1979)	Values, beliefs and expectations that members come to share.
Ouchi (1981)	Set of symbols, ceremonies and myths that communicate underlying values and beliefs of the organization to its employees.
Louis (1983)	Three aspects: some (1) content (meaning and interpretation) (2) peculiar to (3) a group.
Siehl and Martin (1983)	Glue that holds together an organization through shared patterns of meaning. Three component systems: context or core values, forms (process of communication, e.g: jargon), strategies to reinforce content (e.g. rewards, training programs).
Uttal (1983)	Shared values (what is important) and beliefs (how things work) that interact with an organization's structures and control systems to produce behavioral norms (the way we do things around here).

Problems in comparing culture and climate studies have sometimes made identification of such similarities difficult. Methodological differences have limited opportunities for comparison because of the distinctive goals of climate and culture research. Whereas culture has emerged as the explanation of choice for many researchers because of the potential for *rich detail* it offers (Morey and Luthans, 1985), climate has been a vehicle for *summary description*. Use of qualitative methods to study culture yield details which often are not explicitly linked to a particular level or frame of reference and are unlikely to be tested for consistency across units. In contrast, consensus is a key issue in climate research.

As discussed above, the blurring of climate and culture has been an issue, especially to researchers concerned with climate (Glick, 1982; Schneider, 1985). Based upon the notion of symbolic interactionism, Ashforth (1985) distinguishes between shared assumptions (culture) and shared perceptions (climate) and argues that culture 'informs' climate (p. 842) by helping individuals to define what is important and make sense of their experiences. Whether a member describes a boss who fails to communicate clearly as cold and unfeeling (a personality-based attribution) or as doing his or her job (in an organization which rewards people for operating on a 'need to know' basis) can be largely a function of the world-view one comes to hold from talking with other employees and accepting their norms. Thus we might expect organizations with strong cultures to have member consensus in descriptions of it. Increasing concern over the origins of both climate and culture and ways in which one reinforces the other is evident in the current organizational literature. To date, there is little empirical research examining the two together.

By comparing Tables 1 and 2, striking differences between climate and culture also appear:

1. Climate is descriptive, culture is largely normative.
2. Climate is a summary description and culture research operationalizes the construct as rich detail.
3. Climate exists in all organizations (at least at the individual level); but many organizations have no culture (strong norms may be absent).
4. All individuals in an organizational setting experience a climate. Not all individuals are part of a culture.
5. Climate is attached to individual perceptions. To understand its effects, levels of analysis shift upward to collectivities. Culture is a group or social-unit phenomenon. To understand its processes, levels of analysis shift downward to individuals.

From these contrasts and comparisons, two conclusions can be drawn:

1. there are sufficient similarities between the concepts of climate and culture for research on one to inform us about the other
2. the differences between the two are sufficient to maintain their distinctiveness in conceptualization and operationalization.

EMERGING TRENDS IN RESEARCH ON CLIMATE IN ORGANIZATIONS: RESEARCH INTO SOCIALIZATION AND SOCIAL CONSTRUCTION

Though we have argued for a distinction between climate and culture, socialization and social construction are becoming shared conceptual underpinnings for each. A central question raised by Schneider (1983) and Schneider and Reichers (1983) is how it is that individuals who are confronted with a vast array of stimuli in the work environment come to have relatively homogeneous perceptions of it. Initial conceptions of climate (e.g. Forehand and Gilmer, 1964) took a structuralist view and argued that climate emerged from a common experience of an objective reality. Inconsistent relations between structure and climate (Berger and Cummings, 1979) have been interpreted to mean that structure cannot be the sole explanation of similarity in climate-related perceptions (Schneider and Reichers, 1983). Although some of the inconsistency in structure–climate relations might be accounted for by variability in assessment methods (e.g. shifts in organization or unit focus, use of different scales), social processes and individual differences could also be a factor.

Schneider and Reichers (1983) offer an alternative to the notion of a structural etiology to climate by arguing that organizational processes (such as selection into the organization) and individual processes (such as attraction to and attrition from the organization) combine to produce relatively homogeneous members in any one organization. Members have similar perceptions and attach similar meanings to organizational events because in some ways these members are themselves similar to each other. The selection–attraction–attrition model (SAA) works in several ways. People are attracted to organizations they anticipate will in some ways match their personalities or self-concepts (Super, 1953; Holland, 1973) and from which they can obtain desired outcomes (Wanous, 1980). Organizations also often try hard to attract people who will 'fit in'. Given the imperfect nature of the selection process, a second mechanism is in place to weed out mismatches, through both voluntary and involuntary terminations. Attrition tends to increase further homogeneity with a resulting decrease in individual differences, both in personality and behavior patterns, as well as in perceptions and interpretations of the situation. The SAA model suggests that climates differ because the people within social units differ.

Schneider and Reichers (1983) propose another parallel explanation for the origin of climate based upon Mead's (1934) writings on the origins of identity and meaning. Arguing that identity and meaning derive from the social context of behavior (underpinnings to the notion of symbolic interactionism), Schneider and Reichers argue that newcomers engage in sensemaking to organize their new experiences into some personally meaningful structure, adjust their own self-perceptions and behavior to accommodate the new setting, and in doing so have a tendency to adopt the attitudes and world-view of the group of which the new member is a part. Social interactions help newcomers understand the meaning of the new work setting, and without such an interaction consensus regarding situational perceptions is unlikely. From a symbolic interactionist perspective, climates emerge due to an interaction between persons—and consistent with Glick (1985) might take on a reality of their own through this process.

The general trend toward identification of subclimates rather than overall organization-wide climates (e.g. Joyce and Slocum, 1984) suggests that the SAA process and that of symbolic interactionism occur within subunits more consistently than they do on an organization-wide basis. It must be noted that in culture research where degree of consensus has been investigated, the evidence suggests that organizations may be more likely to have subcultures than an overall organizational culture (Cooke and Rousseau, in press). Similar processes may underlie this pattern for both culture and climate.

The emergence of symbolic interactionism and socialization as mechanisms for the creation of shared climate perceptions links climate and culture through common social processes. This trend suggests that research into descriptive beliefs and social norms and values can inform both the climate and culture literatures.

CONCLUSION

Climate in organizations is a construction by researchers of individual perceptions of the settings in which they behave. Construction means to form by putting together parts into a larger whole. Climate as a molar perception (Schneider, 1985) invariably reflects some combination of discrete perceptions. Psychological climate as a measure of individual perceptions reflects assessments of broad categories of setting characteristics (e.g. trust, communication) rather than specific, micro-details (e.g. how much a person trusts an immediate superior during a post-performance appraisal feedback session, how clearly that superior communicated the feedback during the session). As such, climate at all levels from individual to aggregate, collective, and organizational, has summary qualities.

Climate in organizational research is a multidimensional assessment of situational perceptions. It serves as an umbrella concept covering and bringing together specific topics where perceptual measures are the mainstay. Leadership and influence, reward systems, and interpersonal support are among the many concepts within organizational science. Concepts from each serve double duty, both in their own specific field and as part of the larger set of dimensions representing climate. As with the multi-dimensional concept of climate, research in these subfields employs perceptual data at many levels and with many of the same concerns regarding aggregation bias and consensus (Roberts *et al.*, 1978). Climate research informs the many subfields where perceptual data and aggregation are commonly used. Its contribution is threefold: (1) to provide summary descriptors of situational perceptions where the context of behavior is an important factor; (2) to explicate the determinants and etiology of the summary perceptions which few organizational research areas fail to employ; and (3) to develop the methodology and decision rules for aggregation and combination of perceptual data in research involving multiple levels.

Researchers construct climate not only by asking individuals to provide responses to summary categories, but also in the combinations that climate data are subject to based on similarity, group membership, or a common frame of reference. The construction of climate across units and levels introduces a multilevel quality to the climate construct, requiring not only explication of the specific level to which climate is attached, but also specification of different causal models at each level. Psychological climate, almost by definition, is a product of individual differences as well as situational factors. In explaining variance in individual-level perceptions, we would expect individual differences to play a substantial role. In contrast, unit-level climate, where individual data are combined based on membership in the same formal unit and meeting criteria for consensus or accuracy, may be less affected by individual differences and more by common situational features. Thus, researchers trying to account for psychological climate need not be explaining the same pool of variance as those studying climate attached to a larger unit.

Climate has been constructed by the researcher to mean some very distinct things. It would facilitate our interpretation of each study employing the climate concept if researchers would specify which climate type they are studying and attempt in their validation of the climate measure to test for the relative impact of situational, individual and social interaction characteristics on that climate measure. Unless the measure 'behaves' in a fashion consistent with the type of climate it purports to tap (e.g. unit-level climates potentially being influenced largely by interaction or selection of similar people, and psychological climate by individual differences), climate research will bog down in an emphasis on method and an atheoretical proliferation of climate types.

Extension of the climate concept into new research areas such as safety and whistleblowing indicates its continued viability as a theoretical construct, as well as its value as a source of methodological advances in assessing psychologically meaningful descriptions of situations. As an insider's or constituent's experience of the organization, climate remains a durable concept in organizational research.

ACKNOWLEDGMENTS

I appreciate the contributions Robert Cooke and Curtis Cost have made to this chapter. Bill Glick and Ben Schneider also provided cogent criticism and helpful comments which I gratefully acknowledge.

REFERENCES

Abbey, A. and Dickson, J. W. (1983) R & D work climate and innovations in semiconductors. *Academy Management Journal*, **26**, 362–368.

Anderson, J. C. and Narus, J. A. (1986) Toward a better understanding of distribution channel working relationships. In K. Backhaus and D. T. Wilson (eds) *Industrial Marketing: A German–American Perspective*. Berlin: Springer-Verlag, 320–336.

Angle, H. L. and Perry, J. L. (1986) Dual commitment and labor–management relationship climates. *Academy of Management Journal*, **29**, 31–50.

Argyris, C. (1958) Some problems in conceptualizing organizational climate: A case study of a bank. *Administrative Science Quarterly*, **2**, 501–520.

Ashforth, B. E. (1985) Climate formation: Issues and extensions. *Academy of Management Review*, **4**, 837–847.

Barley, S. R. (1983) Semiotics and the study of occupational and organizational cultures. *Administrative Science Quarterly*, **28**, 393–413.

Bass, B. M., Valenzi, E. R., Farrow, D. L. and Solomon, R. J. (1975) Management styles associated with organizational, task, personal, and interpersonal contingencies. *Journal of Applied Psychology*, **60**, 720–729.

Becker, H. S. and Geer, B. (1970) Participant observation and interviewing: A comparison. In W. Filstead (ed.) *Qualitative Methodology*. Chicago: Rand-McNally, 133–142.

Berger, C. J. and Cummings, L. L. (1979) Organizational structures, attitudes, and behavior. In B. M. Staw (ed.) *Research in Organizational Behavior*, **1**, 169–208.

Brass, D. J. (1981) Structural relationships, job characteristics, worker satisfaction, and performance. *Administrative Science Quarterly*, **26**, 331–348.

Campbell, J., Dunnette, M. D., Lawler, E. E. III and Weick, K. E. (1970) *Managerial Behavior, Performance, and Effectiveness*. New York: McGraw-Hill.

Colby, K. M. (1973) Simulations of belief systems. In R. C. Schank and K. M. Colby (eds) *Computer Models of Thought*. San Francisco: Freeman, 251–286.

Colligan, M. S. and Murphy, L. R. (1982) A review of psychogenic illness in work settings. In M. J. Colligan, J. W. Pennebaker, and L. R. Murphy (eds) *Mass Psychogenic Illness*. Hillsdale, N.J.: Lawrence Erlbaum, 33–55.

Cooke, R. A. and Rousseau, D. M. (1981) Problems of complex systems: A model of system problem solving applied to schools. *Educational Administration Quarterly*, **17**, 15–41.

Cooke, R. A. and Rousseau D. M. (1988) Behavioral norms and expectations: a quantitative approach to the assessment of organizational culture. *Group and Organizational Studies* (in press).

Drexler, J. A. Jr (1977) Organizational climate: Its homogeneity within organization. *Journal of Applied Psychology*, **65**, 96–102.

Forehand, G. A. and Gilmer, B. V. H. (1964) Environmental variation in studies of organizational behavior. *Psychological Bulletin*, **62**, 228–240.

Friedlander, R. and Margulies, N. (1969) Multiple impacts of organizational climate and individual value systems upon job satisfaction. *Personnel Psychology*, **31**, 783–811.

Gavin, J. R. (1975) Organizational climate as a function of personal and organizational variables. *Journal of Applied Psychology*, **60**, 135–139.

Gavin, J. R. and Howe, J. G. (1975) Psychological climate: Some theoretical and empirical considerations. *Behavioral Science*, **20**, 228–240.

Gertz, C. (1973) *The Interpretation of Cultures.* New York: Basic Books.

Glick, W. H. (1985) Conceptualizing and measuring organizational and psychological climate: Pitfalls in multilevel research. *Academy of Management Review*, **10**, 601–616.

Goldstein, K. M. and Blackman, S. (1978) *Cognitive Style.* New York: John Wiley.

Holland, J. L. (1973) *The Psychology of Vocational Choice*, revised edition. Waltham, MA: Blaisdell.

James, L. R. (1982) Aggregation bias in estimates of perceptual agreement. *Journal of Applied Psychology*, **67**, 219–229.

James, L. R., Hater, J. S., Gent, M. J. and Bruni, J. R. (1978) Psychological climate: Implications from cognitive social learning theory and interactional psychology. *Personnel Psychology*, **31**, 783–811.

James, L. R. and Jones, A. P. (1974) Organizational climate: A review of theory and research. *Psychological Bulletin*, **81**, 1096, 1112.

James, L. R. and Sells, S. B. (1981) Psychological climate: Theoretical perspectives and empirical research. In D. Magnusson (ed.) *Toward a Psychology of Situations: An interactional perspective.* Hillsdale, N.J.: Lawrence Erlbaum, 275–295.

Jones, A. P. and James, L. R. (1979) Psychological climate: Dimensions and relationships of individual and aggregated work environment perceptions. *Organizational Behavior and Human Performance*, **23**, 201–250.

Joyce, W. F. and Slocum, J. W. Jr (1979) Climates in organizations. In S. Kerr (ed.) *Organizational Behavior.* Columbus, OH: Grid, 317–333.

Joyce, W. F. and Slocum, J. W. Jr (1982) Climate discrepancy: Redefining the concepts of psychological and organizational climate. *Human Relations*, **35**, 951–972.

Joyce, W. F. and Slocum, J. W. Jr (1984) Collective climate: Agreement as a basis for defining aggregate climates in organizations. *Academy of Management Journal*, **27**, 721–742.

Kroeber, A. I. and Kluckhohn, C. (1952) *Culture: A critical review of concepts and definitions.* New York: Vintage Books.

Lammers, C. J. and Hickson, D. J. (1979) Methodological convergences? In C. J. Lammers and D. J. Hickson (eds) *Organizations, Alike and Unalike.* London: Routledge & Kegan Paul, 389–401.

Lewin, J. (1936) *Principles of Topological Psychology.* New York: McGraw-Hill.

Litwin, G. and Stringer, R. (1968) *Motivation and Organizational Climate.* Boston, Mass.: Harvard University Press.

Louis, M. R. (1983) Organizations as culture-bearing milieux. In L. R. Pondy, P. Frost, G. Morgan and T. C. Dandrige (eds) *Organizational Symbolism.* Greenwich, CT: JAI Press.

Martin, J. and Siehl, C. (1983) Organizational culture and counterculture: An uneasy symbiosis. *Organizational Dynamics*, **12** (Autumn), 52–64.

Mead, G. H. (1934) *The Social Psychology of George Herbert Mead.* A. Strauss (ed.) Chicago: The University of Chicago Press.

Micelli, M. P. and Near, J. P. (1985) Characteristics of organizational climate and perceived wrongdoing associated with whistleblowing. *Personnel Psychology*, **38**, 525–544.

Moos, R. (n.d.) *The Social Climate Scales: An overview.* Palo Alto, CA: Consulting Psychologists Press.

Moos, R. H. (1978) Social environments of university student living groups: Architectural and organizational correlates. *Environment and Behavior,* **10**, 109–126.

Morey, N. C. and Luthans, F. (1985) Refining the displacement of culture and the use of scenes and themes in organizational studies. *Academy of Management Review,* **10**, 219–229.

Near, J. P. and Micelli, M. P. (1985) Organizational dissidence: The case of whistle-blowing. *Journal of Business Ethics,* **4**, 1–16.

Neisser, U. (1976) *Cognitions and Reality,* San Francisco: Freeman.

Nisbett, R. E. and Wilson, T. D. (1977) Telling more than you can know: Verbal reports on mental processes. *Psychological Review,* **84**, 231–259.

Payne, R. L., Fineman, S. and Wall, T. D. (1976) Organizational climate and job satisfaction: A conceptual synthesis. *Organizational Behavior and Human Performance,* **16**, 45–62.

Payne, R. L. and Mansfield, R. (1973) Relationships of perceptions of organizational climate to organizational structure, context, and hierarchical position. *Administrative Science Quarterly,* **18**, 515–526.

Payne, R. and Mansfield, R. (1978) Correlates of individual perceptions of organizational climate. *Journal of Occupational Psychology,* **51**, 209–218.

Pritchard, R. D. and Karasick, B. W. (1973) The effects of organizational climate on managerial job performance and job satisfaction. *Organizational Behavior and Human Performance,* **9**, 126–146.

Roberts, K. H., Hulin, C. L. and Rousseau, D. M. (1978) *Developing an Interdisciplinary Science of Organizations.* San Francisco: Jossey-Bass.

Rousseau, D. M. (1978) Characteristics of departments, positions, and individuals: Contexts for attitudes and behavior. *Administrative Science Quarterly,* **23**, 521–540.

Rousseau, D. M. (1985) Issues of level in organizational research: Multi-level and cross-level perspectives. In L. L. Cummings and B. M. Staw (eds) *Research in Organizational Behavior,* **7**, 1–37.

Schnake, M. E. (1983) An empirical assessment of the effects of affective response in the measurement of organizational climate. *Personnel Psychology,* **36**, 791–807.

Schneider, B. (1972) Organizational climate: Individual preference and organizational realities. *Journal of Applied Psychology,* **56**, 211–217.

Schneider, B. (1975) Organizational climates: An essay. *Personnel Psychology,* **36**, 19–39.

Schneider, B. (1985) Organizational Behavior. *Annual Review of Psychology,* **36**, 573–611.

Schneider, B. (1983) An interactionist perspective on organizational effectiveness. In D. Whetten and K. S. Cameron (eds) *Organizational Effectiveness: A comparison of multiple models.* New York: Academic Press.

Schneider, B. and Hall, D. T. (1972) Toward specifying the concept of work climate: A study of Roman Catholic Diocesan priests. *Journal of Applied Psychology,* **56**, 447–455.

Schneider, B., Parkington, J. J. and Buxton, V. M. (1980) Employee and customer perceptions of service in banks. *Administrative Science Quarterly,* **25**, 252–267.

Schneider, B. and Reichers, A. E. (1983) On the etiology of climates. *Personnel Psychology,* **36**, 19–39.

Schneider, B. and Snyder, R. (1975) Some relationships between job satisfaction and organizational climate. *Journal of Applied Psychology,* **60**, 318–328.

Schul, P. L., Little, T. E., Jr and Pride, W. M. (1985) Channel climate: Its impact on channel members' satisfaction. *Journal of Retailing,* **61**, 9–38.

Solomon, E. E. (1986) Private and public sector managers: An empirical investigation of job characteristics and organizational climate. *Journal of Applied Psychology,* **71**, 247–259.

Sproull, L. S. (1981) Beliefs in organizations. In P. C. Nystrom and W. H. Starbuck (eds) *Handbook of Organizational Design*. London: Oxford University Press, Vol. 2, 203–224.

Stahl, S. M. and Lebedun, (1974) Mystery gas: An analysis of mass hysteria. *Journal of Health and Social Behavior*, 15, 44–50.

Super, D. E. (1953) A theory of vocational development. *American Psychologist*, 8, 185–190.

Trice, H. M. and Beyer, J. M. (1984) Studying organizational cultures through rites and ceremonials. *Academy of Management Review*, 9, 653–669.

Uttal, B. (1983) The corporate culture vultures. *Fortune*, 17 October.

Wallace, A. F. C. (1970) *Culture and Personality*. New York: Random House.

Wanous, J. P. (1980) *Organizational Entry: Recruitment, selection, and socialization of newcomers*. Reading, Mass.: Addison-Wesley.

Zohar, D. (1980) Safety climate in industrial organizations: Theoretical and applied implications. *Journal of Applied Psychology*, 65, 96–102.

International Review of Industrial and Organizational Psychology 1988
Edited by C. L. Cooper and I. Robertson
© 1988 John Wiley & Sons Ltd

Chapter 6

APPROACHES TO MANAGERIAL SELECTION

Ivan T. Robertson
*Department of Management Sciences,
University of Manchester Institute of Science and Technology, UK*
and
Paul A. Iles
*Department of Management and Administrative Studies,
Huddersfield Polytechnic, UK*

Devising and using methods to assess and select people for jobs is one of the major activities within the industrial–organisational psychology field, and managerial selection is a topic of considerable interest to both researchers and practitioners, with much time and energy expended in improving the quality of managerial selection and assessment decisions. No previous review however has attempted to focus specifically on *managerial* selection and assessment. The most recent general reviews of personnel selection methods are Muchinsky (1986), Anderson and Shackleton (1986), Schmitt *et al.* (1984b) and Hunter and Hunter (1984) who have conducted comprehensive meta-analyses.

As far as the term 'manager' is concerned, one approach is to adopt a 'nominalist' position, as taken by Stewart (1976) in regarding a manager as, 'anyone above a certain level, roughly above foreman whether... in control of staff or not', due to a primary interest being in 'the jobs that companies call managerial and which form part of the management hierarchy for selection, training and promotion' (Stewart, 1976, p. 4). Another approach is to classify employees as managers, not by possibly misleading job titles, but on the basis of the functions and outputs demanded of their jobs (Boyatzis, 1982). In this sense, 'a person in a management job contributes to the achievement of organisational goals through planning, coordination, supervising and decision making regarding the investment and use of corporate human resources' (Boyatzis, 1982, p. 16). This is close to the definition offered by Drucker (1974) of managers as those people who give direction to their organisations, provide leadership and make decisions about the way the organisation will use the resources it has available. Similarly, Anderson defines management as 'the process of defining organisational goals and making decisions about the efficient and effective use of organisational resources in order to ensure high organisation performance'

(Anderson, 1984, p. 9). We have taken a broad view of relevant studies and as well as including work where the term manager has been used have included several studies where the functions of the job holder seemed to be *in large part* managerial though the title of manager may not have been used.

The first section of this chapter reviews studies on the nature of management work and the tasks, roles, skills and functions characteristic of managerial work. We go on to review the state of the art in management selection, in terms of those methods most often employed in practice, those most often studied by researchers, and the evidence for the validity of these methods in predicting managerial performance. We also examine some recent developments in less traditional areas (e.g. measurement of cognitive style, matching managers to strategies, entrepreneurialism and intrapreneurship, and selecting managers for expatriate assignments) and examine some studies on the processes by which selection decisions are made and the impact of these processes on candidates.

THE NATURE OF MANAGERIAL WORK

Managerial Roles

After a decade or more of sustained criticism of the 'classical functions' approach to the nature of managerial work (e.g. Mintzberg 1973; 1975), recent reviews of management work have gone some way to re-establishing the value of this approach to management (e.g. Carroll and Gillen, 1987; Hales, 1986) and to begin to establish closer links with the literature on management skills and competencies (e.g. Boyatzis, 1982; Anderson, 1984).

Much of the dissatisfaction with the 'classical' approach, describing managerial work in terms of planning, organising, commanding, coordinating, controlling, etc. (Fayol, 1949), stemmed from its failure to specify exactly what it is that managers actually do, and what skills are necessary to accomplish managerial tasks effectively. Observational studies of managerial work, beginning with Carlson's (1951) study of ten Swedish executives, began to reveal a picture of managerial work as pressurised rather than calm, interactive rather than deskbound, reactive rather than proactive, and dealing with 'hot information' gleaned orally rather than strategic planning using formal information systems. This approach to managerial work received its clearest support in Mintzberg's work, where he stated that management work was characterised by 'brevity, variety and fragmentation' (Mintzberg, 1973) and that 'if you ask a manager what he does, he will most likely tell you that he plans, organises, coordinates and controls. Then watch what he does. Don't be surprised if you can't relate what you see to these four words' (Mintzberg, 1975).

Mintzberg's initial work based on intensive shadowing of five chief executives in five US companies, together with an analysis of their diaries, activity patterns, mail and contacts, confirmed the pattern of brevity, variety, fragmentation, interruptions and preference for oral communications first noted by Carlson (1951). Mintzberg derived a conceptual model of managerial work identifying ten roles, three informational, three interpersonal and four decisional.

Most attempts to test Mintzberg's work have concentrated on his 'role' framework, though Kurke and Aldrich (1983), in a one-week observation study of four top executives from the US public and private sector, confirmed the picture of brevity, variety and fragmentation depicted by Mintzberg (1973). A recent British observational study of production managers and general managers in charge of manufacturing units in over twenty companies reinforces many of Mintzberg's conclusions about the interactive, varied, wide ranging nature of managerial work (Lawrence, 1984).

However, difficulties over Mintzberg's work have been noted in the literature. The basis on which the tripartite division is made is unclear, and analysis of how the roles might be carried out in practice, and what skills are necessary to implement them, is lacking. (See Shapira and Dunbar, 1980; and Carroll and Gillen, 1987).

McCall and Segrist (1980) asked managers to rate the importance of each role to their supervisory performance, finding support for the construct validity of six of the roles but much overlap between four roles and other work activities. They contended that 'managers' perceptions of relative role importance across levels and functions were sufficiently similar to support Mintzberg's contention that managerial jobs are essentially alike' (McCall and Segrist, 1980, p. 10), a conclusion disputed by Stewart (1982). In a similar study, Lau, Newman and Broedling (1980) developed a 50-item questionnaire to tap Mintzberg's ten roles, adding an eleventh role of 'technical expert', devised on the basis of interviews, observations and diary analysis in a study of 210 US government managers. Subsequent factor-analysis showed that four factors accounted for most of the variance: (a) leadership and supervision; (b) information-gathering and dissemination; (c) technical problem-solving; (d) executive decision-making–planning–resource allocation. Shapira and Dunbar (1980) used an in-basket simulation study with two Israeli samples (54 MBA students and 112 lower- and middle-level managers). Their analysis showed that the ten roles could be meaningfully divided into two (rather than three) facets—'informational' roles and 'decisional' roles. No separate 'interpersonal' category emerged. In line with Mintzberg's suggestion (Mintzberg, 1973, p. 130), evidence of a 'hierarchical' effect was noted in that middle managers gave greater priority to the figurehead role, and more often assumed the roles of leader, disseminator and entrepreneur, rather than disturbance-handler.

These links between hierarchical level and role have also been noted by Lau and colleagues, as well as effects of managerial function and sector. For example, Lau and Pavett (1980) compared public sector US navy managers and private-sector managers using the 50-item questionnaire devised by Lau, Newman and Broedling (1980). Factor analysis showed that five dimensions characterised most of the variance in managerial roles in both sectors—leadership and supervision; information-gathering and dissemination; technical problem-solving; decision-making–planning–resource allocation and negotiation. Both sectors reported informal, fragmented, non-reflective work, with public-sector managers reporting more formal meetings. Similarities and differences emerged over perceived knowledge, skills and abilities. Pavett and Lau (1983) reviewed earlier work on the influence of hierarchical level on managerial work including the suggestions of Mintzberg (1980) that chief executives were more focused on 'external' roles and lower-level managers on 'internal' roles. Minzberg also suggested that sales managers needed to give greater salience to interpersonal roles, staff managers to informational roles, and production managers to decisional roles. In a study of 180 private sector managers, drawn from various US companies and functional specialities, they found that higher-level managers rated the liaison, spokes-person and figurehead roles as more important than other levels, while lower levels gave greater importance to the 'leader' role. Several other differences emerged—for example, R & D managers rated the technical expert role, sales managers the interpersonal roles, and staff and financial managers the infor-mational roles as relatively more important. 'Conceptual' skills were seen as relatively more important by higher-level managers, whilst 'human' skills were rated as most important at all levels.

Clearly this study, in showing links between hierarchical level, functional speciality, role importance and perceived skill requirements, goes some way to undermine any universal view of managerial roles and skills, though the conclusions are limited by the 'self-report' nature of the study and its failure to relate skill possession to effective performance.

Paolillo (1987) studied 352 US sales, production and staff managers from various industries, examining the role profiles of managers in different functional areas. He showed that six of the ten Mintzberg roles were in fact influenced by functional area. This study seems to confirm that functional area is linked to the extent to which the various managerial roles are displayed. A further study, this time using a 'functions' approach, also indicates the links between hierarchical level and management work. Hughes and Sizler (1985) showed that the importance of directing and controlling remained constant across all levels, but that the importance of planning and organising increased, and the importance of staffing decreased, with rises in managerial level.

Managerial Networks, Interactions and Functions

Kotter (1982a,b) studied fifteen high-level US general managers in various US corporations through in-depth observation, interviews, questionnaires and diary analysis, confirming the picture presented by Mintzberg (1973) of frequent informal meetings, short disjointed conversations and much emphasis on jokes and non-work topics. Kotter (1982a,b) connects managerial responsibilities with the formation and maintenance of a network of relationships; in order to advance personal 'agendas' managers act by making others feel obligations, by estab-lishing reputations, and by manipulating symbols. Kotter reveals a concern with the role of leaders in shaping 'organisational culture' that relates his work to, for example, Peters and Waterman (1982) and Deal and Kennedy (1982)—e.g. 'they used meetings, language, stories about the organisation as symbols in order to communicate messages indirectly' (Kotter, 1982a, p. 74). Kotter (1982a) emphasises the need for managers to process much information quickly and to persuade others to get their own agendas implemented, with much need for wheeler-dealing, quick thinking, and encouraging others to identify with them, but less emphasis on advance planning or decision-making.

Luthans, Rosenkrantz and Hennessey (1985), pointing out that studies such as Mintzberg (1973) and Kotter (1982a) combined actual observations of what managers do with very small numbers and little in the way of statistical analysis, sought to relate managerial activities to managerial success. Their study used trained participant observers to observe the behaviours of 52 managers in a state revenue department, a manufacturing plant and a police department, and employed the Leader Observation System developed by Luthans and Lockwood (1984). The authors showed that 'interaction with outsiders' and 'socialising/ politicking' were two activities associated particularly with 'successful' managers, as measured by a promotion index of level over tenure. The kind of organisation in which the manager worked had some effect, in that socialising/politicking were particularly related to success in the state revenue department, but managing conflict was related to success in the manufacturing plant.

This study supports Mintzberg (1973) and Kotter (1982a) in its emphasis on the importance of 'networking' and face-to-face politicking activities to managerial success (though of course actual performance was not measured). The four top managers studied *did* however seem to spend time planning/coordinating and decision-making, in line with the attention given to it by the 'classical functions' school of Fayol (1949), from which attention had been deflected by Mintzberg (1973). Hales (1986) argues that Kotter's work can be translated into more skill-based terminology, more in line with other research; e.g. setting agendas = planning, network-building = making contacts; network utilising = influencing; implementing agendas = decision-making. He also argues that the work of Kotter (1982a), Mintzberg (1973), Stewart (1982) and Sayles (1965) can be integrated to identify a common set of managerial elements which resemble the supposedly outdated 'management functions', namely: acting as a figurehead and unit leader; allocating resources; handling disturbances; monitoring workflows; negotiating; innovating; planning; controlling and directing subordinates. Mahoney, Jerdee and Carroll (1963; 1965) reported in a study of 452 managers that managerial time can be allocated to a set of eight basic 'PRINCESS' managerial functions (Planning, Representing, Investigating, Negotiating, Coordinating, Evaluating, Supervising, Staffing).

The conclusions of Hales (1986) resembles the analysis of managerial jobs in New York City by Allan (1981) who constructed a task statement questionnaire, distributed to 1476 managers, based on a job analysis. Managers indicated the relative importance of, and time spent in, each task, and 57 tasks were identified as a 'common core', verified through interviews and observation of 120 managers at work. Higher-level managers reported a greater variety of important activities, dealing with long-range matters of considerable importance to the organisation as a whole (e.g. proposing changes in laws or regulations, setting, recommending or developing policy). Additional analysis of the 57 tasks revealed six dimensions, namely: (1) supervision; (2) harmonising; (3) information handling; (4) analytical-evaluative; (5) change initiating; (6) monitoring. Links between hierarchical level and dimensions were also observed. The study, as Allan (1981) acknowledges, did not distinguish between effective and ineffective managers nor did it analyse attributes and abilities necessary to do the job effectively.

Some studies exist which show that skill in performing the various classical functional areas does relate to managerial success or unit performance, for example, in Gillen and Carroll's (1985) study of 103 unit managers in ten industrial enterprises. In the Sohio studies, Boehm (1981) showed that problem-solving skills were the most important to a manager's performance ratings but adaptability, planning and reasoning skills were also important when the situation was ambiguous, with interpersonal skills being only moderately important for this sample (most skills related to the ability to cope with change and manage uncertainty). The AT & T assessment centre studies showed that skill in planning/decision-making as measured in an assessment centre was one of the strongest predictors of managerial success (Bray, Campbell and Grant, 1974) while Boyatzis (1982) found that goal-setting/planning skills related to managerial effectiveness.

The work reviewed above has focused on attempting to understand the nature of managerial work and, in some cases, to identify determinants of successful performance. We move now from an examination of studies of managerial work in general to a more direct examination of specific attempts to predict management performance. Research into the selection of managers, like all personnel selection research, utilises both predictor and criterion measures.

Criteria

As Muchinsky (1986) points out, criteria are conceptually of greater importance than predictors since knowledge of what to predict or how to measure it is a necessity. Personnel selection research typically employs a rather limited range of criteria representing individual worth or benefit to an organisation, principally job performance as measured by supervisory ratings (Monahan and Muchinsky, 1983). Criteria have been characterised in terms of composite v. multiple criteria (Dunnette, 1963), dynamic v. static criteria (Bass, 1962), 'soft' v. 'hard' criteria, and proximal v. distal criteria (Schmitt and Schneider, 1983), as well as in terms of relevance, reliability, freedom from bias and practicality (Thorndike, 1949). Schmitt and Schneider (1983) report that for managerial and professional jobs, most experienced psychologists agree that between one and two years should elapse before collecting criterion data after job entry.

They also argue in favour of some global index of effectiveness as the appropriate dependent variable, with a focus on organisational goals and outcomes and use of behaviour-oriented ratings scales as criteria only where there is an explicit and measured link between behaviour and outcome.

This focus on organisational effectiveness (and consequently organisational analysis as well as job analysis) emphasises the use of more objective measures of managerial performance. One such criterion might be absenteeism, but different measures of absenteeism are often found to be unrelated to one another, and company records are often inaccurate or incomplete (for example, distinguishing between authorised or unauthorised absence for managers). Again, the use of turnover as a criterion often conflates voluntary and involuntary turnover.

Advancement, promotion or salary progression (apparently 'hard' measures, in fact the result of subjective appraisals) are popular measures of managerial performance, especially with assessment centre research. These indices are no guarantee of effective performance, but may in fact reflect organisational socialisation or tenure. These problems of criteria contamination, subtle criteria contamination, and self-fulfilling prophecy effects will be discussed in the section on assessment centres. These problems led Klimoski and Strickland (1977) to argue for other criteria, such as nominations of individuals on 'value to the organisation', estimates of replacement costs, measures of management objectives achieved, critical contribution to the organisation, and peer and subordinate ratings. One approach to selection criteria which has been used by Sackett and Harris (1984) has been to validate the use of 'honesty questionnaires' by looking at monthly shrinkage across chain stores, while Schmitt and Schneider (1983) argue for more use of organisational performance variables (e.g. impact on training function, comparison of relative contributions of different interventions such as personnel selection, training, job enrichment, etc. to organisational performance).

Another direction in criteria research and development is pointed to by Herriot (1986a) who argues for an interest in the individual employee's job satisfaction, as well as her job performance, and by Robertson and Smith (1988), who also argue for attention to other criterion variables such as individual job satisfaction in the context of a perspective of the dynamic, interactive nature of the person–work situation derived from Bandura's (1986) notion of 'reciprocal determinism' between person, situation and behaviour.

Other recent developments relevant to a discussion of criteria include the critical reanalysis of the concept of 'dynamic criteria' by Barrett et al. (1985), concluding that they were rare phenomena overemphasised in the literature, and arguing that research should be focused on removing sources of criteria unreliability. Dickinson (1987) discusses multi-trait–multi-method and person perception designs used to investigate performance ratings distortions by isolating those factors that distort ratings, thus leading to improvements in the quality of performance ratings. He developed a design combining both approaches, illustrating each design with examples and using the design to isolate the influence of rater, ratee and context factors on rating quality. Steel and Mento (1986) examined the impact of situational constraints (e.g. job-induced obstacles, social obstacles, policy or environmental constraints) on subjective and objective criteria of managerial job performance in a field study of branch managers in a financial institution. The effects of constraints on supervisory appraisals, self-ratings and objective performance criteria were investigated, and significant effects reported, with significant differences between groups of managers from high and low constraint settings in supervisor appraisals, and on one objective measure of performance.

Space does not permit a thorough separate discussion of the issue of criteria and the interested reader is referred to material on performance measurement and appraisal for further information (Landy and Farr, 1980; Latham, 1986). For the remainder of this review criterion-related issues are discussed as they arise in subsequent sections. Particular consideration is given to criterion issues in a later section on assessment centres.

Selecting Managers

The selection and assessment of managers is fundamentally concerned with the prediction of job performance; this necessarily implies the use of 'predictors' of various kinds. Over the past 50 years much research has accumulated on the reliability and validity of predictors of various kinds though little is known about the processes by which some predictors actually work. In addition, other important features of predictors, such as their impact on candidates are substantially under-researched.

Many predictors have been and are used in managerial selection and assessment, including interviews, analytic tests and inventories (e.g. cognitive ability tests, perceptual-motor tests, personality and interest inventories, projective tests), analogous tests (e.g. work samples, situational simulations), computer-assisted tests, biodata and accomplishment records, references, graphology, astrology, self-assessment, supervisor assessment, peer assessment, and assessment centres employing some combination of these techniques.

There are various ways of characterising predictors. Robertson (1986) suggests a classification system based on the principle that future work behaviour can be predicted from three factors; from predictors based on the past behaviour of the person (biodata, references, supervisory/peer evaluations), from predictors based on the present behaviour of the person (interviews, tests, work sample tests, self-assessments, assessment centres) and predictors based on the expectancies a person holds about their own future behaviour and competencies (e.g. situational interviews, self-efficacy scales). This classification system is used as our basis for reviewing work on the selection of managers.

Usage of Predictors for Management Selection

Robertson and Makin (1985) conducted a survey on the use of predictors for management selection in a sample of 108 UK organisations, drawn from an existing mailing list based on the Times 1000 index. A summary of their findings is given in Table 1.

Current Research Interests

Monahan and Muchinsky (1983) examined personnel selection studies published during 1950–79 in one academic/professional journal, showing that studies focusing specifically on professional and managerial jobs were highest during the 1960s, where the number of studies published grew to more than four times the rate of publication in the 1950s. In the 1970s however, trades, craft, sales, managerial and professional jobs seemed to be studied with more or less equal frequency.

Table 1—Usage of Selection Methods

	Usage				
	Never	Less than half of applicants	Half of applicants	More than half	Always
	%	%	%	%	%
Interviews	1.0	9.8	4.9	2.0	81.4
References	3.7	14.0	2.8	11.2	67.3
Cognitive tests	70.8	19.8	3.1	1.0	5.2
Personality	64.4	23.8	3.0	5.0	4.0
Assessment centre	78.6	14.6	4.9	1.9	—
Biodata	94.2	2.9	1.0	—	1.9

This survey shows that references and interviews are extremely popular with practitioners, though researchers have demonstrated the low validity of both of these selection instruments (see Muchinsky, 1986). Anecdotal evidence suggests that similar conclusions would apply in other countries though we could not trace any published work.

Schmitt *et al.* (1984b) surveyed all selection validity studies published in two journals between 1964 and 1982, namely the *Journal of Applied Psychology* and *Personnel Psychology* (both international journals edited and published in the USA but with contributions mostly from US researchers. 366 conceptually independent validity coefficients relating to specific predictor–criteria pairs were identified from an original sample of 840 non-independent coefficients, and the distribution of these coefficients across different occupational groups is shown in Table 2:

Table 2—Percentages of Validity Coefficients as a Function of Occupational Groups

Occupational group	*Percentage of coefficients*
Professional	22
Managerial	25
Clerical	10
Sales	14
Skilled labour	13
Unskilled labour	16

Derived from Schmitt *et al.*, 1984b.

It is possible to derive the number of validity coefficients produced for management groups using specific predictor types, as in Table 3:

Table 3—Validity Studies on Managers from *Personnel Psychology* and *Journal of Applied Psychology*, 1964–1982

Predictor	No. of validity coefficients
Biodata	4
Assessment centres	15
Personality	17
Cognitive tests	22
Supervisor/peer assessment	24
Work sample	3

* Based on averages across independent samples.
(From Schmitt *et al.*, 1984.)

State of the Art

Several reviews have attempted to summarise the large amount of information available on predictors and to generate conclusions about the validity of specific predictors for specific criteria. Some such reviews have been narrative reviews (e.g. Reilly and Chao, 1982; Muchinsky, 1986) and others have used meta-analysis techniques (e.g. Hunter and Hunter, 1984; Schmitt *et al.*, 1984b); in general similar conclusions can be drawn.

For all occupational groups, work-sample tests, an 'ability composite' (general mental ability and psychomotor ability), supervisor/peer assessments, assessment centres, biodata and general mental ability tests produce the highest validity coefficients.

It should be noted that these results are for a range of occupational groups and a range of criteria, not specifically for managerial groups. In addition, some predictors predict some criteria better than others (e.g. biodata seem to predict salary much more accurately than tenure, and assessment centres seem to predict promotions or salary progression much more accurately than job performance). Validity is not the only evaluative standard by which to judge predictors (see Muchinsky, 1986; and Robertson and Smith, 1988).

In the next section, specific predictors classified according to past/present/future orientation are reviewed, with specific reference to the selection of managers.

PAST-ORIENTED PREDICTORS

References

References, despite their longstanding popularity and widespread use, remain under-researched. For example, Beason and Bolt (1976) found that 82 per cent of all responding organisations used reference checks, while Kingston (1971) in a survey of UK managerial selection found that 88 per cent of companies requested references. The survey of management selection techniques by Robertson and

Makin (1986) found that references were used 'on some occasions' by over 96 per cent of their UK sample of 108 organisations, with some tendency for larger companies to use them less frequently (e.g. 17 per cent never using them).

As Muchinsky (1979) points out, most studies report low average validity coefficients (e.g. Reilly and Chao, 1982 report average validity coefficients of 0.18 for rated performance, 0.08 for turnover, 0.14 across all criteria), except for a study by Carroll and Nash (1972) which reported a correlation with clerical job performance of 0.64, using a specially constructed forced choice rating form. Muchinsky (1986) reviews the uses to which references may be put, likelihood of adverse impact and ways of reducing it, and the impact of movements for freedom of information and disclosure rights.

A major problem with reference letters is their homogeneity and lack of discrimination. Recent research includes that of Knouse (1983) who, in a study of the ratings of 98 personnel directors, found that a subjects' chances of being recommended (in this case, a management graduate for an unspecified job) increased if specific performance examples were provided. Paunonen, Jackson and Oberman (1987), in a simulated employment interview with student judges for 'professional' jobs, found a major effect of a 'level of competence' manipulation as conveyed through reference reports. Jones and Harrison (1982) compared the ratings given on the headteacher's report form used in Royal Navy officer selection with training performance criteria, finding that a composite score for seven individual rating scales correlated 0.36 with overall training performance (n = 263). The authors concluded that reference reports could contribute usefully to selection if certain conditions were met, such as those identified by Carroll and Nash (1972); namely that the recommender is of a similar sex, race and nationality to the recommendee, has enough time to observe the recommendee, and that the old job and job applied for are similar in content. If these conditions were met, reference reports might provide information on 'samples' of characteristic job relevant behaviour.

Biodata

The use of biodata (historical pieces of information about an individual) for selection purposes is based on the premise that past activities, interests and behaviour as sampled by means of a biographical inventory are predictive of future behaviour. Items (whether verifiable or conjectural) correlating with job performance criteria are typically retained.

The usage of biodata for management selection in the UK seems low but increasing. The survey by Robertson and Makin (1986) revealed that only 6 per cent of respondents, all large companies, reported using it.

In general, the predictive validity of biodata seems consistently high, with Reilly and Chao (1982) reporting an average validity coefficient of 0.35 and a validity coefficient of 0.38 for specifically managerial jobs (based on seven studies). Hunter and Hunter (1984) report validity coefficients for various criteria of 0.26 to 0.37, with Schmitt et al. (1984b) reporting an average validity coefficient of 0.24 (0.53 for salary).

Muchinsky (1986) reviews biodata in terms of their applicability, development costs and possible 'adverse impact' (where some kinds of item content, e.g. inner city addresses, may have adverse impact). In a specifically managerial study, Ritchie and Boehm (1977) developed a biodata key with lower-level women employees and validated it against assessed potential for middle management, as indexed by overall assessment centre ratings. Applied to male and female managerial samples, biodata showed significant validity coefficients for both subgroups, but only for college graduates. Similar types of life experience seemed predictive of subsequent managerial success for both men and women.

Few biodata studies with managerial samples have been published, though Anderson and Shackleton (1986) cite work by Savage (1985) with thirteen UK studies as reporting impressive validity coefficients. Childs and Klimoski (1986) showed that biodata could predict career success (as indexed by career, job and personal success) two years after the completion of the biographical inventory by participants on real-estate courses, with factors obtained through factor analysis predicting different facets of 'career success'. Shaffer, Saunders and Owens (1986) in a study of US college freshmen showed that biodata responses seemed consistent and accurate, using a five-year test–retest design and employing external observers (parents) for verification. Neiner and Owens (1985) reported that biodata could predict job choice among college graduates.

Drakeley, Herriott and Jones (1988) found that biodata predicted training performance in samples of Royal Navy officers as well as a composite score of four psychometric apptitude tests and as well as an overall assessment centre rating. Though elements of the assessment centre were more successful in predicting a 'leadership' criterion, biodata added to the overall predictive power of the procedure. Unlike test scores or assessment centre ratings biodata predicted voluntary withdrawal from training. The authors distinguished 'motivational' from 'achievement' biodata items in that the former (e.g. membership of uniformed youth organisations) predicted voluntary withdrawal and the latter (e.g. achievement at school) predicted training success.

Part of the explanation for biodata's predictive power might lie in the behavioural similarities between itemised behaviour and criteria behaviour (e.g. Asher, 1972) with itemised behaviour acting as 'samples' of relevant behaviour (Wernimont and Campbell, 1968). In addition, early life success might raise self-esteem or self-efficacy expectations through successful performance accomplishments which make later success more likely (e.g. Bandura, 1986). For example, Hall's (1971) 'psychological success' model of career development proposes that successful performance leading to the attainment of valued goals increases feelings of psychological success and self-esteem, increasing involvement in the task and the setting of future goals. As Drakeley et al., (1988) acknowledge, many biodata items will reflect access to opportunity structures. Following Barclay (1982) such denial of access to successful performance accomplishments, role models or verbal encouragements for women may lead to lowered self-efficacy expectations and under-utilisation (a finding reported by Hackett and Betz [1982] with regard to 'career self-efficacy').

Biodata seem useful as pre-screening devices, especially for organisations with large numbers of applicants, but seems less suitable for the selection of internal candidates for promotion or tiering purposes since many biodata items may lack face validity with candidates doubting their relationship to job success. In a study of 233 managerial candidates for entry into the management development programme of a major UK clearing bank, Robertson *et al.* (1988) found that the use of biodata for internal tiering purposes was negatively regarded by a group of managers rejected by this technique, with considerable doubts as to its usefulness, fairness or accuracy being expressed. Given the static, fatalistic nature of biodata (it being impossible to rewrite history!), counselling and feedback on strengths and weaknesses seem difficult, if not impossible. This may have negative impacts on well-being, morale and work commitment.

The importance of certain kinds of college experience is shown by Howard (1986), who studied samples of middle-aged and young managers in ten different organisations and used two longitudinal samples of AT & T managers graduating in the 1950s and 1970s to examine the relationship between college experience and management potential, as demonstrated in assessment centre performance. College major fields of study, extra-curricular activities and level of higher education accounted for most of the variance in performance. As Howard (1986) acknowledges, longitudinal research in both college and work environments is needed to identify causality in the development of managerial competence. A focus on pre-work life history (e.g. college and school activities and interests) whilst appropriate for many entry level positions and graduate recruitment activities should not obscure the important role played by prior work experiences in predicting later work success. For example, Berlew and Hall (1966) found that an important predictor of career success in managers was the experience of 'psychological success' in the first year of work, even after taking individual differences into account. The work of Robertson *et al.* (1988) and London (1985) shows how different career experiences, including experiences of selection and assessment techniques, may impact on such variables as career identity, well being, and work commitment. Wakabayashi and Graen (1984) showed in a longitudinal study of Japanese managers' career progress that the measured quality of supervisor-graduate exchanges as measured by the vertical exchange scale contributed to the prediction of both bonus and promotion criteria. Jasolka, Beyer and Trice (1985), in a study of financial and status success in a large US corporation, found that demographic characteristics were related to financial success.

In a variation of the biodata approach tied specifically to work experience, Hough, Keyes and Dumette (1983) and Hough (1984) developed an 'accomplishment record' for government attorneys using information about past work behaviour based on self-reported descriptions of past accomplishments. These are reported in terms of job-related dimensions drawn from critical incident workshops. Significant criteria-related concurrent validities were reported (overall validity coefficient of 0.25) with little evidence of adverse race or sex effects. As the authors point out, unlike biodata, accomplishment records are open to modification via feedback, training and developmental opportunities. Such scores seemed unrelated to traditional aptitude test measures, grades or school quality and seemed to provide unique information. This method would seem promising for managerial selection, but no evidence of its use has been reported. Clearly its use is limited to candidates with some prior work experience (not necessarily in the same field).

Supervisory/Peer Evaluations

Schmitt *et al.* (1984) report an average validity of 0.43 for supervisory/peer evaluations across all occupational groups, with peer evaluation alone providing an average validity of 0.41 (Reilly and Chao, 1982) and 0.49 (Hunter and Hunter, 1984). Schmitt *et al.* (1984) based their average validity coefficient on 31 validities, of which 24 came from managerial groups. They reported that supervisory/peer evaluations show most predictive power with status change as the criterion (mean validity 0.51), predicting performance ratings reasonably well also (0.32).

Supervisory evaluations seem to have low development needs and high administrative convenience, and to be acceptable to most candidates. Peer evaluations also seem to have low development needs and reasonable administrative convenience, but appear to be less acceptable to candidates. For example, Cederblom and Lounsbury (1983) investigated university faculty acceptance of peer-evaluation schemes, showing that user acceptance was related strongly to perceived friendship bias and perceived feedback value, with correlations with perceived validity, perceived effects on morale, and satisfaction with previous peer ratings. Since peer evaluations seem to be a reliable and valid predictor (several raters in close contact with each other able to observe a range of criteria relevant behaviour, often not available to supervisors) the authors suggest several ways of increasing its acceptance. These include increasing its perceived feedback value by specifying performance criteria more fully. Love (1981) compared peer nominations, peer rankings and peer ratings in a sample of police officers, showing significant reliability and criterion-related validity (supervisory ratings) for all three methods. User acceptance was still negative for all methods, however, in that participants did not see it as fair, likeable or accurate, and did not endorse its use for promotion purposes.

Mumford (1983) has examined theories put forward to account for the striking validity of peer evaluations (such as those obtained for managerial groups by Kraut, 1975; Roadman, 1964) concluding that hypotheses based on friendship, psychometric reliability, observational opportunities and implicit personality theories do not fully account for its validity. From an examination of studies showing strong validity coefficients, factor-analytic investigations, and experimental studies attempting to manipulate the validity of peer evaluations, he puts forward a social comparison theory framework. He further proposes that peer evaluations should be particularly effective for managerial personnel and that they would be particularly useful under standardised observational conditions such as assessment centres or in training programmes. This use of peer evaluations means that, though most useful for internal candidates, they can be used for external candidates too. Fletcher and Dulewicz (1984) describe a UK managerial assessment centre which incorporates a Peer Voting exercise (interestingly, peer voting for 'preferred boss' correlated significantly with the overall assessment rating, while peer voting for 'project colleague' did not, suggesting that participants were looking for different qualities in the two roles). Hart and Thompson (1979) also report on an assessment centre employing peer assessment. Tziner and Dolan (1982; 1985) used a peer nomination score to identify Israeli female army officer potential while on NCO training. They showed that in two samples peer-nomination scores appeared to be a more valid predictor of officer training grade obtained than general intelligence, superior evaluation or interview evaluation of 'fitness to command'. A 'composite score' was the most predictive. The authors relate the usefulness of the peer nomination measure to the lengthy exposure time, multiple judges, and exposure to criterion-relevant behaviours.

Schmitt and Hill (1977) investigated the effects of race/sex composition on peer ratings in the context of a managerial assessment centre, and showed that the peer ratings for black females were adversely affected on ratings of 'forcefulness' and 'communication skills' by the sex/race composition of other members of the group. Muchinsky (1986) and Schmitt and Noe (1986) argue that it is likely that racial bias is to be expected in peer assessments, in terms of similarities and stereotypes. Little hard evidence of bias, or of differential validity across subgroups, exists.

Supervisory assessments seem more acceptable to candidates, but are limited to internal candidates. Their use for purposes other than prediction has been discussed elsewhere (e.g. Latham, 1986). Norton, Balloun and Konstantinovich (1980) discuss their use for predicting managerial success with non-managerial employees, in the context of extrapolating assessments of managerial skills from non-managerial behaviour. The authors argue that in this situation construct, content and criterion related validity studies are seldom applicable to supervisory ratings of promotability.

A study by Siegal (1982) elicited paired comparison evaluations for twenty savings and loan association branch managers, with peer evaluations obtained from sixteen managers and supervisory evaluations from four officers. Inter-judge agreement within and between groups was high, extending to certain independently measured psychological characteristics. Peer evaluations assisted the officers in making promotional decisions by providing an additional perspective (managers were not aware of their partial input into promotional decisions) though the high correlation between mean peer and superior ratings (0.84) supports the inference that these two samples made their ratings from relatively similar characteristics.

Prior superior evaluations can be made as part of the input to an assessment centre process. (Tziner and Dolan [1982] showed that prior superior evaluation of expected success as an officer had a low validity of 0.16 against training success in an Israeli female military officer assessment centre.) As Bernadin and Buckley (1981) suggest, one of the reasons for leniency in supervisors ratings is a decision by the superior to avoid the unpleasant consequences surrounding discussion of a poor rating. This may be one reason why assessment centres, with 'outside' raters providing feedback, may be more acceptable.

PREDICTORS BASED ON THE PRESENT

Self-Assessment

Some studies which have examined the value of self-assessment of ability or talent conclude that it is of little use for selection purposes in organisations (e.g. Thornton, 1980; Reilly and Chao, 1982). Reilly and Chao (1982) in their review of eight studies, reported an average weighted validity coefficient of 0.15 for three studies reporting validity coefficients with overall criteria. Mabe and West (1982), however, reported a mean validity coefficient of 0.29 for self-assessments in their meta-analytic study.

Levine, Flory and Ash (1977) suggest that self-assessment is limited as a personnel selection technique because people will be motivated to produce an inflated or lenient picture of their own abilities. Muchinsky (1986) argues that this will be more true of unemployed people than of current job holders, so that criterion-related validity studies relying on concurrent designs (as nearly all have done) will produce a more positive view of the validity of self-assessment than predictive validity studies. In addition, it is often argued that people are unable to make accurate or reliable estimates of their own ability. In a review of the literature Makin and Robertson (1983) concluded that people's self-assessments corresponded more closely with objective assessments when the factor being assessed was straightforward and well understood (e.g. for typists 0.59 for simple copy typing, 0.07 for typing tables). As Muchinsky (1986) points out, the value of self-assessments could be to provide estimates of ability where objective measures do not exist. Managerial ability could be included here, but we could find no studies of the accuracy of self-assessment in this context. Recent developments in personality theory suggest that self concepts and self-evaluations play a major role in future behaviour (Bandura, 1986) and it may be that better designed self-assessment instruments, such as measurements of managerial self-efficacy, will be more predictive of future performance.

Muchinsky (1986) considers self-assessment to be reasonably fair for racial subgroups, to have low costs, and to be broadly applicable to all occupational groups. Given the pervasive problems of inflation bias and low validity, he considers it to have at best an ancilliary role in personnel selection. It may however have a more general role in the selection process in that decisions to apply for and accept a job involve self-assessments and comparison of oneself, one's abilities, interests and needs, with the requirements and characteristics of the job. Realistic job previews (e.g. Wanous, 1980) seem a useful way of assisting people to make a more accurate assessment of the match between their own characteristics and those of the job. Self-assessment also plays a major part in organisational career planning and career development activities (e.g. Hall and Goodale, 1986) and plays a growing role in assessment centre technology for managerial selection and development, especially with more 'developmental' assessment centres (e.g. Hart and Thompson, 1979; Gratton, 1985). Since Makin and Robertson (1983) have argued that degree of leniency in self-assessment is influenced by perceived consequenses to the assessor, and that accuracy is influenced by the purpose of the assessment, then self-assessment may have a more useful part to play in 'developmental' rather than 'selection' assessment centres. Mabe and West (1982) have shown that much of the variability in the validity coefficients could be accounted for by such conditions of measurement as instructions guaranteeing anonymity and emphasising comparisons with others.

Personality and Interest Inventories and Tests

Schmitt et al. (1984b) report an average validity for personality tests of 0.15, lower than the average validity for managerial groups of 0.21 reported by Ghiselli (1973). Muchinsky (1986) notes that there has been a rekindling of interest in the use of 'new wave' personality tests designed to enable assessments among the adult working population to be made, rather than a reliance on traditional 'clinical' tests (see also Bernardin and Bownas, 1984). For example, a new factor-analytic-based, self-report questionnaire has been developed in Britain as an assessment device for use in managerial and professional selection and coun-selling, the Occupational Personality Questionnaire (OPQ), e.g. Saville and Munro (1986). Swinburne (1985; 1986) has compared the OPQ and the 16PF of Cattell on the extent to which they measure similar aspects of personality, their acceptability to management, and the usefulness of the feedback obtained. Swinburne (1985) examined the correlations between the 16PF and OPQ with a group of 70 managerial/professional staff. Saville and Munro (1986) reported on a study of 230 people in managerial, supervisory and clerical levels that the OPQ factor scales were considerably more reliable than those of the 16PF (alternate form reliabilities), with the OPQ factor scales not well represented in the 16PF.

As Schmitt and Noe (1986) point out, personality test validities for managerial positions may be greater than for other occupations, given the greater contribu-tion to effective performance made by motivation and interpersonal skills. Bentz (1984) in a review of Sear's personality assessment programme with store and manufacturing managers reported validity coefficients ranging between 0.20 and 0.30 against ratings of store performance, training evaluations, and self-report measures, with similar patterns for majority and minority subgroups. Cornelius (1973) reviewing the use of projective tests for personnel selection reported that a greater percentage of studies reported validity coefficients above 0.30 (75 per cent) than for personality inventories. Tziner and Dolan (1985) report a multi-predictor study into Israeli military officer potential among women, using final grade in training as a criterion. A global score of 'fitness to command' as assessed through various projective tests correlated 0.28 and 0.26 with the criterion in two large scale samples (after correction for restriction of range). In a similar study using an overall personality evaluation as part of an assessment centre, Tziner and Dolan (1982) report that the personality measure showed non-significant validity (0.06). The use of personality inventories as part of an assessment centre seems quite common; for example, Moses (1984) reports on an AT & T assessment programme which incorporates personality inventories and projective measures. Muchinsky (1986) discusses the limitations of personality inventories with regard to administrative use (e.g. limited access, need for trained administrators, possible low-face validity). No clear evidence of adverse impact has been demonstrated. The renewed enthusiasm for using personality tests in selection does not seem to have spread to the use of interest tests for selection purposes, perhaps because of their low reported validity (Ghiselli, 1973; Muchinsky, 1986).

McClelland's work on achievement motivation and the 'leadership motive pattern' (LMP) of moderate to high need for power, low need for affiliation and high activity inhibition has generated several recent research studies. McClelland and Boyatzis (1982) examined TAT protocols for 237 AT & T managers at entry, and correlated the scores against levels of promotion eight and sixteen years later, finding a significant, though low, relationship between the LMP and managerial success (for non-technical managers only). Stahl (1983) using a job-choice exercise to measure the LMP and employing 172 respondents drawn from several different samples showed that those scoring high in 'managerial motivation' (high need for power and achievement) were more likely to be managers or leaders in campus, with opposite results for those with low managerial motivation. No race or sex differences were found in a nationwide Air Force cadet sample of 1417 people. Given that significant differences in motivation were observed in the college sample, Stahl (1983) contended that early identification of managerial motivation was possible. Cornelius and Lane (1984) showed, with 39 managers in a profit-making, professionally-oriented service organisation involved in language teaching, that LMP was significantly related to language centre status but not to subordinate morale or administrative job performance as indexed by company records. The authors concluded that the motivation to influence others as captured in the LMP may not be critical for managerial success in technical or professional settings (as in McClelland and Boyatzis, 1982). In their study Cornelius and Lane (1984) found that need for achievement correlated significantly with climate factors relating to standards of excellence.

Ghiselli (1971) has produced a self-description inventory providing measures on 13 traits, designed specifically for predicting managerial performance. Some of the scales (e.g. supervisory ability, decisiveness, need for occupational achievement) predicted managerial performance well.

Gough (1984) has also developed a managerial potential scale for the California Psychological Inventory (CPI) evaluating items against criteria of managerial performance as indexed by performance ratings of 200 military officers and an index of 'managerial interests' obtained from 49 young male bank managers. The resulting managerial potential (MP) scale of 34 items correlated 0.20 with criteria rankings in a new sample of 143 military officers. As the author acknowledges, additional direct evidence in non-military settings is needed, as well as longitudinal studies on college student managerial progress.

The studies reviewed above do suggest that management performance may be predictable from personality characteristics—though it is certainly premature to specify a definite set of traits that are universally linked with managerial success. In fact, in view of the differences between managerial jobs discussed in the earlier section of this chapter this may never be feasible. Recent evidence is emerging however, that success in some of the specific managerial roles (e.g. leadership) discussed earlier is linked to specific personality traits (see Lord, DeVader and Alliger, 1986).

INTERVIEWS

Most reviews of the predictive validity of interviews have concluded that, in general, interviews have poor predictive power as compared with other assessment procedures. (Arvey and Campion, 1982; Reilly and Chao, 1982; Hunter and Hunter, 1984). For example, the meta-analysis of Hunter and Hunter (1984) reported a mean validity of 0.14, with correlations with supervisor ratings and training success superior to those with promotion or length of tenure.

Some recent work has been done to 'structure' interviews in order to increase predictive validity, and these seem to be quite promising (e.g. the patterned interview of Janz, 1982; Orpen, 1984; the situational interview of Latham et al., 1980; Latham and Saari, 1984). In general, a 'structured' interview reduces the number of possibilities open to participants (e.g. in terms of content, order, etc.), producing a method closer to other psychometrically valid devices. Early research by Maas (1965) showed greater reliability for a 'patterned expectation interview' employing behavioural examples of typical traits required in a rating scale. Mayfield et al. (1980) in the US life insurance industry also employed a highly structured approach with applicants rated on a set of specific questions. Arvey et al. (1987) report interview validity coefficients of up to 0.61 after correction with sales clerks. The 'situational' interview of Latham et al. (1980) and Latham and Saari (1984) is discussed more fully in the section on 'future-oriented predictors'.

Despite the generally poor validity of interviews, they are very widely used in managerial selection; for example, Robertson and Makin (1986) reported that 81 per cent of UK companies surveyed always used them to select managers, with only 1 per cent never using them. This may be because the interview is not only used to assess candidates' suitability but to provide job information and clarify applicant questions, as well as it's being applicable for selection into all types of jobs. Herriot (1987a,b) argues that its popularity in part derives from the recognition by organisations, if not by psychologists, that selection is a social process of feedback, accommodation and negotiation with applicants making decisions as well as organisations. The interview serves as a useful, if imperfect, vehicle for this purpose.

Since interviews are highly subjective, interviewer biases, prejudices and feelings are a significant factor affecting interview decisions leading to potential unfairness and adverse impact against racial minorities and women (Arvey, 1979). Many studies of interview fairness reporting effects of lower evaluations given to women and minorities with comparable credentials have however used college students as simulated interviewers evaluating job applicant resumés, and such findings may not be generalisable to field settings. Little evidence of differential validity has been reported (Schmitt and Noe, 1986) but some evidence suggests that 'role congruence' may be an important factor in that individuals seeking 'out of role' jobs (not congruent with racial or gender stereotypes) may receive lower recommendations (Schmitt and Noe, 1986). Since managerial positions are assumed to require 'masculine' characteristics, this is likely to lead to discrimination against women in respect to managerial jobs. Forsythe et al. (1985) used hiring recommendations from 77 personnel administrators to determine the effect of female applicant dress on selection decisions for management positions. Masculinity of dress had a significant effect on interviewers' selection decisions. Heilman and Stropeck (1985a) found that in an experimental study with MBA students, physical attractiveness proved advantageous for women in non-managerial (clerical) positions but disadvantageous for women in managerial positions (management trainee). For males, however, appearance had no effects whatsoever, in contrast to previous research which had shown that attractiveness benefited men regardless of job type. Heilman and Stopeck (1985b) have also presented findings on the effect of appearance on the way corporate managerial success is explained. Attributions of success to ability for males were enhanced by good looks, while females' ability attributions were negatively affected. Judgements of capability were similarly affected, but rate of corporate ascent did not interact with appearance or sex (in this study working people from a range of occupations acted as raters). Heilman and Martell (1987) have also shown that in certain conditions exposure to successful women in previously male-dominated occupations can reduce sex bias in selection decisions in a study of applicants for a finance manager trainee job, using students as selectors. Taylor and Ilgen (1981) found that exposure in terms of contact or experience with successful women in one field had favourable consequences for personnel decisions made about another woman in a different field.

Gilmore, Beehr and Love (1986) manipulated applicant sex, attractiveness, type of job and type of rater experimentally in a study of interview decisions for entry-level management trainee jobs, using resumés and interview transcripts. Physical attractiveness had the broadest effect on employment decisions, with no main effect for applicant sex. Professional interviews were biased in favour of female applicants and rated job applicants less leniently than student interviewers.

Kinicki and Lockwood (1985) studied the factors recruiters use in evaluating job applicants in a study of 24 recruiters conducting interviews with 91 students. Interview impression and attraction to the applicant significantly predicted an assessment of the candidates' interviewing skills and their suitability for hire, with 'interview impression' consisting of ability to express ideas, job knowledge, appearance and drive. Gender similarity was also significantly related to suitability for hire, but less so than for the other two. Relevant work experience, academic achievement and interview impression were significantly correlated with interviewing skills, with applicant sex not related to any criterion.

In general, it seems as if interviewers rely on impressionistic rather than verifiable information in making employment decisions, and consequently rater errors may be common. Impressions of attraction and liking are likely to be conveyed through non-verbal behaviour, with evidence that tone of voice and eye contact affect judgements of applicant qualifications, training and experience, and likelihood of being invited for further interviews (Dipboye and Wiley, 1977). Edinger and Patterson's (1983) review suggests that increased smiling, eye contact, gestures and head nods by an applicant produce more favourable interview outcomes. However, as noted above, many studies have used role-playing or video-taped simulations and student evaluators. One study using interviews for a real job opening (research assistant) and using individuals with training and experience in making personnel decisions by Giffard, Ng and Wilkinson (1985) showed that social skill was reasonably accurately inferred by interviewers through rate of gesturing, time spent talking, and formality of dress, whereas applicant motivation was poorly inferred (perhaps because social skill is encoded more clearly in non-verbal behaviour).

The concentration of research on non-verbal behaviour as a mediator of impressions of personality, motivation and attractiveness may be somewhat misplaced however in the light of the findings by Hollandsworth *et al.* (1979) that utterance content had a greater influence than style on favourable employment decisions. Rasmussen (1984) used a study in which student subjects viewed simulated, video-taped selection interviews in which interviewee non-verbal behaviour, verbal behaviour and resumé credentials were manipulated. Analysis of the ratings of qualifications for the job revealed that resumé credentials had the greatest impact. Parsons and Liden (1984) found that speech characteristics were relatively important cues as compared to personal appearance variables; non-verbal cues in general were highly related to judged qualifications. The kinds of employment sought in this study are so different from managerial jobs (young, casual, seasonal workers) that any generalisation to managerial jobs seems hazardous.

Studies have also examined interviewers. Elliott (1984), in a study of the interview results of candidates for work in an Irish bank, showed that female interviewers saw candidates as better dressed, better groomed, more cooperative, alert and cheerful, and tended to place less significance on test results. Attempts have been made to apply attributional theories to the interview (Herriott, 1981). Other studies have been made of the expectations both selectors and candidates hold about the interview, and candidates' reactions to interview content and interviewer style. These are discussed more fully in Herriott (1987; 1988) and in the section on 'social processes in management selection and assessment' in this chapter.

COGNITIVE TESTS

The validity of cognitive ability tests for personnel selection is well established, with Ghiselli (1973) reporting average validity coefficients for cognitive tests (intellectual, perceptual, spatial and mechanical abilities) for managers varying from 0.21–0.31 for job proficiency criteria. Schmitt *et al.* (1984b) report average coefficients of 0.27 and 0.25 for aptitude and general mental ability tests respectively in their meta-analytic investigation of validity studies published between 1964 and 1982. Hunter and Hunter (1984) report generally higher validities, with an average validity of 0.53 obtained using a combination of cognitive and psychomotor scores. Cognitive ability predicts supervisors' ratings and training success but predicts objective, content-valid work-sample performance even more accurately. Psychological tests have been used to predict a wide range of criterion measures. With supervisory ratings as a criterion a modest but consistent relationship between intelligence and job performance is obtained, but some studies have identified inverse relationships between intelligence and length of employment and non-significant relationships with other criteria (Muchinsky, 1986).

Cognitive tests are generally easy to administer, can be used with groups of candidates, and be administered and scored by people with relatively little training; since many are available 'off the shelf' development needs are low and costs generally are low too. Special aptitude tests are often individually administered and require a higher degree of testing competence by administrators, and are less generalisable in their use than intelligence tests.

There have been many allegations of bias, unfairness and adverse impact against cognitive tests, and it is beyond the scope of this chapter to discuss the issue; for recent reviews see Muchinsky (1986) and Schmitt and Noe (1986). In general minorities do seem to score lower on intelligence tests and adverse impact seems likely to occur. No evidence for the differential validity of cognitive tests is reported by Schmitt and Noe (1986).

Robertson and Smith (1988) argue that the process of psychometric testing may be revolutionised by the use of computer technology, and present a review of computer-assisted testing (CAT). The use of computerised tests in selection and assessment has been restricted largely to military uses, with a slow transfer to industrial and commercial organisations. In general, computerised tests tend to correlate highly with paper and pencil versions, are generally as valid, enable standardisation and administrative control to be increased, allow costs to be reduced, and are generally well received by candidates. In addition, modern computer technology can make tests dynamic and enable cognitive processes to be studied. However, Robertson and Smith (1988) also discuss some disadvantages of CAT such as problems of equivalence and the maintenance of standards. Schmitt and Noe (1986) note that cognitive tests seem most valid for complex jobs like managerial jobs, a claim confirmed by Hunter and Hunter (1984). On this basis then, CAT may play an increasingly significant role in managerial selection.

WORK-SAMPLE TESTS

Work-sample tests require applicants to perform a sample of the job in question, and published work shows that validities for work samples are quite high. For example, Schmitt et al. (1984b) report an average validity of 0.38, with Robertson and Kandola (1982) reporting median validities of 0.24–0.44. However, work-sample tests have been used mainly with non-managerial jobs, except for the use of 'situational exercises' (Muchinsky, 1986) such as in-tray/in-basket simulations, group discussion and decision-making exercises, oral presentations, management games, case studies and one-to-one role plays (e.g. counselling, interviewing, customer complaints, fact-finding) often used in assessment centres. Gill (1979) reports validities for in-trays ranging from 0.27–0.44 against job performance ratings as well as reviewing evidence in favour of its high face validity in graduate recruitment and adequate inter-rater reliability. He also cites evidence in favour of minimal adverse impact, and of its use as a 'trainability test' of management potential. For group discussion exercises Robertson and Kandola (1982) report a median validity of 0.35 with job performance criteria, while they report median validity coefficients for 'situational decision making' (typically in-basket exercises) of 0.48. In general, work samples show good validities across a range of criteria, with the best validity obtained with wages as a criterion. For managerial groups work-sample tests do not require much in the way of special equipment, but development needs may be quite high. It is somewhat surprising how ubiquitous the group discussion and in-tray exercises are, suggesting that more attention could be given to developing specifically managerial work sample tests.

This extra effort might be repaid by the extra benefits work-sample tests seem to give over other predictors. For example, work samples provide candidates with a 'taste' of a job and allow them to make a more realistic assessment of their own suitability, perhaps particularly useful for internal candidates. Downs *et al.* (1978), with a trainability test in a non-managerial sample, showed that even when offered a job, candidates who performed badly at work-sample tests did not tend to select the job, suggesting accurate self-assessment. In addition, applicant reaction to work-sample tests seems very favourable in that they have high face validity (Robertson and Kandola, 1982; Cascio and Phillips, 1979) and this use of analogous work samples may account for the high face validity and acceptability of assessment centres for managerial selection. Dulewicz, Fletcher and Wood (1983) report data on applicant reactions to individual exercises, showing that most of the exercises, but especially the in-tray, business decisions simulation and business plan presentation were very favourably regarded. Work-sample tests also seem to produce less adverse impact against minority groups than many other predictors (e.g. Kesselman and Lopez, 1979; Cascio and Phillips, 1979), though evidence for specific managerial work samples is lacking.

One problem identified by Robertson and Kandola (1982) is that predictive validity may attenuate over time, especially if working methods change with job experience. It has also been argued (e.g. Sackett, 1987) that content validity approaches to developing job sample tests cannot be used as an appropriate strategy for entry-level posts where substantial training and developmental experiences will be provided, since candidates have little or no experience of the job in question. This may be the case with graduate recruitment into management trainee posts. However a trainability-testing or job-learning approach can be used even with inexperienced applicants. In this approach candidates are given instruction, including a demonstration of how to perform the work sample (Robertson and Downs, 1979; for a recent meta-analysis of trainability testing, see Robertson and Downs, 1988). Little use has been made of this procedure for management selection. Gill (1982) reports a study where management studies students undertook two short, in-basket exercises with a prioritising and decision-making training procedure interposed between them. Peformance in both skills was found to be unrelated to intelligence but gain in performance was curvilinearly associated with intelligence in respect of both skills, with an inverted U shape for decision-making.

ASSESSMENT CENTRES

Assessment centres, described by Finkle (1976) as involving assessment in groups, assessment by groups, and the use of multiple techniques with emphasis on situational exercises, represent perhaps the most comprehensive and specific method for attempting to predict *managerial* performance. This emphasis on multiple techniques, multiple assessors and situational exercises is traced by Thornton and Byham (1982) back to the use of such techniques by the German military before 1941, the British War Office Selection Board after 1942, the UK

Civil Service Selection Board, and the US Office of Strategic Services. The first application of such techniques to the identification of industrial managerial potential was with the Management Progress study conducted at AT & T in 1956 (Bray and Howard, 1985).

The original purpose of the assessment centre was to identify potential for first-line supervision, especially where the position in question demands skills and qualities quite different from the position from which incumbents are usually recruited, and where the candidate is not in a position to demonstrate those skills on the job. Assessment centres have been used for many purposes, such as to aid in the selection of school administrators (Schmitt et al., 1984a), military officers (e.g. Tziner and Dolan, 1982; Borman, 1982; Herriott et al., 1985; Wingrove et al., 1985), to identify talent among women and minorities so as to facilitate affirmative action goals (e.g. Moses and Boehm, 1973; Huck and Bray, 1976; Ritchie and Moses, 1983), to identify talent more generally so as to influence management development programmes, training, job assignments, mentoring and career planning (e.g. Boehm, 1982; Boehm and Hoyle, 1977; Gratton, 1985) and to diagnose individual strengths and weaknesses so as to prepare detailed feedback and follow up with specific development plans (e.g. Boehm, 1982; Boehm and Hoyle, 1977; Gratton, 1985).

Typically, an assessment centre is developed through identifying its purpose (e.g. selection, identification, diagnosis), identifying the participants (e.g. by self-nomination, supervisor nomination, through screening by tests, biodata or interviews) and analysing the position under consideration through a systematic job analysis (or family of positions for more general 'identification' programmes). In this respect, it is interesting to compare US and UK practice. In the USA, job analyses of a standard kind seems to be used (e.g. interviews, checklists, critical incident workshops). In the UK repertory grid techniques are much favoured, following Kelly (1955). For example, the centres described by Gratton (1985), Dulewicz, Fletcher and Wood (1983) and Fletcher and Dulewicz (1984) used repertory grid techniques as part of the job analysis. Further details of the use of repertory grid techniques for this and other purposes can be found in Stewart and Stewart (1981), Smith and Stewart (1978) and Smith (1980).

The use of assessment centres in the United States is widespread, and survey research and informal reports suggest that their usage is increasing in the UK (Robertson and Makin, 1986; Bridges, 1984). A previous survey by Gill, Ungerson and Thakur (1973) found that 7 per cent of companies used assessment centres, while Bridges (1984) found that 19 per cent of UK companies used them, with 65 per cent of user organisations having begun to use them in the previous five years. Robertson and Makin (1986) reported that 21 per cent of companies used assessment centre-type exercises at least sometimes.

Most of the validity evidence for an assessment centre is positive (Muchinsky, 1986), with Schmitt et al. (1984b) reporting that assessment centre ratings have an average validity of 0.41, and Hunter and Hunter (1984) reporting a mean validity of 0.43. Hunter and Hirsch (1987) report similar results from a meta-analysis by Gaugler et al. (1986). Bray and Howard (1986) indicate that assessment centres can predict 25 years subsequently the level managers reach in their organisation (American Telephone and Telegraph Company) while similar long-term predictability has been reported in the UK for civil servants (Anstey 1977) and naval officers (Gardner and Williams, 1973).

Most of the published work has indicated that use of assessment centre technology does not adversely affect the hiring rate of minority groups. For example, Moses and Byham (1975) found that assessment centres were as predictive of subsequent managerial promotions for women as for men, using a sample of women evaluated in the Bell System programme between 1969 and 1971. The distribution of ratings was similar for men and women, as were the most predictive dimensions. Ritchie and Moses (1983) found that assessment centre predictions of over 1000 women managers were significantly related to career progress seven years later, and confirmed the similar rating distributions of potential for men and women managers and substantial similarities in the relationships between specific dimension ratings and progress for both men and women. Russell (1985) also showed that sex of the assessee had almost no impact on the way in which the overall assessment rating (OAR) is arrived at for the ten assessors studied in an entry selection centre. Huck and Bray (1976) found no significant differences in the correlations of overall assessment rating with criteria of overall job performance and potential for advancement with samples of black and white women. However, white females received significantly higher ratings for some dimensions and ratings of administrative skills and effective intelligence had higher relationships with job performance for whites, with sensitivity being more closely related to performance ratings for blacks.

In recent years doubts have been raised about the assessment centre paradigm. Assessment centres are time-consuming and expensive to run, requiring at least one or two days of both assessee and assessor time, travel and accommodation costs, training costs and clerical costs. They are of limited applicability, being unsuitable as a means of shortlisting candidates, and seem most useful for identifying individuals with managerial potential rather than for use in selection for clerical, professional or blue-collar jobs. Cascio and Sibley (1979), in a utility study, compared productivity gains from using assessment centres, multiple interviews and random selection. The results indicated that costs were relatively insignificant in comparison to monetary gains.

More damaging criticism has come over the interpretation of the validity evidence for the assessment centre. As Muchinsky (1986) points out, most assessees receive a single overall rating after enumeration of individual ratings across all of the multiple exercises, so that it is difficult to distil out how much of the variance in rating is due to each contributing source of information. Similarly, Robertson (1986) has noted that in many studies assessment centres are treated as if they were a single predictor, whereas in fact they incorporate several different predictors and they should be treated separately in validity assessments. Some studies have estimated the respective contributions made to the overall criterion score by the various *dimensions* (e.g. Moses and Boehm [1975] showed that leadership, decision-making and organising and planning showed the highest correlations with management level for both men and women, while Huck and Bray [1976] showed that the factors of administrative skills and effective intelligence, but not sensitivity, had higher correlations with job performance ratings for whites than for blacks). Schmitt *et al.* (1984a) also reported leadership, oral communications, organisational ability, decisiveness, judgement and problem analysis to correlate most highly with job performance. Other studies have examined the relative contributions of the *exercises*; for example, Tziner and Dolan (1982) found that the most valid predictors in an Israeli officer centre for women officers in terms of a training performance criterion were verbal intelligence scores, role play rating, leaderless group discussion rating and field command game rating. The situational exercises improved prediction beyond that of intelligence test score and accounted for a significant, unique portion of variance. Fletcher and Dulewicz (1984) found that psychometric tests made useful contributions but seemed less influential than the simulation exercises in the assessor's decisions. Borman (1982) in a study of the use of assessment centres for predicting military recruiter performance found that ratings for the oral presentation, parent interview, in-basket, and interviews provided the highest validities, with lower validities for structured interview ratings and pencil-and-paper test scores of personality and interests.

Difficulties with assessment centres emerge with the way attribute or dimension ratings are used to arrive at the overall assessment rating. The requirements of differentiating and integrating 15–25 pieces of information (dimensions) into an overall rating seem beyond assessors, with assessors' dimensional ratings being dominated by a single common underlying factor. Sackett and Hakel (1979) showed that only a few dimensions were required to predict most of the variance in the OAR for each assessor. Russell (1985) extended the work of Sackett and Hakel (1979) by examining facets of the decision processes used by 46 assessors in a centre used for the selection of entry-level managers. He found that assessors' perceptions were dominated by a single factor (generally either interpersonal or problem-solving skills). In addition a derived factor structure represented the concepts underlying the 18 dimensional ratings better than the prior category groupings. Assessor judgement processes did not appear to coincide with the centre designers' view of how the dimensional ratings grouped together or how assessors use the dimensional ratings to arrive at an OAR.

Further doubts have been cast on the group decision-making process typically used in assessment centres, when assessors, having observed participants, pool their observations and arrive at overall ratings. Both Borman (1982) and Tziner and Dolan (1982) found that a statistical composite of individual ratings or a mechanical aggregation of data produced a higher validity coefficient than clinical consensus judgements made after discussion. Sackett and Wilson (1982) showed that discussion changed the OAR only rarely. Wingrove *et al.* (1985) showed that the validity of the ratings was no higher after discussion than before in a UK naval officer assessment centre, using training performance as a criterion. What changes there were were explicable by common group influence processes. In addition, officer rank of the exception to the majority had some effect (Herriot *et al.*, 1985).

Some studies have been done on promotional decisions in managerial assessment. In a series of studies London and Stumpf (e.g. London and Stumpf, 1983; Stumpf and London 1981a,b; London and Stumpf, 1986) have used survey, interview and in-basket simulations to investigate management promotion decisions.

Other empirical work has cast doubt on the rationale behind assessment centre design and practice. Sackett and Dreher (1982) and Robertson *et al*. (1987) have demonstrated that within-exercise ratings of different dimensions correlate more closely with each other than do across exercise ratings of the same dimensions, suggesting that the main factors emerging represent exercises rather than dimensions.

Silverman *et al* . (1986) provide an empirical examination of the use of two different assessment centre methods in this context.

Robertson *et al*. (1987) relate their findings to work-sample tests and suggest focusing directly on exercises as work samples, with each exercise assessed by behaviourally-based rating scales. This suggestion is very similar to previous suggestions by Sackett and Dreher (1984), who argue in favour of identifying critical managerial roles though job analysis and designing exercises based on these roles. Zedeck and Cascio (1984) argue that rather than have 'dimension-driven' assessment centres, assessment centre dimensions be given a secondary role and centres be driven by tasks and behaviour representative of the managerial position. This also has the advantage of relating assessment centre design more closely to the role analysis offered by Mintzberg (1973), and related more specifically to level and function by Pavett and Lau (1980), Lau and Pavett (1983) and Paolillo (1987).

From the review of the nature of managerial work at various levels and within various functions reviewed earlier, it seems clear that many important managerial roles and behaviours are not being attended to in many present centres, especially where the focus is on more senior levels. The dimensions often used seem to represent fairly basic managerial skills and qualities appropriate to early career but less appropriate for senior levels where different roles and skills became important. In addition, given the studies relating managerial roles and skills to managerial function (e.g. Paolillo, 1987; Lau and Pavett, 1983; Pavett and Lau, 1980), greater consideration needs to be given to task analyses that reflect different divisional and functional responsibilities, with consequent variation. One way of thinking about this might be to use a strategy of 'targeted career development' (London, 1985) requiring a thorough job analysis at each target level so as to identify the particular skills, competencies and abilities required at each level.

Redesigning assessment centres on the basis of managerial roles and tasks would also allow the other benefits of assessment centres to be retained, such as the development of assessors' observational, evaluative and communication skills, a benefit often claimed for assessment centres (e.g. Thornton and Byham, 1982). One study which addresses these claims directly is by Lorenzo (1984) who showed that experienced assessors after three monthly training and assessor experience were more proficient in interviewing a source person to obtain relevant information, verbally presenting and defending information about other's managerial qualifications, and communicating this information in written reports. In addition, experienced assessors' ratings of video-taped ratees' managerial abilities displayed better psychometric properties. This study gives some support to the notion that participation in an assessment centre improves assessors' ability to acquire information and communicate it (though assessors seemed no more proficient in observing behaviour in this study).

The results concerning the psychometric properties of assessment centres (e.g. Sackett and Dreher, 1982) do not, of course, invalidate previous studies demonstrating the criterion-related, validity of assessment centres. Questions have, however, also been raised here (though most apply also to *any* method of managerial selection). As Muchinsky (1986) and Turnage and Muchinsky (1984) point out, there is much opportunity for criterion contamination, with knowledge of assessment centre performance biasing supervisor evaluations. Even in the few studies where the assessment centre decision has been withheld to examine the correlation with managerial success some years later (e.g. Huck and Bray, 1976; Bray, 1982), they point out that most criterion measures used in assessment centre research is of the 'status quo' variety (Klimoski and Strickland, 1977). Assessors, often knowledgeable about the types of people who succeed in their company in terms of background, personality, etc., may give higher evaluations to those who 'fit the mould'.

It does seem to be the case that assessment centre evaluations predict promotability and salary progression most accurately (Schmitt *et al.*, 1984). Turnage and Muchinsky (1984) in a study of industrial supervisors found that centre ratings were unrelated to ranked or rated performance, transfers, quits or discharges but were predictive of who got promoted—a finding similar to Klimoski and Strickland (1981). However, other criteria have also produced positive evidence for the predictive validity of assessment centres, e.g. training performance criterion used in military studies by Tziner and Dolan (1982) and Borman (1982), rated performance criterion used with school administrators by Schmitt *et al.* (1984a).

Sackett (e.g. Sackett, 1987; Sackett and Dreher, 1981; Dreher and Sackett, 1981) has also discussed issues with regard to content validity arguing that most approaches to content validity have focused on job analysis leading to exercise construction and dimension selection as the basis for determining content validity. He contends that content validity requires more than the careful construction of exercises (stimuli). He also claims that how the materials are presented and how responses to them are evaluated are also critical to any judgment of content validity. Dreher and Sackett (1981) claim that an assessment centre can be viewed as a sample, a measure of a candidate's current level of competence, or as a sign, a prediction of a candidate's potential for performance at some time in the future after subsequent training and experience; content validity is conceptually appropriate only when the centre is being used as a 'sample', so where centres are being used, for example, to select individuals for entry into an extensive training programme, they are being used as predictors of future performance, not as measures of current competence. Thus criterion-related validity, not content-related validity, is appropriate.

The variability in assessment centre practice noted by Sackett (1987) reinforces the point about the inadvisability of treating the assessment centre as a single predictor and the need to consider each predictor separately. Turnage and Muchinsky (1984) have also argued that it is doubtful if one can ever establish the 'true' relationship between assessment centre evaluation and job performance, given the multiple sources of criterion distortion often demonstrated. They also admit that psychometrically 'clean' evaluations of assessment centres may be impossible to obtain, and assessment centres may partially operate by raising individual's expectations and self-esteem on nomination, generating a self-fulfilling prophecy whereby candidates seek to perform both in assessment and on the job at a level substantiating this evaluation. This point raises the question of the 'impact' of assessment centre procedures, and indeed of selection techniques more generally, an area examined in Robertson *et al.* (1988) and discussed below.

Klimoski and Brickner (1987) contend that though assessment centres seem to make valid predictions of managerial success for a variety of purposes and in numerous contexts, it is not clearly established why this is so. They consider alternative explanations such as actual criterion contamination (the 'crown prince/kiss of death' phenomenon), subtle criterion contamination (e.g. Klimoski and Strickland, 1977), a self-fulfilling prophecy explanation (e.g. Turnage and Muchinsky, 1984) due to raised self-efficacy perceptions consequent on selection, performance or feedback (Schmitt *et al.*, 1986); a managerial intelligence explanation and a performance consistency explanation (whereby in practice judgements of traits are bypassed by assessors in favour of judgements of past performance as assessed through biodata or by interview or of present performance in managerial roles as assessed through exercises).

FUTURE-ORIENTED PREDICTORS

Recent research in personality (e.g. Bandura, 1986) and work motivation (Locke and Henne, 1986) indicates that work behaviour is to some extent predictable from intentions and expectations about future behaviour and competencies. However, few selection methods, except perhaps the interview, in a rather unsystematic way, explicitly focus on intentions, goals, expectancies and other future-oriented variables, so that research on future-oriented predictors is much less comprehensive.

One promising approach is the situational interview as developed by Latham and colleagues (Latham *et al.*, 1980; Latham and Saari, 1984; Schmitt and Ostroff, 1986) where candidates are asked about their intentions as to how they would behave in hypothetical job situations. These situations are derived from 'critical incidents' identifying behaviours critical to effective performance in an initial job analysis. Candidates' expressed intentions about their behaviour are then scored by comparisons with a scoring guide developed by job experts for evaluating responses, with illustrations provided of specific benchmarks. In a study of 49 hourly workers and 62 white male supervisors, Latham *et al.* (1980) reported good internal consistency, inter-rater reliability, and validity coefficients. Using peer and supervisor job performance evaluations as criteria, Latham and Saari (1984) showed significant correlations between what employees said they would do and what others observed them doing, but not between current performance and what they said they had done in the past. A correlation between interview performance and current job performance with new hires of 0.40 was also obtained with a small sample of 29.

Schmitt and Ostroff (1986) also used a situational interview as part of a strategy of developing selection tests operationalising the 'behavioural consistency' notion of Wernimont and Campbell (1968) with a sample of 43 emergency police telephone-operator applicants. A collection of critical incidents was translated into relevant interview questions in which job applicants were asked to indicate how they would behave in specific situations (translated into questions where job candidates could show some knowledge and experience). Schmitt and Ostroff (1986) evaluated the applicants on knowledge, skills and abilities generated through prior job analysis with the use of standardised BARS-type rating scales (Smith and Kendall, 1963). Content validity data is presented, but no concurrent or predictive validity data.

None of the above research has been on specifically managerial samples, and all has used small samples. A study by Robertson *et al*. (1988) of internal candidates for entry into a management development programme in a major UK clearing bank showed that a situational interview was reasonably well received, though not as well endorsed for accuracy or fairness or use for selection as most assessment centres studied within the same programme. Considerable differences emerged in the reaction of a group rejected for further tiering on the basis of their situational interview performance and one selected for further tiering and the two groups differed significantly on several other personal variable measures, particularly some measures of commitment to work.

REVIEW OF CURRENT APPROACHES

In general, it seems fairly clear that a set of techniques provides the best predictions of future work performance, namely ability tests, work samples, biodata, supervisor/peer ratings, and assessment centres. For managerial selection, the best method would seem to be the assessment centre, but if large numbers of external candidates are involved, a combination of biodata and ability tests might be more appropriate, at least as a pre-screening device. These methods have low cost and are easy to administer, though some concern exists over their fairness in terms of the probability that some adverse impact will occur. For the selection and placement of internal personnel, peer and supervisory evaluations have low costs, are easy to administer and have reasonably high validities if care is taken over the appropriate rating scales. Accomplishment records and situational interviews would seem to be promising techniques also for both internal and external candidates, especially given their apparently reasonable face validity and fairness (though for entry-level jobs such as management trainees it will be necessary to formulate protocols and interview questions to which inexperienced candidates can still respond in a meaningful way). If assessment centres were to be used in a genuinely diagnostic way, with a real impact on staff development, their use for internal candidates has added benefits over peer or supervisor ratings. In addition, assessment centres, given their high validity seem ideal for use at senior levels, where the value of successful performance warrants a heavy investment into the selection procedure, and appear also to be the technique with the highest face validity and user acceptability, and least adverse impact against women or racial minorities.

It is interesting to note that the ceiling for validity coefficients for a single predictor is approximately 0.5; while Hunter and Hunter (1984) have shown that by combining two specific, closely related predictors (mental ability and psychomotor ability) mean validity coefficients are increased by comparison with a single predictor. Little material is available on the relationships between various predictors, and therefore any possible gain in validity that might be achieved using several predictors is unclear (though this may be one reason for the high validity of assessment centres).

It is also interesting to note that strategies for designing selection methods seem to follow one of three basic procedures, and that methods with high validities can be found in all three categories. In one approach, typified by some biodata questionnaires, raw empiricism is used to identify biodata items linked to criterion success without regard for theoretical rationale. In another, behaviour is used as a *sign* to predict future performance, such as with psychometric tests, while in another, such as with work samples, behaviour is used as a *sample* to predict future performance with the predictor being as close to the criterion as possible (Wernimont and Campbell, 1968).

Latham and Saari (1984) believe that their situational interview produced significant validity because of adherence to the advice of Wernimont and Campbell (1968) to develop predictors that are realistic samples of job behaviour and as close to the criterion as possible through using job analysis to derive both observable behaviours as performance criteria and to derive interview questions. In addition, Hough (1984) attempted to follow a 'sample' approach to developing the accomplishment record, while assessment centre designers have recently been urged to adopt this approach (e.g. Sackett and Dreher, 1984; Herriot, 1986; Robertson *et al.*, 1987) instead of using exercises as vehicles for the observation of 'signs' or attributes/dimensions. Schmitt and Ostroff (1986) describe procedures designed specifically to operationalise the behavioural consistency approach advocated by Wernimont and Campbell (1968) through relying on consistencies between relevant dimensions of job behaviour and pre-employment samples obtained in simulated job exercises. It does appear that the development of predictors based on this approach has not only led to the generation of novel, and apparently valid, predictors (e.g. situational interview, accomplishment record) and established predictors that are highly valid (e.g. assessment centres, work-sample tests) but has also generated predictors that have high face validity and user acceptability (e.g. work samples, assessment centres), minimal adverse impact on women or racial minorities (the evidence is clearest for work-sample tests and assessment centres, but promising for situational interviews and accomplishment records) and perhaps minimal damaging psychological impact. The justifiable enthusiasm for job-sample exercises of various kinds should not deflect attention from the value of using biodata or ability tests of similarly high validity and lower cost, though it is clear that costs in terms of face validity and user acceptability, and perhaps impact and fairness, will be incurred using these methods, suggesting that they are much less appropriate for internal candidates and need careful monitoring for use with external candidates.

NON-STANDARD PREDICTOR—CRITERIA RELATIONSHIPS

Selecting Managers to Fit Business Strategies

There has been recent interest, but little in the way of empirical research, in the concept of matching managers, in terms of skills, background and personal attributes, to strategies (e.g. Szilagyi and Schweiger, 1984; Herbert and Deresky, 1986). With the growth of interest in 'strategic human resource management' (e.g. Devanna et al., 1981; Fombrun et al., 1984; Hall and Goodale, 1986; Sparrow and Pettigrew, 1986) has come an interest in 'strategic staffing', including the linkage of staffing policies to business strategies by means of matching managerial qualities to job requirements.

In theory this 'matching' strategy should involve a thorough job analysis of what is involved in implementing a particular strategy, but there is often a lack of specificity in translating the generic strategies into relevant behaviours. Miles and Snow (1978) formulated four global strategies associated with different degrees of domain defence or expansion, while Porter (1980) emphasised three generic strategies. Leontiades (1980; 1982) identified various steady-state or evolutionary strategies associated with various growth stages of the business. Specific job requirements, in terms of what activities are actually involved in implementing a particular strategy, are often lacking. Similarly, the conceptual base for many of these general strategic models, the product life-cycle conceptualisation, has come into question, as has the evidence linking strategic choice to organisational performance (Szilagyi and Schweiger, 1984). Similar lack of clarity exists about the translation of strategic choice or job requirements into managerial skills or personal characteristics. Often this translation is left at the level of managerial function, such as the assertion that 'prospector' or growth/expansion strategies will be best implemented by managers with a marketing or R & D background, whereas finance managers or accountants might best implement more defensive or steady-state strategies (e.g. Miles and Snow, 1978). Or else assertions are made at the level of personality attributes rather than behavioural skills, often cast in the form of 'managerial prototypes'. For example, Wisserma et al. (1980) sought to establish links between strategies based on product life-cycle to leadership styles and also asserted links to personal characteristics but with little empirical evidence. Leontiades (1980; 1982) also identified managerial prototypes associated with growth stages, but with little specificity in terms of skills or behaviours. What empirical research there is, such as that of Gupta and Govindarajan (1982; 1984), has also tended to focus on personality characteristics, finding that strategic business unit strategy implementation was related to tolerance for ambiguity, or that locus of control was related to strategic decision making (Miller, De Vries and Touleuse, 1982).

Szilagyi and Schweiger (1984) argue that the benefits of appropriate managerial selection in facilitating the implementation of particular strategies have yet to be empirically determined, and that this will involve the identification and evaluation of key job requirements and their translation into critical managerial skills, knowledge and behaviours, perhaps with the use of assessment centre technology. The kinds of skill and knowledge they feel will be worth investigating are still left at a rather general level. The authors also stress the importance of considering wider organisational contingencies relating to structure, culture, power, etc. Other areas not mentioned by the authors but probably worthy of empirical investigation would include 'cognitive style' (see below).

Ten Dam (1986) also speculates, on the basis of a literature review and his consulting experience, on how to identify 'strategic mentality' (defined as the ability to think, decide and act strategically) and assess it for the purposes of assigning candidates to management positions. One empirical attempt to assess 'helicopter ability' through assessment centre technology, is described by Fletcher and Dulewicz (1984). A study by Herbert and Derelsky (1986) goes some way to relate generic strategy to role content, finding that each strategy was related to a particular pattern of roles and activities. However the authors fail to distinguish between 'successful' and 'unsuccessful' strategy implementers.

Assessing Managers for Intrapreneurialism/Entrepreneurialism

This position of theoretical interest combined with a lack of empirical evidence also characterises much of the recent interest in 'intrapreneurialism' or corporate internal entrepreneurialism (e.g. Pinchot, 1985; de Chambeau and McKenzie, 1986). Most of the empirical research on entrepreneurs and entrepreneurialism, as well as often failing to distinguish between 'successful' and 'unsuccessful' entrepreneurs, or between entrepreneurs and small business people, has focused on personality characteristics. A variety of such characteristics, usually measured by personality inventories have been identified, (e.g. Hull, Bosley and Udell, 1980; Sexton and Bowman, 1984; Harris, 1985; 1986; Smith and Miner, 1985). A more recent and thorough study of aspiring entrepreneurs using interviews and psychometric scales by Cromie (1987) showed that both male and female UK entrepreneurs were motivated by autonomy, achievement and job satisfaction, and both scored high on need for achievement and internal locus of control. Women were less motivated by money and more by career dissatisfaction and a wish to combine career and child rearing. Based on his organisational experience, Maxon (1986) argues that innovators, entrepreneurs and intrapreneurs have different profiles on the Myers–Briggs Type Indicator (MBTI) (Myers, 1962).

Indicators of Cognitive Style

Robertson (1985) has reviewed evidence on individual differences in information processing strategies adopted by people in problem solving and decision making activities. A variety of cognitive style dimensions have been identified, such as the field-dependence/field independence dimension of Witkin (1976), the work of Guilford on convergent and divergent thinking (Guilford, 1967), that of Kagan on reflective-impulsive styles (Kagan et al., 1964) and the work of Driver and his colleagues (Driver and Rowe, 1979).

A link between modes of thinking and brain activity has been made by Mintzberg (1976) and Taggart and Robey (1981) specifically in the context of managerial thinking and decision-making, but it is not yet clear whether brain functioning can be related to cognitive strategy in any straightforward way.

Mintzberg (1976) contended that a fundamental difference might exist between formal managerial planning and informal managing, with each category associated with left and right hemisphere processes. Effective managers are seen to revel in ambiguity, disorder and complexity, in contrast to formal strategic planners, a theme later taken up by Peters and Waterman (1982) in their study of 'excellent' companies. Taggart and Robey (1981) present a model of dual information processing as a way to understand managerial decision styles, drawing on neurological evidence, Eastern philosophy and, importantly, Jung's typology of personality (Jung, 1971), operationalised using the Myers–Briggs Type Inventory (MBTI, Myers, 1962). The implication is that successful management depends on the use of a full range of processing skills, involving both left hemisphere (verbal and analytical) processes and right hemisphere (spatial and intuitive) processes.

Schweiger (1983) takes issue with several of the points made by Robey and Taggart (1981) with regard particularly to the development of various instruments purporting to measure 'managerial cognitive style'.

Much recent work, and much consulting practice especially in the UK, seems to make use of the MBTI (Maxon, 1986; Church and Alie, 1986; Martin and Bartol, 1986; Berry, 1986; Gratton, 1987). For example, Gratton (1987) quotes evidence that managers frequently exhibit an ESTJ profile whereas research scientists frequently exhibit an INTP profile, managers being more extraverted and interested in facts rather than possibilities, and oriented towards thinking rather than feeling, and sensing rather than intuition. Church and Alie (1986) attempted to explore relationships between managers' personality characteristics and their management levels and job foci, finding, for example, that middle managers prefered sensing but upper managers intuition. It would seem useful to conduct further research on managerial effectiveness using the MBTI as a predictor, as conceivably managers may be most effective if their cognitive styles match job requirements.

Mullen and Stumpf (1987), on the basis of interview observations of large numbers of executives and business students participating in two behavioural simulations, identified two informational processing styles related to how managers chose to attend and to interpret information relating to strategic issues. Mullen and Stumpf (1987) relate these styles to personality type and vocational preference, and to the cognitive styles identified by the MBTI. The authors claim that general managers' positions seemed dominated by convergers, but argue also for involving evolvers and searchers in strategic management through specific recruitment and selection. They also argue that further research is needed to identify the most effective styles, whether different styles are more effective in particular situations, and whether managers can alter their predominant style.

Another theory—and measure—of cognitive style used widely in organisational research is the Adaption–Innovation theory of Kirton (1976) and the Kirton Adaption–Innovation Inventory (KAI), a 32-item, self-report inventory. Kirton (1984) cites evidence that entrepreneurs score more highly on 'innovativeness' than government employees, and Foxall (1986) showed that marketing and engineering managers scored more innovatively than production operations and accounting/finance managers, though with specific subgroups being identified within the engineering group. Kirton and McCarthy (1987) argue that the identification of similarities in preferred ways of working and their associated personality characteristics constitutes a 'cognitive climate' within occupational groups and organizations, with implications for stress, turnover and job satisfaction. They also argue that cognitive styles as measured by the KAI might be identified as part of the selection process, in terms of building work teams which include a variety of problem-solving styles. However, it is not clear that the KAI in fact measures style, rather than level, of creativity. Goldsmith and Matherly (1987) report that KAI scores correlate significantly with Torrance's Creative Motivation scale (Torrance, 1971) and Smith and Schaeger's (1969) Creativity Scale, which are regarded as measures of level of creative ability. Alternatively, it may be that tests purporting to measure level of creativity in fact measure creative style.

Another approach to information processing styles which has been specifically related to managerial decision-making is that of Driver and Streufert (e.g. Driver and Rowe, 1979; Streufert and Swezy, 1986). Streufert and Swezy (1986) review research on complexity theory, with complex subjects searching for more different kinds of information when faced with a decision problem and being less certain after they had made a decision. Complex subjects seemed better able to plan and engage in more strategic actions, especially at optimal environmental load levels, with higher levels of strategic planning performance being a linear function of the proportion of cognitively complex persons in a decision-making group. Later research has related cognitive complexity to communication, leadership information orientation, perception and job performance in applied problem-solving tasks in some task environments (Streufert and Swezy, 1986). Much of this work has clear implications for management selection. Streufert and Swezy (1986) also extend, more speculatively, complexity theory to the information-processing characteristics of the organisation itself, as well as to the information processing of organisational personnel.

Assessing Managers for Team Roles

Some recent interest, especially in the UK, has been shown in matching not just specific job tasks but team roles to personality characteristics of managers (Mabey and Hunter, 1986). This is often based on the analysis of work teams and the attributes required by team members to optimise team performance by Belbin (1981), who has identified eight team roles for optimum performance. Much of this work is promising, but formal validation, rather than the informal 'face validity' reported from training cases and consultancy experience, needs to be done. Other promising predictors for team role success would seem to be 'cognitive style' as identified by Mullen and Stumpf (1987), or assessed through the KAI (Kirton, 1984) or MBTI (Church and Alie, 1986).

Assessing Managers for Expatriate Assignments

Most of this literature is very general and prescriptive, focused mainly at the level of personality traits, with many of the managerial qualities cited as necessary for expatriate success being useful qualities for managers generally, such as zeal for work, alertness, foresight, flexibility, empathy (e.g. Baligra and Baker, 1985). Heyes (1974) surveyed the opinions of expatriate executives for success factors. Miller (1977) examined expatriate US executives perceptions of successful, higher-level expatriate managers.

Since one third of expatriate managers resign prematurely, research in this area is likely to have significant pay-offs. Brown (1987) reports on the Overseas Assignment Inventory (OAI) developed by Moron, Stath and Beger Inc. to identify individuals better able to cope with overseas assignments. (A 71-item questionnaire, assessing expectations, attitudes, attributes and motivations empirically demonstrated to be related to successful overseas adjustment.)

Social Processes in Managerial Selection and Assessment

There has been increasing emphasis on the two-way, negotiable nature of recruitment and selection decisions (e.g. de Wolff and van den Bosch, 1984; Herriot, 1985; 1986b; 1987) and increasing realisation that social processes in recruitment, assessment and selection are not most appropriately treated as distorting intrusions which cause bias, and decrease reliability and validity (Herriott, 1987) but rather that selection *is itself* a social process. There has also been increasing recognition of selection and assessment procedures as interventions into peoples' lives and careers not as socially, or psychologically neutral processes (Robertson *et al.*, 1988).

One area of interest has been the effects of organisational recruitment practices on applicants' perceptions and decisions, recruitment practices being of interest as the initial episode in the developing relationship between the individual and the organisation (Herriot, 1988). Each party is seen by Herriott as having expectations regarding behaviour during the selection procedure itself.

Herriott and Rothwell (1981) found that career information issued by organisations to engineering students had an impact on candidates intentions to apply; while Quaglieri (1982) found with a sample of business graduates in trainee management and accountancy jobs that informal sources of job information and referral were perceived as providing more specific and accurate job information. (This was confirmed in a study by Breaugh and Mann [1984] of social service workers, in that employee referrals had more realistic job expectations and longer tenure than those recruited through direct applications or newspaper advertisements.)

There have also been studies of candidates' reactions to interview procedures in recruitment and selection. For example, Schmitt and Coyle (1976) found applicants' perceptions of recruitment practices, in particular perceptions of the interviewer's personality, manner and adequacy of job information presented, predicted the applicants' acceptance of a job offer. Glueck (1973) found that for one-third of a student sample, recruiter behaviour acted as a major reason for selecting a particular employer. Using two experimental investigations with student subjects and using simulated recruitment interviews, Rynes and Miller (1983) showed that recruiter behaviour was consistently interpreted as a signal regarding chances of a job offer, while job attributes exerted a clear influence on perceived job desirability. Powell (1984) found through path analysis with 200 graduating college students that perceived job attributes but not perceived recruiter behaviour determined the probability of accepting a job offer. Harn and Thornton (1985) however, in a study of graduating college students following employment interviews at a college placement centre, found that three factors—non-directive counselling behaviours, listening skills and interpersonal sensitivity—were related to perceived recruiter warmth and thoughtfulness, whilst listening skill was related to applicant willingness to accept a job offer. This relationship was moderated by the degree to which the applicant saw the recruiter as a representative of the organisation (see also Keenan and Wedderburn, 1980; Liden and Parsons, 1986; Taylor and Bergmann, 1987). The impact of recruitment activities in post-employment reactions has been less well examined, though the realistic job preview literature indicates a significant effect on tenure and retention (Premack and Wanous, 1985), and Taylor and Bergmann (1987) also believe it may affect the speed with which new employees adapt to the organisation.

Other studies have examined applicant reactions to other aspects of the recruitment and selection process. Those of particular relevance to managerial selection and assessment include work on assessment centres (e.g. Teel and DuBois, 1983; Dulewicz, Fletcher and Wood, 1983; Dodd, 1987; Robertson et al., 1988), biodata and situational interviews (Robertson et al., 1988). There are some signs that applicants prefer selection devices which sample behaviour and ensure behavioural consistency between predictor and criterion (e.g. assessment centres, work samples, possibly situational interviews) over paper-and-pencil tests used as 'signs' of potential (e.g. ability tests, biodata). Applicants may believe their privacy invaded if they perceive themselves to have no control over how it will be used (Fusilier and Moyer, 1980). It seems, overall, that candidates will be more satisfied with a selection procedure, and more likely to accept it, if recruiters provide useful job information, behave warmly and sympathetically towards them in any selection encounter, and use selection procedures with face validity, and possibly lower adverse impact on minorities also (Herriot, 1987). This may well impact on subsequent job behaviour, satisfaction and tenure. Fo example, Wanous (1976) showed that business school students changed their expectations held before entering an organisation by a lowering of their expectations of intrinsic rewards. The meta-analytic review of twenty studies of realistic job previews by Premack and Wanous (1985) supports the effects of realistic job previews in lowering applicant expectations, increasing the probability of self-selecting out before entry, decreasing turnover, and increasing commitment, job satisfaction and performance.

Perhaps more research has been done on candidate reactions to assessment centres than to any other selection method. Thornton and Byham (1982) suggested that applicant reactions should be investigated in the short, medium and long term; for example, reactions in terms of stress, self-esteem, motivation and career development. Nirtaut (1977) surveyed organisations concerning assessment centre reactions and possible adverse effects on candidates, concluding that no company reported negative reactions from candidates and few adverse effects (some companies reported discouragement from low performers, and the mismatch between high scorers' promotion expectations and limited opportunities also sometimes caused problems). Early research by Kraut (1972) and Bourgeois *et al.* (1975) also suggested that participants' reactions to assessment centres are favourable, with such centres having high face validity, high acceptability, providing useful feedback and enabling participants to obtain a realistic view of their strengths and weaknesses. Dodd (1977) has reviewed many such studies generally indicating positive reactions and overall endorsements, especially its use for developmental purposes. Data collected on the basis of a standardised questionnaire suggested by Dodd (1977) have more recently confirmed this general picture (Dulewicz, Fletcher and Wood, 1983), though interestingly Teel and Dubois (1983) found that if their small sample was subdivided into high and low scorers, then high scorers were more generally positive in their view of assessment centres, with low scorers tending to rate centre accuracy and fairness more negatively. High scorers were more likely to claim perceived career benefits, pointing to possible demoralising effects on low scorers.

Robertson *et al.* (1988) have carried out a much larger-scale study of candidates' reactions to three assessment centres used for internal tiering purposes in a major UK clearing bank, confirming many of the findings of Teel and DuBois (1983) in that, in general, such centres were well received, in terms of perceived fairness, accuracy, usefulness and developmental value, but high scorers selected for further tiering were generally more positive in their endorsements, especially over the centre's value for selection rather than for career development or training-needs identification. However, unlike Teel and DuBois (1983), little difference was noted between groups over perceptions of behaviour in the centre being like 'real life'. Interesting differences emerged between candidates' reactions to different centres, in that in general candidates rejected for tiering at senior levels saw their particular centre more negatively than those rejected at lower levels.

IMPACT ON CANDIDATES

Thornton and Byham (1982) have raised questions as to the impact of assessment centres on candidates' self-esteem, motivation, morale and work commitment, but little definitive research evidence exists. Until recently it has not been viewed as a major dimension by which to judge selection techniques. Both Thornton and Byham (1982) and Dreher and Sackett (1983) focus on the potential consequences of rejection decisions for the individual job-seeker, the organisation and society as a whole.

Few studies however have gone beyond a study of candidate reactions to examine the impact of assessment centre reactions on candidates. Schmitt, Ford and Shultz (1986) showed that changes in self-perceived ability were related to performance in particular assessment centre exercises, even in the absence of performance feedback, suggesting that 'self-assessment' plays a significant role in assessment centre participation. Noe and Steffy (1987), pointing out that the impact of assessment centre evaluation on subsequent career behaviour and job attitudes has been little studied, produced evidence on assessment centre evaluations, attitudes towards the assessment centre process, job involvement, career exploration and career planning. The evaluation appeared to have an impact on individuals' motivation to experiment with managerial skills and seek further work experiences and job and career-related information, perhaps due to its acting as a realistic job preview (Wanous, 1980).

Robertson *et al.* (1988) studied candidates' exposure to an assessment centre, as well as to biodata and situational interview selection methods, with three groups of individual variables, namely work commitment (e.g. work and job involvement, career and organisational commitment), psychological well-being (e.g. self-esteem, mental health) and personal agency (e.g. self-efficacy, locus of control) with results suggesting an 'impact' effect, especially on those variables grouped under 'work commitment'.

CONCLUSIONS

Managerial performance can be seen as a function of the person, the situation, and the interaction between the two. This interactionist view of human behaviour is best represented in Social Learning Theory (Bandura, 1986). Personnel selection methods are means of identifying appropriate people, and information about the person can be derived from the past present or future, with most predictors employing information derived from the past or the present. The joint influence, of personal characteristics and situational factors, is also apparent in different approaches to personnel selection. Some approaches attempt to examine directly personal qualities of ability, motivation or personality, such as tests of cognitive ability or personality; others involve placing the person in a situation that simulates the job for which he or she is being assessed, such as work-sample tests. Other approaches, such as biodata, cannot be so neatly classified—for instance, pure biodata items generate information about the person, but other biodata approaches also incorporate situational considerations by more directly sampling relevant work behaviour, as in the 'accomplishment record' (Hough, 1984).

In terms of what personal qualities seem useful predictors of managerial performance, most of the evidence indicates the importance of cognitive ability and analytical reasoning skills (Schmitt *et al.*, 1984; Hunter and Hunter, 1984; Klimoski and Brickner, 1987) with some evidence that a straightforward linear relationship between cognitive ability and performance should not be expected (Muchinsky, 1986). It is clear, however, that other personal characteristics, such as personality and motivational variables, attitudes, intentions and expectancies, are also important in managerial work.

Sample-based approaches to predicting performance, such as work-sample tests or assessment centres, attempt to place people in job-relevant situations and assess their performance. Such approaches are limited by the nature of the sample selected, which creates particular problems in the case of managerial work, given its wide variation in scope and discretion and its dynamic and evolving nature (Stewart, 1982). Many assessment centre-type exercises, for instance, have focused on simulating the work of lower- or middle-level managers, and have not fully captured the range and importance of tasks and skills appropriate even to these levels.

There appears to be a parodox in analyses of managerial performance and selection in that the meta-analysis studies of Hunter and Hunter (1984) and

Schmitt *et al.* (1984) appear to show that managerial jobs are broadly similar and that the validities of at least some of our methods of personnel selection are much the same regardless of the specific job. Perhaps this is due to the common influence on both predictor and criterion measures of cognitive ability. On the other hand the analysis of managerial work by level and function, and most people's experience suggests that organizations feel that they have distinctive requirements for prospective managers (Herriot, 1986a).

The assessment centre, work sample and situational interview are processes which ensure that content validity considerations are at least attended to in the generation of work samples, and 'sampling' approaches to predicting work performance also appear not only to have high validity but, in comparison to 'sign' approaches, less adverse impact on minority groups and more favourable applicant reactions, with some evidence of less malignant psychological impact. In addition, they appear to provide a better basis for counselling and developmental feedback, particularly useful for internal candidates. In addition to considerations of cost, questions of applicability may place limits to their usefulness in their narrow focus on the work sample. The dynamic nature of managerial work may make it difficult to predict performance in *future* jobs which are difficult to sample adequately; the less knowledge one has of the target position, the less adequately can a work sample be generated.

Since this is an international review, it is interesting to compare national differences in research interests and selection practices. It is interesting to note that there seem to be variations in the usage of predictors in different countries. For example, graphology appears to be more widely used in Israel (Caspi, 1988) and Continental Europe than in the UK or the USA. US research has tended to focus on the prediction of job performance, productivity questions and, under the impact of federal legislation, on questions of fairness and adverse impact on minority groups and women. This legislative impetus, which has led in part to a renewed interest in job analysis, content validity, and the devising of novel approaches to personnel selection such as the situational interview and the accomplishment record, has been less evident in European contexts. In addition US research interest has had a relatively narrow focus on a limited range of criteria and on economic benefit to the employing organisation. In UK and Continental Europe however, greater interest has been shown in selection research in questions of job satisfaction, psychological impact, psychological well-being, mutual decision making, and the social nature of the selection process as a whole (e.g. Holloway, 1984; de Wolff and van den Bosch, 1984). This interest has led to a greater interest in social psychological theory. In general, perhaps, the field could benefit from greater integration with psychological theorising in other areas of psychology which could increase our knowledge of how certain predictors work. For example, understanding of cognitive ability tests and tests of cognitive style might benefit from greater familiarity with the literature on cognitive processes, while our understanding of assessment centres could benefit from greater integration with theory and research on group processes, person perception and cognitive information processing.

The person–situation perspective mentioned above helps focus attention on the important role played by other people in managerial jobs, since most managerial work is carried out with and through other people. Significant 'others' in a managers' job situation include peers, bosses and subordinates, and the recent interest in the assessment of people for work-team roles and in boss–subordinate matches (e.g. Mabey and Hunter, 1986) is to be welcomed, especially as research by Wakabayashi and Graen (1984) has shown the importance of leader–subordinate dyadic exchanges for managerial success.

This importance of dyadic relationships has been shown in recent British work on the different role relationships of 'chairman' and general managers in the National Health Service (Stewart, 1987) which show that though the two roles are dependent on each other, the amount of role-sharing and the type of relationship identified (executive, partner, mentor, consultant, distant) vary widely. As well as re-emphasising the elements of choice present in managerial jobs and the potential scope and variety in a managerial role, this study focuses on the important influence of the 'chairman' role on general managerial job performance and success. More generally, it directs attention to the importance of dyadic relationships in managerial work, to social processes of role-making and role-shaping in determining managerial job performance, to the extent of choice and flexibility in managerial jobs, and to the importance of other people in a managers' job situation. It is our contention that selection and assessment research, focusing on managers, has not given sufficient consideration to such issues.

REFERENCES

Allan, P. (1981) Managers at work: a large-scale study of the managerial job in New York City government. *Academy of Management Journal*, **24**, 613–619.

Anderson, C. R. (1984) *Management: Skills functions and organisational performance.* Dubuque, IA: WM C Brown.

Anderson, N. and Shackleton, V. (1986) Recruitment and selection: A review of developments in the 1980s. *Personnel Review*, **15**, 19–26.

Anstey, E. (1977) A 30-year follow-up of the CSSB procedures with lessons for the future. *Journal of Occupational Psychology*, **50**, 149–159.

Argyris, C. (1960) *Understanding Organizational Behavior*. Homewood, Ill.: Dorsey.

Arvey, R. D. (1979) Unfair discrimination in the employment interview: legal and psychological aspects. *Psychological Bulletin*, **86**, 736–765.

Arvey, R. D. and Campion, J. E. (1982) The employment interview: a summary and review of recent literature. *Personnel Psychology*, **35**, 281–322.

Arvey, R. D., Miller, H. E., Gould, R. and Burch, P. (1987) Interview validity for selecting sales clerks. *Personnel Psychology*, **40**, 1–12.

Asher, J. J. (1972) The biographical item: can it be improved? *Personnel Psychology*, **25**, 251–269.

Baliga, G. M. and Baker, J. C. (1985) Multinational corporate policies for expatriate managers: selection, training, evaluation. *SAM Advanced Management Journal*, **504**, 31–38.

Bandura, A. (1986) *Social Foundations of Thought and Action*. Englewood Cliffs, N J: Prentice-Hall.

Barclay, L. (1982) Social learning theory: A framework for discrimination research. *Academy of Management Review*, **7**, 587–594.

Barling, J. and Beattie, R. (1983) Self-efficacy beliefs and sales performance. *Journal of Organizational Behavior Management*, **5**, 41–51.

Barrett, G. V., Caldwell, M. S. and Alexander, R. A. (1985) The concept of dynamic criteria: a critical reanalysis. *Personnel Psychology*, **38**, 41–56.
Bass, B. M. (1962) Further evidence on the dynamic character of criteria. *Personnel Psychology*, **15**, 93–97.
Bass, B. (1985) *Leadership and Performance Beyond Expectations*. New York: Free Press.
Baxter, J. C. Brock, B., Hill, P. C. and Rozelle, R. M. (1981) Letters of recommendation. A question of value. *Journal of Applied Psychology*, **66**, 296–301.
Beason, G. and Bolt, J. A. (1976) Verifying applicants' backgrounds. *Personnel Journal*, **55**, 345–8.
Belbin R. M. (1981) *Management Teams*. London: Heinemann.
Bentz, U. J. (1984) Explorations in executive behaviour. Paper presented in symposium titled 'Back to the Basics: Describing leaders' at 92nd annual meeting of the American Psychological Association, Toronto, Ontario.
Berlew, D. and Hall, P. (1966) The socialisation of managers: effects of expectations on performance. *Administrative Science Quarterly*, **11**, 207–223.
Bernardin, H. J. and Bownas, P. (1984) *Personality Assessment in Organisations*. New York: Praeger.
Bernardin, H. J. and Buckley, M. R. (1981) Strategies in rater training. *Academy of Management Review*, **6**, 205–212.
Berry, M. (1986) Organisation development. *Training Officer*. November, 326–329.
Boehm, V. R. (1981) What do managers really do? Paper to annual meeting of the AACSB Graduate Admissions Council, Toronto.
Boehm, V. R. (1982) Assessment centres and management development. In K. Rowland and G. Ferris (eds) *Personnel Management*. London: JAI Press.
Boehm, V. R. and Hoyle, D. F. (1977) Assessment and management development. In J. Moses and W. C. Byham, (eds) *Applying the Assessment Center Method*. Elmsford. New York: Pergamon.
Borman, W. C. (1982) Validity of behavioral assessment for predicting military recruiter performance. *Journal of Applied Psychology*, **67**, 3–9.
Boyatzis, R. R. (1982) *The Competent Manager: A Model for Effective Performance*. New York: John Wiley.
Bray, D. W., Campbell, R. J. and Grant, P. L. (1974) *Formative Years in Business: A long term AT and T study of managerial lives*. New York: John Wiley.
Bray, D. and Howard, A. (1986) Managerial lives in transition: Advancing age and changing times (forthcoming).
Breaugh, J. A. and Mann, R. B. (1984) Recruiting source effects: a test of two alternative explanations. *Journal of Occupational Psychology*, **57**, 261–267.
Bridges, A. (1984) Assessment centres: Their use in industry in Great Britain. Unpublished MSc dissertation. Department of Management Sciences, UMIST.
Brown, R. (1987) How to choose the best expatriates. *Personnel Management*, June, 67.
Bruner, J. S., Goodnow, J. and Austin, G. A. (1956) *A Study of Thinking*. New York: John Wiley.
Caldwell, D. F. and Spivey, W. A. (1983) The relationship between recruiting source and employee success: an analysis by race. *Personnel Psychology*, **36**, 67–72.
Carlson, S. (1951) *Executive Behaviour*. Stockholm: Strombergs.
Carroll, S. J. and Gillen, D. J. (1987) Are the classical management functions useful in describing managerial work? *Academy of Management Review*, **1**, 38–51.
Carroll, S. J. and Nash, A. N. (1972) Effectiveness of a forced choice reference check. *Personnel Administration*, **35**, 42–46.
Caspi, A. (1987) *Personal communication*.
Cascio, W. F. and Philips, N. F. (1979) Performance testing: a rose among thorns? *Personnel Psychology*, **32**, 751–766.

Cascio, W. F. and Sibley, V. (1979) The utility of the assessment center as a selection device. *Journal of Applied Psychology*, **64**, 107–118.

Cattell, R. B. and Eber, H. W. (1962) *Manual for the Sixteen Personality Factor Questionnaire*. NFER Publishing.

Cederblom, D. and Lounsbury, J. W. (1980) An investigation of user acceptance of peer evaluation. *Personnel Psychology*, **33**, 567–579.

Childs, A. and Klimoski, R. J. (1986) Successfully predicting career success: An application of the biographical inventory. *Journal of Applied Psychology*, **71**, 3–8.

Church, L. M. and Alie, R. E. (1986) Relationships between managers' personality characteristics and their management levels and job foci. *Akron Business and Economic Review*, **17**, 29–45.

Cornelius, E. T. III (1983) The use of projective techniques in personnel selection. In K. Rowland and G. R. Ferris, (eds) *Research in Personnel and Human Resources Management*, Vol 1. Greenwich CT: JAI Press.

Cornelius, E. T. III and Lane, F. B. (1984) The power motive and managerial success in a professionally oriented service industry organisation. *Journal of Applied Psychology*, **69**, 32–39.

Cromie, S. (1987) Motivations of aspiring male and female entrepreneurs. *Journal of Occupational Behaviour*, **8**, 251–261.

Deal, T. E. and Kennedy, A. A. (1982) *Corporate Cultures*, Reading, Mass.: Addison-Wesley.

De Chambeau, F., Fanbrun, C. and McKenzie, F. (1986) Intapreneurship. *Personnel Journal*, July.

Devanna, M. A. and Tichy, N. (1981) Human resources management: a strategic perspective. *Organisational Dynamics*, Winter, 51–67.

De Wolff, C. J. and van den Bosch, G. (1984) Personnel selection. In P. J. D. Dreath, H. Thierry, P. J. Willems and C. J. de Wolff (eds) *Handbook of Work and Organisational Psychology*, Vol 1. Chichester: John Wiley.

Dipboye, R. L. and Wiley, J. W. (1977) Reactions of college recruiters to interviewee sex and self-presentation style. *Journal of Vocational Behaviour*, **10**, 1–12.

Dickinson, T. L. (1987) Designs for evaluating the validity and accuracy of performance ratings. *Organizational Behavior and Human Decision Processes*, **40**, 1–21.

Dodd, W. E. (1977) Attitudes towards assessment center programs. In J. L. Moses and W. C. Byham (eds) *Applying the Assessment Center Method*. New York: Pergamon.

Downs, S., Farr, R. M. and Colbeck, L. (1978) Self-appraisal: a convergence of selection and guidance. *Journal of Occupational Psychology*, **51**, 271–278.

Drakeley, R. J., Herriot, P. and Jones, A. (1988) Biographical data, training success, and turnover. *Journal of Occupational Psychology* (in press).

Dreher, G. F. and Sackett, P. R. (1983) *Perspectives on Employee Staffing and Selection: Readings and Commentary*. Irwin.

Driver, M. and Rowe, A. J. (1979) Decision-making styles: a new approach to management decision making. In C. L. Cooper (ed.) *Behavioural Problems in Organisations*. Englewood Cliffs, N.J.: Prentice-Hall.

Drucker, P. (1974) *Management: Tasks, Responsibilities, Practices*. New York: Harper and Row.

Dulewicz, V., Fletcher, C. and Wood, P. (1983) A study of the internal validity of an assessment centre and of participants' background characteristics and attitudes: A comparison of British and American findings. *Journal of Assessment Center Technology*, **6**, 15–24.

Dunnette, M. D. (1966) *Personnel Selection and Placement*. Belmont, CA: Wadsworth.

Dunnette, M. D. (1963) A modified model for rest validation and selection research. *Journal of Applied Psychology*, **47**, 317–332.

Edinger, J. A. and Patterson, M. L. (1983) Nonverbal involvement and social control. *Psychological Bulletin*, **93**, 30–56.

Elliott, A. G. P. (1984) Sex and decision-making in the selection interview: a real life study. *Journal of Occupational Psychology*, **54**, 265–273.

Fanbrun, C., Tichy, N. M. and Devanna, M. A. (1984) *Strategic Human Resource Management*. New York: John Wiley.

Fayol, H. (1949) *General and Industrial Management* (trans. C Stars) London: Pitman.

Feldman, J. M. (1981) Beyond attibution theory: cognitive processes in performance appraisals. *Journal of Applied Psychology*, **66**, 127–148.

Finkle, R. B. (1976) Managerial assessment centers. In Dunnette M.D. (ed.) *Handbook of Industrial and Organisational Psychology*, Chicago: Rand-McNally.

Fletcher, C. and Dulewicz, V. (1984) An empirical study of a UK based assessment centre. *Journal of Management Studies*, **211**, 83–97.

Foxall, G. R. (1986) Managerial orientations of adaptors and innovators. *Journal of Managerial Psychology*, **1**, 24–28.

Forsythe, S., Drake, M. F. and Cox, C. E. (1985) Influence of applicants' dress on interviewers' selection decisions. *Journal of Applied Psychology*, **70**, 374–378.

Fusilier, M. R. and Hoyer, W. D. (1980) Variables affecting perceptions of invasion of privacy in a personnel selection situation. *Journal of Applied Psychology*, **65**, 623–626.

Gardner, K. E. and Williams, A. P. O. (1973) A 25-year follow-up of an extended interview procedure in the Royal Navy: Part 1. *Occupational Psychology*, **47**, 1–13.

Gaugler, B. B., Rosenthal, D. B., Thornton, G. C. and Bentson, C. (1986) Meta-analysis of assessment center validity. Unpublished manuscript. Colorado State University.

Ghiselli, E. E. (1972) The validity of aptitude tests in personnel selection. *Personnel Psychology*, **26**, 461–477.

Gifford, R. N. C. and Wilkinson, M. (1985) Non-verbal cues in the employment interview: links between applicant qualities and interviewer judgements. *Journal of Applied Psychology*, **70**, 4, 729–736.

Gill, R. W. T. (1979) The in-tray (in-basket) exercise as a measure of management potential. *Journal of Occupational Psychology*, **52**, 185–197.

Gill, R. W. T. (1982) A trainability concept for management potential and an empirical study of its relationship with intelligence for 2 managerial skills. *Journal of Occupational Psychology*, **55**, 139–148.

Gill, D., Ungerson, B. and Thakur, M. (1973) *Performance appraisal in Perspective: A survey of current practice*. London: Institute of Personnel Management.

Gillen, D. J. and Carroll, S. J. (1985) Relationship of managerial ability to unit effectiveness in more organic versus more mechanistic departments. *Journal of Management Studies*, **22**, 668–676.

Gilmore, D., Beehr, T. A. and Lane, K. G. (1986) Effects of applicant sex, applicant physical attractiveness, type of rater and type of job on interview decisions. *Journal of Occupational Psychology*, **59**, 103–109.

Glueck, W. F. (1973) Recruiters and executives: how do they affect job choice? *Journal of College Placement*, **33**, 77–78.

Goldsmith, R. E. and Matherly, T. A. (1987) Adaption–innovation and creativity: a replication and extension. *British Journal of Social Psychology*, **26**, 79–82.

Gough, H. G. (1984) A managerial potential scale for the California Psychological Inventory. *Journal of Applied Psychology*, **69**, 233–240.

Gratton, L. (1985) Assessment centres: theory research and practice. *Human Resources Management, Australia*, **23**, 10–14.

Gratton, L. (1987) How can we predict management potential in research scientists? *R & D Management*, **17**, 87–97.

Guilford, J. P. (1967) *The Nature of Human Intelligence*. New York: McGraw-Hill.

Gupta, A. K. and Govindarajan, V. (1982) An empirical examination of linkages between strategy, managerial characteristics and performance, *Proceedings of the National meeting of the Academy of Management*. New York, 31–35.

Gupta, A. K. and Govindarajan, V. (1984) Business Unit Strategy, managerial characteristics and business unit effectiveness at strategy implementation. *Academy of Management Journal*, **27**, 25–41.

Hackett, H. G. and Betz, N. E. (1981) A self-efficacy approach to the career development of women. *Journal of Vocational Behaviour*, **18**, 326–339.

Hales, C. P. (1986) What do managers do? A critical review of the evidence. *Journal of Management Studies*, **23**, 88–115.

Hall, D. T. (1971) A theoretical model of career subidentity development in organisational settings. *Organisational Behaviour and Human Performance*, **6**, 50–75.

Hall, D. J. and Goodale, J. (1986) *Human Resource Management Strategy Design and Implementation*. Glenview, Ill: Scott-Foresman.

Harn, T. J. and Thornton, G. C. III (1985) Recruiter counselling behaviours and applicant impressions. *Journal of Occupational Psychology*, **54**, 165–173.

Harris, P. R. (1985) *Managers in Transition*. San Francisco: Jossey-Bass.

Harris, P. R. (1986) Intrapreneurialism – a timely concept. *Leadership and Organisational Development Journal*, **6**, 3–20.

Hart, G. L. and Thompson, P. M. (1979) Assessment centers: for selection or development? *Organizational Dynamics*, 63–77.

Hayes, R. D. (1974) Expatriate selection: insuring success and avoiding failure. *Journal of International Business Studies*, 5, 40·46.

Heilman, M. E. and Saruwatari, L. R. (1979) When beauty is beastly: the effects of appearance and sex on evaluations of job applicants for managerial and non-managerial jobs. *Organizational Behavior and Human Performance*, **23**, 360–372.

Heilman, M. E. and Stopeck, M. H. (1985a) Being attractive: advantage or disadvantage? Performance-based evaluations and recommended personnel actions as a function of appearances, sex, and job type. *Organizational Behavior and Human Decision Processes*, **35**, 202–215.

Heilman, M. E. and Stopeck, M. H. (1985b) Attractiveness and corporate success: different causal attributions for males and females. *Journal of Applied Psychology*, **70**, 2, 379–388.

Heilman, M. F. and Martell, R. F. (1986) Exposure to successful women: antidote to sex discrimination in applicant screening decisions? *Organizational Behavior and Human Decision Processes*, **37**, 376–390.

Herbert, T. T. and Deresky, H. (1986) Should general managers fit their business strategies? *Organizational Dynamics*, 40–51.

Herriot, P. (1981) Towards an attributional theory of the selection interview. *Journal of Occupational Psychology*, **54**, 165–173.

Herriot, P. (1986a) Managerial recruitment: Selection or negotiation? Paper to the International Congress on the benefits of Psychology. Lausanne, Switzerland.

Herriot, P. (1986b) Graduate recruitment. Getting it right. Paper to the Annual Conference of the Institute of Personnel Management. Harrogate, England.

Herriot, P. (1987) The selection interview. In P. B. Warr (ed.) *Psychology at Work*, 3rd edition. Harmondsworth: Penguin.

Herriot, P. (1988) Selection as a social process. In J. M. Smith and I. T. Robertson (eds) *Advances in Selection and Assessment*. Chichester: John Wiley.

Herriot, P., Chalmers, C. and Wingrove, J. (1985) Group decision making in an assessment centre. *Journal of Occupational Psychology*, **58**, 309–312.

Herriot, P. and Rothwell, C. (1981) Organizational choice and decision theory: effects of employers' literature and selection interview. *Journal of Occupational Psychology*, **54**, 17–31.

Herriot, P. and Rothwell, C. (1983) Expectations and impressions in the graduate selection interview. *Journal of Occupational Psychology*, **56**, 303–314.

Herriot, P. and Wingrove, J. (1984) Decision processes in graduate pre-selection. *Journal of Occupational Psychology*, **57**, 269–276.

Holland, J. L. (1973) *Making Vocational Choices: A Theory of Careers*. Englewood-Cliffs, N.J.: Prentice-Hall.

Hollandsworth, J. R., Kazelskis, R., Stevens, J. and Dressel, M. C. (1979) Relative contributions of verbal articulative and non-verbal communication to employment decisions in the job interview setting. *Personnel Psychology*, **32**, 359–367.

Holloway, W. (1984) Fitting work: psychological assessment in organisations. In J. Henriques *et al. Changing the Subject – Psychology, Social Regulation and Subjectivity*, London: Methuen.

Hough, L. M. (1984) Development and evaluation of the 'Accomplishment Record' method of selecting and promoting professionals. *Journal of Applied Psychology*, **69**, 135–146.

Hough, L. M., Keyes, M. A. and Dunnette, M. D. (1983) An evaluation of three 'alternative' selection procedures. *Personnel Psychology*, 261–276.

Howard, A. (1986) College experiences and managerial performance. *Journal of Applied Psychology*, **71**, 530–552.

Huck, J. R. and Bray, D. W. (1976) Management assessment center evaluations and subsequent job performance of white and black females. *Personnel Psychology*, **29**, 13–30.

Hull, D., Bosley, J. J. and Udell, G. G. (1980) Renewing the hunt for the heffalump. Identifying potential entrepreneurs by personality characteristics. *Journal of Small Business Management*, **18** (1), 1–18.

Hughes, G. D. and Singler, C. M. (1985) *Strategic Sales Management* Reading, Mass.: Addison-Wesley.

Hunter, J. E. (1986) Cognitive ability, cognitive aptitudes, job knowledge and job performance. *Journal of Vocational Behaviour*, **29**, 340–362.

Hunter, J. E. and Hunter, R. (1984) Validity and utility of alternative predictors. *Psychological Bulletin*, **96**, 72–98.

Hunter and Hirsch (1987) Applications of meta-analysis. In C. L. Cooper and I. T. Robertson. *International Review of Industrial and Organizational Psychology*. Chichester: John Wiley.

Imada, Ä (1982) Social interaction, observation and stereotypes as determinants of differentiation in peer ratings. *Organizational Behaviour and Performance*, **29**, 397–415.

Janz, T. (1982) Initial comparisons of behaviour description interviews versus unstructured interviews. *Journal of Applied Psychology*, **67**, 577–580.

Jasolka, G., Beyer, J. M. and Trice, H. M. (1985) Measuring and predicting managerial success. *Journal of Vocational Behaviour*, **26**, 189–205.

Jones, A. and Harrison, E. (1982) Prediction of performance in initial officer training using reference reports. *Journal of Occupational Psychology*, **55**, 35–42.

Jung, C. E. (1978) *Psychological Types*. New York: Harcourt, Brace.

Kagan, J., Rosman, B. L., Day, D., Albert, J. and Phillips, N. (1964) Information processing in the child: significance of analytic and reflective attitudes. *Psychological Monographs*, **78**.

Keenan, A. and Wedderburn, A. A. I. (1980) Putting the boot on the other foot. Candidate's description of interviewers. *Journal of Occupational Psychology*, **53**, 81–89.

Kelly, G. A. (1955) *The Psychology of Personal Constructs*. Vol. 1, *A Theory of Personality*. New York. W. W. Norton.

Kesselman, G. A. and Lopez, P. E. (1979) The impact of job analysis on employment test validation for minority and non minority accounting personnel. *Personnel Psychology*, **32**, 91–108.

Kingston, N. (1971) *Selecting Managers: a survey of current practice in 200 companies*. London: British Institute of Management.

Kinicki, A. J. and Lockwood, C. A. (1985) The interview process: An examination of factors recruiters use in evaluating job applicants. *Journal of Vocational Behaviour*, **26**, 117–125.

Kirton, M. J. (1976) Adaptors and innovators: a description and measure. *Journal of Applied Psychology*, **61**, 622–629.

Kirton, M. J. (1984) Adaptors and innovators – why new initiatives get blocked. *Long-Range Planning*, **17**, 137–143.

Kirton, M. J. and McCarthy, R. M. (in press) Cognitive climate and organisations. *Journal of Occupational Psychology*.

Klimoski, R. J. and Strickland, W. J. (1977) Assessment centers – valid or merely prescient? *Personnel Psychology*, **30**, 353–361.

Klimoski, R. J. and Strickland, W. J. (1981) A comparative view of assessment centers: a case analysis. Unpublished manuscript.

Klimoski, R. and Brickner, M. (1987) Why do assessment centers work? The puzzle of assessment center validity. *Personnel Psychology*, **40**, 243–260.

Knouse, S. B. (1983) The letter of recommendation: specificity and favourability of information. *Personnel Psychology*, **36**, 331–341.

Kotter, J. P. (1982a) *The General Managers*. New York: Free Press.

Kotter, J. P. (1982b) What effective general managers really do. *Harvard Business Review*, **60**, 156–167.

Kraut, A. I. (1975) Prediction of managerial success by peer and training staff ratings. *Journal of Applied Psychology*, **60**, 14–19.

Kraiger, K. and Ford, J. K. (1985) A meta analysis of ratee race effects in performance ratings. *Journal of Applied Psychology*, **70**, 1, 56–65.

Kurke, C. B. and Aldrich, H. E. (1984) Mintzberg was right! A replication and extension of the nature of managerial work. *Management Science*, **29**, 975–984.

Landy, F. J. and Farr, J. L. (1980) Performance rating. *Psychological Bulletin*, **87**, 72–107.

Latham, G. P. (1986) Job performance and appraisal. In C. L. Cooper and I. T. Robertson (eds) *International Review of Industrial and Organizational Psychology*. Chichester: John Wiley.

Latham, G. P. and Saari, L. M. (1984) Do people do what they say? Further studies on the situational interview. *Journal of Applied Psychology*, **69**, 569–573.

Latham, G. P., Saari, L. M., Purcell, E. D. and Campion, M. A. (1980) The situational interview. *Journal of Applied Psychology*, **65**, 422–427.

Lau, A. W., Newman, A. R. and Broedling, L. A. (1980) The nature of managerial work in the public sector. *Public Management Forum*, **19**, 513–521.

Lau, A. and Pavett, C. (1980) The nature of managerial work: A comparison of public and private sector managers. *Group and Organisation Studies*, **5**, 453–466.

Lawrence, P. (1984) *Management in Action*. London: Routledge & Kegan Paul.

Leontiades, M. (1982) Choosing the right manager to fit the strategy. *Journal of Business Strategy*, **3** (2), 58–69.

Leontiades, M. (1980) *Strategies for Diversification and Change*. Boston: Little, Brown.

Levine, E. L., Flory, A. and Ash, R. A. (1977) Self-assessment in personnel selection. *Journal of Applied Psychology*, **62**, 428–435.

Liden, R. C. and Parsons, C. K. (1986) A field study of job applicant interview perceptions, alternative opportunities and demographic characteristics. *Personnel Psychology*, **39**, 109–122.

Locke, E. and Henne, D. (1986) Work motivation theories. In C. L. Cooper and I. T. Robertson. *International Review of Industrial and Organisational Psychology*. Chichester: John Wiley.

London, M. (1985) *Developing Managers*. San Francisco: Jossey-Bass.

London, M. and Stumpf, S. A. (1983) Effects of candidate characteristics on management promotion decisions: an experimental study. *Personnel Psychology*, **36**, 241–259.

London, M. and Stumpf, S. A. (1984) Promotion decisions. *Management Decision (UK)*, **24**, 21–25.

Lorenzo, R. V. (1984) Effects of assessorship on managers' proficiency in acquiring, evaluating and communicating information about people. *Personnel Psychology*, **37**, 617–634.

Love, K. G. (1981) Comparison of peer assessment methods: reliability, validity, friendship bias, and user reaction. *Journal of Applied Psychology*, **66**, 451–457.

Luthans, F. and Lockwood, P. L. (1984) Toward an observation system for measuring leader behaviour in natural settings. In J. G. Hunt, D. Hosking, C. Schnesheim and R. Stewart (eds) *Leaders and managers: international perspectives on managerial behaviour and leadership*. New York: Pergamon Press.

Luthans, F., Rosenkrantz, S. and Hennessey, H. (1985) What do successful managers really do? An observation study of managerial activities. *Journal of Applied Behavioural Science*, **21**, 255–270.

Mass, J. B. (1985) Patterned expectation interview: reliability studies on a new technique. *Journal of Applied Psychology*, **49**, 431–433.

Mabe, P. and West, S. (1982) Validity of self-evaluation of ability: a review and meta-analysis. *Journal of Applied Psychology*, **67**, 280–296.

Mabey, W. and Hunter, R. (1986) Using personality measures to improve selection. *Guidance and Assessment Review*, **2**, 1–4.

McCall, M. W. and Segrist, L. A. (1980) *In Pursuit of the Manager's Job: Building on Mintzberg*. Grensboro, N.C.: Center For Creative Leadership.

McClelland, D. C. and Boyatzis, R. E. (1982) Leadership motive patterns and long-term success in management. *Journal of Applied Psychology*, **67**, 737–743.

Mahoney, T. A., Jerdee, T. H. and Carroll, S. J. (1963) *Development of Managerial Performance: a Research Approach*. Cincinnati: South Western.

Mahoney, T. A., Jerdee, J. H. and Carroll, S. J. (1965) The job of management. *Industrial Relations*, **4**, 97–110.

Makin, P. J. and Robertson, I. T. (1983) Self-assessment, realistic job previews and occupational decisions. *Personnel Review*, **12**, 21–25.

Martin, D. C. and Bartol, K. M. (1986) Holland's vocational preference inventory and the Myers Briggs Type Indicator as predictors of vocational choice among Master's of Business Administration. *Journal of Vocational Behaviour*, **29**, 51–65.

Mayfield, E. C., Brown, S. H. and Hamstra, B. W. C. (1980) Selection interviewing in the life insurance industry: an update of research and practice. *Personnel Psychology*, **33**, 725–740.

Miles, E. and Snow, C. C. (1978) *Organisational Strategy, Structure and Process*. New York: McGraw-Hill.

Miller, E. C. (1977) Managerial qualities of personnel occupying overseas management positions as perceived by US expatriate managers. *Journal of International Business Studies*, **8**, 57–69.

Miller, D., Ket de Vries, F. R. K. and Touleuse, J. M. (1982) Top executive locus of control and its relationship to strategy making, structure, and environment. *Academy of Management Journal*, **25**, 237–253.

Mintzberg, H. (1973) *The Nature of Managerial Work*, New York: Harper and Row.

Mintzberg, H. (1975) The manager's job: folklore and fact. *Harvard Business Review*, **53**, 49–61.

Mintzberg, H. (1976) Planning on the left side and managing on the right. *Harvard Business Review* , **54**, 49–58.

Monahan, C. J. and Muchinsky, P. M. (1983) Three decades of personnel selection research: a state of the art analysis and evaluation. *Journal of Occupational Psychology*, **56**, 215–225.

Moses, J. L. (1984) Using clinical methods in a high level management assessment center. In J. Bernardin and D. Bownas (eds) *Personality Assessment in Organisations*. New York: Praeger.

Moses, J. L. and Boehm, V. R. (1975) Relationship of assessment center performance to management progress of women. *Journal of Applied Psychology*, **60**, 527–529.

Maxon, J. (1986) Innovators, entrepreneurs and intrapreneurs: food for thought. *Industrial and Commercial Training*, **18**, 13–16.

Muchinsky, P. M. (1979) The use of reference reports in personnel selection: a review and evaluation. *Journal of Occupational Psychology*, **52**, 287–297.

Muchinsky, P. M. (1986) Personnel selection methods. In Cooper, C. L. and Robertson, I. T. *International Review of Industrial and Organizational Psychology*. Chichester: John Wiley.

Mullen, T. P. and Stumpf, S. A. (1987) The effect of management styles on strategic planning. *Journal of Business Strategy*, 60–75.

Mumford, M. D. (1983) Social comparison theory and the evaluation of peer evaluations: a review and some applied implications. *Personnel Psychology*, **36**, 867–882.

Myers, I. (1962) *Manual: The Myers–Briggs Type Indicator*. Palo Alto Cal.: Consulting Psychologists Press.

Neiner, A. G. and Owens, W. A. (1985) Using biodata to predict job choice among college graduates. *Journal of Applied Psychology*, **71**, 127–136.

Nirtaut, D. J. (1977) Assessment centers: an examination of participant reaction and adverse effects. *Journal of Assessment Center Technology*, **1**, 18–23.

Noe, R. A. and Steffy, B. D. (1987) The influence of individual characteristics and assessment center evaluation on career exploration behaviour and job involvement. *Journal of Vocational Behavior*, **30**, 187–202.

Nortan, S. D., Ballon, J. L. and Konstantinovich, B. (1980) The soundness of supervisory ratings as predictors of managerial success. *Personnel Psychology*, **33**, 377–388.

Orpen, C. (1984) Patterned behavior description interviews versus unstructured interviews: a comparative validity study. *Journal of Applied Psychology*, **70**, 774–776.

Paolillo, J. (1987) Role profiles for managers in different areas. *Group and Organisation Studies*, **12**, 109–118.

Parsons, C. K. and Liden, R. C. (1984) Interview perception of applicant qualifications: A multivariate field study of demographic characteristics and non verbal cues. *Journal of Applied Psychology*, **69**, 557–568.

Pavett, C. and Lau, A. (1983) Managerial work: The influence of hierarchical level and functional speciality. *Academy of Management Journal*, **26**, 170–177.

Paunonen, S. V., Jackson, D. N. and Oberman, S. N. (1987) Personnel selection decisions: effects of applicant personality and the letter of reference. *Organizational Behavior and Human Decision Processes*, **40**, 96–114.

Peters, T. J. and Waterman, R. H. (1982) *In Search of Excellence*. New York: Harper and Row.

Pinchot, G. (1985) *Intrapreneuring*. New York: Harper and Row.

Porter, M. E. (1980) *Competitive Strategy*. New York: Free Press.

Powell, G. (1984) Effects of job attributes and recruiting practices on applicant decisions: a comparison. *Personnel Psychology*, **37**, 721–731.

Premack, S. L. and Wanous, J. P. (1985) A meta-analysis of realistic job preview experiments. *Journal of Applied Psychology*, **70**, 706–719.

Quaglieri, P. L. (1982) A note on variations in recruiting information obtained through different sources. *Journal of Occupational Psychology*, **55**, 53–55.

Rasmussen, K. G. (1984) Nonverbal behavior, verbal behavior resume credentials and selection interview outcomes. *Journal of Applied Psychology*, **69**, 551–556.

Reilly, R. R. and Chao, G. T. (1982) Validity and fairness of some alternative employee selection procedures. *Personnel Psychology*, **35**, 1–62.

Ritchie, R. J. and Boehm, V. R. (1977) Biographical data as a predictor of men's and women's management potential. *Journal of Vocational Behaviour*, **11**, 363–368.

Ritchie, R. J. and Moses, J. L. (1983) Assessment center correlates of women's advancement into middle management: A 7-year longitudinal analysis. *Journal of Applied Psychology*, **68**, 227–231.

Roadman, H. E. (1964) An industrial use of peer ratings. *Journal of Applied Psychology*, **48**, 211–214.

Robertson, I. T. (1985) Human information processing strategies and style. *Behaviour and Information Technology*, **4**, 19–29.

Robertson, I. T. (1986) Assessing managerial potential. In G. Debus and H. W. Schroiff (eds) *The Psychology of Work and Organisation*. Amsterdam: Elsievier Science Publishers BV (North-Holland).

Robertson, I. T. and Downs, S. (1979) Learning and the prediction of performance: Development of trainability testing in the United Kingdom. *Journal of Applied Psychology*, **64**, 42–50.

Robertson I. T. and Downs, S. (1988) Work sample tests of trainability: a meta-analysis. (Under review.)

Robertson, I. T. and Kandola, R. S. (1982) Work sample tests: validity, adverse impact and applicant reaction. *Journal of Occupational Psychology*, **55**, 171–182.

Robertson, I. T. and Makin, P. J. (1986) Management selection in Britain: a survey and critique. *Journal of Occupational Psychology*, **59**, 45–57.

Robertson, I. T., Gratton, L. and Sharpley, D. (1987) The psychometric properties and design of managerial assessment centres: dimensions into exercises won't go. *Journal of Occupational Psychology*, **60**, 187–195.

Robertson, I. T. and Smith, J. M. (1988) Personnel selection methods. In J. M. Smith and I. T. Robertson *Advances in Selection and Assessment*. Chichester: John Wiley.

Robertson, I. T., Iles, P. A., Gratton, L. and Sharpley, D. S. (1988) *The Psychological Impact of Personnel Selection Methods on Candidates* (in preparation).

Robey, D. and Taggart, W. (1981) Measuring manager's minds: The assessment of style in human information processing. *Academy of Management Review*, **6**, 375–383.

Russell, C. J. (1985) Individual decision processes in an assessment center. *Journal of Applied Psychology*, **704**, 737–746.

Rynes, S. L., Heneman, H. G. and Schwab, D. P. (1980) Individual reactions to organizational recruiting: a review. *Personnel Psychology*, **33**, 529–542.

Rynes, S. L. and Lawler, J. (1983) A policy capturing investigation of the role of expectancies in decisions to pursue job alternatives. *Journal of Applied Psychology*, **68**, 620–631.

Rynes, S. L. and Miller, H. E. (1983) Recruiter and job influences on candidates for employment. *Journal of Applied Psychology*, **68**, 147–154.

Sackett, P. R. (1987) Assessment centers and content validity: some neglected issues. *Personnel Psychology*, **40**13–25.

Sackett, P. R. and Dreher, G. F. (1982) Constructs and assessment center dimensions: some troubling empirical findings. *Journal of Applied Psychology*, **67**, 401–410.

Sackett, P. R. and Dreher, G. F. (1984) Situation specificity of behavior and assessment center validation strategies: a rejoinder to Neidig and Neidig. *Journal of Applied Psychology*, **69**, 187–190.

Sackett, P. R. and Hakel, M. D. (1979) Temporal stability and individual differences in using assessment information to form overall ratings. *Organizational Behavior and Human Performance*, **23**, 120–137.

Sackett, P. R. and Wilson, M. A. (1982) Factors affecting the consensus judgement process in managerial assessment centers. *Journal of Applied Psychology*, **67**, 10–17.

Savage, A. (1985) Biographische fragebogenals methode der personal auswahl. In H. Schuler and W. Stehle (eds) *Beitrage zur Organisation Psychologie*, Band 2. Stuttgart: Verlag Für Angewandte Psychologie.

Saville, P. and Munro, A. (1986) The relationship between the factor model of the Occupational Personality Questionnaires and the 16PF. *Personnel Review*, 15, 30–34.

Sayles, L. R. (1964) *Managerial Behavior*. New York: McGraw-Hill.

Schmitt, N. and Coyle, B. W. (1976) Applicant decisions in the employment interview. *Journal of Applied Psychology*, 61, 184–192.

Schmitt, N., Ford, K. J. and Stults, D. (1986) Changes in self-perceived ability as a function of performance in an assessment center. *Journal of Occupational Psychology*, 59, 327–336.

Schmitt, N. and Hill, T. E. (1977) Sex and race composition of assessment center groups as a determinant of peer and assessor ratings. *Journal of Applied Psychology*, 62, 3, 261–264.

Schmitt, N. and Noe, R. A. (1986) Personnel selection and equal employment opportunity. In C. L. Cooper and I. T. Robertson (eds) *International Review of Industrial/Organisational Psychology*. Chichester: John Wiley.

Schmitt, N. and Ostroff, C. (1986) Operationalising the 'behavioural consistency' approach: selection test development based on a content-oriented strategy. *Personnel Psychology*, 39, 91–108.

Schmitt, N. and Schneider, B. (1983) Current issues in personnel selection. In K. Rowland and G. Ferris (eds) *Research in Personnel and Human Resources Management*. Vol. 1. JAI Press.

Schmitt, N., Noe, R., Merrit, H. R. and Fitzgerald, M. (1984a) Validity of assessment center ratings for the prediction of performance ratings and school climate of school administrators. *Journal of Applied Psychology*, 69, 207–213.

Schmitt, N., Gooding, R. Z., Noe, R. A. and Kirsch, M. (1984b) Meta-analyses of validity studies published between 1964 and 1982 and the investigation of study characteristics. *Personnel Psychology*, 37, 407–422.

Schweiger, D. (1983) Measuring manager's minds: a critical reply to Robey and Taggart. *Academy of Management Review*, 8, 143–151.

Sextan, D. L. and Bowman, N. B. (1984) Entrepreneurship education: suggestions for increasing effectiveness. *Journal of Small Business Management*, 22, 2, 12–18.

Shaffer, G. S., Saunders, V. and Owens, W. A. (1986) Additional evidence for the accuracy of biographical data: long term retest and observer ratings. *Personnel Psychology*, 39, 791–809.

Shapira, Z. and Dunbar, R. (1980) Testing Mintzberg's managerial roles classification using an inbasket simulation. *Journal of Applied Psychology*, 65, 87–95.

Siegal, L. (1982) Paired comparison evaluations of managerial effectiveness by peers and supervisors. *Personnel Psychology*, 35, 843–852.

Silverman, W. H., Dalessio, A., Woods, S. B. and Johnson, R. L. (1986) Influence of assessment center methods on assessor ratings. *Personnel Psychology*, 39, 565–579.

Smith, N. and Miner, J. B. (1984) Motivational considerations in the success of technologically innovative entrepreneurs. In J. A. Hornaday, F. Tarpley, J. Timmons and K. Vesper (eds) *Frontiers of Entrepreneurship Research*, Vol. 5. Welleseley, Mass.: Batison College.

Smith, J. M. and Schaefer, C. E. (1969) Development of a creativity scale for the adjective check list. *Psychological Reports*, 25, 87–92.

Smith, J. M. (1980) An analysis of 3 managerial jobs using repertory grids. *Journal of Management Studies*, 17, 205–213.

Smith, J. M. and Stewart, B. J. M. (1978) Repertory grids: A flexible tool for establishing the content and structure of a manager's thoughts. *Management Bibliographies and Reviews*, 3, 209–226.

Smith, P. C. and Kendall, L. M. (1963) Retranslation of expectations: an approach to the construction of unambiguous anchors for rating scales. *Journal of Applied Psychology*, **47**, 149–155.

Sparrow, R. and Pettigrew, A. M. (1986) Britain's training problems: the search for a strategic human resources management approach. *Human Resource Management*, **25**, 1–19.

Steel, R. P. and Mento, A. J. (19??) Impact of situational constraints on subjective and objective criteria of managerial job performance. *Organisational Behavior and Human Decision Processes*, **37**, 254–265.

Stahl, M. J. (1983) Achievement, power and managerial motivation: selecting managerial talent with the job choice exercise. *Personnel Psychology*, 775–789.

Stewart, A. and Stewart, V. (1981) *Tomorrow's Managers Today*. London: Institute of Personnel Management.

Stewart, R. (1976) *Contrasts in Management*. Maidenhead: McGraw-Hill.

Stewart, R. (1982) A model for understanding managerial jobs and behavior. *Academy of Management Review*, **7**, 7–13.

Stewart, R. (1987) Chairmen and general managers: a comparative study of different role relationships. Paper presented to the British Academy of Management, University of Warwick, September.

Streufert, S. (1970) Complexity and complex decision-making: convergences between differentiation and integration approaches to the prediction of task performance. *Journal of Experimental Social Psychology*, **6**, 694–509.

Streufert, S. and Swezey, R. W. (1986) *Complexity, Managers and Organisations*. Orlando, Florida: Academic Press.

Stumpf, S. A. and London, M. (1981a) Management promotions: individual and organisational factors influencing the decision process. *Academy of Management Review*, **6**, 539–549.

Stumpf, S. A. and London, M. (1981b) Capturing rater policies in evaluating candidates for promotion. *Academy of Management Journal*, **24**, 752–766.

Swinburne, P. J. (1985) A comparison of the OPQ and 16PF in relation to their occupational application. *Personnel Review*, **14**, 29–33.

Swinburne, P. J. (1986) Personality questionnaires as a source of learning in management education and training: a comparison of the OPQ and 16PF. *Personnel Review*, **15**, 32–35.

Szilagyi, A. D. and Schweiger, D. M. (1984) Matching managers to strategies: a review and suggested framework. *Academy of Management Review*, **9**, 626–637.

Taggart, W. and Robey, D. (1981) Minds and managers: on the dual nature of human information processing and management. *Academy of Management Review*, **6**, 187–195.

Taylor, M. S. and Ilgen, D. R. (1981) Sex discrimination against women in initial placement decisions: A laboratory investigation. *Academy of Management Journal*, **24**, 859–865.

Taylor, M. S. and Sniezek, J. A. (1984) The college recruitment interview: topical content and applicant reactions. *Journal of Occupational Psychology*, **57**, 157–168.

Taylor, M. S. and Bergmann, T. J. (1987) Organisational recruitment activities and applicant's reactions at different stages of the recruitment process. *Personnel Psychology*, **40**, 261–271.

Teel, K. S. and Dubois, H. (1983) Participant's reactions to assessment centres. *Personnel Administrator*, March, 85–91.

Ten, Dam, H. W. (1986) Strategic mentality. *Leadership and Organisation Development Journal*, **7**, 27–32.

Thorndike, L. J. (1949) *Personnel Selection: test and measurement technique*. New York: John Wiley.

Thornton, G. C. III (1980) Psychometric properties of self appraisals of job performance. *Personnel Psychology*, **33**, 263–271.

Thornton, G. C. III and Byham, W. C. (1982) *Assessment Centres and managerial performance*. London: Academic Press.

Torrance, E. P. (1971) *Technical Norms Manual for the Creative Motivation Scale*. Athens GA: Georgia Studies of Creative Behaviour, University of Georgia.

Turnage, J. J. and Muchinsky, P. M. (1984) A comparison of the predictive validity of assessment center evaluations versus traditional measures in forecasting supervisory job performance: Interpretive implications of criterion distortion for the assessment paradigm. *Journal of Applied Psychology*, **69**, 595–602.

Tziner, R. A. and Dolan, S. (1982) Validity of an assessment center for identifying future female officers in the military. *Journal of Applied Psychology*, **67**, 728–736.

Tziner, A. and Dolan, S. (1985) Identifying female officer potential – an exploration in predictors' pay off. *Industrial Relations (Canada)*, **40**, 87–98.

Wakabayashi, M. and Graen, G. B. (1984) The Japanese career progress study: a 7-year follow-up. *Journal of Applied Psychology*, **69**, 603–614.

Wanous, J. P. (1976) Organisational entry: from naive expectation to realistic beliefs. *Journal of Applied Psychology*, **61**, 22–29.

Wanous, J. P. (1980) *Organisational Entry*. Reading, Mass.: Addison-Wesley.

Wernimont, P. F. and Campbell, J. P. (1968) Signs, samples, and criteria. *Journal of Applied Psychology*, **52**, 372–376.

Wingrove, J., Herriot, P. and Glendinning, R. (1984) Graduate pre-selection: a research note. *Journal of Occupational Psychology*.

Wingrove, J., Jones, A. and Herriot, P. (1985) The predictive validity of pre and post discussion assessment centre ratings. *Journal of Occupational Psychology*, **58**, 189–192.

Winter, B. and Herriot, P. (in preparation) Aptitude, self-efficacy and situation as predictors of success in training.

Wisserma, J. G., Van der Pol, H. W. and Messer, H. M. (1980) Strategic management archetypes. *Strategic Management Journal*, **1**, 37–47.

Witkin, H. A. (1976) Cognitive style in academic performance and in teacher–student relations. In S. Messick (ed.) *Individuality in Learning*. San Francisco: Jossey-Bass.

Zedeck, S. and Cascio, W. F. (1984) Psychological issues in personnel decisions. In M. Rosenzweig and L. Porter (eds) *Annual Review of Psychology*, **35**, Palo Alto, Ca: Annual Reviews.

International Review of Industrial and Organizational Psychology 1988
Edited by C. L. Cooper and I. Robertson
© 1988 John Wiley & Sons Ltd

Chapter 7

PSYCHOLOGICAL MEASUREMENT: ABILITIES AND SKILLS

Kevin R. Murphy
Department of Psychology
Colorado State University
USA

The accurate measurement of cognitive and psychomotor skills and abilities is, or should be, an important concern to industrial and organizational psychologists. Measures of ability and skill provide basic data for making decisions about selection, classification and training. There is now considerable evidence that the use of ability tests in selection can lead to substantial increases in productivity (Schmidt *et al.*, 1979; Hunter and Schmidt, 1982; Hunter and Hunter, 1984: see, however, Murphy, 1986d). Comparable analyses have not been performed in the domain of skill measures, but it is likely that the impact of valid skill measures on productivity is also substantial. This chapter discusses the measurement of cognitive and psychomotor abilities and skills in occupational settings. For the most part, I shall focus on research published during the period 1977–86. The dates are somewhat arbitrary, but this period represents a time of rapid change in the theory, methods and technology of psychometrics and psychological testing. One aim of this chapter is to assess the degree to which these changes have affected ability and skill measurement in occupational settings.

Given the importance of the topic, our knowledge regarding the use of ability and skill measures in the field is surprisingly patchy and disorganized. In 1982, the National Academy of Sciences published a wide-ranging evaluation of cognitive ability tests; on the whole, they concluded that cognitive ability tests were more economical, valid and fair than existing alternatives (Wigdor and Garner, 1982). This report contains an excellent history of employment testing (Hale, 1982), as well as a partial survey of current testing practices (Friedman and Williams, 1982). Temopyr (1981) provides additional information about employment testing in the US; Robertson and Makin (1986) survey methods of management selection in Britain. Finally, several authors allude to the use of ability or skill tests in countries other than the US or Britain, but very little detail is given (Droege, 1984; Haritos-Fatouros, 1984; Raymond and Mailick, 1985; Porteous, 1986). In general, this literature suggests that:

(a) We don't know what testing practices are actually followed in organizations—it is difficult to answer even simple questions such as 'How many organizations use skill or ability tests?' More complex issues, such as the types of test that are used for different decisions, or the overall effects of tests on organizational decisions, are a matter of anecdote and conjecture.

(b) Cognitive ability tests are not widely used in personnel selection, but their use may be increasing as the result of recent research on the validity and utility of these tests.

(c) Systematic knowledge about the measurement of skill in occupational settings is fragmentary. We know a good deal about the *methods* of skill measurement, but little is published in professional or scientific journals about the application of those methods.

(d) Ability and skill testing is extremely important in the military and in government, where tests are given to hundreds and thousands of applicants and incumbents, but is likely to be a small-scale operation in most occupational settings. Some organizations perform research on the development, validation, and use of tests, but others use whatever tests and testing procedures are available and convenient.

Given the issues listed above, it is difficult to describe in any coherent way the actual practice of ability and skill measurement in occupational settings. This review focuses on scientific progress (or lack of progress) in ability and skill measurement over recent years. For the most part, I shall discuss research reported in scientific journals, but shall also discuss several studies, books and chapters written for personnel managers. It is important to emphasize that this review does not focus on the state of the art of ability and skill testing *as practised in the field*. As noted earlier, systematic information regarding actual testing practices in the private sector is hard to come by. This review will, however, summarize literature that is typically consulted by industrial and organizational psychologists interested in ability and skill testing.

This review is divided into three sections. First, the measurement of cognitive ability is discussed, and the impact of Item Response Theory and computerized testing technology is assessed. Second, measures of psychomotor ability are reviewed. The boundaries between psychomotor and physical abilities are not easily drawn; this section therefore overlaps somewhat with a broad literature describing physiologically-based measures of fitness, speed, etc. but is by no means exhaustive in its coverage of physical ability measurement. The third section describes the measurement of skill, in both blue-collar and managerial/professional jobs.

COGNITIVE ABILITY

In the 1960s and 1970s, cognitive ability tests were certainly not regarded as the 'cutting edge' in selection research. The validity of paper-and-pencil ability tests was assumed to be generally low (but unstable), and in the US, government regulations seemed to discourage the use of ability tests (Hale, 1982). Boehm (1982) suggests that this combination of regulation and unimpressive results forced validation research to 'go underground', in the sense that investigators became less interested in publishing their results, especially negative ones. Research on validity generalization (Schmidt and Hunter, 1977) and on the impact of valid selection tests on workforce productivity (Schmidt *et al.*, 1979) led to a renewed interest in the use of cognitive ability tests, and to a more detailed examination of the relationship between measured abilities and job performance.

Validity of Cognitive Tests

Application of validity generalization procedures to cognitive ability testing in a wide variety of settings has consistently led to three conclusions:

(a)   The variation in validity coefficients is not much greater than the variation one would expect on the basis of sampling error.

(b)   When corrected for attenuation, the mean validity coefficient is reasonably large.

(c)   The confidence interval around this mean *r* rarely includes values less than or equal to zero.

Representative applications of validity generalization to populations of computer programmers, petroleum workers and law enforcement officers are presented in Schmidt, Gast-Rosenberg and Hunter (1980), Schmidt, Hunter and Caplan (1981), and Hirsh, Northrop and Schmidt (1986). There are several other applications of the method in the research literature, but these three are sufficient to illustrate the application of validity generalization.[1] Results of meta-analysis such as these have convinced Schmidt and Hunter (1981) that cognitive ability tests are valid for predicting performance in essentially all jobs. It is important to note here that the term 'valid' merely implies a positive correlation between test score and job performance that is greater than some arbitrarily small numbers. Schmidt, Hunter and their colleagues typically set $r = .10$ as this minimum cut-off, but under certain conditions (e.g. large variation in performance levels), a criterion of $r = .01$ or even $r = .001$ would do just as well.

Comparisons of the validity of cognitive ability tests to that of alternative predictors of job performance have yielded inconsistent results. Reilly and Chao (1982) suggested that interviews, self-assessment, reference checks, academic records, expert judgements and projective tests are less valid and/or fair than cognitive ability tests, but that biodata and peer evaluations showed levels of validity comparable to those achieved using standard ability tests. Schmitt *et al.* (1984) analysed validity studies published between 1964 and 1982, and found that cognitive ability tests showed consistent evidence of validity, but that work samples, assessment centers and supervisor/peer evaluations provided more valid predictions of performance. Hunter and Hunter (1984), on the other hand, concluded that cognitive ability tests were the most valid predictors of success in entry-level jobs. In an extensive meta-analysis, they estimated the average correlation between scores on cognitive ability tests and judgemental measures of job proficiency to be $r = .53$. This estimate is corrected for attenuation in the

---

1.   This chapter does not include a comprehensive review of research on validity generalization, much of which is methodological rather than substantive. The technique is reviewed only to the extent that it affects decisions regarding the use of ability or skill tests.

criterion; the mean observed r is in the .20–.35 range, depending on the data-set included in one's analysis. Finally, Hunter and Hirsh (1987) suggest that the corrected validity and cognitive ability tests in predicting work sample performance is greater than .70.

The question of whether ability tests represent the best predictor, or merely one of the best predictors is somewhat academic. All of the major meta-analyses have led to the conclusion that cognitive ability tests are useful in a wide variety of jobs, and that these tests are likely to be cost-effective in most settings.

IMPLICATIONS OF VALIDITY GENERALIZATION FOR ABILITY MEASUREMENT

Validity generalization research has clearly led to a change in psychologists assessment of the value of cognitive ability tests. The proposition that we should drop ability testing, or that there is some simple alternative that is equally cost-effective in a wide variety of settings would no longer receive serious support in the scientific community. Validity generalization has not, however, led to a renaissance in ability testing. Between 1977 and 1986, scientific journals contained reference to few new tests proposed or developed for occupational settings; in this period there were few papers suggesting or illustrating specific abilities that should be measured to better predict job success. In part, this is due to the fact that existing tests provide very adequate measures of several well-defined abilities. This relative lack of progress in ability measurement may also, however, reflect a sense of complacency that comes from the apparent uniformity of validity generalization results. If we accept the conclusion that cognitive tests are valid predictors in essentially all jobs, (cf. Schmidt and Hunter, 1981) validation research loses some of its urgency.

In a very important paper, Schmidt, Hunter and Pearlman (1981) suggested that major differences in the tasks performed in different jobs do not moderate the validity of selection tests. They obtained validity data from five job families, ranging from stenography-related to production and stock clerks and showed that the validity of each of eight classes of ability tests did not vary substantially as a function of the job or of the job family; this same pattern has been replicated elsewhere (Burke, Raju and Pearlman, 1986).

Table 1—Pooled Validity Coefficients for Eight Test Types[a]

Test Type	Average r	Corrected r
General mental ability	.24	.50
Verbal ability	.19	.40
Quantitative ability	.24	.50
Reasoning ability	.21	.44
Perceptual speed	.22	.47
Memory	.19	.39
Spatial/mechanical ability	.14	.30
Clerical aptitude	.25	.57

[a] Data are taken from Schmidt, Hunter and Pearlman (1981).

Schmidt *et al.* (1981) noted that validity does not vary greatly from job family to job family. Average correlations from Schmidt *et al.* (1981) are shown in Table 1; these correlations suggest an additional conclusion that validity does not vary greatly from test to test. These and similar data (cf. Zedeck and Cascio, 1984) lead to the questions of whether: (a) general ability tests are equally valid for all jobs; (b) a person who scores high on a test will do better in any job than a lower-scoring candidate; and (c) all cognitive tests are equally valid in all jobs. Proponents of validity generalization have not, in general, made such sweeping claims (Schmidt *et al.*, 1985) although all three positions are implied by their work (Schmidt and Hunter, 1981). The one moderator of validity that has been recognized in the literature is job complexity, broadly defined as the extent to which the job imposes information-processing demands. Hunter (1980) and Hunter and Hunter (1984) note that the validity of cognitive ability tests increases as the information-processing demands of the job increase. Gutenberg *et al.* (1983) noted the same phenomenon, and also noted that the validity of two-hand dexterity tests from the GATB increases as information-processing demands of the job decrease. There may be other moderators that have not been detected to date. Osburn *et al.* (1983) note that the power to detect true differences in validity is low in many validity generalization analyses. In a subsequent analysis, Sackett, Harris and Orr (1986) showed that small differences in validity (i.e. .10 or less) are difficult to detect regardless of the number of studies or the sample size, and that moderate differences (i.e. .20) will not be reliably detected with a small number of studies, or with small samples. (See also Kemery, Mossholder and Roth, 1987; Spector and Levine, 1987.) Finally, James, Demaree and Mulaik (1986) question the logic of using validity generalization analyses to show that no moderators of validity exist, and show that even if the logic of the procedure is accepted, validity generalization analyses are biased in favor of the finding that validities are constant across situations.

The data cited by Hunter and Hunter (1984) and Gutenburg *et al.* (1983) suggest a gross difference in levels of validity across jobs, but do not address a more interesting question. Within any given job type, do validities vary as a function of the specific ability being measured? If so, different ability measures will be useful for different jobs. If not, a single measure of general ability might be sufficient for most, if not all positions. The data in Table 1 do not adequately address the question. For example, although the average validity of verbal ability tests is equal to that of memory tests, it is possible that administering *both* types of tests would yield more accurate prediction than using either test alone. Hunter and Hunter (1984) note that relatively few studies employ measures of multiple abilities, making it difficult routinely to test the hypothesis that measuring multiple abilities is more or less cost-effective than measuring general mental ability alone. In principle, however, meta-analysis could be used to estimate the correlations between different types of ability measures, in much the same way that predictor-criterion correlations are now estimated; given estimates of the predictor intercorrelations, together with validity estimates, it would be easy to test any number of hypotheses about the incremental validity of different test types. (See Schmidt, Hunter and Caplan [1981] for an illustration of this sort of analysis.)

Validity generalization research has led to an increasing emphasis on cognitive ability in its general sense, but may also have led to a *decreasing* emphasis on identifying and measuring the specific abilities required by the given job. Validity generalization research suggests that the validity of cognitive tests can be established by simply showing that the job in question is a member of a broad job family for which validity generalization has been demonstrated (Pearlman, 1980; Pearlman, Schmidt and Hunter, 1980; Schmidt, Hunter and Pearlman, 1981). Detailed job analyses are not encouraged, making it unlikely that careful attention will be paid to the actual ability requirements of individual jobs. This approach is appropriate if all jobs require the same ability or abilities, but may not represent the optimal use of information about the abilities of job applicants.

One Ability or Many?

Several studies have applied utility equations to estimate the effects of using ability tests in personnel selection (Hunter and Schmidt, 1982; Murphy, 1986; Schmidt *et al.*, 1979; Schmidt *et al.*, 1984). Other studies have used path analysis in an attempt to assess the causal impact of cognitive ability on performance (Hunter, 1983; Schmidt, Hunter and Outerbridge, 1986). All of these studies are notable for the fact that they treat cognitive ability as a unitary trait; in these studies the terms 'ability', 'cognitive ability' and 'general mental ability' are used interchangeably.

Whereas personnel psychologists have emphasized general mental ability, researchers in the area of intelligence have in recent years deemphasized general mental ability, and have turned their attention to the specific abilities that underlying cognition. For example, for the first time in its history, the authors of the Stanford-Binet have specified a multidimensional model of intelligence, and now provide measures of several separate abilities in addition to an overall IQ (Thorndike, Hagen and Sattler, 1986). Other assessment batteries have pursued a similar course (Kaufman, Kamphaus and Kaufman, 1985); although different tests are based on different models, most intelligence tests now measure specific as well as general abilities.

Modern theories, models and definitions of intelligence are rarely dominated by a single factor (g), but rather specify many different abilities, components, and even types of intelligence (Sternberg, 1982; Gardner, 1983; Guilford, 1985; Horn, 1985; Humphreys, 1985). Sternberg and Detterman (1986) asked 24 sets of experts to answer the question: 'What is intelligence?' Only one of the resulting essays (A. Jensen's) took the position that intelligence should be regarded as a unitary trait. Thus, the trends in intelligence research are diverging from those in personnel selection research. Intelligence researchers are moving away from the concept of general ability almost as quickly as personnel psychologists are moving toward it.

Measures of specific cognitive abilities

The best measures of factorially distinct cognitive abilities are probably those included in the kit of 'factor-referenced' tests provided by the Educational Testing Service (ETS, 1976). A longstanding program of research has identified marker tests that are known to have substantial loadings of well-defined cognitive factors (French, Ekstrom and Price, 1963; Ekstrom, French and Harman, 1975; 1976; 1979). The kit contains marker tests for several of the 23–25 cognitive factors identified by ETS researchers; examples include Flexibility of Closure, Associational Fluency, Logical Reasoning, and Associative Memory. Several of the abilities measured by tests in the kit are similar to those used by Fleishman and his associates in their attempts to construct taxonomies of human perform-ance. Fleishman and Quaintance's (1984) description of these efforts is essential reading for researchers interested in occupational ability testing.

A few new cognitive ability tests have been developed that may be useful in occupational settings. For example, the Graduate Record Examinations now contain items that measure analytic ability (Powers and Swinton, 1981); similar tests might be useful in selection for jobs that require inference or unstructured decision making. Colberg (1985) proposed the logic-based measurement of verbal ability (see also Colberg, Nester and Trattner, 1985); it is not yet clear whether logic-based tests are superior to traditional tests of induction and deduction. Finally, Toquam et al. (1985) discuss several tests of memory and spatial ability. Tests have also disappeared, notably the Professional and Administrative and Career Examination (PACE), which had been given to over 200,000 college graduates applying for jobs in the federal government, but which was withdrawn as the result of a consent decree in a lawsuit alleging discrimination in employment (Oligan and Wilcox, 1982).

Assessing Ability Requirements

It is an article of faith among personnel psychologists that performance will be maximized when the abilities of workers best fit the requirements of the job. (See, however, Schoenfeldt, 1982.) Determining this fit is not easy since, as Dunnette (1976; 1982) notes, the taxonomies that describe the ability domain are very different from those that describe the job or task domain (see also Peterson and Bownas, 1982). Determining the abilities required by a specific job, except in its most trivial sense (i.e. a job that involves driving trucks requires truck-driving ability), requires careful analysis. Three approaches have been used to establish ability requirements; (a) direct judgement, (b) derived ability profiles, and (c) the use of models or theories that specify ability–performance links and the conditions that moderate those linkages.

The Minnesota Job Requirements Questionnaire (MJRQ) is an example of a direct judgement method, in which supervisors are asked to judge the extent to which each of several abilities is required in a given job (Desmond and Weiss, 1970; 1973). Functional Job Analysis (FJA) also requires direct judgement, although the ability dimensions involved in a FJA are not likely to be as finely separated as with the MJRQ (Olson et al., 1981). The *Dictionary of Occupational Titles* (DOT) includes judgements regarding the extent to which each of the abilities measured by the General Aptitude Test Battery (GATB) is required in several thousand jobs (Field and Field, 1977). There is some evidence that these ratings are reliable (Cain and Greed, 1983), but these ratings may not discriminate well between jobs (Dunnette, 1976; Murphy, 1986b). Murphy (1986b) used direct judgements of ability requirements to cluster jobs, and found this method to be superior to clustering on the basis of GATB profiles from the DOT. Caution must be observed, however, in interpreting the results of direct judgements. Mabe and West (1982) suggest that people are poor judges of their *own* ability; supervisors may find it even harder to judge the abilities of others.

The use of job analysis data to derive ability requirements is a common step in assessing synthetic validity (see Mossholder and Avery [1984] for a useful review of synthetic validity techniques.) The Position Analysis Questionaire (PAQ) is particularly useful for this purpose (McCormick, Jeanneret and Williams, 1972; McCormick, DiNisi and Shaw, 1979; Sparrow et al., 1982). The PAQ database contains descriptions of practically every type of job along 32 specific and 13 general worker-oriented dimensions, as well as GATB information for each job. It is therefore possible to estimate the validity of each GATB subtest for most jobs, given a set of scores on the PAQ. The J-coefficient represents another approach that is likely to lead to the derivation of specific ability requirements (Primoff, 1959; Hamilton, 1981; Trattner, 1982; Hamilton and Dickinson, 1987). Although not designed specifically as a method of establishing multiple ability requirements, the J-coefficient approach often involves deriving these requirements (to estimate the correlation between specific tests and job components) as an intermediate step. Finally, Cunningham et al. (1983) discuss empirical relationship between scores from the Occupational Analysis Inventory and GATB requirements listed in the DOT.

A third approach to determining ability requirements is essentially a prescriptive one, in which a model is constructed linking different abilities to different types of tasks, and in which ability requirements are defined in terms of that theoretical structure. For example, Murphy and Kroeker (1986) constructed a model that describes links between general mental ability and more basic information processing abilities and criteria such as skill acquisition, task proficiency, individual team performance and team task performance for the enlisted population in the Navy. Potential changes in these relationships over time are described in Murphy (1986a). Peterson (1985) has constructed a more elaborate model that maps six types of cognitive and psychomotor tests onto a criterion space that contains both training and performance measures. The potential of this approach for specifying ability requirements of jobs is obvious, but has not yet been empirically demonstrated.

Advances in the Theory and Technology of Ability Measurement

Two relatively recent advances have begun to change the face of psychological measurement, especially in cognitive ability domains; they are (a) the development of item response theory, and (b) the use of computers in test administration. Item Response Theory (IRT) suggests a very different approach to the construction, scoring and evaluation of tests that which has dominated ability measurement since Binet's time. The use of computers in administering tests allows psychologists to operationalize procedures based on item-response theory, and has opened the door to measuring abilities that are not adequately tapped by paper-and-pencil tests.

Item-response theory

Item response theory, also known as latent trait theory, attempts to relate responses to individual test items to an underlying latent trait or ability. As applied to ability testing, the theory assumes that the probability of answering a test item correctly is a function of the ability measured by that item. This function often takes the form of a normal ogive, and is often described in terms of parameters that indicate the difficulty of the item, the discriminating power of the item, and the probability of guessing the correct answer. The basic ideas of item response theory can be traced back to the work of Lazarfeld (1959; 1960) and Rasch (1960); extended discussions of the theory and its applications have been available for nearly 20 years (Lord and Novick, 1968).

Item-response theory and its applications to practical testing problems are discussed at some length by Hambleton (1983), Hulin, Drasgow and Parsons (1983) and Lord (1980). All three books require some mathematical sophistication; of the three, Hulin, Drasgow and Parsons (1983) is probably most accessible. Those entirely new to the theory might find Allen and Yen's (1979) presentation a useful introduction to the concepts and terms employed in IRT. A special issue of the journal *Applied Psychological Measurement* (Fall, 1982) is devoted to IRT and its application; that issue provides another useful introduction to the topic.

Item-response theory represents a 'new wave' in psychometrics. Issues that are central to the classic true-score theory of psychometrics (i.e. reliability, correlation for attenuation, validity of composite tests) have received little attention in recent years; modern psychometric research had focused largely on the estimation and interpretation of IRT parameters (Traub and Lam, 1985). However, IRT has had very little impact on occupational ability testing (Hakel, 1986). Three applications that have been mentioned in the applied psychology literature are in scale equating (Hulin, Drasgow and Komocar, 1982), in determining whether item pools are undimensional, or approximately undimensional (Drasgow and Lissak, 1983; Parsons and Hulin, 1982), and in assessing item and test bias (Ironson and Subkoviak, 1979; Ironson and Guion, 1982). Of these three applications, the assessment of bias is most likely to be relevant to occupational ability measurement. Bias indices derived from IRT must be viewed with caution, however, since questions have been raised regarding the statistical bases of these measures (Traub and Lam, 1985).

The practice of occupational ability testing does not appear to have kept up with progress in psychometric theory. Psychometricians have for the most part either abandoned classic true score theory (e.g. Lumsden, 1976), or have moved on to a theory they regard as more fruitful (i.e. IRT). Personnel psychologists cling stubbornly to a psychometric theory that has changed little since Gulliksen (1950). For example, proponents of validity generalization refer to the correlation between test scores and performance measures corrected for attentuation in the criterion ($r_{yy} = .60$ is assumed) as the 'estimated true validity' (see, for example, Pearlman, Schmidt and Hunter, 1980, p. 387). This interpretation assumes that the figure .60 represents *the* reliability of performance measures. Generalizability theory, another advance largely ignored in occupational ability testing, suggests that the concept of 'true validity' is not a useful one, since there are many different reliabilities, depending on both the conditions of measurement and the way in which information is to be used (Cronbach *et al.*, 1972).

The current state of occupational ability testing is not one of sophistication, at least with regard to the psychometric concepts that dominate the field. There is, however, reason for optimism. The availability of computerized adaptive tests is slowly forcing personnel psychologists to learn and apply the theory that underlies those tests.

Computerized testing

It is becoming increasingly common to administer and score tests via computer, rather than using traditional paper-and-pencil tests. In some applications, paper-and-pencil tests are, in effect, transcribed directly on to computer files, and a computer terminal is used for testing; research suggests that administering the same test via computer *v.* via paper-and-pencil does not affect test scores (Elwood, 1969; Johnson and Mihal, 1973; Katz and Dalby, 1981). More recent literature on computerized testing has reported testing applications that are considerably more sophisticated than merely using the computer terminal as a stand-in for an answer sheet. In particular, computerized testing has made adaptive testing both possible and practical.

In scanning the literature on computerized ability, three things stand out: (a) this technology allows one to capitalize on the strengths of item response theory; (b) this technology allows one to measure both aspects of test behavior (e.g. response latency) and cognitive abilities (e.g. dynamic processing abilities) that are difficult to otherwise measure; and (c) most of the practical applications of this technology are occurring in the military, with few applications in the private sector.

The marriage of computerized testing and item-response theory has made *fully* adaptive or tailored testing possible. The basic idea in tailored testing is that individuals should respond only to those items that are at a level of difficulty appropriate to their ability level, since items that are extremely easy or extremely difficult for that person provide little information. This is not a new idea; tests such as the Stanford–Binet have used an adaptive testing strategy for years. Computerized tests allow for a more sophisticated strategy, in which the choice of *each* test item is determined by an estimate of the examinee's ability, and in which ability estimates can be revised on the basis of each item response until they converge at some stable value.

Applications of tailored testing in personnel selection and assessment were reported as early as 1977 (Urry, 1977), and the potential of this technology has been pointed out by many reviewers (e.g. Tenopyr and Oeltjen, 1982; Hakel, 1986), but to date there have been few papers reporting the application of this technology in the private sector. There have, however, been several reports dealing with the use of computerized adaptive testing in the military (Sands and Gade, 1983; Hakel, 1986). A major effort is underway to develop a computerized adaptive test that can be substituted for the Armed Services Vocational Aptitude Battery (ASVAB). The ASVAB, which is used for making selection and placement decisions for enlisted personnel in the armed services, is the most widely-used multiple-aptitude test battery in the US (Murphy, 1984a); the scope of current efforts to develop a computerized adaptive version of the test (CAT-ASVAB) is therefore considerably larger than that of most other test-development projects. Validation of CAT-ASVAB subtests is discussed in McBride and Martin (1983) and Moreno *et al.* (1984); Sands (1985) provides an overview of progress to date in the CAT-ASVAB project. Similar efforts to develop computerized adaptive tests in the German Federal Armed Forces are discussed by Wildgrube (1985).

The use of computers as testing devices makes it possible to measure abilities that are very difficult to measure with paper-and-pencil tests. Considerable progress has been reported in two areas; (a) the measurement of basic information-processing abilities, and (b) the measurement of spatial visualization. Cory, Rimland and Bryson (1977) describe a series of computerized Graphic Information Processing (GRIP) tests; progress in the measurement of visual memory, figure recognition, perceptual speed, memory span and speed of mental processing is reviewed by Cory (in press). Barrett *et al.* (1982) discuss additional applications of computerized testing in measuring information-processing abilities.

Hunt and Pellegrino (1985) distinguish between static and dynamic spatial visualization and reasoning. Computerized tests allow subjects to view complex objects in motion and to predict the effects of that motion at different points in time (Pellegrino and Hunt, in press). It is not clear whether static and dynamic spatial abilities are *empirically* distinct, but Hunt and Pellegrino (1985) note that regardless of the correlation between these two abilities, computerized testing may be preferable because of its flexibility.

Computerized test interpretation has long been popular in the area of personality measurement (Butcher, Keller and Bacon, 1985). For example, several programs exist that will generate a narrative report, based on the subjects' responses to the MMPI. As you might expect, these reports are not universally popular among clinicians (Matarazzo, 1986), although advantages of this method have been noted (Murphy, 1987). Vale, Keller and Bentz (1986) discuss a computerized narrative interpretation system designed for personnel tests. It is too soon to tell whether this application of computers will generate the same controversy among personnel psychologists as it has among clinical and counseling psychologists.

Summary

By the mid-1970s, personnel psychologists were generally pessimistic about written cognitive ability tests. These tests were regarded by many as biased, as poor (or at least uncertain) predictors, and as having a minor impact on the effectiveness of organizations. All of this has changed dramatically, but strangely enough, occupational ability testing has hardly changed at all. Major advances in the theory and technology of testing have had little apparent impact on testing practices in private-sector organizations. Over the last ten years, research on the nature and measurement of cognitive ability has proliferated. Several handbooks of intelligence have been published (e.g. Sternberg, 1982; Wolman, 1985).

Jensen (1980) has offered a thorough but controversial examination of the issue of bias in mental testing. The journal *Intelligence* has become a major outlet for basic and applied research on human ability, and benchmark tests, such as the Stanford–Binet, have been radically revised. Despite these advances in basic research, conceptual, theoretical or technological advances in occupational ability testing have been few and far between. The progress that has been noted has occurred mostly in the military.

There are several reasons for the lack of progress in occupational ability testing. First, we already measure relevant abilities well with very simple tests and measurement techniques. For example, the Wonderlic Personnel Test, which can be administered and hand-scored in 15–20 minutes, is an impressively accurate predictor of performance in a wide variety of jobs (Murphy, 1984b). It might be difficult to improve substantially on the accuracy of predictions based on the Wonderlic. Second, our thinking about the relationship between ability and performance has not progressed beyond the most rudimentary stage (e.g. it is better to have lots of ability than to have little). Hunter (1983) and Schmidt *et al.* (1986) have begun to test causal models linking ability to performance, but these models have not yet incorporated separate abilities or multiple domains of ability. Given the state of our thinking with regard to ability-performance relationship, it is not altogether surprising that little progress has been made in the domain of cognitive ability measurement.

PHYSICAL AND PSYCHOMOTOR ABILITY

A logical starting-point for any discussion of physical and psychomotor ability testing is the work of Fleishman and his associates. Fleishman and Quaintance's (1984) *Taxonomies of Human Performance* has already been mentioned; this book is a valuable source of information about physical and psychomotor ability in general, and about the methods used to determine ability requirements for a wide variety of tasks. Table 2 lists 33 separate psychomotor, physical and sensory abilities used by Fleishman and his colleagues for classifying tasks and forming performance-oriented taxonomies. Definitions of these abilities are presented in Appendix B of Fleishman and Quaintance (1984).

The distinction between psychomotor and physical abilities in Table 2 is somewhat fuzzy. Note, for example, that multilimb coordination is classified as a psychomotor ability, whole gross body coordination is classified as a physical proficiency factor.

Measuring Physical and Psychomotor Abilities

The typical measurement strategy in physical/psychomotor domain is quite different from that in the cognitive ability domain. Cognitive ability test typically require subjects to respond to multiple items; one basis for evaluating these tests is the internal consistency of item responses. Physical and psychomotor ability tests are almost always performance tests, and the concept of a test item often does not apply. For example, one of the best measures of stamina is step test, in which a subject steps up and down ten times from a 20-inch step; th

Table 2—Psychomotor, Physical and Sensory Abilities—Fleishman Taxonomy

Psychomotor Ability	Physical Proficiency	Sensory Acuity
Control precision	Static strength	Near vision
Multilimb coordination	Explosive strength	Far vision
Response orientation	Dynamic strength	Visual color
Rate control	Trunk strength	discrimination
Reaction time	Extent flexibility	Night vision
Arm–hand steadiness	Dynamic flexibility	Peripheral vision
Manual dexterity	Gross body coordination	Depth perception
Finger dexterity	Gross body equilibrium	Glare sensitivity
Wrist–finger speed	Stamina	General hearing
Speed of limb movement		Auditory attention
Selective attention		Sound localization
Time sharing		Speech hearing
		Speech clarity

From Fleishman and Quaintance (1984).

difference in heart rate before and after the step test is inversely related to stamina (Fleishman, 1964; Tuxworth and Shahnaway, 1977). A number of simple physical ability tests are discussed in Fleishman (1964) and Larson (1974).

The factor structure of physical and psychomotor ability tests is different from the factor structure of most cognitive ability tests in an important way—there is no general factor that dominates physical or psychomotor ability tests (Fleishman, 1964; 1978). Thus, at least in Fleishman's view, it makes no sense to talk about hiring on the basis of physical or psychomotor ability, without specifying the precise abilities involved. This view is not universally held; Arnold et al. (1982) suggest that a general strength measure might be feasible and useful. Nevertheless, one way in which the physical and psychomotor ability literature differs from research on cognitive ability is the degree to which highly specific rather than broad and general abilities dominate.

The degree of specificity of psychomotor and physical abilities has posed special problems when assessing the convergent validity of multiple methods of measuring a given ability. For example, a wide variety of assessment techniques have been used in measuring different types of strength; it is difficult to identify multiple methods that provide equivalent measures of any given type of strength (Campion, 1983). On the other hand, Wilmore and Davis (1979) claim to have developed field tests for the selection of state troopers that provide equivalent measurement to those and provided by complex laboratory tests.

For all their simplicity, physical and psychomotor ability tests are often highly reliable (Fleishman, 1964). Several studies also support the validity of these tests. For example, Chaffin, Herrin and Keyserling (1978) showed that several physical strength tests could be used to predict the likelihood of back injury in strenuous jobs. One problem pointed out in this study is that strength tests may screen out the large majority of both older applicants and female applicants, thus increasing the likelihood of discrimination. Reilly, Zedeck and Tenopyr (1979) used measures of body density, balance and static strength to predict training outcomes, performance evaluation outcomes, and accident rates among craft workers. Arnold et al. (1982) used a construct-oriented strategy to demonstrate the validity and utility of strength tests. Finally, Hogan (1985) and Jones and Prien (1978) provide additional evidence for the criterion-related validity of physical and psychomotor ability tests.

In studies on the utility of cognitive ability tests, the costs of testing are often so trivial that they can be ignored. The same is not necessarily true for physical and psychomotor tests. For example, Hogan (1985) was able to demonstrate a respectable level of validity for physical ability tests used to screen for driver training, but noted that a number of expensive or complicated tests were needed for effective prediction.

Applications in public service occupation

Measures of physical ability are frequently employed in selecting police officers (Evans, 1980; Maher, 1984; Hogan and Quigley, 1986) and fire fighters (Considine et al., 1976; Ronan, Anderson and Talbert, 1976; Whisenard, 1979). These measures often consist of carrying out strenuous physical activities that resemble behaviors or situations that might be encountered on the job. Examples include (a) scaling a wall, (b) crawling through windows, (c) running a set distance, (d) running an obstacle course, (e) hauling or dragging a dummy, (f) climbing stairs, (g) pushing an automobile a set distance, and (h) swimming a set distance (Eisenberg and Murray, 1975; Considine et al., 1976; Hernandez, 1983; Maher, 1984). A variety of methods are used for scoring these tests; the time required to complete each task is often the primary determinant of the applicant's test score (Evans, 1980; Maher, 1984).

Police and fire departments frequently use height and weight requirements as surrogates for physical ability standards (Evans, 1980; Hogan and Quigley, 1986). These requirements are based on the assumption that height and/or weight place some limit on either the applicant's strength and ability to perform strenuous tasks, or the applicant's ability to avoid hazardous or dangerous situations. For example, in the 1970s over 90 per cent of all police departments set minimum height requirements, based largely on the assumption that larger officers would be better able to control violent suspects and less likely to be assaulted themselves. Subsequent research has shown that these assumptions are incorrect; there is no correlation between officer height and likelihood of assault, or of the suspect resisting arrest (Evans, 1980).

Because height and weight requirements are likely to screen out women and some minorities from police and fire jobs, these requirements have been challenged in the courts (Hogan and Quigley, 1986). Police and fire departments have rarely been able to establish the job-relatedness or the necessity of these requirements (Evans, 1980; Hogan and Quigley, 1986), and are starting to abandon these requirements in favor of physical ability tests (e.g. obstacle courses, arrest-resistance simulators). Even these tests have been attacked in court, on the basis that they do not sample actual job behavior. For example, police departments sometimes use ¼–1 mile running tests, arguing that police work involves foot-chases of fleeing suspects. Research has shown, however, that foot chases are typically brief (e.g. less than 80 yards) and are rarely carried out over level terrain (Hogan and Quigley, 1986). Thus, the physical ability tests used in police and fire departments cannot be accepted at face value, but must be validated in the same way that other tests (e.g. cognitive ability tests) are validated. This is rarely done (Evans, 1980; Hogan and Quigley, 1986).

Setting Physical Ability Requirements

A variety of methods, ranging from the methods of biophysics to a negotiated settlement between labor and management, can be used to set minimum and maximum ability and workload standards (Larson, 1974). One very useful finding in research from Fleishman's taxonomy project is that rating scales can be used by subject-matter experts to determine physical and psychomotor ability requirements for a variety of tasks and jobs (Campion, 1983; Fleishman and Quaintance, 1984). For example, Hogan *et al.* (1980) showed that rating scales provided reliable and valid measurement of the physical effort in both general and narrowly specified tasks. Decision trees have also proved useful in determining physical ability requirements (Mallamad, Levine and Fleishman, 1980). Procedures used for determining ability requirements of tasks are described in some detail in Fleishman and Quaintance (1984). Behaviorally-anchored rating scales for several ability dimensions are included in the appendices of this useful volume.

SKILL MEASUREMENT

There is a certain affinity between physical/psychomotor ability measurement and skill measurement, in that both approaches typically require the examinee to *do* something; measures of skill or ability are based on the quantity or quality of that performance. The essential difference between abilities and skills is that skills are; (a) learned over a relatively short period of time, and (b) goal-directed. Skills are more like physical abilities than cognitive abilities, in that there is no general skill factor; skills are task-specific rather than general. In addition, the term 'skill' usually connotes physical or motor performance (Adams, 1987). Finally, skills seem likely to be measured for more diverse reasons than abilities; skill measures are likely to be used as both predictors and criteria.

Training in industry is largely focused on the enhancement of specific job-related skills (Fitts, 1962; Hinrichs, 1976; Wexley, 1984); the question of whether to hire on the basis of ability or skill depends largely on the amount of time and effort the employer is willing to spend on training. Adams (1987) reviews 100 years of research on the learning and retention of motor skills, and cautions that research on cognitive learning may not generalize well to the motor skill domain. One useful generalization that can be drawn from research on motor skill learning is that procedural skills (e.g. assembling complex machines) are more easily forgotten than continuous control skills (e.g. tracking) (Fleishman and Parker, 1962; Mengelkoch, Adams and Gainer, 1971; Schendel and

Hagman, 1982). Thus, it is likely that the test-retest reliability of measures of procedural skills will be lower than that of measures of continuous control skills.

Skill Measurement in Non-exempt Jobs

Research on skill measurement in non-exempt jobs can be organized under three headings: (a) descriptions of occupational competency testing programs, (b) research on work samples, and (c) research on validation strategies in skill measurement.

Competency testing programs

Several large-scale testing programs are devoted to the measurement of occupational competency. The testing program of the National Occupational Competency Institute (NOCTI) provides the best example of this type of skill measurement. NOCTI offers three separate testing programs: (a) a testing program for vocational education teachers in over 60 separate specialities, (b) a testing program for vocational education students, and (c) a competency testing program for experienced workers. Tests used for measuring vocational skills and students are described below.

There are currently 29 NOCTI tests available in the Student Occupational Competency Achievement Test (SOCAT) program; 42 others are in preparation. Although the tests vary according to the occupational specialty involved (e.g. auto body, computer programming, refrigeration), the tests typically include three components; (a) a multiple-choice job achievement (i.e. job knowledge) test, (b) a performance test, and (c) a scholastic ability test. For example, the Commercial Foods test include a 184-item written test covering food preparation and service, safety, equipment, purchasing, management skill, and specialty service, and a three-hour performance test that involves preparing a salad, an entrée and a quick bread, and serving them. Structured rating forms are used to evaluate performance on the performance tests.

The NOCTI testing program is reviewed by Baldwin (1978). At the time of the review, little information was available regarding the reliability and validity of the SOCAT tests. Since then, evidence of reliability has been provided for most of the tests; internal consistency reliabilities in the .80–.90 range are typical for SOCAT tests.

Several other testing programs exist on a somewhat smaller scale than the NOCTI program. For example, the Ohio Vocational Education Achievement Test program offers 38 occupational tests in areas such as data processing, farm management and small engine repair. The American Association for Vocational Instructional Materials offers the VCM tests—criterion-referenced job knowledge and performance tests in 17 separate areas (e.g. apparel sales, carpenter, physical therapist assistant). The NTE tests assess skill and knowledge of students in teacher education programs (Nelson, 1978); NTE tests are available in 26 specialists areas (e.g. agriculture, mathematics, music education). The validity of the various tests mentioned above will be discussed later in this chapter.

Work samples

Work samples provide what may be the most valid method of predicting job performance (Reilly and Chao, 1983; Schmitt *et al.*, 1984). They are also used by many researchers (e.g. Schmidt *et al.*, 1986) as a *measure* of job performance; current efforts to develop new performance measures in the armed services use work samples as a benchmark against which new performance measure will be evaluated (see Hakel, 1986, for a brief overview of Project A, a project that includes these criterion development efforts). Work-sample testing has the advantage of face validity (McClelland, 1973); these tests often appear quite reasonable to both examinees and managers, increasing the likelihood that test results will be accepted by all involved, and decreasing the likelihood of complaints, lawsuits, etc.

Siegel (1986) reviews research on the reliability and validity of work-sample tests. It is interesting to note that research on the *construct* validity of these tests has rarely been conducted in the last 35 years. Several studies in the 1950s were concerned with determining what is measured by work-sample tests; recent research has been more concerned with the criterion-related validity of work sample tests. I shall return to this issue in the next section.

Campion (1972) presented evidence that scores from work-sample tests are related to a variety of job performance measures. Cascio and Phillips (1979) demonstrated that work-sample tests also predict turnover. These tests also show less adverse impact on racial minorities than do cognitive ability tests (Brugnoli, Campion and Basen, 1979). Asher and Sciarrino (1974) suggest that criterion-related validity is maximized when there is a point-to-point correspondence between the predictor and the criterion. In its extreme form, this statement is a logical consequence of classical reliability theory, since strict point-to-point correspondence implies that the predictor and the criterion are parallel tests. Nevertheless, even when predictors and criterion *are* clearly different, work sample tests are very likely to yield moderate to large validities (Asher and Sciarrino, 1974).

A distinction is sometimes made between motor-work sample tests and verbal-work samples. The former includes bench tests and various hands-on demonstrations of skill; the latter include leadership group discussions, in-baskets, and verbal job knowledge tests. Both types of tests show similar levels but different patterns of validity. Motor-work samples predict job proficiency measures better than they predict measures of success in training. Verbal-work samples predict training outcomes better than they predict job proficiency (Asher and Sciarrino, 1974; Robertson and Kandola, 1982).

Work samples are often used as trainability tests (Siegel and Bergman, 1975). A trainability test is one where applicants receive brief training in a particular task, and then are tested for their ability to perform the task. Robertson and Downs (1979) review the literature on trainability tests and discuss the application of this technique in UK. Robertson and Mindel (1980) report the successful use of a trainability test for skilled jobs. They note that there is little evidence concerning the reliability or psychometric quality (e.g. construct validity) of trainability tests. Unfortunately, this comment applies equally well to work sample tests in general. There is a clear need for research on the psychometric properties of work sample tests.

Validation strategy

The most common method of demonstrating the validity of tests of various skills is a content validity strategy. For example, there are no studies of the criterion-related or construct validity of the NOCTI tests; validity is inferred for these tests on the basis of the test construction procedures. Typically, these tests are constructed using panels of subject-matter experts, who work from lists of specific occupational competencies to develop test items. Reliability studies are typically carried out to assess the internal consistency of test items, but no empirical methods are used to demonstrate construct or even criterion-related validity. A similar strategy is followed in some applications of physical ability tests (Evans, 1980; Maher, 1984; Hogan and Quigley, 1986).

Lawshe's (1975) content validity ratio, and several variants of this approach have been applied in the evaluation of skill tests and training programs. Bownas, Bosshardt and Donnelly (1985) used expert judgement to determine the fit between training curriculum content and task requirements. Ford and Wroton (1982) reported a similar application of expert judgement to assess the content validity of training programs. Distefano, Pryer and Craig (1980) used the content validity ratio to determine the job relatedness of a job knowledge test. Faley and Sundstrom (1985) report a more sophisticated application of the same basic idea. They used the PAQ to assess the representativeness of the behavioral content of a training program, by applying the PAQ to both the job and the training program. The similarity of the PAQ profiles provides a measure of content validity.

The use of content validity strategy has been criticized by Guion (1977; 1978); Fitzpatrick (1983) suggests that content validity is simply not a useful term, since there is no adequate way of defining the content validity of a test. The crux of this argument is that validity is a characteristic of the inferences that are based on test scores, not a property of the test itself. Test scores are certainly affected by the content of a test, but are also affected by the type of responses required by the test, the conditions of measurement, and the examinee's state of mind when responding to the test. For example, asking a chef how to prepare a sauce is not the same thing as having him or her prepare the sauce (Guion, 1977). Similarly, the ability to perform is not the same thing as actual on-the-job performance (Murphy, 1986a). Even the legal system recognizes the likelihood that the setting and administration of job-like tasks used in a work sample differs from the job itself, and that content validity arguments must take this into account (Hogan and Quigley, 1986; Nathan and Cascio, 1986).

Ridgway's (1980) analysis suggests that even a combination of content and criterion-related validity is not sufficient to establish the validity of measurement. (See also Murphy and Davidshofer, 1988.) Ridgway (1980) examined a test made up of multidimensional scheduling tasks that was known to predict performance in a job that consisted mainly of scheduling. Through facet analysis, the test was shown to measure visual scanning ability rather than scheduling ability.

Landy (1986) agrees that the traditional emphasis on *types* of validity is misplaced; test validation is always a matter of hypothesis testing, and multiple methods might be used to test almost any hypothesis. Thus, the particular context in which a validity study is carried out (e.g. personnel selection, skill measurement) does not dictate the validation strategy that must, or even should be followed. Any validity strategy is potentially useful in a wide variety of settings. Landy's (1986) argument also implies, however, that any *single* validation strategy may not be sufficient to establish the validity of a test. Both abilities and skills represent construct, and multiple validation methods are typically required to establish the construct validity of any test.

The evidence that the skill measures reviewed here actually measure job-related skills is not impressive. Skill measurement seems to be one of the last bastions of content validity. It is not that there is any sizable body of evidence *against* the validity of skill measures. It is just that the available evidence deals only with the stimulus content of the test. Content-oriented validation strategies are recognized in the *Standards for Educational and Psychological Testing* (1985) and the *Principles for the Validation and Use of Personnel Selection Procedures* (1987) as appropriate strategies for obtaining information about test validity, but the *sole* use of content-oriented strategies is clearly not consistent with current professional standards. Content-oriented strategies are viewed by many psychologists as the weakest method of test validation; the failure to apply a wider variety of methods when validating measures of job-related skill is a potentially serious mistake.

Skill Measurement in Managerial and Professional Jobs

In blue-collar jobs, skill measures often involve hands-on performance tests. In managerial jobs, the closest equivalent to a hands-on test is provided by situational tests. Examples include the leaderless group discussion (Bass, 1954), the in-basket (Frederiksen, 1962) and business simulations (Wolfe, 1976). Recent research on the measurement of managerial skills is most often encountered in the context of assessment centers.

Assessment center research

The assessment center is regarded by many as one of the success stories of organizational psychology (Finkle, 1976; Hinrichs, 1978). Assessment procedures employed by the staff of the Office of Strategic Services (forerunner of the CIA) during World War II were adapted after the war to managerial assessment, and are now widely employed in both the public and private sector. Although assessment procedures vary from setting to setting, most assessment centers include simulations or situational tests designed to assess critical managerial skills.[1]

The distinction between managerial skills and abilities is not clear-cut (Thornton and Byham, 1982), in part because the tasks, goals, procedures, etc.

---

1. As with validity generalization research, this chapter does not include a comprehensive review of assessment center research. Research relevant to managerial skill measurement is reviewed.

that comprise a manager's job are not as well defined as those that define most blue-collar jobs. This can be illustrated by considering the types of dimensions that are typically measured in assessment centers. Table 3 lists 14 dimensions that were measured in an assessment center used by AT & T. This mix of abilities (e.g. scholastic aptitude), skills (e.g. decision-making), dispositional variables (e.g. energy), and dimensions that might reflect abilities, skills or dispositional variables (e.g. awareness of social environment) is not atypical (Thornton and Byham, 1982), nor is the large number of dimensions measured. Some assessment centers measure 25 or more separate dimensions.

Table 3—Fourteen Dimensions Measured by a Managerial Assessment Center

1.	Oral communication
2.	Leadership
3.	Energy
4.	Self-objectivity
5.	Tolerance of uncertainty
6.	Range of interests
7.	Decision-making
8.	Awareness of social environment
9.	Behavioral flexibility
10.	Inner work standards
11.	Resistance of stress
12.	Need for advancement
13.	Organization and planning
14.	Scholastic aptitude

From Ritchie and Moses (1983).

Evaluations of the reliability and validity of assessment center ratings have been almost universally favorable. Assessment center ratings are generally reliable, both over raters (Sackett and Hakel, 1979) and over time (Schmidt, 1977). These ratings are correlated with a variety of performance measures (Hunter and Hunter, 1984), and are generally thought to be fair to minorities (Huck and Bray, 1976) and to women (Moses and Boehm, 1975; Ritchie and Moses, 1983). Finally, assessment centers, although expensive, are still thought to be highly cost-effective (Cascio and Silbey, 1979; Burke and Frederick, 1986; Casio and Ramos, 1986).

Although most often encountered in the United States, the assessment center method has also been applied in other countries, e.g. Japan (Wakabayashi, 1980). Thornton and Byham (1982) provide a comprehensive review of assessment center research through the early 1980s. A more recent discussion of longitidinal assessment center research, specifically the Management Progress Study and the Management Continuity Study at AT & T, is presented in Howard (1986). Both Thornton and Byham (1987) and Howard (1986) document impressive evidence for the long-term criterion-related validity of assessment center ratings. One particularly important finding is that assessment center ratings account for variance in managerial performance measures that is not accounted for by cognitive ability tests alone (Tziner and Dohlan, 1982). Thus, assessment centers measure some skills, abilities or personality traits that are related to performance and are empirically distinct from general mental ability.

Sackett and Dreher (1982, 1984) have questioned the construct validity of assessment center ratings. They note that the exercises included in assessment centers (e.g. in-basket, leaderless group discussions, situational tests) are usually designed to measure multiple performance dimensions. However, factor analyses of assessment center ratings almost invariably yield exercise factors rather than factors that correspond to the dimensions those exercises were meant to measure. This phenomenon is similar to the halo error that is widely discussed in research on performance rating. Assessment center ratings appear to be dominated by a general evaluative factor (cf. Murphy, 1982). Thus, a person who appears to do well in an exercise will generally receive high ratings on all of the dimensions measured by that exercise, whereas a person who does poorly will receive low ratings on all dimensions. This interpretation is consistent with Sackett and Hakel's (1979) finding that assessors attend to only a small amount of information about each ratee when making dimension ratings.

Neidig and Neidig (1984) note that the failure to find dimension factors may reflect true situational inconsistency in behavior. The problem with this argument is that it implies that the dimensions rated are not stable individual difference variables, but rather are inherently unstable. If this is the case why should we be interested in measuring these variables? Skills that are so specific that they do not generalize across assessment exercise may indeed exist, but the utility of measures of these skills is doubtful.

Research on the construct validity of assessment centers has led to substantial changes in assessment center practice (Thornton, personal communication, 5 March, 1987). Assessment centers are starting to employ fewer dimensions with each exercise, and are asking assessors to rate more concrete, specific dimensions (e.g. small-group leadership v. interpersonal effectiveness). It is too soon to tell whether these changes will lead to substantial increases in the validity of assessor ratings, but they clearly represent a step in the right direction.

Testing for Licensing and Certification

Many occupations, ranging from barbers and hairdressers to clinical psychologists, involve professionals selling their services directly to individual members of the public. In most countries, entry into these professions is restricted through licensing or certification requirements. In general, the use of tests that measure job-related skills is a more common component of the licensing process in the US than in Canada or Europe (Slayton and Trebilcock, 1978; Orzack, 1983; Trebilcock and Shaul, 1983).

Approximately 800 occupations are regulated by US state governments, though a variety of licensing and certification boards (Shimberg, 1981b). Licensing and certification generally involve testing, and often include both written and performance tests (Shimberg, 1981b). Although well-constructed tests are available in some professions, in general, testing for licensing and certification is a sorry mess. There is an over-reliance on essay questions and an appalling lack of standardization or adequate scoring criteria (Shimberg, 1972). Validation research is rare, and what research there is often poorly done (Shimberg, 1972; 1981b).

There are several reasons for the sad state of licensing exams. First, state laws often mandate that licensing boards be made up primarily of members of the occupation being tested (Shimberg, 1972). This means that licensing exams are often constructed by individuals who have little or no training in the construction or evaluation of tests. Second, states often do not observe reciprocity in their licensing laws. This means that there may be many different locally-constructed exams or procedures used in each regulated profession. Third, there is little real motivation to construct valid tests. Although in theory the purpose of licensing exams is to protect the public, in fact their purpose is often to restrict entry into a profession, thereby reducing competition and maintaining higher pay and job security for those who hold a license (Shimberg, 1981a; Freidman and Williams, 1982).

CONCLUDING REMARKS

This review has said little about specific tests that are used in occupational settings. Standard reference works, such as the *Mental Measurements Yearbook* and *Test Critiques* provide in-depth evaluations of individual tests. This review has focused on conceptual and theoretical issues in ability and skill measurement. Clearly, there are some problems in this area. Advances in psychometric theory have not yet been incorporated in occupational ability testing. Progress in understanding the nature of intelligence and cognitive ability has been ignored. The construct validity of skill measures is still unknown. Testing for licensing and certification is in a state of disarray. There are, however, reasons for optimism. Personnel psychologists are beginning to incorporate item response theory into their repertoire. Progress is being made in theories and models that link ability to performance. Large-scale efforts are underway to develop and integrate taxonomies of abilities, skills and tasks.

There is an urgent need for more detailed research on the relationship between cognitive ability and performance. We do not really know at present whether there is any utility to considering multiple, specific abilities in personnel selection and classification, or whether we should focus exclusively on measures of general mental ability. It is likely that in some jobs, detailed consideration of the abilities required by the job will *not* be worthwhile; we do not yet know enough about the ability domain to tell which jobs fit in this category.

Skill measurement deserves more attention than it currently receives. In particular, we need to examine the construct validity of work samples and situational tests. Content validity is not accepted as the sole method of validating ability tests, and should not be accepted as the sole method of validating skill tests. Finally, psychologists should exert more pressure to increase the quality of licensing exams. In some states, the examinations that are used for licensing psychologists are of questionable quality. We need to 'clean up our act', and to set some sort of example for other professions in which examinations are used to control entry into the field.

ACKNOWLEDGEMENT

Thanks to Jeanette Cleveland and George Thornton for their valuable comments and input.

REFERENCES

Adams, J. A. (1987) Historical review and appraisal of research on the learning, retention, and transfer of human motor skills. *Psychological Bulletin*, **101**, 41–74.

Allen, M. J. and Yen, W. M. (1979) *Introduction to Measurement Theory*. Monterey, Cal.: Brooks/Cole.

Arnold, J. D., Rauschenberger, J. M., Soubel, W. G. and Guion, R. M. (1982) Validation and utility of a strength test for selecting steelworkers. *Journal of Applied Psychology*, **67**, 588–604.

Asher, J. J. and Sciarrino, J. A. (1974) Realistic work sample tests: A review. *Personnel Psychology*, **27**, 519–533.

Baldwin, T. S. (1978) Review of National Occupational Competency Testing program. In O. K. Burus (ed.) *Eighth Mental Measurements Yearbook*. Highland Park, N.J.: Gryphon Press.

Barrett, G. V., Alexander, R. A., Doverspike, D., Cellar, D. and Thomas, J. C. (1982) The development and application of a computerized information-processing test battery. *Applied Psychological Measurement*, **6**, 13–29.

Bass, B. M. (1954) The leader group discussion. *Psychological Bulletin*, **51**, 465–492.

Boehm, V. R. (1982) Are we validating more but publishing less? (The impact of governmental regulation on published validation research – an exploratory investigation). *Personnel Psychology*, **35**, 175–187.

Bownas, D. A., Bosshardt, M. J. and Donnelly, L. F. (1985) A quantitative approach to evaluating curriculum content sampling adequacy. *Personnel Psychology*, **28**, 563–575.

Brugnoli, G. A., Campion, J. E. and Basen, J. A. (1979) Racial bias in the use of work samples for personnel selection. *Journal of Applied Psychology*, **64**, 119–123.

Burke, M. J. and Frederick, J. T. (1986) A comparison of economic utility estimates for alternative SDy estimation procedures. *Journal of Applied Psychology* **71**, 334–339.

Burke, M. J., Raju, N. S. and Pearlman, K. (1986) An empirical comparison of the results of five validity generalization procedures. *Journal of Applied Psychology*, **71**, 349–353.

Butcher, J. N., Keller, L. S. and Bacon, S. F. (1985) Current development and future directions in computerized personality assessment. *Journal of Consulting and Clinical Psychology*, **53**, 803–815.

Cain, P. S. and Green, B. F. (1983) Reliabilities of selected ratings available from the Dictionary of Occupational Titles. *Journal of Applied Psychology*, **68**, 155–165.

Campion, J. E. (1972) Work sampling for personnel selection. *Journal of Applied Psychology*, **56**, 40–44.

Campion, M. A. (1983) Personnel selection for physically demanding jobs. *Personnel Psychology*, **36**, 527–550.

Cascio, W. F. and Phillips, N. F. (1979) Performance testing: A rose among thorns? *Personnel Psychology*, **3** 751–766.

Cascio, W. F. and Ramos, R. A. (1986) Development and application of a new method for assessing job peformance in behavioral/economic terms. *Journal of Applied Psychology*, **71**, 20–28.

Cascio, W. F. and Silbey, V. (1979) Utility of the assessment center as a selection device. *Journal of Applied Psychology*, **64**, 107–118.

Chaffin, D. B., Herrin, G. D. and Keyserling, W. K. (1978) Preemployment strength testing: An updated position. *Journal of Occupational Medicine*, **20**, 403–408.

Colberg, M. (1985) Logic-based measurement of verbal reasoning: A key to increased validity and economy. *Personnel Psychology*, **38**, 374–359.

Colberg, M., Nester, M. A. and Traftner, M. H. (1985) Convergence of the inductive and deductive models in the measurement of reasoning. *Journal of Applied Psychology*, **70**, 681–694.

Considine, W., Misner, J.E., Boileau, R. A., Punian, C., Cole, J. and Abbatiell, A. (1976) Developing a physical performance test battery for screening Chicago fire fighter applicants. *Public Personnel Management*, **5**, 7–14.

Cory, C. H. (in press) Testing perceptual and reasoning abilities. In R. Dillon (ed.) *Testing: Theoretical and Applied Perspectives*. New York: Praeger.

Cory, C. H., Rimland, B. and Bryson, R. A. (1977) Using computerized tests to measure new dimensions of abilities: An exploratory study. *Applied Psychological Measurement*, **1**, 101–110.

Cronbach, L. J., Gleser, G., Nanda, H. and Rajaratnam, N. (1972) *The Dependability of Behavioral Measurements: Theory of generalizability for scores and profiles*. New York: John Wiley.

Cunningham, J. W., Boese, R. R., Neeb, R. W. and Pass, J. J. (1983) Systematically derived work dimensions: Factor analysis of the Occupational Analysis Inventory. *Journal of Applied Psychology*, **68**, 232–252.

Desmond, R. E. and Weiss, D. J. (1970) *Measurement of Ability Requirements of Occupations*. Research Report No. 34, Work Adjustment Project, University of Minnesota, Minneapolis.

Desmond, R. E. and Weiss, D. J. (1973) Supervisor estimation of abilities required in jobs. *Journal of Vocational Behavior*, **3**, 181–194.

Distefano, M. K., Pryer, M. W. and Craig, S. H. (1980) Job-relatedness of a prooftraining job knowledge criterion used to assess validity and test fairness. *Personnel Psychology*, **33**, 785–793.

Drasgow, F. and Lissak, R. I. (1983) Modified parallel analysis: A procedure for examining the latent dimensionality of dichotomously scored items. *Journal of Applied Psychology*, **68**, 363–373.

Droege, R. C. (1984) The General Aptitude Test Battery and its international use. *International Review of Applied Psychology*, **33**, 413–416.

Dunnette, M. D. (1976) Aptitude, abilities, and skills. In M. Dunnette (ed.) *Handbook of Industrial and Organizational Psychology*. Chicago: Rand-McNally.

Dunnette, M. D. (1982) Critical concepts in the assessment of human capabilities. In M. Dunnette and E. Fleishman (eds) *Human Performance and Productivity; Human capability assessment*. Hillsdale, N.J.: Lawrence Erlbaum.

Eisenberg, T. and Murray, J. M. (1974) Selection. In O. Stahl and R. Stanfenberger (eds) *Police Personnel Administration*. Washington, D.C.: Police Foundation.

Ekstrom, R. B., French, J. W. and Harman, H. H. (1975) *An Attempt to Confirm Five Recently Identified Cognitive Factors*. Princeton, N.J.: Educational Testing Service.

Ekstrom, R. B., French, J. W. and Harman, H. H. (1976) *Manual for Kit of Factor-referenced Cognitive Tests*. Princeton, N.J.: Educational Testing Service.

Ekstrom, R. B., French, J. W. and Harman, H. H. (1979) Cognitive factors: Their identification and replication. *Multivariate Behavioral Research Monographs*, **79-2**.

Elwood, D. L. (1969) Automation of psychological testing. *American Psychologist*, **24**, 287–288.

ETS Kit of Factor-referenced Cognitive Tests (1976) Princeton, N.J.: Educational Testing Service.

Evans, D. H. (1980) Height, weight, and physical agility requirements – Title VII and public safety employment. *Journal of Police Science and Administration*, **8**, 414–436.

Faley, R. H. and Sundstron, E. (1985) Content representativeness: An empirical method of evaluation. *Journal of Applied Psychology*, **70**, 567–571.

Field, T. and Field, J. (1977) *The Classification of Jobs According to Work Trait Factors: An addendum to the 1977 edition of the Dictionary of Occupational Titles*. Athens, Georgia: VDRAE Service Bureau.

Finkle, R. B. (1976) Managerial assessment centers. In M. Dunnette (ed.) *Handbook of Industrial and Organizational Psychology*. Chicago: Rand-McNally.

Fitts, P. M. (1962) Factors in complex skill training. In R. Glaser (ed.) *Training Research and Education*. Pittsburg, Penn.: University of Pittsburg Press.

Fitzpatrick, A. R. (1983) The meaning of content validity. *Applied Psychological Measurement*, **7**, 3–13.

Fleishman, E. A. (1964) *The Structure and Measurement of Physical Fitness*. Englewood Cliffs, N.J.: Prentice-Hall.

Fleishman, E. A. (1978) Relating individual differences to the dimensions of human tasks. *Ergonomics*, **21**, 1007–1019.

Fleishman, E. A. and Parker, S. F. (1962) Factors in the retention and relearning of perceptual-motor skill. *Journal of Experimental Psychology*, **64**, 215–276.

Fleishman, E. A. and Quaintance, M. K. (1984) *Taxonomies of Human Performance: The description of human tasks*. New York: Academic Press.

Ford, J. K. and Wronton, S. P. (1982) A content validity ratio approach to determining training needs. Presented at *Annual Conference of American Psychological Association*, Washington, D.C.

Fredericksen, N. (1962) Factors in in-basket performance. *Psychological Monographs*, **76** (22 Whole No. 541).

French, J. W., Ekstrom, R. B. and Harman, H. H. (1963) *Kit of Reference Tests for Cognitive Factors*. Princeton, N.J.: Educational Testing Service.

Friedman, T. and Williams, E. B. (1982) Current uses of tests for employment. In A. Wigor and W. Garner (eds) *Ability Testing: Uses, consequences and controversies*. Washington, D.C.: National Academy Press.

Gardner, H. (1983) *Frames of Mind*. New York: Basic Books.

Guilford, J. P. (1985) The structure-of-intellect model. In B. Wolman (ed.) *Handbook of Intelligence*. New York: John Wiley.

Guion, R. M. (1977) Content validity – the source of my discontent. *Applied Psychological Measurement*, **1**, 1–10.

Guion, R. M. (1978) Content validity in moderation. *Personnel Psychology*, **31**, 205–214.

Gulliksen, H. (1950) *Theory of Mental Tests*. New York: John Wiley.

Gutenberg, R. L., Avery, R. D., Osburn, H. G. and Jeanneret, P. R. (1983) Moderating effects of decision-making/information-processing job dimensions on test validities. *Journal of Applied Psychology*, **68**, 602–608.

Hakel, M. D. (1986) Personnel selection and placement. *Annual Review of Psychology*, **37**, 351–380.

Hale, M. (1982) History of employment testing. In A. Wigor and W. Garner (eds) *Ability Testing: Uses, consequences and controversies*. Washington, D.C.: National Academy Press.

Hambleton, R. K. (1983) *Applications of Item Response Theory*. Vancouver, British Columbia: Educational Research Institute of British Columbia.

Hamilton, J. W. (1981) Options for small sample sizes in validation: A case for the J-coefficient. *Personnel Psychology*, **34**, 805–816.

Hamilton, J. W. and Dickinson, T. L. (1987) Comparison of several procedures for generating J-coefficients. *Journal of Applied Psychology*, **72**, 49–54.

Haritos-Fatourous, M. (1984) Research studies on testing in Greece: A review. *International Review of Applied Psychology*, **33**, 351–370.

Hernandez, E. (1983) Physical ability remedial training. *Journal of Police Science and Administration*, **11**, 42–45.

Hinrichs, J. R. (1976) Personnel training. In M. Dunnette (ed.) *Handbook of Industrial and Organizational Psychology*. Chicago: Rand-McNally.

Hinrichs, J. R. (1978) An eight-year follow-up of a management assessment center. *Journal of Applied Psychology*, **63**, 596–601.

Hirsh, H. R., Northrop, L. C. and Schmidt, F. L. (1986) Validity generalization results for law enforcement occupations. *Personnel Psychology*, **39**, 399–420.

Hogan, J. C. (1985) Tests for success in diver training. *Journal of Applied Psychology*, **70**, 219–224.

Hogan, J. C. and Quigley, A. M. (1986) Physical standards for employment and the courts. *American Psychologist*, **41**, 1193–1217.

Hogan, J. C., Ogden, G. D., Gebhardt, D. L. and Fleishman, E. A. (1980) Reliability and validity of methods for evaluating perceived physical effort. *Journal of Applied Psychology*, **65**, 672–679.

Horn, J. L. (1985) Remodeling old models of intelligence. In B. Wolman (ed.) *Handbook of Intelligence*. New York: John Wiley.

Howard, A. (1986) College experiences and managerial performance. *Journal of Applied Psychology*, **71**, 530–552.

Huck, J. R. and Bray, D. W. (1976) Management assessment center evaluations and subsequent job performance of white and black females. *Personnel Psychology*, **26**, 191–212.

Hulin, C. L., Drawgow, F. and Komocar, J. (1982) Applications of item response theory to analysis of attitude scale translations. *Journal of Applied Psychology*, **67**, 818–825.

Hulin, C. L. Drasgow, F. and Parsons, C. K. (1983) *Item Response Theory: Application to psychological measurement*. Homewood, Ill.: Dow Jones-Irvin.

Humphreys, L. G. (1985) General intelligence: An integration of factor, test, and simplex theory. In B. Wolman (ed.) *Handbook of Intelligence*. New York: John Wiley.

Hunt, E. B. and Pellegrino, J. W. (1985) Using interactive computing to expand intelligence testing. *Intelligence*, **9**, 209–236.

Hunter, J. E. (1980) *Validity Generalization for 12,000 Jobs: An application of synthetic validity and validity generalization to the General Aptitude Test Battery*. Washington, D.C.: US Employment Service, Department of Labor.

Hunter, J. E. (1983) A causal analysis of cognitive ability, job knowledge and supervisory ratings. In F. Landy, S. Zedeck and J. Cleveland (eds) *Performance Measurement and Theory*. Hillsdale, N.J.: Lawrence Erlbaum.

Hunter, J. E. and Hirsh, H. R. (1987) Applications of meta-analysis. In C. L. Cooper and I. T. Robertson (eds) *International Review of Industrial and Organizational Psychology*. Chichester: John Wiley.

Hunter, J. E. and Hunter, R. F. (1984) Validity and utility of alternative predictors of job performance. *Psychological Bulletin*, **96**, 72–98.

Hunter, J. E. and Schmidt, F. L. (1982) Fitting people to jobs. In M. Dunnette and E. Fleishman (eds) *Human Performance and Production: Human Capability assessment*. Hillsdale, N.J.: Lawrence Erlbaum.

Ironson, G. H. and Guion, R. M. (1982) Adverse impact from a psychometric perspective. *Journal of Applied Psychology*, **67**, 419–432.

Ironson, G. H. and Subkoviak, M. J. (1979) A comparison of several methods of assessing item bias. *Journal of Educational Measurement*, **16**, 209–225.

James, L. A., Demaree, R. G. and Mulaik, S. A. (1986) A note on validity generalization procedures. *Journal of Applied Psychology*, **71**, 440–450.

Jensen, A. R. (1980) *Bias in Mental Testing*. New York: Free Press.

Johnson, D. F. and Mihal, W. L. (1973) The performance of blacks and whites in manual vs. computerized testing environments. *American Psychologist*, **28**, 694–699.

Jones, M. A. and Prien, E. P. (1978) A valid procedure for testing the physical abilities of job applicants. *Personnel Administration*, **23** (9), 33–38.

Katz, L. and Dalby, J. T. (1981) Computer and manual administration of the Eysenck Personality Inventory. *Journal of Clinical Psychology*, **37**, 586–588.

Kaufman, A. S., Kamphaus, R. W. and Kaufman, N. L. (1985) New directions in intelligence testing: The Kaufman Assessment Battery for Children. In B. Wolman (ed.) *Handbook of Intelligence*. New York: John Wiley.

Kemery, E. R., Mossholder, K. W. and Roth, L. (1987) The power of the Schmidt and Hunter additive model of validity generalization. *Journal of Applied Psychology*, **72**, 30–37.

Landy, F. J. (1986) Stamp collecting versus science: Validation as hypothesis testing. *American Psychologist*, **41**, 1183–1192.

Larson, L. A. (1974) *Fitness, Health, and Work Capacity: International standards for assessment*. New York: Macmillan.

Lawshe, C. H. (1975) A quantitative approach to content validity. *Personnel Psychology*, **28**, 563–575.

Lazarfeld, P. F. (1959) Latent structure analysis. In S. Koch (ed.) *Psychology: A study in a science*, Vol. 3. New York: McGraw-Hill.

Lazarfeld, P. F. (1960) Latent structure analysis and test theory. In H. Gulliksen and S. Messick (eds) *Psychological Scaling: Theory and applications*. New York: John Wiley.

Lord, F. M. (1980) *Applications of Item Response Theory to Practical Testing Problems*. Hillsdale, N.J.: Lawrence Erlbaum.

Lord, F. M. and Novick, M. R. (1968) *Statistical Theories of Mental Test Scores*. Reading, Mass.: Addison-Wesley.

Lumsden, J. (1976) Test theory. *Annual Review of Psychology*, **27**, 251–280.

Mabe, P. A. and West, S. G. (1982) Validity of self-evaluation of ability: A review and meta-analysis. *Journal of Applied Psychology*, **67**, 280–296.

Maher, P. T. (1984) Police physical ability tests: Can they ever be valid? *Public Personnel Management*, **13**, 173–183.

Mallamad, S. M., Levine, J. M. and Fleishman, E. A. (1980) Identifying ability requirements by decision flow diagrams. *Human Factors*, **22**, 57–68.

Matarazzo, J. D. (1986) Computerized clinical psychological test interpretations: Unvalidated plus all mean and no sigma. *American Psychologist*, **41**, 14–24.

McBride, J. R. and Martin, J. T. (1983) Reliability and validity of adaptive ability tests in a military setting. In D. Weiss (ed.) *New Horizons in Testing: Latent trait test theory and computerized adaptive testing*. New York: Academic Press.

McClelland, D. C. (1973) Testing for competence rather than for intelligence. *American Psychologist*, **28**, 1–14.

McCormick, E. J., Jeanneret, P. R. and Mecham, R. C. (1972) A study of job characteristics and job dimensions as based on the Position Analysis Questionaire (PAQ). *Journal of Applied Psychology*, **56**, 374–368.

Mengelkoch, R. F., Adams, J. A. and Gainer, C. A. (1971) The forgetting of instrument flying skills. *Human Factors*, **13**, 397–405.

Moreno, K. E., Weitzel, C. D., McBride, J. R. and Weiss, D. J. (1984) Relationship between corresponding Armed Services Vocational Aptitude Battery (ASVAB) and computerized adaptive testing (CAT) subtests. *Applied Psychological Measurement*, **8**, 155–163.

Moses, J. L. and Boehm, V. R. (1975) Relationship of assessment center performance to management progress of women. *Journal of Applied Psychology*, **60**, 527–529.

Mossholder, K. W. and Arvey, R. D. (1984) Synthetic validity: A conceptual and comparative review. *Journal of Applied Psychology*, **69**, 322–333.

Murphy, K. R. (1982) Difficulties in the statistical control of halo. *Journal of Applied Psychology*, **67**, 161–164.

Murphy, K. R. (1984a) Review of Armed Services Vocational Aptitude Battery. In D. Keyser and R. Sweetland (eds) *Test Critiques*, Vol. 1 Kansas City, Missouri: Test Corporation of America.

Murphy, K. R. (1984b) Review of the Wonderlic Personnel Test. In D. Keyser and R. Sweetland (eds) *Test Critiques*, Vol. 1 Kansas City, Missouri: Test Corporation of America.

Murphy, K. R. (1986a) *A Developmental Theory of Job Performance: Application in two Navy ratings*. Unpublished report, Colorado State University.

Murphy, K. R. (1986b) *Predictor-based Taxonomy of Navy Ratings: A preliminary study*. Unpublished report, Colorado State University.

Murphy, K. R. (1986c) When your top choice turns you down: Effects of rejected offers on the utility of selection tests. *Psychological Bulletin*, **99**, 133–138.

Murphy, K. R. (1987) The accuracy of clinical vs. computerized test interpretations. *American Psychologist* **42**, 192–193.

Murphy, K. R. and Davidshofer, C. O. (1988) *Psychological Testing: Principles and applications*. Englewood Cliffs, N.J.: Prentice-Hall.

Murphy, K. R. and Kroeker, L. (1986) *Dimensions of Job Performance*. Unpublished report, Colorado State University.

Nathan, B. R. and Cascio, W. F. (1986) Introduction: Technical and legal standards. In R. Berk (ed.) *Performance Assessment: Methods and Applications*. Baltimore: Johns Hopkins Press.

Neidig, R. D. and Neidig, P. J. (1984) Multiple assessment centers exercise and job relatedness. *Journal of Applied Psychology*, **69**, 182–186.

Nelson, E. A. (1985) Review of NTE programs. In J. Mitchell (ed.) *Ninth Mental Measurements Yearbook*. Lincoln, Nebraska: Buros Institute of Mental Measurements.

Oligan, J. D. and Wilcox, J. C. (1982) The controversy over PACE: An examination of the evidence and implications of the Leuvano consent decree for employment testing. *Personnel Psychology*, **35**, 659–676.

Olson, H. C., Fine, S. A., Myers, D. C. and Jennings, M. C. (1981) The use of functional job analysis in establishing performance standards for heavy equipment operators. *Personnel Psychology*, **34**, 351–364.

Orzack, L. H. (1983) International authority and national regulations: Architects, engineers, and the European Economic Community. *Law and Human Behavior*, **7**, 251–264.

Osburn, H. G., Callender, J. C., Greener, J. M. and Ashworth, S. (1983) Statistical power of tests of the situational specificity hypothesis in validity generalization studies: A cautionary note. *Journal of Applied Psychology*, **68**, 115–122.

Parsons, C. K. and Hulin, C. L. (1982) An empirical comparison of item response theory and hierarchical factor analysis in applications to the measurement of job satisfaction. *Journal of Applied Psychology*, **67**, 826–834.

Pearlman, K. (1980) Job families: A review and discussion of their implications for personnel selection. *Psychological Bulletin*, **87**, 1–28.

Pearlman, K., Schmidt, F. L. and Hunter, J. E. (1980) Validity generalization results for tests used to predict job proficiency and training success in clerical occupations. *Journal of Applied Psychology*, **65**, 373–406.

Pellegrino, J. W. and Hunt, E. B. (in press) Computer-controlled assessment of static and dynamic spatial reasoning. In R. Dillon (ed.) *Testing: Theoretical and Applied Perspectives*. New York: Praeger.

Peterson, N. G. (1985) Mapping predictors to criterion space: Overview. *Proceedings of the 27th Annual Conference of the Military Testing Association*, 867–872.

Peterson, N. G. and Bownas, D. A. (1982) Skill, task structure, and performance acquisition. In M. Dunnette and E. Fleishman (eds) *Human Performance and Productivity: Human capability assessment*. Hillsdale, N.J.: Lawrence Erlbaum.

Porteous, M. A. (1986) A survey of Irish psychologists attitudes toward tests. *International Review of Applied Psychology*, 35, 231, 238.

Powers, D. E. and Swinton, S. S. (1981)Extending the measurement of graduate admission abilities beyond the verbal and quantitative domains. *Applied Psychological Measurement*, 5, 141–158.

Primoff, E. S. (1959) Empirical validation of the J-coefficient. *Personnel Psychology*, 12, 413–418.

Principles for the Validation and Use of Personnel Selection Procedures (1987) College Park, Maryland: Society for Industrial and Organizational Psychology.

Rasch, G. (1960) *Probabilistic Models for Some Intelligence and Attainment Tests*. Copenhagen: Neilson and Lydiche.

Raymond, H. and Mailich, S. (1985) *International Personnel Policies and Practices*. New York: Praeger.

Reilly, R. R. and Chao, G. T. (1982) Validity and fairness of some alternative employee selection procedures. *Personnel Psychology*, 35, 1–62.

Reilly, R. R., Zedeck, S. and Tenopyr, M. L. (1979) Validity and fairness of physical ability tests for predicting performance in craft jobs. *Journal of Applied Psychology*, 64, 262–274.

Ridgway, J. (1980) Construct validity through facet analysis: Scheduling tests do not necessarily measure scheduling ability. *Journal of Applied Psychology*, 53, 253–263.

Ritchie, R. J. and Moses, J. L. (1983) Assessment center correlates of women's advancement into middle management: A 7-year longitudinal analysis. *Journal of Applied Psychology*, 68, 227, 231.

Robertson, I. T. and Downs, S. (1979) Learning and the prediction of performance: Development of trainability testing in the United Kingdom. *Journal of Applied Psychology*, 64, 42–50.

Robertson, I. T. and Kandola, R. S. (1982) Work sample tests: Validity, adverse impact and applicant reaction. *Journal of Occupational Psychology*, 55, 171–183.

Robertson, I. T. and Makin, P. J. (1986) Management selection in Britain: A survey and critique. *Journal of Occupational Psychology*, 59, 45–57.

Robertson, I. T. and Mindel, R. M. (1980) A study of trainability testing. *Journal of Occupational Psychology*, 53, 131, 138.

Ronan, W. W., Anderson, C. L. and Talbert, T. L. (1976) A psychometric approach to job performance: Fire fighters. *Public Personnel Management*, 5, 409–442.

Sackett, P. R. and Dreher, G. F. (1982) Constructs and assessment center dimensions: Some troubling empirical findings. *Journal of Applied Psychology*, 67, 401–410.

Sackett, P. R. and Dreher, G. F. (1984) Situation specificity of behavior and assessment center validation strategies: A rejoinder to Neidig and Neidig. *Journal of Applied Psychology*, 69, 187–190.

Sackett, P. R. and Hakel, M. D. (1979) Temporal stability and individual differences in using assessment information to form overall ratings. *Organizational Behavior and Human Performance*, 23, 120–137.

Sackett, P. R., Harris, M. M. and Orr, J. M. (1986) On seeking moderator variables in the meta-analysis of correlational data: A Monte Carlo investigation of statistical power and resistance to Type I error. *Journal of Applied Psychology*, 71, 302–310.

Sands, W. A. (1985) An overview of the accelerated CAT-ASVAB program. *Proceedings of the 27th Annual Conference of the Military Testing Association*, 19–22.

Sands, W. A. and Gade, P. A. (1983) An application of computerized adaptive testing in U.S. Army recruiting. *Journal of Computer Based Instruction*, **10**, 87–89.

Schendel, J. D. and Hagman, J. D. (1982) On sustaining procedural skills over a prolonged retention interval. *Journal of Applied Psychology*, **67**, 605–610.

Schmidt, F. L. and Hunter, J. E. (1977) Development of a general solution to the problem of validity generalization. *Journal of Applied Psychology*, **62**, 529–540.

Schmidt, F. L. and Hunter, J. E. (1981) Employment testing: Old theories and new research findings. *American Psychologist*, **36**, 1128, 1137.

Schmidt, F. L., Gast-Rosenberg, I. and Hunter, J. E. (1980) Validity generalization results for computer programmers. *Journal of Applied Psychology*, **65**, 643–661.

Schmidt, F. L., Hunter, J. E. and Caplan, J. R. (1981) Validity generalization results for two job groups in the petroleum industry. *Journal of Applied Psychology*, **66**, 261–273.

Schmidt, F. L., Hunter, J. E., McKenzie, R. C. and Muldrow, T. W. (1979) Impact of valid selection procedures on work-force productivity. *Journal of Applied Psychology*, **64**, 609–626.

Schmidt, F. L., Hunter, J. E. and Outerbridge, A. N. (1986) Impact of job experience and ability on job knowledge, work sample performance, and supervisory ratings of job performance. *Journal of Applied Psychology*, **71**, 432–439.

Schmidt, F. L., Hunter, J. E. and Pearlman, K. (1981) Task differences as moderators of aptitude test validity in selection: A red herring. *Journal of Applied Psychology*, **66**, 166–185.

Schmidt, F. L., Mack, M. J. and Hunter, J. E. (1984) Selection utility in the occupation of U.S. Park Ranger for three modes of test use. *Journal of Applied Psychology*, **69**, 490, 497.

Schmidt, F. L., Pearlman, K., Hunter, J. E. and Hirsh, H. R. (1985) Forty questions about validity generalization and meta-analysis. *Personnel Psychology*, **38**, 697–798.

Schmitt, N. (1977) Inter-rater agreement in dimensionality and construction of assessment center judgements. *Journal of Applied Psychology*, **62**, 171–176.

Schmitt, N., Gooding, R. Z., Noe, R. D. and Kirsh, M. (1984) Meta-analysis of validity studies published between 1964 and 1982 and the investigation of study characteristics. *Personnel Psychology*, **37**, 407–422.

Schoenfeldt, L. F. (1982) Intra-individual variation and human performance. In M. Dunnette and E. Fleishman (eds) *Human Performance and Productivity: Human capability assessment*. Hillsdale, N.J.: Lawrence Erlbaum.

Shimberg, B. (1972) *Occupational Licensing: A public perspective*. Washington, D.C.: Public Affairs Test.

Shimberg, B. (1981a) *Licensure: What vocational educators should know*. Columbus, Ohio: National Center for Research in Vocational Education.

Shimberg, B. (1981b) Testing for licensure and certification. *American Psychologist*, **36**, 1138–1146.

Siegel, A. I. (1986) Performance tests. In R. Berk (ed.) *Performance Assessment: Methods and applications*. Baltimore: Johns Hopkins Press.

Siegel, A. I. and Bergman, B. A. (1985) A job learning approach to performance prediction. *Personnel Psychology*, **28**, 325–339.

Slayton, P. and Trebilcock, M. J. (1978) *The Professions and Public Policy*. Toronto, Canada: University of Toronto Press.

Sparrow, J., Patrick, J., Spurgeon, P. and Barwell, F. (1982) The use of job component analysis and related aptitudes in personnel selection. *Journal of Occupational Behavior*, **55**, 157–164.

Spector, P. E. and Levine, E. L. (1987) Meta-analysis for inter-rating study outcomes: A Monte-Carlo study of its susceptibility to Type I and Type II errors. *Journal of Applied Psychology*, **72**, 3–9.

Standards for Educational and Psychological Testing (1985) Washington, D.C.: American Psychological Association.

Sternberg, R. J. (1982) *Handbook of Human Intelligence*. Cambridge: Cambridge University Press.

Sternberg, R. J. and Detterman, D. K. (1986) *What is Intelligence? Contemporary viewpoints on its nature and definition*. Norwood, N.J.: Ablex Publishing Corporation.

Tenopyr, M. L. (1982) The realities of employment testing. *American Psychologist*, **36**, 1120–1127.

Tenopyr, M. L. and Oeltjen, P. D. (1982) Personnel selection and classification. *Annual Review of Psychology*, **33**, 581–618.

Thorndike, R. L., Hagen, E. P. and Sattler, J. M. (1986) *Technical Manual for the Stanford-Binet Intelligence Scale*, 4th edition. Chicago: Riverside Publishing Corporation.

Thornton, G. C. and Byham, W. C. (1982) *Assessment Centers and Managerial Performance*. London: Academic Press.

Toquam, J. L., Dennette, M. D., Corpe, V. A. and Houston, J. (1985) Adding to the ASVAB: Cognitive paper-and-pencil measures. *Proceedings of the 27th Annual Conference of the Military Testing Association*, 885–890.

Traub, R. E. and Lam, Y. R. (1985) Latent structure and item sampling models for testing. *Annual Review of Psychology*, **36**, 19–48.

Trebilcock, M. J. and Shaul, J. (1983) Regulating the quality of psychotherapeutic services: A Canadian perspective. *Law and Human Behavior*, **7**, 265–278.

Trattner, M. H. (1982) Synthetic validity and its application to the uniform guidelines validation requirements. *Personnel Psychology*, **35**, 383–397.

Tuxworth, W. and Shahnaway, H. (1977) The design and evaluation of a step test for the rapid prediction of physical work capacity in an unsophisticated industrial work force. *Ergonomics*, **20**, 181–191.

Tziner, A. and Dohlan, S. (1982) Validity of an assessment center for identifying future female officers in the military. *Journal of Applied Psychology*, **67**, 728–736.

Urry, V. W. (1977) Tailored testing: A successful application of latent trait theory. *Journal of Educational Measurement*, **14**, 181–196.

Vale, C. D., Keller, L. S. and Bentz, V. J. (1986) Development and validation of a computerized interpretation system for personnel tests. *Personnel Psychology*, **39**, 525–542.

Wakabayashi, M. (1980) *Management Career Progress in a Japanese Organization*. Ann Arbor, Michigan: UMI Research Press.

Wexley, K. N. (1984) Personnel training. *Annual Review of Psychology*, **35**, 519–551.

Whisenard, P. M. (1979) Personnel management. In J. Bryan and R. Picard (eds) *Managing Fire Services*. Washington, D.C.: International City Management Association.

Wigdor, A. K. and Garner, W. R. (1982) *Ability Testing: Uses, consequences, and controversies*. Washington, D.C.: National Academy Press.

Wildgrube, W. (1985) News about CAT in the General Federal Armed Forces. *Proceedings of the 27th Annual Conference of the Military Testing Association*, 96–101.

Wolfe, J. (1976) The effects and effectiveness of simulations in business policy teaching applications. *Academy of Management Review*, **1**, 47–56.

Wolman, B. (1985) *Handbook of Intelligence*. New York: John Wiley.

Zedeck, S. and Casio, W. F. (1984) Psychological issues in personnel decisions. *Annual Review of Psychology*, **35**, 461–518.

International Review of Industrial and Organizational Psychology 1988
Edited by C. L. Cooper and I. Robertson
© 1988 John Wiley & Sons Ltd

Chapter 8

CAREERS: A REVIEW OF PERSONAL AND ORGANIZATIONAL RESEARCH

Michael J. Driver
University of Southern California
Los Angeles, California
USA

INTRODUCTION

Given the extreme range and volume of career research, only certain aspects will be covered here. I shall begin with a fundamental analysis of the fragmentation problem among theories in the area and suggest the relevance of differences in career definition as a step toward better integration.

Research dealing with the basic issue of career definition will be reviewed next. I shall then examine individual concerns such as personality factors in careers and the process of career choice. Next, I turn to a more organizational focus and review early career issues such as socialization, and later career issues such as career change. The review will conclude with a look at organization–person congruence models, societal trends and career management and the status of career management practice in organizations.

METATHEORETICAL ISSUES

In his critique of the career field, Schein (1986) essentially focuses on four problems: (a) fragmentation, (b) culture bias, (c) lack of integration via theory and confrontation, and (d) 'tool' obsession.

While not wishing to underplay the importance of US bias and tool preoccupation in some career research, it seems to me that the central problem of this field is addressed by Schein's emphasis on extreme fragmentation enhanced by lack of integrating theory.

That the career field is fragmented is hardly surprising given its history. Sonnenfeld and Kotter (1982) have traced the various themes which have dominated career research from the inception of the twentieth century. The first model to gain ascendancy was the social structure view that individual career choices are constrained by socioeconomic class membership. In the 1920s came the emergence of a more psychological view stressing personality traits, such as interests, as determinants of career choice. During the 1950s a more dynamic concept of career stages, dictated by organization focus, took hold. Finally, they see a current interest in internal life cycle stages as a guide in the career process.

In a similar vein, Arthur (1984) isolates five streams of activity in career research:

1. *Vocational guidance*—which assumes people are 'fixed' and organizations can at best select, but not change people.
2. *Human resource management*—assuming people can adapt to organization needs.
3. *Human potential movement*—which focuses on the individual's need to grow and sees organizations as often becoming impediments.
4. *Women's and minority rights*—which sees a white male culture bias distorting the field.
5. *Life/career stage models*—which posit orderly change processes in careers.

Finally, Hall (1986) divides the career field into career planning, concerned with the individual; and career management, concerned with the organization.

In conducting this review the fragmentation due to these varied streams was extremely obvious. Journals such as the *Journal of Vocational Behavior* seemed heavily focused on individual issues with a strong bias toward vocational guidance or trait orientations. *Human Development* was clearly focused on life-cycle models. Organization behavior journals such as *Academy of Management Review* tended toward career management, organizational socialization and career stage models. Theoretical and empirical integration efforts did emerge as will be stressed subsequently. However, they tended to stay 'within streams' rather than cross-streams.

In addition to factors such as diverse training and reference groups, I suggest a major problem here is basic definition. Each career research stream seems to have its own definition of careers. John Davis and I (1987) have tried to capture the underlying dimensions of this issue (as seen in Figure 1). We suggest that two basic issues concerning the definition of careers are:

(a) Do career choices change over time or stay constant?
(b) Are career choices externally generated or internal processes?

One can then locate the various streams in a two-dimensional metatheoretical space as seen in Figure 1. The one exclusion is the women's and minority view which, along with Schein's US bias factor, should also be factored in. A fourth factor in career definition not seen in Figure 1 is the work/non-work dimension: how much should career definition expand to include non-work activity? Describing the basis of the field's fragmentation is possibly helpful, but we wish to go further. Are there any integrating models which can begin to pull it all together? I suggest that there may well be.

The career concept model was developed precisely to deal with the definitional differences in the career realm (Driver, 1979; 1980; 1982). The model suggests four basic concepts held by people (including career researchers) concerning careers:

Figure 1 A metatheory space for career models.

CAREER CHOICE FREQUENCY

	Constant	Changing
Inner	Vocational guidance Trait theory	Life cycle stages Human potential
SOURCE OF CAREER CHOICE		Luck
External	Sociological determinism	Organizational career stages Human resource planning

1. *Steady-state*—career choice is made once for a life-time commitment to an occupation.
2. *Linear*—career activity continues throughout life as one moves up an occupational ladder.
3. *Spiral*—career choice evolves through a series of occupations (7–10-year durations) where each new choice builds on the past and develops new skills.
4. *Transitory*—career choice is almost continuous—fields, organizations, jobs change over 1–4-year intervals with variety the dominant force.

In our view, each stream tends to favor, consciously or otherwise, a particular career concept. The vocational guidance/trait stream generally focuses on a Steady-State view of careers in which initial choice of field is vitally important. The organizational career stage theories have taken strongly Linear views on the 'need' to advance and avoid plateaux. The life-cycle and human potential views seem heavily Spiral in their emphasis on inner forces winning through over time as identity unfolds. Finally, a stream not much discussed in the literature, stressing luck, seems well tuned to the Transitory model.

In the material reviewed below, these researcher career concepts will be made as clear as possible. The hope is that each career research stream can begin to recognize its own bias and begin to expand awareness to other career concepts. Our research (e.g. Driver and Coombs, 1983) has shown the existence of people working with *all* four concepts. Clearly any theory or stream focused on only one concept will miss a major segment of career phenomena. A truly integrative career research field needs theories encompassing all types of career definition.

Related to the career concept issue is a second fragmentary force—academic discipline. As Hall (1986) has noted, the field falls into individual focus research with a psychological discipline base (and at least four career concept variants), and organizational research with a sociological discipline base. As the contributors to Arthur's book *Working With Careers* (1984) assert, organizations tend toward what I would call Linear career concepts. Thus, much of the organizational career literature in the past has tended to focus on processes aimed at enhancing Linear careers. In the 1980s, organization behavior career researchers such as Bailyn (1984) and Hall (1986) have revised this trend. They are calling for a more Spiral approach in organizations—or even for a pluralistic approach which would permit many career concepts to flourish.

Unfortunately, the individual and organizational focused research streams are not in close communication. A major need in the career area is for the psychological richness (in theory and method) of the individual theorists to connect better with the growing insights of organizational theorists as to how organizations operate and change in shaping careers. An excellent case example of this process is shown by Campbell and Moses' (1986) analysis of how changes in AT & T are changing career definitions of AT & T employees (see below).

FUNDAMENTAL CAREER DEFINITION RESEARCH

Work–Non-Work

There seems to be a growing consensus that careers involve both work and non-work activities. Super (1986) sees a career as involving six roles: child, student, leisurite, citizen, worker, and homemaker. Over time he suggests that the intensity and breadth of involvement in all these roles change in important ways. Hopefully, research can follow his lead in defining the essential roles in a career. It is not clear yet what set of roles is most helpful. For instance, Sundby (1980) defines four roles—worker, mate, parent and self-developer. A main task ahead will be to define which roles are most useful in defining a career.

On a narrower focus, work continues on the work–leisure activity front. Shaffer (1987) has developed a taxonomy of relationships between work and leisure which could be productive. Research and theory continues to support the notion that leisure activity can compensate for meaningless work. Driver and Coombs (1983) found that individuals with Transitory career concepts in a company with very Steady-State values were not totally alienated—they derived meaning from avocational activity. Levinson (1984) describes a case in which a person, bored at work, builds his real career in his avocation. If Spenner (1985) is right that work complexity is not increasing, the highly educated workers of the future may indeed need to turn to avocations to fulfil career needs.

Another theme receiving attention is the family–work arena. Anderson-Kulman and Paludi (1986) have reviewed the problems faced by working mothers. It is clearly seen as a strain (Hardesty and Betz, 1980) in which family cooperation (Gray, 1983) and good day-care (Perry, 1982) help. Despite the strain, working mothers have high self-esteem (Birnbaum, 1971) and equivalent life satisfaction to non-working women (Warr and Perry, 1982).

Anderson-Kulman and Paludi cite Belsky *et al.*'s (1982) conclusions that working mothers have no adverse effect on children, and Hoffman's data (1980) that working mothers have positive effects on female adolescent children. However, more recent work by Belsky (*Time Magazine*, 1987) seems to cast doubt on this. It appears that some day-care may be adverse. The effect of working mothers on middle class family dynamics seems neutral (Wright, 1978) but may be negative for lower-class families (Nye, 1974). Overall, Anderson-Kulman and Paludi concluded that there is a reciprocal relationship between mother's job satisfaction and family harmony.

Career Concepts

Research directly using the Driver Career Concept model has been sparse but confirmatory. Driver and Coombs (1983) found meaningful frequencies in all four career concepts in a large sample of technical and business administration people. In general, those individuals whose career concepts fit the organization culture (Steady-State) reported high productivity, morale and life satisfaction. Those most out of line (i.e. Linear) reported the opposite. Coombs and Driver (1986) have found that there are interesting age differences in career concepts. The Transitory is most prevalent among younger workers, Steady-State and Linear are most frequent among middle aged, and Spiral is dominant among older workers. Tie-ins with life-cycle models are explored. Prince (1984) examined a version of the career concept model and found that work was more central for Linears as opposed to Steady-State or Transitory persons. Linear and Transitory persons had higher energy than Steady-State. Linear and Steady-State individuals show more organizational commitment than Transitory people.

Latack and D'Amico (1985) used actual job moves among youths to measure concepts (as opposed to the career concept questionnaire, Driver and Brousseau, 1981) used in the studies described above. They found that Steady-State youths enter high status occupations with moderate aspirations. Transitories enter lower-status organizations with low aspirations and Linears simply show high aspirations. In their youth sample, 70 per cent were Linear, 15 per cent Steady-State and 4 per cent Transitory. Some caution is needed in interpreting these studies since a distinction must be made between the ideal career concept a person wants (as measured by questionnaire), and the actual careers pursued or expected.

McKinnon (1987) expanded the career concepts model to study engineers. He described three patterns: a managerial Linear, a technical Linear and a technical Steady-State. The latter accounted for 50 per cent of his sample. They were older and less educated (BS only) than Linears and not interested in organizational advancement. They were interested in getting on to new challenging projects with considerable influence over the job. The two Linear types differed in cognitive style—the managerial being less detailed and complex—but they were similar in wanting to go up a ladder.

It may be noted that despite calls for 'Spiral' career approaches by organization behavior analysts, this concept has emerged least clearly in current concept research.

Several studies not overtly using the concept model, have shed light on career concept issues. For instance, Steiner and Farr (1986) find a strong Linear orientation among engineers. Rynes (1987) also finds a majority of an engineer sample hopeful of a Linear career. In fact, Badawy (1981) finds a majority of engineers do go into management. In other occupations the Linear orientation is not so prevalent. For instance, Burke (1985) reports that 40 per cent of a police sample (and only 12 per cent of a teacher sample) exhibit 'careerist' orientation—which is similar to the Linear in Cherniss's model (1980).

The degree of Linear orientation among managers is a matter of considerable controversy. Direct measures of career concepts among MBA's shows a marked increase in the percentage of Linears over the last ten years (Driver, 1985). No large samples using direct measures of concepts have occurred, but by extending the career concept model to include key motives much light on general trends can be shed. Prior research (Driver and Coombs, 1983) has linked career motives and career concepts. In particular, the motivation to get ahead in management and make money is uniquely tied to the Linear concept. In contrast, the Steady-State concept is tied to motives such as security, and the Spiral and Transitory concepts to motives such as novelty.

This linkage allows one to look at studies of career motives as clues to career concept patterns. One of the most interesting data sets has been developed by Astin and Greene (1987). Their work shows a massive shift from Spiral-like concerns with developing a 'philosophy of life' to a very Linear focus on financial well being and administrative responsibility. This shift began in 1975 and shows no signs of leveling off.

In contrast, research by Miner and Smith (1987) seems to suggest that motivation to manage (Linear) has declined from 1960 to 1980. However, Bartol et al. (1980) found the opposite—a rise in this Linear-type motivation using the same instrument. Disputes about scoring methods arose (Miner et al., 1985; Bartol and Schneier, 1985). However, the Bartol and Schneier view that Miner's results suffer from a too narrow baseline—one college in Oregon—seems most relevant. National trends seem to be largely Linear among managers and engineers as seen above.

Some of the confusion on Linear trends may also be due to the fact that in the 1960s and early 1970s there was a decline of Linear-type motives (Driver, 1985). Some of Miner's data may reflect this earlier pattern. The 'turnaround' to increasing Linear orientation occurred around 1975 for college freshman and probably reached MBA's around 1980. This fall from 1960 to 1975, followed by a rise of Linear thinking may explain why studies of 'baby boomers' (Russell, 1982; Hall and Richter, 1985) report values of autonomy, self-development, entrepreneurism and work–family balance. Such non-Linear values did peak for early baby boomers in the early 1970s. But the trend now seems reversed.

Work Values

Given the close tie-in of work values and career concepts, a look at research in this realm seems in order. MacNab and Fitzsimmons (1987) conducted an exemplary integrative study comparing three research approaches: needs, values and preferences. They found high convergent validity and a strong advancement (Linear) orientation showing in all three methods for their sample.

Further afield, Krau (1987) finds an overall Linear value pattern in Israel but notes interesting ethnic and religious differences which suggest some Spiral dominance in certain groups. Berger (1986) also analysed subgroup differences in work values for Mexican-Americans. The study confirmed prior Anglo results that women emphasize social–emotional work qualities (Bentell and Brennan, 1986) while men stress Linear values such as pay and promotion, as well as security and independence (Bush and Bush, 1978). Berger confirmed a male focus on advancement, prestige, security and safety. Also confirmed were white-collar *v.* blue-collar differences. In general, white-collar individuals stressed advancement, prestige, security and safety more than blue-collar.

In general, a Linear value trend seems to be surfacing, even beyond the US.

Career Anchors

Another framework for integrating career research might be Schein's career anchor theory (1971). His five basic anchors are assumed to be differential bases for careers—and hence lead to varied concepts of careers. The five basic anchors are managerial, technical, security-oriented, autonomy-oriented and entrepreneurial. De Long (1985) has factor-analysed these anchors into two dimensions: a management autonomy cluster, and a security technical cluster. These two dimensions could easily tie into a Linear *v.* Steady-State construct. Indeed, Prince (1984) has factor-analysed career concepts into two groups: stayers and movers (i.e. Linear, Spiral and Transitory).

However, purely quantitative analyses of these models can be deceptive since vagaries of samples are notorious. A more promising direction might be to attempt to integrate career concepts and motives into a 'minimum set' of useful dimensions for describing career orientations. By a minimal set I mean a number of categories which does justice to human complexity, yet avoids proliferation of an operationally useless number of categories.

Derr (1986) has attempted to provide 5 orientations which might be a prototype for a minimal set:

Getting ahead—A fusion of the Linear career concept and the managerial anchor;
Getting secure—a fusion of the Steady-State concept and the security anchor;
Getting high—the Spiral concept;
Getting free—a fusion of the Transitory concept and the autonomy anchor;
Getting balanced—a unique focus on work/non-work balance.

The career concept model has also proposed subdividing concepts by motives. There could be two Steady-State patterns—competence and security-oriented; two Linear types—power and achievement-oriented; two Transitory types—identity seeking and novelty-oriented; and several Spiral types—self-development and nurture/mentor oriented (see Driver, 1979). At present a usable minimal set remains an important target for career research.

Organizational Commitment

A final definitional issue concerns the role of organizational identity or commitment in careers. There is a stream of research on organizational commitment which views this aspect of a career as a very positive indicator—both for individuals and organizations (see Mowday et al., 1974). It is seen as a good indication of work satisfaction as well as a predictor of performance. In this view, factors which reduce commitment, such as education, are seen as problematic since commitment is such a strong value (Mottaz, 1986).

However, from a career concept view, this construction of commitment becomes an extreme case of Steady-State thinking—in which organization *and* occupation are essential in career definition. Prince (1984) and Driver and Coombs (1983) find that organizational commitment is a strong correlate of Steady-State concepts. The problem here is that there are career concepts for which commitment is low, yet self-satisfaction is not low (e.g. Transitory in Driver and Coombs, 1983).

It would therefore seem useful to broaden research on organizational commitment to include a more positive view of those non-Steady-State people for whom low commitment may *not* be a sign of trouble (see the idea of resilience, below). On the other hand, this stream of research does suggest the importance of including organizational loyalty as a part of at least some career definitions.

PERSONALITY AND CAREERS

Although we have looked at certain personality factors above, there are many interesting streams of research on personality and careers that do not impinge directly on career definitional issues. I shall review first personality development models and then turn to adult personality factors.

Development Theory

Despite the consensus on the 1980s being the era of life-cycle theories, the research literature reviewed here seems to be dominated by one model—the Erikson view. Although it is a life-cycle theory, the Erikson model focuses on the central issue of careers—identity—but once in a lifespan. For Erikson, once the identity problem has been resolved in one's twenties, or early thirties, one should move on to relationships—e.g. intimacy. As a result, research based on Erikson has tended to view career choice as a one time event—a Steady-State view.

One of the most pervasive variants of Erikson's model was developed by Marcia (1966) with the terms diffuse, foreclosed, moratorium and achieved identity. She defined diffuse as having no identity, foreclosed as reaching an easy, externally given identity with no inner choice, moratorium as still searching and achieved as an inner identity based on self-search. Using Marcia's interview method Larkin (1987) found that diffuse and moratorium types had higher fear of success than the focused/foreclosed and achieved identity types. Grotevant and Thorbecke (1982) found the achieved type to correlate well with Holland's measure of identity. Using an objective measure of Marcia's types, Neimeyer and Metzlar

(1981) found the achieved identity types to be more complex in their thinking about careers. The positive side of the Marcia's work is its emphasis on moving from external identities (foreclosed) to real identity as warmly advocated by Shepard (1986).

What this research suggests is that the person with an achieved, self-realized identity is superior to the more fearful, simplistic types. This clearly favors a Steady-State or possibly Linear view of careers and has come under attack as too narrow a view of the identity process. Gilligan (1982), for instance, has noted that Erikson's model is male-oriented. She suggests that for women, relationship issues precede rather than follow identity issues.

In a far more sweeping revision, Logan (1986) suggests a recapitulation model of the basic Erikson concept. Just as Erikson sees early childhood problems such as trust and autonomy recapitulating in the identity crisis, so Logan suggests that identity issues can reoccur at later life stages when a person is apparently focusing on relationships. Identities can be reshaped even after they are 'achieved' in early adulthood. Logan shows how this view of Erikson is compatible with Levinson's and Gould's models of life-cycle change. It can only be hoped that this view of Erikson can receive research analysis and lead to a view of career identity which can admit to change—even from 'achieved' status.

Another line of developmental research stems from the work of Owens (1979) on life history. Using a largely empirical grouping method Owens found 15 male and 17 female groups with similar background factors. Membership in groups tied into subsequent career patterns. The number of Owens' life-history groups possibly exceeds the 'minimum set' for practical research. Many of these groupings are tantalizing in their affinity for some of the simpler theoretical models underlying career choice. For instance, the 'upward mobile' group suggests the Linear concept; the 'analytic adaptive' group seems like the technical anchor of Schein; the 'virile extravert' may relate to the realist of Holland. The potential for integrative research tying these groups to more parsimonious models is clear.

Neiner and Owens (1985) in fact do tie in life-history factors to the Holland interest groups. Using actual job choices they find connections linking life history groups to the Holland categories. For instance, the life-history factors: academic achievement, science interest and social intraversion connect to the investigative interest group. Eberhart and Mushinsky (1982) did similar analyses using proposed work areas for students.

A possible problem in this life-history approach is its fairly Steady-State orientation. Davis (1984) has suggested that there is some change in life-history groups over seven years. From our view this is positive since it permits some people to shift patterns as their life unfolds—supporting Spiral or Transitory concepts of career.

Adult Personality. 1: Interests

Research on interests is dominated by the overarching Holland schema—which will be considered later. But some further developments on the Strong Campbell Vocational Interest Blank have occurred.

Hill and Hansen (1986) studied sex differences in managers and technical managers. In general, managers show no sex differences (Donnell and Hall, 1980). However, Hill and Hansen found that for technical managers, females were higher on Artistic interests, while males were higher on Realistic interests. They also find technical managers were more Investigative and less Enterprising than general managers (which ties in with McKinnon's data, see above).

On a broader front, Fouad *et al.* (1986) challenge the previous notion (e.g. Hansen and Campbell, 1985) that there are no cross-cultural differences in interests for occupations. On the contrary, they suggest that only if an occupation has universal norms (e.g. science, accounting, etc.) will one see similarity across cultures. As evidence, their data show similar interests for Mexican and American accountants but not for attorneys whose roles in their two countries are quite dissimilar.

Adult Personality. 2: Achievement Motives

Farmer (1985) conducted a major review and extension of understanding in the area of achievement motivation. She breaks the motive into three parts: level of aspiration (LOA), need for competence, and centrality of work/career. The connection of this construct with the Linear concept should be clear.

Her review of LOA research suggests that high aspiration is a function of higher social status, urban location, intelligence, self-esteem, independence and the support of parents and teachers. Her own data for women support these findings (except for independence) and add the factors of race and a supportive attitude on women working.

Past research on competence motivation suggests a positive role of social status, self esteem, being male, intrinsic (*v.* instrumental) values and parent–teacher support. Fear of success has a negative effect. In her data she confirms only the support variable, but adds location (urban), math ability, independence and competitiveness. Career centrality has been linked to sex, intelligence, self-esteem, intrinsic values, support and competence. Her data confirm the latter two, and add race and independence.

One can conclude that sex differences in LOA antecedents are minimal, but that for competence and career centrality, sex differences are sizeable. In particular, the female factors in competence motivation suggest the pattern needed to break the 'female stereotype' to be discussed below.

While very intriguing research, it would be more synergistic if it had not such a stand alone quality. For instance, it would be interesting to tie LOA to concepts like Linear *v.* Steady-State (e.g. is it the absolute level aimed for, or the number of steps on the way that make the difference?). Also, connecting career centrality with the broader work/non-work construct would be most interesting.

Adult Personality. 3: Self-efficacy and Locus of Control

It might seem strange to link these two concepts; however, internal locus of control refers to a belief in self-causation which comes very close to self-efficacy.

Differences due to locus of control continue to emerge in research. On a very general level the internal locus person is more satisfied with work, supervisors and promotions. They are more involved in work and see work as important (Stout, Slocum and Cron, 1987). The internals are more career satisfied but nevertheless initiate more job moves (Hamner and Vardi, 1981). Internals do more self-exploration and have more career information (Noe and Steffy, 1987).

The self-efficacious person also emerges with a 'glow'—they use wider ranges of career choice (Rotburg *et al.*, 1987), and are higher in their integration of vocational material (Neville *et al.*, 1986). Lack of a sense of self-efficacy has been blamed as a cause of females not breaking out of traditional jobs. The implication here is that internal, self-efficacious people make 'better' career choices. There are two problems here. One is: what is cause, and what is effect? Andrisani and Nestel (1976), for instance, find that upward mobility correlates with increased internal locus of control. The question is whether internal locus contributes to success (Linear), or the reverse. Perhaps, Hall has the best answer with his notion that success breeds success—i.e. the two are reciprocal.

A more thorny issue concerns what are 'good' career choices. Are we to assume that high information use is better? Or, that Linear success is the only kind? We will revisit these issues a bit further on.

Adult Personality. 4: Intelligence

As seen above, intelligence plays a role in LOA, competency and career centrality. It has also been linked to interest patterns in another exemplary integrative study by Lowman, Williams and Leeman (1985). The six Holland interest categories were rationally linked to abilities: The Realistic interest is connected to mechanical and spatial ability, the Investigative to general and verbal intelligence, the Artistic to music and art ability, the Social to interpersonal skill, the Enterprising to leadership ability and the Conventional to clerical skill.

The results confirmed the Enterprising, Conventional and Social linkages. Artistic interest broke into separate music and art aptitude factors. Investigative interest tied to general, arithmetic and mechanical, but not verbal, ability. Realistic interests related to no abilities.

In general, the data support a link between content of career choice and ability. It also raises some question about the meaningfulness of the Realistic category which may bear further subdivision. It is also possibly worth noting how relatively sparse are intelligence related studies of career choice. Does this betoken a preference for heart over head in career studies (cf. Shepard, 1984)?

Adult Personality. 5: Cognitive Style

In strong contrast to sparse intelligence related studies, there seems to be a major interest in cognitive styles in career research. Perhaps one reason for this flurry of interest in style is the long standing interest in vocational guidance in constructs like vocational maturity which includes quasi-stylistic factors such as career planning, exploration, decision skill and vocational information. The underlying premise of this maturity construct seems to be the assumption that the more rational the career choice the better (Super, 1980). The assumption has been challenged (Phillips *et al.*, 1984), but a preponderance of opinion in this stream of research seems to favor 'rationality'. This debate naturally suggests an investigation of decision-style in career choice.

Harren (1979) proposed a style model contrasting rational with intuitive and dependent styles. Unlike the orderly information-oriented rational style, the intuitive relies on feeling and little data whereas the dependent style gets direction from others with little internal processing.

The normative flavor of this model is revealed in Phillips and Strohmeyer's (1982) conclusion that the dependent style is not 'effective' in career decisions. However, Bud and Daniels (1985) report the intuitive style is 'surprisingly' not unadaptive in career thinking. Blustein (1987) counters with the suggestion that for well-informed students absence of rational style may not matter, whereas for less sophisticated students, style will matter. He supports this with less-informed students where the rational style positively correlated with vocational maturity while the other two styles showed negative correlations.

The problem surfacing here is one that occurred early in the general cognitive style literature. In particular, Witkin's field independence model had a strong normative bias—and ultimately was found to correlate heavily with intelligence.

Much of the other work on style has tried to avoid this normative, intelligence like bias, taking instead the view that all styles are 'good' for certain types of information settings (see Driver, 1975). The point here is whether a rational approach is always best. Shepard (1984) strongly argues for a more intuitive 'path with a heart'. One could find sociologically-minded defenders of the idea that careers should be fitted to the needs of society—which could favor a dependent style.

The ultimate issue again is: what is a good career choice? Is it one that is logical, one that feels good, one that contributes to society, one that maximizes personal growth or power? Unless we can develop a framework for resolving this question it may be wise to avoid premature closure on any one criterion of what makes a good choice.

Nevertheless, the analysis of styles in the choice process seems a very promising direction of research. It can lead to a far better descriptive analysis of the choice process than earlier efforts. This is clearly seen in the line of research building on the Kelly personal construct model (Bodden, 1970). In this approach vocational areas and attributes are grouped into classes yielding scores on differentiation—the number of distinct categories of thought; and integration—the amount of linkage among categories.

The evolution of this research stream paralleled the earlier work on general cognitive complexity in its initial focus on differentiation, which is still seen in more recent studies; e.g. Brown's (1987) result that using one's own vocational constructs yields a more differentiated structure than using experimenter developed attributes.

However, as Winer and Gati (1986) note, some time ago we (Schroder, Driver and Streufert, 1969) emphasized the danger in equating complexity with pure differentiation. One could have many cognitive dimensions to work with yet deal with any one situation very simplistically if the dimensions were not connected and only one dimension was brought to bear at a time. The distinction between these two complexity factors is shown by the negative correlation usually found between them (Neimeyer and Metzler, 1987).

In fact, most studies of this type do stress integration following Cochran's lead (1977). Research has shown that the more integrated the vocational concept system is, the more one finds:

1. Rapid information processing (Cochran, 1977).
2. More information values (Adams-Webber, 1979).
3. More active exploration of identity (i.e. achieved or moratorium types in Marcia's framework) (Neville et al., 1986).
4. More self-efficacy (Neville et al., 1986).

High integration with low differentiation has been associated with better recall of information on vocations (Neville et al., 1986). Whereas, high integration and high differentiation has been linked to the 'achieved identity' of Marcia's typology.

One might be tempted to see a 'master integration' occurring here: the high-complexity person as the nexus of self-efficacy, achieved identity, rational decision process, etc. However, some caution is urged.

First, the Kelly object sorting methodology almost forces a conflict between differentiation and integration. This has caused many of us in the cognitive style area to seek other methods of measuring integration independent of differentiation (see Schroder et al., 1969; Streufert and Streufert, 1979). Also, the tendency to exalt the complex style may be biased. At this stage in career research can we be sure that simpler styles will always make poor or false career choices?

Finally, the focus on complexity in vocational constructs, while highly relevant to careers, is fraught with a problem noted by Winer and Gati (1986). The problem is that complexity across a particular content domain varies within a person. For instance, Winer and Gati found more complexity underlying rejected occupations than selected occupations. One implication of this finding is that 'achieved' or focused identity may be tied to simpler structures, while uncertainty generates more complexity. I shall pursue this issue later.

Another reaction to the Winer and Gati result is to worry about the generality of complexity scores based on one content domain. In our work (e.g. Driver and Streufert, 1969) we have tried to assess the complexity of a presumed central cognitive processing unit which remains relatively stable across content areas and over time. The complexity of this central processor is most accurately measured when a person is dealing with new information and past memory is minimalized. Becoming too domain specific allows the complexity of past experience (i.e. memory traces) to impact and distort the central processor's own structure. We suggest that the most general measure of cognitive structure—i.e. the central processor's structure—might give the most stable measure of career-related complexity since in our work this measure has predicted choice behavior in many varied settings. The general 'decision style' of a person (Driver and Mock, 1975) might give a broader insight into how people cope with all aspects of careers compared to a more domain specific technique.

At present, only a few studies have explored this general decision style model in relation to career issues. The four basic styles in this model are:

(a) *Decisive*—low differentiation, low integration
(b) *Flexible*—high differentiation, low integration
(c) *Hierarchic*—low differentiation, high integration
(d) *Integrative*—high differentiation and integration

Prince (1979) has linked these general styles to career concepts. The Decisive style was correlated with the Linear career concept while the Steady-State concept was negatively correlated with the Integrative style. Olson (1979) reports similar findings. More recently Coombs (1987) has found a consistent style-concept pattern, e.g. Spiral and Transitory correlations with Flexible and Integrative styles.

Schutt (1979) has found interesting connections between Holland interest patterns and style. For instance, the Enterprising orientation correlates with Decisive style while the Investigative correlates with the Integrative style. Finally, Owens (1979) finds general style variables helpful in defining life-history groupings and Strong Campbell Vocational Interest areas. For instance, Integrative style is linked to interests such as psychiatry, personnel, computer programming and law. One other interesting result in Owens work is a connection of Decisiveness and conformity to the female role. Bartunek and Louis (1985) have found that experienced MBAs had higher Flexible and Integrative scores, and lower Decisive scores than inexperienced MBAs. They found differential reactions to socialization at work for each style. They also reported how various factors contributed to style change at work. (This is reviewed in more detail below.)

In sum, after seeing the diversity of these studies of personality and career choice, I strongly endorse Schein's (1986) call for efforts to integrate these varied personality patterns into a minimal set which can propel career research onto a new level.

CAREER CHOICE PROCESSES

Career Indecision

We now wish to shift the focus from studies of factors affecting career processes to research on the process itself. A transitional topic concerns 'career indecision'.

This topic has been a prime focus in traditional vocational guidance literature. Osipow (1976) has developed a scale concerning decidedness which is similar to the maturity measures of Super *et al.* (1981) and Crites (1973). It also resembles Holland's identity scale (Holland *et al.*, 1980) and even Marcia's concept of achieved identity. Integrative studies have linked these measures.

Graef *et al.* (1985) found the Super, Holland and Osipow scales highly intercorrelated. Grotevant and Thorbeck (1982) and Savickas (1985) empirically linked Marcia's achieved identity and Holland's scales. Fuqua and Seaworth (1987) again find high intercorrelation among decidedness scales as well as a strong relation between all of them and anxiety. Even the complexity model gets on board as Niemeyer and Metzler (1987) find high differentiation tied to indecision.

However, the research literature does raise some caveats on any premature closure on the idea that career decidedness is the 'ultimate state' for career happiness. Hartman *et al.* (1983) found that the indecision variable was not very stable over time. They suggest three 'types': decided, developmentally undecided, and chronic undecided. Hartman *et al.* (1985) found the chronic undecided type had more anxiety, less stable self-perception and more external locus of control than the other two types. However, Hartman *et al.* (1986) also found that the unreliability of the decidedness construct increases from decided, to developmentally undecided, to chronic undecided.

The connection of this research to career concept theory is quite intriguing. If we equate decided with Steady-State, and undecided—particularly chronic undecided—with Transitory or Spiral concepts, this line of research can lift itself above a normative plane in which decided equals good. It may allow fascinating possible insights into the affective and personality dynamics of diverse, yet legitimate 'undecided' career orientations.

Another line of effort here as seen in Graef *et al.* (1985) is work on the antecedents of the Super, Holland and Osipow approaches to decidedness. The three measures did not share similar background factors and in some cases they showed rather socially undesirable associations. The Osipow 'decided' type and much of the super 'mature' person pattern showed correlation with low GPA and, in addition, the Super mature type showed poor social adjustment. Westbrook *et al.* (1985) also found no correlation of maturity and academic success although they do see some connection of maturity with students own satisfaction with their career processes. In a more positive vein, Healey *et al.* (1985) report the 'mature' students (in Crites' model) to be older, have a higher GPA and better college jobs.

Several comments are in order. While it seems clear that a major distinction in career states (or concepts, if you prefer) does exist (e.g. decided Steady-State *v.* undecided Transitory), it is by no means clear that one is superior to the other. For instance, undecidedness may be a wholesome, workable state for chronic Transitory people who have found a proper career setting. On the other hand, we hardly deny that for Steady-State (or Linear) people, undecidedness may be indeed a highly traumatic, anxiety-producing and undesirable state. Putting the decidedness variable in a broader context would illuminate career choice research.

Career Planning

The research on career planning has been mainly covered under previous headings with a few scattered exceptions. One such area concerns sex differences in planning. Brenner and Tomkievicz (1979) found males doing more planning; whereas Rynes and Rosen (1983) found no sex differences. A similar concern for sex difference exists concerning the use of career information. Yanico and Hardin (1986) found that women estimated their vocational knowledge in non-traditional work areas as less than did men. In fact, real knowledge showed no sex effect. Whether those sex factors can be subsumed under broader sex differences (e.g. in cognitive style) should form an interesting research target.

Interventions in Career Process

There continues to be considerable research on interventions to improve career choice processes, despite Holland's (1981) concern that these interventions have little effect.

One general trend is for intervention to produce more decidedness and more positive feeling about career processes (e.g. Remer *et al.*, 1984; Neimeyer and Ebben, 1985; Slaney and Lewis, 1986). Neimeyer and Ebben found that interventions such as the Holland search processes, computer interactive systems and providing vocational information *decreased* complexity. Thus, as noted above, decidedness may actually link to cognitive simplicity, not complexity. A further point is that at least one of these interventions (Ramer *et al.*, 1984) also found an increase in a 'rational' style. It may be that intervention to improve decidedness and rationality decrease complexity.

A counter-trend, however, is found in a few studies showing more explorations after intervention—possibly implying greater complexity. For instance, assessment center feedback (Noe and Steffy, 1987) and problem-solving training (Jepson *et al.*, 1982) increase exploration. And the vocational information treatment in the Neimeyer and Ebben study seemed to produce a slight increase in complexity in a follow-up time period.

It appears that very structured interventions may produce a stable but simple 'identity', whereas more open interventions may raise complexity. Along these lines, Robbins and Tucker (1986) found that 'unstable' types (i.e. non-steady-state) worked better in more open interactive career workshops compared to structured techniques. Would not an interesting line of research be to study effects and affinities of different career orientation types for different types of intervention?

But again, we must ask: by what criteria do we judge the goodness of intervention? Until the field examines the issue of how to define 'good' careers, projections of each researcher's definition will continue to be dominant. I would suggest that the use of a descriptive model, such as career concepts or career anchors, could help us take a broader, less uni-focused, normative view of 'goodness in career choice'.

EARLY CAREER ISSUES

Socialization and the Effect of Work

Several theoretical approaches to socialization have recently surfaced. Reichers (1987) has suggested an interactive framework for viewing the process. He suggests that person factors such as field dependence, tolerance of ambiguity, and affiliation needs will increase the rate of socialization. Environmental facilitators would include task interdependence, orientation programs, training, performance evaluation and mentoring.

Hopefully, new research will focus on this model since certain factors (e.g. tolerance of ambiguity) might work opposite to the role suggested by Reichers and certain personality factors (e.g. general decision style) may be a useful addition in his model (see below).

Morrison and Hock (1986) also propose an interactive model seeing work experience as the major factor in shaping careers. They cite an extensive literature showing how work alters personal factors such as locus of control, authoritarianism, well-being and mental health. In particular they cite studies (such as Kohn and Schooler, 1982; Brousseau, 1983) showing deleterious effects of overly simple work. They propose that careers should be shaped by exposing people to incrementally increasing complexity in work—a view shared by Brousseau (1984). They correctly note that this will require extremely effective job analysis and design. However, they do not focus, as Brousseau does, on the need to specifically measure and design complexity on the job. They do, however, stress the importance in selection of measuring changeable, as well as invariant, characteristics. Complexity of style clearly seems to be of the former class (see Bartunek and Louis, 1985) underlining the potential value in the cognitive complexity approach.

Another aspect of the Bartunek and Louis study deserves a summary at this point. They expected that inexperienced MBAs would be more affected by socialization aids (e.g. training) as opposed to work itself; while the opposite would be true for experienced MBAs. The prediction held for inexperienced MBAs and initially for experienced MBAs. However, over time socialization aids were seen retroactively as important by experienced MBAs, as well as work.

As noted above, interesting differences in decision style also emerged. For instance, formal training decreased complexity for all MBAs; whereas relation factors, such as buddy relations and mentoring, increased complexity for experienced MBAs. Curiously many factors that attracted complex styles initially at work (e.g. task variety) actually were associated with declining complexity over time. This study may have uncovered support for the premise in complexity theory that too great a rate of change in environmental complexity can produce a decline in personal complexity (see Driver and Streufert, 1969).

Success Factors in Different Types of Career

(a) Female careers

Gutek *et al.* (1986) have provided a thorough review of women at work so only a quick look will be given to this topic here. They note that despite a major influx of women into the world's workforce, sex segregation of jobs is still pandemic. For instance, Von Glinow and Kryczkowska (1985) found no increase in the tiny percentage of women on boards or serving as officers in major corporations. Females are also portrayed in company brochures in typically 'female stereotype' jobs.

The problem of unequal pay is also still prevalent. In the face of this, women appear to be developing increasingly less stereotypical views of their potential work roles. For instance, recently Foss and Slaney (1986) found that more liberal women had higher self-efficacy and chose non-traditional jobs for their daughters. Being a working mother, although a great strain due to simultaneous competing role elements, tends to foster this liberal attitude (e.g. Hoffman, 1974).

(b) Entrepreneur careers

Derr (1984) proposes an interesting typology of entrepreneurs and suggests varied orientations in each. He proposes a small business type who is social and focused on one area; a technical entrepreneur who is a craftsman also focused on one area; an administrative type who pursues not income but new projects inside a company; an adventurer who seeks diverse ventures, risk and profit and an artist driven by creativity. In particular, the distinction of a variety oriented, risk seeking type *v.* a one-venture security-oriented type seems very useful since they are often grouped together and yet differ profoundly in career orientation (e.g. Steady-State *v.* Transitory).

Bowen and Hesrick (1986) reviewed the entrepreneur literature particularly for women. They note a lack of general trends in predicting entrepreneurial success. For instance, some studies suggest entrepreneurs are not highly educated, others suggest they are; some are risk-takers, some aren't. Bowen and Hesrick suggest that some of this inconsistency may be due to the different types of industry studied, e.g. high-tech *v.* low-tech. However, attention to distinctions among types of entrepreneurs such as Derr has proposed might yield much clearer results on success factors in this career area.

(c) Managerial careers

Studies on factors in manager success are not particularly frequent. Howard (1984) found that linear motives, tolerance for ambiguity, dominance and independence predicted managerial success. Jaskolke and Beyer (1985) stressed sociological factors such as education, years with a company and job involvement as success factors.

One important distinction which seems needed in this literature is between levels of management. Dalton and Thompson (1986) provide an impressive analysis of the demands of four organizational levels—apprentice, individual contributor, manager and director. They point out that moves from individual contributor to manager require a relinquishment of technical, inside oriented self-absorption and instead a broader focus on others, the outside world and administration. Moves from manager to director require increased skills in providing vision, representing the organization, exercising power and sponsoring new talent. Kotter (1982) provides a similar role analysis for managers.

Given the discrete job demands at different levels, one would expect greater focus and precision in looking for success factors at each level. Top-level factors have received considerable attention. Bennis and Nanus (1986) provide great insight into the traits needed by top leaders. They find that vision, particularly a positive self-regard, a great ability to ask questions and listen, a strong results focus, and a capacity to create clear, compelling goals are essential qualities. Levinson and Rosenthal (1984) agree with most of these findings and would add a willingness to take risks, to take charge and to combine thinking and doing. Dropping down a level, Kotter (1982) finds traits like being sociable (a networker), being stable and optimistic, above average in IQ, moderately analytical as well as having the pervasive Linear motives of power and achievement are vital in successful general managers.

The changes between levels in required traits suggests a great need for deeper analysis of succession planning and management development that has been typical. Sorcher (1985) describes the actual processes used in succession planning but gives only some general ideas on what traits are involved in the failure to make it to the top (e.g. lack of integrity, selfish, too political, rigid, unpleasant). Brady and Helmich (1984) provide great insight into the relative merits of inside vs. outside succession, but only touch on the issue of personality factors in succession.

One of the more intriguing lines of work which concerns executive cognitive style seems to be gaining interest. Streufert (1986) has stressed a unique integrative complexity among successful managers. Weick (1983), on the contrary, stresses a strong action focus. I have proposed that a combination style using integration under moderate stress and a more simplistic Decisive style under high pressure may be the unique 'executive style' (Driver, 1986). However, future research here may reveal that types of industries and even stages of organization life-cycle may relate to optimal management cognitive style.

(d) Expatriate careers

One area of emerging interest concerns careers outside one's own culture (Conway and Von Glinow, 1986). The US expatriate seems to have a more difficult time adjusting than European or Japanese (Dunn, 1980; Tung, 1982). The key problem seems to be family and personal adjustment.

Prior experience seems to help an expatriate as well as traits of empathy, respect, flexibility, tolerance, interest in local cultures, and task skills. It may be expected that more culture-specific adaptation factors (e.g. success factors for Africa v. Japan) may emerge as this research area develops. Mendenhall and Oddou (1985) begin to address the issue of cultural difference as well as proposing a fairly complex model of expatriate success. They suggest three dimensions of success:

(a) *Self-oriented*—capacity to change means of gratification, capacity to reduce stress and competence.
(b) *Other-oriented*—capacity to relate and to communicate.
(c) *Perceptual*—absence of rigidity and ethnocentric judgement.

Each of these factors needs to be adjusted for 'cultural toughness'; i.e. Asian and African sites seem tougher than others (Torbiorn, 1982).

While a promising start, it might prove useful to connect this line of research more to general personality models—e.g. cognitive styles. It might also be useful to describe cultures on dimensions tied to measurable expatriate personality traits—e.g. if cultures vary in their typical information processing complexity, matching cultures to expatriate decision style might be quite helpful (Meshkati and Driver, 1986).

LATER CAREER ISSUES

Plateauing

Although some earlier work (Bray and Howard, 1980) suggests that plateaued managers adjust well, there is growing concern that plateauing may be a very serious problem. Near (1985) reports that plateaued managers were more absent, had poorer relations with superiors, and impaired health. The plateaued manager had poorer education which tallies with prior data on education and management advancement.

Some of the differences in data on plateauing may be due to age. Hall (1986) reviews studies which show that younger plateaued managers are more adversely affected than older. I would also point to the probability that Linear type people would be most hurt by plateauing, while Steady-State would be least bothered.

Career Change

One response to the mid-career problems has been to increasingly advocate career change (Hall, 1986). Hall sees the primary problem in mid-career being a constriction of opportunity. He sees early career stages as being driven by short run performance goals (achievement). Success breeds more success (Howard, 1984). However, at mid-career, chances to perform run out. Hall suggests that some might cope by shifting energy to non-work channels. Others might benefit by shifting jobs laterally (Bailyn and Lynch, 1983), or even downward (Hall and Isabella, 1985).

The central idea here is that as the gap between expectations and reality widens, a new career search can begin (Mihal et al., 1984). This new career search may focus more on finding deeper identity or on adaptability or resilience (London and Stumpf, 1986).

It is clear that Hall is advocating a 'Spiral'-type solution in which new identities are developed over a lifespan, as Logan has suggested. Hall points to the Spiral-type career structure at Digital Equipment (Kidder, 1981) as a prototype. If one is a Spiral or Transitory-type person, these solutions make sense. The problem here is whether truly Linear types can make a meaningful career concept changes. We have found that many apparent Linears are 'closet Spirals or Transitories' waiting for a chance for the organization to approve of lateral moves. For them, the Hall-type solution is excellent. For 'true' Linears, career change may be a hard solution.

For many Steady-State people, Lorsch and Takayi (1986) may have hit a key solution to mid-life problems. They note that successful plateaued managers have had histories of 'mainline' assignments which leave them committed even when no further linear movement is possible. This ties in with Brousseau's (1978) finding that strong task identity and significance impart greater energy. It also ties in with our proposition that for Steady-State persons' 'centrality' (in Schein's [1971] terms—being in the center of the action—is a substitute for advancement.

For the true Linear, perhaps threat of job loss may cause a self-renewal process and shift to another career concept (e.g. Latack and Dozier, 1985). At this stage the factors enhancing concept change, particularly for Linears, remain a prime target for research.

A final line of research on career change concerns factors that facilitate change. Stout, Slocum and Cron (1987) support Louis's (1980) premise that if either a boss or a subordinate have experienced change and the other has not, things go better. Too much change (i.e. both parties) is disruptive (Latack, 1984). Spousal support also seems crucial in career change and is reported to be present for most changers (Anderson-Kulman *et al.*, 1986). Studies show that after the change, husbands are more at home, marriages improve, self-concepts are better, but social activity decreases. Here again one wonders if this picture would be so idyllic for true Linears.

Job Loss

Fryer and Payne (1986) have recently surveyed this area thoroughly, as have Latack and Dozier (1986) and De Frank and Ivancevich (1986). There is considerable consensus that job loss lowers happiness and increases the frequency of depression, mental illness and physical illness. Less clear but possible consequences are higher death rates, suicide, lowered self-esteem and family disorders. Greenhalgh (1985) even notes that survivors of layoffs show increased anxiety and disengagement.

In general, over time, the impact of job loss is maximum at first then wears down. A key coping mechanism is active job search, which is enhanced by expectations of success (Kanfer and Holin, 1985).

Factors facilitating coping include age (younger or older are better), being male, non-caucasian, highly active, 'hardy' (Kobasa and Puceitti, 1984)—that is, *not* committed (i.e. not Steady-State)—being well-off, having sound support, advance warning, good reasons for being let go, and being told by one's immediate boss.

It is suggested that if the stress is moderate and support such as outplacement is given, the experience can even lead to growth. Again, a career concept view here is that for the Steady-State and Linear person, these results make sense, but for Transitories of Spirals ('hardy' or 'resilient' types), job loss is simply a challenge to move on—especially if it is not due to personal incompetence.

Retirement

Only one review of retirement came to light by Beehr (1986). Surprisingly, he cites studies showing retirement as non-stressful (Kasl, 1980) and productive of less illness (Minkler, 1981). However, Ekerdt *et al.* (1983) note that retirees tend to ignore health problems.

Again, individual differences surface. Lower-status workers die faster (Hayes *et al.*, 1978). May this be due to prolonged effects of job simplicity *à la* Kohn and Schooler? Committed (i.e. Steady-State, Linear) types show low satisfaction in retirement (Glamser, 1981). In fact, we might suggest that retirement is little or no stress for change-oriented career types.

ORGANIZATION–PERSON CONGRUENCE MODELS

The Holland Model

Considerable research has been marshalled by Holland and his associates (e.g. Gottfredson, 1977) that individuals who choose occupations which fit their interest pattern will fare better in subsequent careers.

One challenge to this view comes from Schwartz *et al.* (1986). They suggest that in most cases, Holland supporters show that Investigative types do better in Investigative settings than non-Investigative types. The problem, they point out, is that Investigative types are generally higher achievers. The real test of the Holland congruence model then would be to determine if a non-Investigative setting favored non-Investigative types. They raise serious questions by finding that Conventional type accountants (a Conventional area) achieve poorer salaries than non-Conventional types.

This type of result raises questions as to whether the very popular Holland scheme—especially in the Realistic (see IQ data above) and Conventional interest categories—could not benefit by cross-fertilization with some other variables (e.g. complexity of interest fields may better sort out patterns).

A more fundamental challenge to the entire congruence concept is put forth by Pazy and Zin (1987). They suggest that psychological needs for consistency moderate the effects of occupation-interest congruence. In their view, if interests match occupations, all is well. However, if there is a mismatch, only those people with secondary interest patterns which are similar (congruent) to primary interests will be disturbed. Those with incongruent (dissimilar) secondary interest patterns will not be disturbed. Congruence of interest patterns is defined as having secondary interests adjacent to one's primary interests in the Holland hexagram. In sum, incongruence between interests and occupation is only a problem for those with 'inner congruence'.

Their research generally supports the proposed model. However, there are some concerns. One, 'job involvement' comes out as being low for situations where occupation and interest are congruent, which is not expected. In contrast, satisfaction variables are predictably high for congruent cases. Some explanation of this oddity seems needed.

Secondly, several interpretations of this general view are plausible. One which they favor is that low inner consistency in interest areas is symptomatic of high tolerance for ambiguity, which makes occupation-interest incongruence a positive event. This view, incidentally, is consistent with my General Incongruity Adaptation Level model (Driver, 1984), not inconsistent as Pazy and Zin assert.

Another interpretation, however, is that since inner incongruent types have two divergent sets of interests, when they are in an occupation not matching their primary interests, it may still match their secondary areas. Further analysis, or perhaps new studies using a direct measure of inner uncertainty tolerance, might clarify these issues.

Career Culture–Career Concept Congruence

Coombs and Driver (1983) directly tested the career concept models' prediction that if a company constructs a culture (Driver, 1980) which resonates with a person's career concept, optimal performance will occur. Using questionnaire analysis, a company was determined to be seen as largely Steady-State in culture—particularly in its reward system. It was expected that Steady-State-type people would report higher commitment, satisfaction and productivity in this company, which they did. They also report more life satisfaction, a not unexpected 'spillover' of work satisfaction into non-work.

As expected, the Linear types reported strong lack of commitment, low satisfaction and productivity and negative spillover into life satisfaction. The Spirals showed only moderate discomfort and were possibly sustained by intrinsic job interest. The Transitory result was most interesting—unexpectedly low negativity and an apparent compensatory good feeling about avocational activities.

Organization Change and Congruence

An exciting new trend may be emerging in the more dynamic fitting of changing occupations or organizational settings with career interests, concepts, etc. Hall (1986), for instance, suggests matching individual life stages to organizational development stages. An illuminating example of this type of matching is described by Campbell and Moses (1986). They describe shifts in AT & T culture which included lower company identity, less promotion from within, changing standards for measuring high potential and a shift from manager to employee as career manager. However, hierarchic structure, work identity, and performance standards remained intact.

They also note that work values changed to less work primacy, less commitment and less need for structure. They concluded that employees' career orientations must change to more short-term, achievement-oriented, self-managed and, above all else, multiple-career oriented. In career concept language, they echo calls by theorists like Hall for a shift to Spiral career concepts. As noted, only further research will clarify whether changes in career concepts to match changing culture can easily occur.

Societal Trends and Careers

On a broader scale, London and Stumpf (1986) examine social trends which they believe might impact careers. They propose that automation is increasingly leading to a declining management role. They also see trends toward off site work, declining hierarchy, and declining work identification. In these trends, they see an imperative toward less concern with advancement and argue that workers today must develop 'career resiliency' as well as greater self-insight.

I would agree that trends at present are not moving in favor of a Linear career concept (Driver, 1985). To the above, I would add a baby boom bulge about to wipe out most possible movement in upper management, a lengthening of retirement decisions, a not very dynamic economic growth forecast, and the increasing passion to trim management levels. One might argue with some of these factors, but overall, trends do favor anything but the Linear career concept.

The problem, as noted earlier, is that almost all signals seem to say that the Linear type of concept is on the rise. It seems then that a major concern for theory, research and practice is to deal with how to either alter career concepts, or set up alternative Linear structures—perhaps in the leisure world?

Career Management Practice in Organization

Gutteridge (1986) has once again provided a thorough review of the states of the art in career management. I would group these practices into four areas:

Person assessment

By far and away the most common tools found in corporations are self-description work books usually used in workshops. There is some small use of professional counselors, but most often human resource people conduct such efforts. The problem with such methods is mainly self-deception (as London and Stumpf note), or self-ignorance. Sometimes discussion with supervisors can correct misperceptions, but often they too perceive through distorted lenses as the performance appraisal literature has pointed out.

A second tool of growing importance is the computer-based, interactive self-assessment method (Miner, 1986). It ha penetrated schools (Meyers and Cairo, 1983), and is beginning to be used by companies (Harris-Bowlsby, 1983). Despite the electronics, the heart of most of these systems is the same—self-assessment—with the same caveats as workbooks.

A possible corrective might be in greater use of professionally developed psychological tests, professional counselor interviews, and where economically defensible—assessment center methods. As Gutteridge notes, these methods are useful if feedback is given to the person by professionally trained personnel.

Even with these conditions, Gutteridge worries about rigid cutoffs and self-fulfilling prophesies if such methods are used to identify 'high potential'. I would tend to agree. I have found that testing works best when embedded in an integrated career management program which includes counseling, developmental programs, and reward systems not totally tied to Linear advancement (Von Glinow *et al.*, 1985).

There is evidence that psychological testing, hopefully purged of the inadequacies of the pre-EEOC era, is coming back into use. It is clearly a superior assessment tool to self- or other analysis (Reilly and Chao, 1982). A very useful line of research would be to evaluate how a developmentally-oriented testing approach impacts career processes in organizations. One of the problems here is the need for more intensive training among HR practitioners, and organization behavior researchers in test theory and practice. The general lack of such training is one of the fragmentors alluded to by Schein as plaguing this field.

Job analysis

Gutteridge mentions very little about job analysis. Unfortunately, as testing is heavily oriented toward selection, so job analysis tends to be driven by compensation needs. A technique known as job profiling has been described by Brousseau (1984) which builds a picture of the ideal incumbent's personality and abilities based on links to specific tasks in a job. Techniques like this, if in wider use, could provide a much needed advance over vague job descriptions or job analysis focused solely on motives or on aptitudes.

Given job analyses tied to measurable person traits, techniques such as job posting might become more useful. Unfortunately, at present, they are often meaningless blinds covering up predetermined decisions on vacancies—as Gutteridge notes.

Matching processes

Gutteridge and Miner both observe a renaissance of interest in skills inventories. After an abortive start, they seem to be getting more user friendly and specific. However, they seem largely focused on specific task competencies which as Morrison and Hock note, are not very useful in more abstract jobs such as in professions or management. The skill inventory technique, wedded to an integrated system, using common job–person dimensions has considerable promise—if it can avoid fossilization.

Perhaps the most critical area for matching is succession planning. Unfortunately, this area is so far rather barren of research at a deeper psychological level. Gutteridge sees most practice as biased and top down with little openness to career management issues.

Development

Gutteridge takes a dim view of formal career ladder systems which he sees as too focused on the past. While I see ladders as out of touch with trends toward loose, organic, Spiral systems, I suggest that ladders of some type are important to Linear people. A challenge of the future may be to invent new types of ladders.

Kram (1986) suggests that mentoring is a vitally important developmental process at all career stages—even late in one's career (Clawson, 1980). However, she notes that cross-sex mentoring can raise problems (Clawson and Kram, 1984). Formal mentoring programs can be poor if the fit between parties is poor. She suggests that mentoring is best introduced into an organization through general OD techniques.

Perhaps use of testing could produce a maximally useful mentoring program. For instance, a Spiral-type person might be very prone to mentoring, while a Linear would be threatened by the role. Also, developmental life stage might be crucial as Davis (1982) notes. Individuals at complementary life stages rather than competitive stages seem to work best in mentoring relationships.

Finally, we note that little research comes to light on the effect of developmental programs such as enrichment, rotation, or training on participants, other than the almost automatic 'feels good' response. This seems a rich field for future research—especially in relation to the effects of such program on career concepts.

In doing career management, Gutteridge suggests going slow and starting small. I agree, but must caution that all too often career programs end up isolated and vulnerable to the first cost reduction pressure. We have suggested that only when career programs become integrated with standard HR practice—such as performance appraisal, reward systems, selection programs and training will the real promise of the career area be met in organizations (Von Glinow *et al.*, 1983).

CONCLUSION

If there is one trend that most impressed the reviewer, it is the continued fragmentation of this field. Even within streams, there seems to be an unfortunate tendency to reinvent measures of constructs rather than first test or build on prior relevant materials. I see a great need for more research comparing and condensing overlapping measures into a hopefully general minimal set of measures. It is through shared measures that most scientific inquiry progresses.

At a broader level, I see a need for theories which embrace the psychological insights of vocational guidance and the growing organizational and sociological sensitivity of organizational theorists. If we are to truly understand organizational careers, the major themes discussed here must somehow begin to merge.

REFERENCES

Adams-Webber, J. (1979) *Personal Construct Theory.* New York: John Wiley.

Anderson-Kulman, R. and Paludi, M. (1986) Working mothers and the family context: predicting positive coping. *Journal of Vocational Behavior*, **28**, 241–53.

Andrisani, P. and Nestel, G. (1986) Internal–external control as a contributor to an outcome of work experience. *Journal of Applied Psychology*, **61**, 156–65.

Arthur, M. (1984) The career concept: Challenge and opportunity for its further application. In M. Arthur, L. Bailyn, D. Levinson and H. Shepard *Working With Careers*, New York: Columbia University School of Business.

Astin, D. and Greene, K. (1987) *The American Freshman: twenty-year trends.* Los Angeles: Higher Education Research Institute, UCLA.

Badawy, M. (1983) Why managers fail. *Research Management*, 26–31.

Bailyn, L. (1984) Issues of work and family in organizations: Responding to social diversity. In M. Arthur, L. Bailyn, D. Levinson and H. Shepard *Working With Careers*. New York: Columbia University School of Business.

Bailyn, L. and Lynch, J. (1983) Engineering as a life-long career: its meaning, its satisfactions, its difficulties. *Journal of Occupational Behavior*, **4**, 263–83.

Barton, K., Anderson, C. and Schneier, C. (1980) Motivation to manage among college business students: a reassessment. *Journal of Vocational Behavior*, **17**, 22–32.

Bartol, K. and Martin, D. (1987) Managerial motivation among MBA students: a longitudinal assessment. *Journal of Occupational Psychology*, **30**, 1–12.

Bartol, K. and Schneier, C. (1985) Internal and external validity issues with motivation to manage research: a reply. *Journal of Vocational Behavior*, **26**, 299–305.

Bartunek, J. and Louis, M. (1986) Information processing activities associated with organizational newcomers' complex thinking. Paper given at the Academy of Management, Chicago.

Beehr, T. (1986) The process of retirement. *Personnel Psychology*, **39**, 31–55.

Belsky, J., Steinberg, L. and Walker, A. (1982) The ecology of day care. In M. Lamb (ed.) *Nontraditional Families.* Hillside, N.J.: Lawrence Erlbaum.

Bennis, W. and Nanus, B. (1986) *Leaders.* New York: Harper and Row.

Bentell, N. and Brenner, O. (1986) Sex differences in work values. *Journal of Vocational Behavior*, **28**, 29–41.

Berger, P. (1986) Differences in importance and satisfaction from job characteristics by sex and occupational type among Mexican–American employees. *Journal of Vocational Behavior*, **28**, 203–213.

Birnbaum, J. (1971) Life patterns, personality and self-esteem in gifted family oriented and career oriented women. PhD Dissertation, University of Michigan.

Blustein, D. (1987) Decision-making styles and vocational maturity—an alternative perspective. *Journal of Vocational Behavior*, **30**, 61–71.

Bodden, J. (1970) Cognitive complexity as a factor in appropriate vocational choice. *Journal of Counseling Psychology*, **17**, 364–68.

Bowen, D. and Hesrich, R. (1986) The female entrepreneur—a career development perspective. *Academy of Management Review*, **11**, 393–407.

Bray, D. and Howard, A. (1980) Career success and life statisfaction of middle-aged managers. In L. Bond and J. Rosen (eds) *Competence and Coping During Adulthood*. Hanover, N.H.: University Press of New England.

Brady, G. and Helmich, D. (1984) *Executive Succession*. Englewood Cliffs, N.J.: Prentice-Hall.

Brenner, O. and Tomkiewicz, J. (1979) Job orientations of males and females: are sex differences declining? *Personnel Psychology*, **32**, 741–50.

Brousseau, K. (1978) Personality and job experience. *Organizational Behavior and Human Performance*, **22**, 235–52.

Brousseau, K. (1983) Toward a dynamic model of job–person relationships. *Academy of Management Review*, **8**, 33–45.

Brousseau, K. (1984) Job–person dynamics and career development. In K. Rowland and G. Ferris (eds) *Research in Personnel and Human Resources*, Vol. 2. Greenwich, CT: JAI Press.

Brown, M. (1987) A comparison of two approaches to the cognitive differentiation grid. *Journal of Vocational Behavior*, **30**, 155–66.

Bud, J. and Daniels, M. (1985) *Assessment of Career Decision Making: Manual*. Los Angeles: Western Psychology Press.

Burke, R. (1985) Career orientations, work experience and health. Paper given at the Academy of Management, San Diego.

Bush, P. and Bush, R. (1978) Women contrasted to men in the industrial sales force. *Journal of Marketing Research*, **15**, 43888.

Campbell, R. and Moses, J. (1986) Careers from an organizational perspective. In D. Hall and Associates (eds) *Career Development in Organizations*. San Francisco, Jossey-Bass.

Cherniss, C. (1980) *Professional Burnout in Human Service Organizations*. New York: Praeger.

Clawson, J. (1980) Mentoring in managerial careers. In C. B. Derr (ed.) *Work, Family, and the Career*. New York: Praeger.

Clawson, J. and Kram, K. (1984) Managing cross-gender mentoring. *Business Horizons*, May–June, 22–32.

Cochran, L. (1977) Differences between supplied and elicited constructs. *Social Behavior and Personality*, **5**, 241–47.

Conway, B. and Von Glinow, M. (1986) The successful expatriate: A comparative study of U.S., European, and Japanese expatriates in ASEAN. Unpublished manuscript, Department of Management and Organization, University of Southern California, Los Angeles.

Coombs, M. (1987) Measuring career concepts: an examination of the concepts, constructs, and validity of the career concept questionnaire. PhD Dissertation, University of Southern California, Los Angeles.

Coombs, M. and Driver, M. (1986) Who are you satisfied employees: A comparison of work attitudes and values with individual development. Paper given at the Academy of Management, Chicago.

Crites, J. (1973) *Theory and Research Handbook for the Career Maturity Scale*. Monterey, CA: CTB, McGraw-Hill.

Dalton, G. and Thompson, P. (1986) *Novations*. New York: Scott, Foresman.

Dannell, S. and Hall, J. (1980) Men and women managers. *Organizational Dynamics*, **8**, 60–77.

Davis, J. (1982) The influence of life stage on father–son work relationships. Doctoral dissertation, Harvard Business School.

Davis, K. (1984) A longitudinal analysis of biographical sub-groups using Owens' Developmental Integration Model. *Personnel Psychology*, **37**, 1–14.

De Frank, R. and Ivancevich, J. (1986) Job loss: an individual-level review and model. *Journal of Vocational Behavior*, **28**, 1–20.

De Long, T. (1985) Comparing rural and urban educators using the variable of career orientation. Unpublished manuscript, Harvard Business School, Boston, Mass.

Derr, C. B. (1984) Entrepreneurs—a career perspective. Paper given at the Academy of Management, Boston.

Derr, C. B. (1986) *Managing the New Careerists*. San Francisco: Jossey-Bass.

Driver, M. (1979) Career concepts and career management in organizations. In C. Cooper (ed.) *Behavioral Problems in Organizations*. Englewood Cliffs, N.J.: Prentice-Hall.

Driver, M. (1980) Career concepts and organizational change. In C. B. Derr (ed.) *Work, Family and the Career*. New York: Praeger.

Driver, M. (1982) Career concepts: a new approach to career research. In R. Katz (ed.) *Career Issues in Human Resource Management*. Englewood Cliffs, N.J.: Prentice-Hall.

Driver, M. (1984) *The Purdue Rutgers Prior Experience Inventory, III (GIAL-SD): Technical Manual*. Santa Monica, CA: Decision Dynamics Corp.

Driver, M. (1985) Demographic and societal factors affecting the linear career crisis. *Canadian Journal of Administrative Science*, December.

Driver, M. (1986) The executive style. Paper given at the Academy of Management, Chicago.

Driver, M. and Brousseau, K. (1981) *The Career Concept Questionnaire*. Los Angeles: Decision Dynamics Corp.

Driver, M. and Coombs, M. (1983) Fit between career concepts, corporate culture, and engineering productivity and morale. *Proceedings, IEEE Careers Conference*, New York: IEEE.

Driver, M. and Davis, J. (1987) Change and consistency in career choice: a career concept integration. Unpublished manuscript, Department of Management and Organization, University of Southern California, Los Angeles.

Driver, M. and Mock, T. (1975) Information processing: decision style theory and accounting information systems. *Accounting Review*, **50**, 490–508.

Driver, M. and Streufert, S. (1969) Integrative complexity. *Administrative Science Quarterly*, **14**, 272–285.

Dunn, F. (1980) *The Successful International Executive*. New York: Transnational Information, Inc.

Eberhardt, B. and Mushinsky, P. (1982) Biodata determinants of vocational typology. *Journal of Applied Psychology*, **69**, 714–727.

Ekerdt, D., Bosse, R. and La Castro, J. (1983) Claims that retirement improves health. *Journal of Gerontology*, **38**, 231–36.

Farmer, H. (1985) A model of career and achievement motivation for women and men. *Journal of Counseling Psychology*, **32**, 363–90.

Foss, C. and Slaney, R. (1986) Increasing nontraditional career choices in women: relations of attitude toward women and responses to a career intervention. *Journal of Vocational Behavior*, **28**, 191–202.

Fouad, N., Hansen, J. and Arias-Garcia, F. (1986) Multiple discriminant analysis of cross-cultural similarity of vocational interests of lawyers and engineers. *Journal of Vocational Behavior*, **28**, 85–96.

Fryer, D. and Payne, R. (1986) Being unemployed. *International Review of Industrial and Organizational Psychology*, **1**, 235–271.

Fugua, D. and Seaworth, T. (1987) The relationship of career indecision and anxiety. *Journal of Vocational Behavior*, **30**, 175–186.

Gilligan, C. (1982) *In a Different Voice: Psychological Theory and Women's Development*. Cambridge, Mass.: Harvard University Press.

Glamser, F. (1981) Predictions of retirement attitudes. *Aging and Work*, **4**, 23–27.

Gottfredson, G. (1977) Career Stability and Redirection in Adulthood. *Journal of Applied Psychology*, **62**, 436–44.

Graef, M., Wells, D., Hyland, A. and Muchinsky, P. (1985) Life history antecedents of vocational indecision. *Journal of Vocational Behavior*, **27**, 276–99.

Gray, J. (1983) The married professional woman. *Psychology of Women Quarterly*, **7**, 235–43.

Greenhalgh, L. (1985) Job insecurity and disinvolvement: Field research on the survivors of layoffs. Paper given at the Academy of Management, San Diego.

Grotevant, H. and Thorbecke, W. (1982) Sex differences in styles of occupational identity formation in late adolescence. *Developmental Psychology*, **18**, 396–405.

Gutek, B., Larwood, L. and Stromberg, A. (1986) Women at work. *International Review of Industrial and Organizational Psychology*, **1**, 217–229.

Gutteridge, J. (1986) Organizational career development systems: The state of the practice. In D. Hall and Associates (eds) *Career Development in Organizations*. San Francisco, Jossey-Bass.

Hall, D. (1986) Breaking career routines: mid-career choice and identity development. In D. Hall and Associates (eds) *Career Development in Organizations*. San Francisco, Jossey-Bass.

Hall, D. and Isabella, L. (1985) Downward moves and career development. *Organizational Dynamics*, **14**, 5–23.

Hall, D. and Richter J. (1985) The baby boom and management: Is there room at the middle? Unpublished manuscript, Boston University, School of Management.

Hamner, J. and Vardi, P. (1981) Locus of control and career self-management among non-supervisory employees in industrial settings. *Journal of Vocational Behavior*, **18**, 13–29.

Hansen, J. and Campbell, D. (1985) *Manual for SVIB-SCII*. Stanford, CA: Stanford University Press.

Hardesty, S. and Betz, N. (1980) The relationship of career salience, attitudes toward women and demographic and family characteristics to marital adjustment in dual career couples. *Journal of Vocational Behavior*, **17**, 242–50.

Harren, V. (1979) A model of career decision making for college students. *Journal of Vocational Behavior*, **14**, 119–33.

Harris-Bowlsby, J. (1985) *Discover for Organizations: Human Resource Development Manual*. Hunt Valley, MD: American College Testing Program.

Hartman, B., Fuqua, D. and Blum, C. (1985) A path analytic model of career indecision. *Vocational Guidance Quarterly*, 231–40.

Hartman, B. Fuqua, D. and Hartman, P. (1983) The predictive potential of the career decision scale in identifying chronic career indecision. *Vocational Guidance Quarterly*, **32**, 103–8.

Hartman, B., Fuqua, D. and Jenkins, S. (1986) The reliability/generalizability of the construct of career indecision. *Journal of Vocational Behavior*, **28**, 142–8.

Haynes, S., Mc Michael, A. and Tyroler, H. (1981) Survival after early and normal retirement. *Journal of Gerontology*. **4**, 23–27.

Healey, C., O'Shea, D. and Crook, R. (1985) The relation of career attitudes to age and career progress during college. *Journal of Counseling Psychology*, **32**, 239–44.

Hill, R. and Hansen, J. (1986) An analysis of vocational interests for female research and development managers. *Journal of Vocational Behavior*, **28**, 70–83.

Hoffman, L. (1974) The effects of maternal employment on the child. *Developmental Psychology*, **10**, 204–28.

Hoffman, L. (1980) The effects of maternal employment on the academic attitudes and performance of school-aged children. *School Psychology Review*, **9**, 319–35.

Holland, J., Daiger, D. and Power, P. (1980) *My Vocational Situation*. Palo Alto, CA: Consulting Psychology Press.

Holland, J., Magoun, T. and Spokane, A. (1981) Counseling psychology: Career interventions research and theory. In M. Rosenzweig and L. Porter (eds) *Annual Review of Psychology*. Palo Alto, CA: Annual Reviews.

Howard, A. (1984) Cool at the top. Paper given at American Psychology Association, Toronto.

Jaskolka, G. and Beyer, J. (1985) Measuring and predicting managerial success. *Journal of Vocational Behavior*, **29**, 189–205.

Jepson, D., Dustin, R. and Miars, R. (1982) The effects of problem-solving training on adolescents' career exploration and career decision-making. *Personnel and Guidance Journal*, November, 149–53.

Kanfer, R. and Hahn, C. (1985) Individual differences in successful job searches following lay off. *Personnel Psychology*, **38**, 835–847.

Kasl, S. (1980) The impact of retirement. In C. Cooper and R. Payne (eds) *Current Concerns in Occupational Stress*. Chichester: John Wiley.

Kealey, D. and Ruben, B. (1983) Cross-cultural personnel selection—criteria, issues, and methods. In D. Landis and R. Brislin (eds) *Handbook of International Training*. Vol. I, *Issues in Theory and Design*. New York: Pergamon.

Kidder, T. (1981) *The Soul of a New Machine*. Boston, Mass.: Little, Brown.

Kobasa, S. and Pucetti, M. (1983) Personality and social resources in stress resistance. *Journal of Personality and Social Psychology*, **40**, 839–50.

Kohn, M. and Schooler, C. (1982) Job conditions and personality. *American Journal of Sociology*, **87**, 1257–86.

Kotter, J. (1982) *The General Managers*. New York: Free Press.

Kram, K. (1986) Mentoring in the workplace. In D. Hall and Associates (eds) *Career Development in Organizations*. San Francisco, Jossey-Bass.

Krau, E. (1987) The crystallization of work values in adolescence—sociocultural approach. *Journal of Vocational Behavior*, **30**, 103–23.

Larkin, L. (1987) Identity and fear of success. *Journal of Counseling Psychology*, **34**, 38–45.

Latack, J. (1984) Career transitions within organizations: an exploratory study of work, non-work, and coping strategies. *Organizational Behavior and Human Performance*, **34**, 296–322.

Latack, J. and D'Amico, R. (1985) Career mobility among young men. In S. Hills, R. D'Amico, D. Ball, J. Golon, J. Jackson, J. Latack, L. Lynch, S. Mangum and D. Shapiro *The Changing Market*. Columbus, OH: Center for Human Resources Research, the Ohio State University.

Latack, J. and Dozier, J. (1986) After the axe falls: job loss as a career transition. *Academy of Management Review*, **11**, 375–392.

Levinson, D. (1984) The career is in the life structure; the life structure is in the career: an adult development perspective. In M. Arthur, L. Bailyn, D. Levinson and H. Shepard (eds) *Working With Careers*. New York: Columbia University School of Business.

Logan, R. (1986) A Reconceptualization of Erikson's theory: the recapitulation of existential and instrumental themes. *Human Development*, **29**, 125–36.

London, M. and Stumpf, S. (1986) Individual and organizational career development in changing times. In D. Hall and Associates (eds) *Career Development in Organizations*. San Francisco, Jossey-Bass.

Lorsch, J. and Takayi, H. (1986) Keeping managers off the shelf. *Harvard Business Review*, July–August, 60–64.

Louis, M. (1980) Career transitions: varieties and communalities. *Academy of Management Review*, **5**, 325–40.

Lowman, R., Williams, R. and Leeman, G. (1985) The structure and relationship of college women's primary abilities and vocational interests. *Journal of Vocational Behavior*, **27**, 298–315.

MacNab, D. and Fitzsimmons, G. (1987) A multi-trait multi-method study of work-related needs, values, and preferences. *Journal of Vocational Behavior*, **30**, 1–15.

Marcia, J. (1966) Development and validation of ego identity status. *Journal of Personality and Social Psychology*, **3**, 551–68.

McKinnon, P. (1987) Steady state people: a third career orientation. *Research Management*, January–February, 26–32.

Mendenhall, M. and Oddou, G. (1985) The dimensions of expatriate acculturation: a review, *Academy of Management Review*, **10**, 39–47.

Meshkati, N. and Driver, M. (1986) A systematic method to analyze the effects of the non-technological infrastructure factors of the industrially developing countries on managerial effectiveness and success. *Proceedings: 30th Meeting of the Human Factors Society*.

Mihal, W., Sorce, P. and Comte, T. (1984) A process model of individual career decision-making. *Academy of Management Review*, **9**, 95–103.

Minkler, M. (1981) Research on the health effects of retirement. *Journal of Health and Social Behavior*, **22**, 117–30.

Miner, J. and Smith, N. (1982) Decline and stabilization of managerial motivation over a 20-year period. *Journal of Applied Psychology*, **67**, 297–05.

Miner, J., Smith, N. and Ebrahimi, B. (1985) Further considerations in the decline and stabilization of managerial motivation. *Journal of Vocational Behavior*, **26**, 290–98.

Minor, F. (1986) Computer applications in career development planning. In D. Hall and Associates (eds) *Career Development in Organizations*. San Francisco, Jossey-Bass.

Morrison, R. and Hock, R. (1986) Career building: learning from cumulative work experience. In D. Hall and Associates (eds) *Career Development in Organizations*. San Francisco, Jossey-Bass.

Mottaz, C. (1986) An analysis of the relationship between education and organizational commitment in a variety of occupational groups. *Journal of Vocational Behavior*, **28**, 214–28.

Mowday, R., Porter, L. and Dubin, R. (1974) Unit performance, situational factors, and employee attitudes in spatially separated work units. *Organizational Behavior and Human Performance*, **12**, 231–48.

Myers, R. A. and Cairo, P. (eds) (1983) Computer-assisted counseling. *The Counseling Psychologist*, **11**, 7–63.

Near, J. (1985) A discriminant analysis of plateaued vs. nonplateaued managers. *Journal of Vocational Behavior*, **26**, 177–88.

Neimeyer, G., and Ebben, R. (1985) The effects of vocational intervention on the complexity and positivity of occupational judgments. *Journal of Vocational Behavior*, **27**, 87–97.

Neimeyer, G. and Metzlar, A. (1987) The development of vocational structures. *Journal of Vocational Behavior*, **30**, 1–17.

Neiner, A. and Owens, W. (1985) Using biodata to predict job choices among college graduates. *Journal of Applied Psychology*, **70**, 127–36.

Nevill, D., Neimeyer, G., Probert, B. and Fukuyama, M. (1986) Cognitive structures in vocational information processing and decision making. *Journal of Vocational Behavior*, **28**, 110–22.

Noe, R. and Steffy, B. (1987) The influence of individual characteristics and assessment center evaluation on career exploration behavior and job involvement. *Journal of Vocational Behavior*, **30**, 187–202.

Nye, F. (1974) Sociocultural factors. In L. Hoffman and F. Nye (eds) *Working Mothers*. San Francisco, Jossey-Bass.

Olson, T. (1979) Career concepts and decision styles. Paper given at the Academy of Management, Atlanta.

Osipow, S. and Reed, R. (1985) Decision-making style and career indecision in college students. *Journal of Vocational Behavior*, **27**, 368–73.

Osipow, S., Carver, C., Winer, J., Yanico, B. and Koschier, M. (1976) *The Career Decision Scale*. Columbus, OH: Marathon Consulting and Press.

Owens, W. and Schoenfeldt, L. (1979) Towards a classification of persons. *Journal of Applied Psychology*, **64**, 569–607.

Pazy, A. and Zin, R. (1987) A contingency approach to consistency: A challenge to prevalent views. *Journal of Vocational Behavior*, **30**, 84–101.

Perry, S. (1978) Survey and analysis of employee sponsored day care in the U.S. PhD Dissertation, University of Wisconsin-Milwaukee.

Phillips, S. and Strohman, D. (1982) Decision-making style and vocational maturity. *Journal of Vocational Behavior*, **20**, 215–22.

Phillips, S., Pazienza, N. and Walsh, D. (1984) Decision Making Styles and Progress in Occupational Decision Making. *Journal of Vocational Behavior*, **25**, 96–105.

Prince, B. (1979) An investigation of career concepts and career anchors. Paper given at the Western Academy of Management, Portland, OR.

Prince, B. (1984) Allocative and opportunity structures and their interaction with career orientation. PhD dissertation, University of Southern California.

Reichers, A. (1987) An interactionist perspective on newcomer socialization rates. *Academy of Management Review*, **13**, 278–87.

Reilly, R. and Chao, G. (1982) Validity and fairness of some alternative employee selection procedures. *Personnel Psychology*, **35**, 1–62.

Remer, P., O'Neill, C. and Gohs, D. (1984) Multiple outcome evaluation of a life-career development course. *Journal of Counseling Psychology*, **31**, 532–40.

Robbins, S. and Tucker, K. (1986) Relation of goal instability to self-directed and interactional career counseling workshops. *Journal of Counseling Psychology*, **33**, 418–24.

Rotberg, H., Brown, D. and Ware, W. (1987) Career self-efficacy expectations and perceived career options in community college students. *Journal of Counseling Psychology*, **34**, 164–70.

Russell, L. (1982) *The Baby Boom Generation and the Economy*. Washington, D.C.: Brookings Institute.

Rynes, S. (1987) Career transitions from engineering to management: are they predictable among students? *Journal of Vocational Behavior*, **30**, 138–54.

Rynes, S. and Rosen, B. (1983) A comparison of males and females reactions to career advancement opportunities. *Journal of Vocational Behavior*, **22**, 105–16.

Savickas, M. (1985) Identity in vocational development. *Journal of Vocational Behavior*, **27**, 329–37.

Schein, E. (1971) The individual, the organization and the career: A conceptual scheme. *Journal of Applied Behavioral Science*, **7**, 401–26.

Schein, E. (1986) A critical look at current career development theory and research. In D. Hall and Associates (eds) *Career Development in Organizations*. San Francisco, Jossey-Bass.

Schroder, H., Driver, M. and Streufert, S. (1967) *Human Information Processing*. New York: Holt, Rinehart, Winston.

Schwartz, R., Andiappan, P. and Nelson, M. (1986) Reconsidering the support for Holland's congruence achievement hypothesis. *Journal of Counseling Psychology*, **33**, 425–8.

Shaffer, G. (1987) Patterns of work and non-work satisfaction. *Journal of Applied Psychology*, **72**, 115–24.

Shepard, H. (1984) On the realization of human potential: A path with a heart. In M. Arthur, L. Bailyn, D. Levinson and H. Shepard *Working With Careers*. New York: Columbia University School of Business.

Slaney, R. and Lewis, E. (1986) Effects of career exploration on career undecided re-entry women: an intervention and follow-up study. *Journal of Vocational Behavior*, **28**, 97–109.

Sonnenfeld, J. and Kotter, J. (1982) The maturation of career theory. *Human Relations*, **35**, 19–46.

Sorcher, M. (1985) *Predicting Executive Success*. New York: John Wiley.

Spenner, K. (1985) The upgrading and downgrading of occupations: issues, evidence, and implications for education. *Review of Educational Research*, **55**, 125–54.

Steiner, D. and Farr, J. (1986) Career goals, organizational reward systems, and technical updating in engineers. *Journal of Occupational Psychology*, **59**, 13–24.

Stout, S., Slocum, J. and Cron, W. (1987) Career transitions of supervisors and subordinates. *Journal of Vocational Behavior*, **30**, 124–37.

Streufert, S. and Streufert, S. (1978) *Behavior in the Complex Environment*. Washington, D.C.: Winston.

Streufert, S. and Swezey, R. (1986) *Complexity, Managers, and Organizations*. Orlando, FL: Academic Press.

Sundby, D. (1980) The career quad: a psychological look at some divergent dual career families. In C. B. Derr (ed.) *Work, Family, and the Career*. New York: Praeger.

Super, D. (1980) A life span life space approach to career development. *Journal of Vocational Behavior*, **16**, 282–98.

Super, D. (1986) Life career roles: self-realization in work and leisure. In D. Hall and Associates (eds) *Career Development in Organizations*. San Francisco, Jossey-Bass.

Super, D., Thompson, A., Lindeman, R., Jordaan, J. and Myers, R. (1981) *Career Development Inventory*. Palo Alto, CA: Consulting Psychology Press.

Time Magazine, 22 June, 1983, p. 63.

Torbiorn, I. (1982) *Living Abroad: Personal Adjustment and Personnel Policy in the Overseas Setting*. New York: John Wiley.

Tung, R. (1982) Selection and training procedures of U.S., European, and Japanese multinationals. *California Management Review*, **25**, 57–71.

Von Glinow, M., Driver, M., Brousseau, K. and Prince, B. (1983) The design of a career-oriented human resource system. *Academy of Management Review*, **89**, 23–32.

Von Glinow, M. and Kryczkowska, A. (1985) The Fortune 500: a caste of thousands. Unpublished manuscript, Department of Management and Organization, University of Southern California.

Warr, P. and Parry, G. (1982) Paid employment and women's psychological well-being. *Psychological Bulletin*, **91**, 498–516.

Weick, K. (1983) Managerial thought in the context of action. In S. Srivastava *The Executive Mind*. San Francisco: Jossey-Bass.

Westbrooke, B., Sanford, E., O'Neill, P., Horne, D., Fleenor, J. and Garren, R. (1985) Predictive and construct validity of six experimental measures of career maturity. *Journal of Vocational Behavior*, **27**, 338–55.

Winer, D. and Gati, I. (1986) Cognitive complexity and interest crystallization. *Journal of Vocational Behavior*, **28**, 48–59.

Wright, J. (1978) Are working women really more satisfied? *Journal of Marriage and the Family*, **40**, 301–13.

Yanico, B. and Haudin, S. (1986) College students self-estimated and actual knowledge of gender traditional and non-traditional occupations. *Journal of Vocational Behavior*, **28**, 229–40.

International Review of Industrial and Organizational Psychology 1988
Edited by C. L. Cooper and I. Robertson
© 1988 John Wiley & Sons Ltd

Chapter 9

HEALTH PROMOTION AT WORK

Michael T. Matteson
and
John M. Ivancevich
College of Business Administration
University of Houston
USA

In recent years there has been a growing multinational awareness of and interest in matters of individual health. The primary, although certainly not exclusive, focus has been on preventive health issues. This is reflected in a variety of lifestyle changes including renewed concern with dietary habits, physical fitness and exercise, moderation and cessation of 'unhealthy' behavior patterns such as smoking, alcohol and drug usage, and a multitude of other considerations thought to be associated with personal physical and mental health. One specific manifestation of this interest in matters of health has been the increase in corporate sponsored programs designed to have a positive impact on employee health and well-being. An examination of what companies are doing in this area, how and why they are doing it, what are the outcomes, and what issues and questions are related to these activities, is the topic of this review. Have important and positive outcomes been derived from health promotion? Or, as has been argued, is it the case that 'danger lurks in the Garden of Health Promotion; all is not well with wellness, and there is much unholy about holistic health' (Becker, 1986, p. 15).

This review is organized in five major sections. In the first section the term workplace health promotion will be defined and a brief discussion of its historical antecedents will be developed. Next, the rationale for such activities will be identified by looking at the presumed benefits of health promotion programs. In the third, and longest section, various types of programs or program components will be identified and described. Certain key issues and questions relating to worksite health promotion will be the focus of the fourth section. These issues include ethical and legal considerations, and questions relating to health-care costs, among others. Finally, research needs relating to workplace health promotion will be examined and a research agenda will be suggested.

DEFINITION AND HISTORY OF HEALTH PROMOTION

Organized activities designed to prevent disease and encourage health can be found under a number of labels including, but not limited to, health enhancement, wellness and health promotion (Matteson and Ivancevich, 1987). While it can be argued (and, indeed, has been), that each of these terms means something different from the others, all relate in general to activities designed to identify, correct and/or prevent specific health problems, hazards, or negative health habits. This includes not only disease identification, but values and lifestyle modification as well.

Health promotion (which is the term we shall use throughout) is a combination of diagnostic, educational and behavior modification activities designed to support the attainment and maintenance of positive health. Health promotion at the work place consists of ongoing activities initiated, endorsed, and funded by an employing organization (Parkinson and Associates, 1982; Davis, 1984; Everly and Feldman, 1984; Fielding, 1984; Terborg, 1986). Typical components of such programs generally include risk assessment, educational and instructional classes, and counseling and referral (Davis, 1984). Specific areas of concern include physical fitness, weight control, dietary and nutritional counselling, giving up smoking, stress management, blood pressure monitoring and control, alcohol and drug-related problems, and general lifestyle modification thought to be related to health. While some health promotion activities are diagnostic in nature (hypertension screening, for example) and others are treatment-oriented (alcohol abuse treatment, for example), most are preventive in their intent.

Identifying the inception of health promotion programs is a difficult task which depends largely on one's definition of health promotion and the philosophical position one takes. Cunningham (1982), for example, cites Asclepius and his ancient Greek temples of healing as a forerunner of health promotion today. Trice and Beyer (1984) suggest that the Industrial Betterment movement with its paternalistic orientation was a precursor to the current health promotion orientation. Shain, Suurvali and Boutilier (1986) trace health promotion to industrial welfarism, citing as early examples the English Quaker businesses, and the United States examples epitomized by Goodyear and Ford Motors.

It is impossible to examine the historical underpinnings of contemporary workplace health promotion programs without emphasizing the important role played by early Employee Assistance Programs (EAPs). Some employers have offered employees services for decades which quite easily fall within the EAP domain. An early example is Macy's Department Store which, in 1917, established a program to assist employees in dealing with personal problems. By 1920 a third of the 431 largest companies in the United States had a full-time welfare secretary (Popple, 1981). A welfare secretary had a variety of responsibilities, but a major role was that of counsellor—listening to problems, offering advice, and in general providing social support.

Contemporary EAPs are a blend of the paternalism of the past and the humanism and pragmatics of the present. Their present form is based less on the welfare secretaries of the turn of the century and more on the industrial alcoholism programs which emerged in the 1940s (Shain and Groeneveld, 1980;

Numeroff, 1983). Today, it is difficult to draw a distinction between EAPs and many programs labeled health promotion. Bezold, Carlson and Peck (1986) argue that today's health promotion programs subsume the earlier EAPs, a position with which we agree.

Since the emergence of the EAPs in the 1940s, numerous successful health promotion programs have been developed and implemented in organizational settings. Early examples include DuPont (1942), Kennecott Copper (1950s), National Aeronautics and Space Administration (1962), and the health and fitness program initiated in 1981 at Xerox (Davis, 1984). While early examples were relatively few in number, the decade of the 1970s was a period of rapid growth for work site health promotion. In 1970 fewer than a hundred companies were actively involved in health promotion on any meaningful scale. Currently, however, as many as 50,000 organizations may be involved in some way (Howe, 1983; Jacobs, 1983). Over 1500 organizations alone support some form of comprehensive fitness program, including over 200 American firms in the Fortune 500 (Rosen, 1985). This acceleration of growth is directly related to the presumed benefits associated with health promotion programs. An examination of these benefits provides a partial rationale for health promotion program popularity.

WHY WORKPLACE HEALTH PROMOTION?

Unquestionably there are a multitude of different reasons why each organization which has elected to embark on health promotion has decided to do so. Some have done so in response to employee requests, some have public and employee relations in mind. For others it represents a natural extension of prevailing management philosophy, while others feel it positively impacts performance and productivity. In some countries (Sweden and Norway, for example) legislation has mandated it. In a very broad sense, however, a crucial component of the decision, directly or otherwise, is related to bottom line considerations.

In virtually every industrialized nation in the world health care costs are not only rising, the rate of increase has for some time been greater than that attributable to inflation. In the United States, for example, between 1981 and 1982 the overall consumer price index increased by 6.5 per cent while medical costs rose 11.6 per cent (Cohen, 1985). In the United States health care costs have steadily increased for several decades, going from 4.4 per cent of gross national product in 1950, to 5.3 per cent in 1960, 7.5 per cent in 1970, 9.4 per cent in 1980, and 10.5 per cent in 1984, with a 1984 per capita expenditure of over $2000 (Gibson and Waldo, 1981; Waldo, 1982; Patton et al., 1986). Expenditures in 1987 approached $400 billion (Renner, 1987).

In the United States, businesses pay approximately one half of those health care costs (Cohen, 1985). When a large industrial concern such as General Motors spends well over $800 million per year (or $175 per vehicle produced) it is not difficult to understand why organizations are interested in anything which may reduce—even slightly—those expenditures (Stacey, 1980). How effective various forms of health promotion programs may be in decreasing health care costs is a question which will be repeatedly addressed in subsequent sections of this review.

In addition to possible reductions of direct health care costs in the form of reduced health and medical insurance premiums and benefits paid, there are other presumed indirect benefits associated with health promotion programs as well, including reductions in absenteeism, tardiness, voluntary and involuntary turnover, accidents and worker's compensation costs. Increases in employee loyalty and commitment, corporate image, creativity, decision-making effectiveness and enhanced labor relations and employee recruitment, are other frequently cited examples of benefits accruing to organizations sponsoring health promotion activities (Terborg, 1986; Matteson and Ivancevich, 1987)

Pelletier (1984) suggests that the conditions which contribute to individual health and well-being are exactly the same conditions which contribute to the organizational health and well being of the incorporated body. The presumed indirect benefits listed above would be, in Pelletier's view, consequences of enhanced employee health. Pelletier makes the additional point that while this is a concept which only recently has gained adherents in the United States, it is one that is well established in numerous other countries. For some time now a number of countries, including Canada, Germany, Japan and the Scandinavian nations, have been active initiators and supporters of workplace health promotion programs. In several countries private organizations and governmental agencies provide direction to employers in developing programs. The implication would seem to be that many nations have been cognisant for some time of the benefits to health promotion that American organizations have only recently discovered.

But are these presumed benefits real, or do they frequently exist primarily in the eyes of the beholder? Are there clearly positive individual and organizational payoffs to corporate health promotion, and if so, are they cost-effective ones? That is, could the same or greater benefits be achieved more effectively (at lower cost) in some other manner? These are important questions for individuals, organizations and industrial and organizational psychology practitioners and researchers. Much of the remainder of this review addresses issues germane to these questions.

HEALTH PROMOTION PROGRAM COMPONENTS

Workplace health promotion programs may be thought of as either narrow or broad spectrum programs. Narrow spectrum programs consist of only one or two components, while the broad spectrum programs may include a half dozen or more types of activities. While the list of possible components is virtually unlimited, we will restrict our discussion in this section to six of the most common ones. We shall examine (1) smoking cessation, (2) hypertension screening and control, (3) stress management, (4) nutrition and weight control, (5) exercise and fitness, and (6) drug and alcohol programs. Our focus will be on a general description of each activity and a review of information relating to how successful these activities are in accomplishing their most direct objective, namely improvement in the condition or behaviors the program addresses. Less directly related outcomes such as a decrease to the organization in health care costs, or improved performance, will be addressed in a subsequent section of this review.

Smoking Cessation

Smoking cessation programs have become, in very recent years, increasingly popular with both employers and employees (smokers and non-smokers). The statistics linking cigarette smoking to increased health problems and expenses and decreased personal and corporate payoffs are significant. It has been estimated, for example, that smokers can cost as much as 30 per cent more than non-smokers in the areas of medical care, premature morbidity and lost time on the job (Cascio, 1982). Danaher (1980) cites an estimate that a smoking employee costs the employing organization $3 per day. Thus a company employing 1000 smokers would incur smoking-related expenses of approximately $750,000 annually. Traditionally, however, organizations have been hesitant to ban smoking in the workplace except in areas where the risk of accidents is greatly increased (Walsh, 1984). A recent survey indicated that 16 per cent of 500 companies had some type of policy limiting smoking, and 2 per cent of these prohibited smoking altogether (Kent and Cenci, 1982).

While variations are possible, there are essentially two different approaches to smoking cessation programs: external and internal. In external programs, the organization contracts with a consultant or proprietary program to provide services for its employees. Internal programs most typically take the form of group skills training, and are usually patterned after external programs differing only in that they are developed and implemented in-house.

Evaluation of smoking cessation programs is not as thorough as it should or could be. In terms of the direct objective of such endeavors (reducing the number of smokers), two major considerations are important. The most obvious, perhaps, is the quit rate. Estimates of quit rates for workplace programs are generally in the 25–60 per cent range (Matteson and Ivancevich, 1987). Metropolitan Life Insurance Company provides four different smoking cessation program options to its employees and reports a quit rate which averaged 35 per cent over four years of the program (Brennan, 1986). Naditch (1986) reports a sustained quit rate one year after a control data program of slightly over 30 per cent. Other results include a 21–35 per cent quit rate reported by Altman et al. (1987), and an amazingly high six-month abstinence rate of 80–91 per cent at three different worksites reported by Stachnik and Stoffelmayr (1983).

The other consideration which must be factored in any evaluation of cessation program success relates to the percentage of the target group which participated. If an organization has 500 smokers, even a quit rate of 60 per cent is not particularly impressive if only 5 per cent of the smokers participated in the program. While most reports of smoking cessation program outcomes include a quit rate, many do not indicate what percentage of the targeted group participated. For those that do, the percentage is usually relatively low. At Metropolitan Life, for example, over the four-year period cited above, only 7.5 per cent of the targeted group participated (Brennan, 1986). At the other extreme, Stachnik and Stoffelmayr (1983) report 47–70 per cent participation at their three worksites, and Klesges and Glasgow (1986) achieved an 88 per cent participation rate at four banks which competed with each other in the same market. Employees of each bank competed against the other three banks. The overall quit rate of 16 per cent which was achieved is most impressive given the high participation rates.

Hypertension Screening and Control

Hypertension is usually defined as blood pressure greater than 140/90 mmHg over several measurements. In the United States each year, businesses lose an estimated 52 million work days to cardiovascular diseases; for every employee who dies as a result of an industrial accident, 50 die from cardiovascular disease (Cohen, 1985). Hypertension is one of the major—and easily detected and controllable—risk factors in heart-related diseases. It is also a fairly common condition among virtually any employee population. Estimates are that as many as 25 per cent of employees are hypertensive (Fielding, 1984). The attractiveness of organizationally-based screening and control programs is that they are easily implemented, relatively inexpensive, and offer potentially significant payoffs, both from humanitarian and monetary perspectives.

A key to the success of work-site programs is control. Screening in and of itself does not yield the follow-up necessary to achieve consistent results; programs which provide for some treatment mechanism have a much greater payoff. The specifics of worksite programs vary, but according to Alderman (1984), successful programs include several components which contribute to their effectiveness:

Educating employees to the dangers of high blood pressure and to the payoffs gained from treatment.
Screening by taking blood pressure measurements of those employees participating.
Referral of employees with elevated pressure readings to community-based medical care or offering on-site treatment.
Follow-up of referred employees to verify that treatment was successful and to monitor the continued progress of the employee.

How effective are workplace hypertension programs? As was the case with smoking cessation programs, the answer is dependent in part on the percentage of the targeted population reached. Unlike smoking cessation efforts however, the number of employees who are hypertensive and who do not participate in screenings can not be readily determined, since hypertension is an asymptomatic problem. Taylor, Agras and Sevelius (1986) examined the data reported from eight worksite programs which screened from 22–98 per cent of the workforce and found, of those screened, that 5–29 per cent were hypertensive. Based on the estimated rate of hypertensives in the working population, these figures indicate that the number of hypertensives identified is about the same as or slightly less than the presumed rate in the population. Thus, the percentage of employees undergoing screening is probably a reasonable estimation of the percentage of the targeted group reached.

For those screened and found to be hypertensive, varying rates of control have been reported in the literature. Examples include 67 per cent in control after 13 months, compared to 30 per cent in control at the baseline period (Baer, Parchment and Kneeshaw, 1981); 49 per cent in control after an unspecified time-period, versus 39 per cent at baseline (Wasserman, 1982); and 63 per cent at four years, and 70 per cent at five years versus 30 per cent at baseline (Alderman and Melcher, 1983). Some data suggest that worksite programs may achieve higher control rates than are achieved in other settings. Thus, for example, Alderman (1984) reports that after one year, 75 per cent of participants in a worksite program were under control, compared to 29 per cent at a private physician's office and 33 per cent at a hospital clinic.

The number of components in a program may also affect success rates. Foote and Erfurte (1983) report the results of a worksite program in which participants were placed into one of four groups: screening only, referral with semi-annual follow-up, referral with frequent follow-up, and on-site treatment. Control rates after three years for the four groups were 47, 62, 56 and 62 per cent, respectively, attesting to the importance of doing more than simple screening. Even the nature of the educational information given participants may effect control rates (Zimmerman et al., 1986).

Stress Management

Stress and stress management are topics of growing interest and concern. This interest is both reflected in and exacerbated by the proliferation of articles in both popular and scientific press. Various estimates of the cost of stress to businesses in the United States alone range from $75–100 billion a year (Ivancevich and Matteson, 1980; Cohen, 1985). The consequences of dysfunctional stress are pervasive and can effect a variety of behaviors which themselves are the target of other health promotion activities, such as smoking, alcohol and drug use, and hypertension (Elliot and Eisdorfer, 1982). When two tranquilizers, Valium and Librium, represent the most frequently prescribed drugs in the world (Rittel-meyer, 1982), it is evident that stress, or at least the perception of it, is a major health concern.

Surveys of health promotion activities in the workplace have documented organizational and employee interest in stress management programs. Fielding and Breslow (1983), in a survey of over 400 companies, uncovered more interest in stress management than in any other type of health promotion program. In another survey, 43 per cent of those queried felt that stress had affected their health in the last year (Silverman, Eichler and Williams, 1987). That excessive stress can have negative individual and organizational consequences has been well documented (see, for example, Beehr and Bhagat, 1985). What has not been nearly as well documented is how effective workplace stress management programs are in helping employees deal more effectively with their stress.

There are a number of ways stress management programs can be categorized. For example, a program can be educational in nature or skill acquisition-oriented, or both. Educational programs are designed primarily to inform employees as to what stress is, how it is experienced, what its effects may be, and to provide general guidelines for avoiding or coping with stress. Skill acquisition approaches, on the other hand, are designed to provide the participant with usable skills and techniques for combating excessive stress. What evaluation research has been done of worksite stress management programs has tended to focus on skill acquisition programs. Examples of skill acquisition program components include relaxation training, biofeedback and various cognitive techniques for dealing with stress, although these are certainly not the only possible components.

In what was the first, and still frequently cited, comprehensive review of stress management techniques, Newman and Beehr (1979) concluded that evaluation research into the effectiveness of stress management techniques was in a poor state of affairs and very few programs or techniques had been evaluated with any degree of scientific rigor. Five years later, Murphy (1984) found some improvement in the existing state of knowledge regarding the effectiveness of organizational stress management programs, noting that both the amount of research and the rigor of the research had increased since the publication of the Newman and Beehr (1979) review. Murphy concluded that although too few studies had been done to draw unequivocal conclusions, such programs appeared 'to offer promise for helping workers cope with stress and exert greater control over physiological and psychological systems which are reactive to stressors' (p. 1).

Several articles, in addition to the two cited above, have reviewed workplace stress management programs in recent years (see, for example, Hilkenberg and Collins, 1982; Brown, 1984; Murphy, 1985; and Singer et al., 1986). Although most studies report varying degrees of program success, much of the research is characterized by methodological, design, and analytical flaws which seriously bring into question its reliability, validity, and generalizability. Problems of inadequate controls, reliance on subjective questionnaire responses of participants, confusion of dependent and independent variables, and lack of longitudinal designs abound. Health promotion evaluation research in general suffers from a lack of behavioral science research rigor; stress management research particularly is in special need of attention. We shall address this question in more detail in the fifth section of this review.

Nutrition and Weight Control

Nutrition and weight control components of health promotion programs can include a wide variety of instructional and lifestyle change classes covering topics such as weight loss, proper nutrition, nutrition counselling, and even healthy cooking. Nutrition programs frequently include a weight control component, but we shall consider these two activities separately.

Nutrition programs typically include one or both of two types of activities. One is educational in nature, providing information and/or instruction in the basics of planning, selecting and preparing healthy and appropriate-sized portions of foods that provide the proper portion of necessary nutrients. Actual cooking classes and demonstrations, as well as provisions for individually tailored weekly or monthly nutritional plans may be part of these kinds of educational effort (Ford and Ford, 1986).

The second type of activity relates to the provision for access to healthy and nutritional foods for company employees. Thus, some organizations provide food service on site for employees which consists of offerings low in fat, calories and cholesterol, and stock vending-machines with nutritional snacks such as raisins, nuts and seeds (Foreyt, Scott and Gotto, 1980). Pelletier (1984) reports on a company which stocks its vending machines with yogurt and granola bars, provides fresh fruit at no charge, makes available a free low-calorie, low-fat, high-fiber lunch, and provides a free popcorn machine, encouraging employees to take popcorn breaks instead of coffee and sweet roll breaks. Some companies provide calorie information on menus at company eating facilities (Salcedo, 1986).

Worksite weight control programs are becoming increasingly popular. Fielding (1982) indicates that 14 per cent of men and 21 per cent of women are obese (defined as being 20 per cent or more over ideal weight). Such programs are not limited in their popularity to just this group of employees, however. Terborg (1986) concludes that much of the popularity stems not from health concerns, but rather from an interest in personal appearance. Weight control programs typically consist of informational lectures, and may include specific diet plans and various behavioral modification activities. Some such programs are contracted externally with commercial or non-profit organizations, while others are operated entirely in-house (Matteson and Ivancevich, 1987).

There has been virtually no evaluation research reported on general nutrition programs, and not a great deal on weight control activities at the workplace. One of the earliest controlled studies of weight control at the workplace was reported by Stunkard and Brownell (1980). Obese participants who stayed with the program lost an average of 7.9 pounds. The attrition rate, however, was a relatively high 50 per cent. This weight loss compares to the 7.6 per cent loss reported by Brennan (1983) in another work setting.

The worksite programs which seem to have been the most successful used competition as a key feature of the program. Feuer (1985) reports on a three-month program which included individual and team competition within the same company, and which utilized small monetary and psychological incentives (a personalized certificate). Of 2500 employees starting the program, 70 per cent completed it, and 90 per cent of those lost an average of 8 pounds, with team members losing more than individuals. Brownell et al. (1984) report on a weight control competition between companies. Company presidents each issued letters challenging the others and weekly progress charts were displayed at each worksite. Average weight losses were 19 and 11 pounds for men and women, respectively. A six-month follow-up indicated that the average participant had maintained 80 per cent of the weight loss achieved during the program. Most impressive was an attrition rate of less than 5 per cent. The attrition rate of 50 per cent reported earlier tends to be more representative (see, for example, Abrams and Follick, 1983).

Exercise and Fitness

In recent years particularly, the number of worksite exercise and fitness programs has increased dramatically. In 1970 there were fewer than two dozen full-time physical fitness specialists employed by United States companies; today, that figure is in excess of 2000 (Matteson and Ivancevich, 1987), and over 50,000 organizations have some type of program promoting employee fitness (Driver and Ratliff, 1982). The potential positive individual health benefits of attaining and maintaining a proper level of physical fitness are widely known and will not be examined here. The level of exercise required to achieve these benefits is relatively modest—20–30 minutes a day, three or four days a week—as demonstrated in research in the United States, Great Britain (Morris *et al.*, 1980), Israel (Epstein *et al.*, 1980), and elsewhere.

The range of possible fitness program activities and levels of organizational involvement and commitment is extensive. Some organizations have invested in multi-million dollar facilities, fully staffed with fitness specialists and offering a multitude of exercise options and instructions. This level of investment is certainly not necessary, however, for a program to provide both individual and organizational benefits. Examples of company activities in the fitness area include jazzercise classes, construction of jogging paths, provisions for daily exercise breaks, providing lockers for employees, and sponsoring fun runs, softball teams, and other similar group activities.

Regardless of the specific nature of the program, the key ingredient of success is getting employees to start and stay with the program. Critical factors which influence participation include such considerations as having knowledgeable program leadership, making participation convenient, providing adequate information and instruction on how and why to keep fit, providing the type of activities which will meet the needs and preferences of participants, establishing specific goals and providing a mechanism to periodically assess those goals, and encouraging support by peers, supervisors, even family, for continued participation (Haskell and Blair, 1982).

That worksite exercise and fitness programs do yield positive results in terms of improvements in physical condition and health is reasonably clear. As one example, Pauly *et al.* (1982) reported on physiological changes achieved by 73 employees participating in a worksite fitness program. Results showed significant improvement in heart rate, blood pressure, cholesterol and triglyceride levels and VO_2 max. Other studies have shown similar results (see, for example, Blair, Jacobs and Powell, 1985; Cady, Thomas and Karwiesky, 1985; and Brownstein and Herd, 1986).

In spite of these positive outcomes, however, there is a less favorable side of the issue. Participation and adherence rates are not particularly encouraging. Studies indicate that 30 per cent or fewer of employees who have the opportunity to participate do so (Shepard, 1983; Fielding, 1984; Oldridge, 1984). Further, those employees who do participate are not necessarily the ones who would gain the greatest benefit. That is, already physically active individuals are the ones most likely to participate in workplace programs; their sedentary counterparts, who would benefit the most, are less likely to become involved. Shephard *et al.* (1980) report that 25 per cent of program volunteers were already physically active (and were more likely to be non-smokers). Based on a literature review, Fielding (1982) concluded that, in general, exercise program participants are at less health risk prior to participation than are non-participants.

Drug and Alcohol Programs

Drug and alcohol programs in the workplace have a longer history than virtually any other component of corporate health promotion. Many of the current programs are modern equivalents to the alcoholism programs of the 1940s which are associated with the genesis of employee assistance programs. That their current focus is not solely on alcohol simply reflects the changing nature of society and the fact that the range of chemical substances readily available for abuse today is far greater than was the case a half century ago. As McClellan (1985) has pointed out, drug use and poly-drug addiction has made the alcoholism program obsolete. The availability of synthetic drugs (including sedative-hypnotic compounds such as Librium and Valium) has further complicated matters.

In addition to being one of the first health promotion components, such programs are also among the most prevalent components. Over 5000 programs in the United States alone cover as many as 15 million employees. Preston and Bierman (1985) report that approximately 12 per cent of the United States workforce has direct access to some type of alcohol or drug abuse program.

The specific direction of individual programs differs greatly. In general, programs identify employees with problems and provide short-term counseling and/or referral to outside sources for long-term assistance. Training is frequently provided supervisory personnel to aid them is identifying and supporting employees as they attempt to deal with their problem (Davis, 1984). DuPont and Basen (1982) suggest that corporate alcohol and drug abuse programs can be grouped into four categories: those providing consultation only, those providing assessment and referral, those offering diagnosis and referral, and those providing diagnosis and treatment (treatment may be either inpatient, out-patient, or both). Clearly, however, some programs do not fit cleanly into such a four category classification schema.

Given the history and prevalence of alcohol and drug abuse programs it is somewhat surprising—and disappointing—that more information is not available relating to the effectiveness of such programs. Undoubtedly this is in part attributable to the sensitive nature of the problems being dealt with, from both individual and organizational perspectives, and the need for confidentiality. None the less, there are few reports in the literature which address the question of workplace alcohol and drug abuse program effectiveness.

Muldoon and Berdie (1980) briefly summarize results obtained from a dozen different company programs. Without exception, improvements are reported in such indices as absenteeism, turnover, productivity, accidents and similar measures, but virtually no information is available regarding control or quit rates for the chemical being abused. Additionaly, most reports lacked a variety of important controls, and relied too heavily on subjective reports.

Pelletier (1984), in an examination of health promotion activities in the workplace, concludes that alcohol and other substance abuse programs are among the most effective of health promotion programs, with success rates for long-term reductions in excessive drinking falling into the 65–80 per cent range. These figures seem to be based mainly on reports in trade and popular press publications and in most cases do not reflect the results of reasonable evaluation research. As we have indicated previously, evaluation of health promotion programs has been far from ideal; alcohol and drug abuse components epitomize this state of affairs very well.

Having identified, and briefly described, some of the more popular components of workplace health promotion programs, we now turn our attention to examining a number of key issues. Each of the issues addressed has implications for individuals and organizations, and each raises questions that industrial and organizational psychologists can contribute to answering.

ORGANIZATIONAL ISSUES

Numerous issues can, and have, been raised regarding health promotion in the workplace. Any selection of a subset of these is to a large extent arbitrary and the following discussion is no exception. We shall consider seven issues that seem to be of particular importance and/or interest to those concerned with health promotion activities generally, and industrial and organizational psychologists, specifically. The first four relate to questions of possible benefits to organizations of health promotion, and include considerations of costs, performance improvement, absenteeism and turnover reduction, and morale and attitude improvements. The latter three address other important issues, specifically those of confidentiality, ethical considerations, and possible unintended—and undesirable—consequences of health promotion activities.

Costs

One of the major objectives which frequently provide the motivation for an organization to undertake health promotion activities is a desire to reduce health-related costs. We have seen earlier in this review that health care costs are a significant factor in doing business, and an interest in reducing these costs or in slowing their increase is understandable. The key question is whether workplace health promotion has a positive effect on costs.

Cost considerations are generally given a great deal of emphasis in evaluating health promotion programs, but there are few well conducted studies reported in the literature. Most reports rely quite heavily on estimated savings or draw conclusions based on theoretical assumptions and not on actual empirical investigations. A distinction must also be made between *cost-effectiveness* and *cost-benefit* approaches (Rossi and Freeman, 1982; Patton *et al.*, 1986). Cost-effectiveness studies determine to what extent program goals were achieved and how much it cost to achieve them; cost-benefit studies ask what the benefit of achieving program goals is, and is the benefit a positive one considering costs?

Of the program components considered in this review, smoking cessation and hypertension programs are among the easiest to evaluate with respect to cost considerations. Several reports have indicated positive cost benefits for smoking cessation programs (see, for example, Fielding, 1982; Brennan, 1983; and Pelletier, 1984). A typical example is that of Metropolitan Life Insurance Company, cited previously. Their one-year success rate is approximately 35 per cent (that is, 35 per cent of participants were still not smoking one year after the program). The program costs less than $200 for each successful quitter, while a smoking employee is estimated to cost $646 annually (Brennan, 1983). Note, however, that the cost of a smoker is an estimated or theoretical one. Similar outcomes have been reported for hypetension programs (Alderman, Green and Flynn, 1980; Ruchlin and Alderman, 1980; Logan, 1981; Brennan, 1983).

Smoking cessation and hypertension programs are not the only components which have been looked at from the standpoint of cost reduction. Cox, Shepard and Corey (1981) and Shephard et al. (1982) offer evidence of cost savings from a fitness program in a Canadian insurance company, estimating a reduction of $132 per year in hospital and medical costs per employee. In a similar study of an American insurance company fitness program Browne et al. (1984) report estimated savings of $1.93 in reduced medical costs for every $1.00 spent on the program. Manuso, cited in Murphy (1985), reports an estimated return of $5.52 for every $1.00 invested in a stress management program.

All of these reports cited above are flawed to some degree. This is not meant so much as a criticism, as it is an indication that, as difficult as it is to do, well-designed and rigorous research into cost issues is lacking. Published reports tend to be anecdotal in nature, based on surveys in which self-selection of respondents contributes to possibly unrepresentative samples, and/or reliance on general theoretical models of associated costs and benefits, rather than program specific data. In spite of these limitations, however, there appears to be little question that health promotion activities *can* be cost effective and yield positive cost benefits. Far more, and better, research remains to be done, however.

Performance Improvement

The term performance improvement as used here relates to *direct* positive changes in employee task performance. Not included, for example, would be a reduction in absenteeism which presumably would contribute to performance by virtue of the fact that an employee was physically present more often. Presumably, healthier workers, because of higher energy levels, will perform better (quantitatively and qualitatively) than their less healthy counterparts. Unfortunately, a presumed link between health promotion programs and enhanced employee performance remains intuitively attractive but largely untested and unverified.

Haskell and Blair (1982) argue that physical activity, such as would be experienced in a fitness or exercise program increases an individual's physical working capacity (PWC) and that even people in sedentary jobs need to meet certain PWC standards if they are to avoid chronic fatigue. They indicate that numerous studies in Germany, Eastern Europe and the Soviet Union supposedly demonstrate that factory and clerical workers show performance improvements as a result of regular exercise breaks, but conclude that most such reports are based on conjecture rather than on data.

The few studies conducted in the United States can be categorized in much the same manner. Naditch (1986) in discussing the STAYWELL health promotion program at Control Data Corporation reports a significant relationship between health risk status as measured in the program and self-reports of work limitations, a subjective, surrogate measure of performance. Bernacki and Baun (1984) report finding, based on a sample of over 3200 white-collar employees, a significant relationship between performance ratings and exercise adherence. The report suggests, however, that the relationship is non-causal in nature, and indeed it appears that the only reasonable conclusion to be drawn is that high performers are more likely to participate in the program than low performers. On balance one must conclude that the performance-health promotion link offers significant opportunities to behavioral science researchers interested in health promotion research.

Absenteeism/Turnover

Once again, a relationship between health promotion and a positive outcome (absenteeism/turnover) is intuitively attractive, and also once again, it must remain not a great deal more than that. It seems reasonable to hypothesize that healthier employees will be absent less due to illness and that increased employee goodwill as a consequence of being provided health promotion activities would also operate to reduce both absences and turnover.

Indeed, there are reports of improvements in both work days missed and turnover. Fielding (1986) cites a number of reports indicating reductions in absence days associated with participation in a variety of different health promotion activities including hypertension programs, fitness and exercise programs, and smoking cessation activities. Similarly, Terborg (1986) summarizes several reports which claim reductions in absenteeism and turnover as outcomes of workplace health promotion. Typical of such studies are the data reported by Browne et al. (1984) in which participants in a fitness program averaged 4.2 sick days in the year prior to the program, and 3.4 days in the year following the start of the program. It is interesting that program nonparticipants in this study averaged 7.3 sick days, further indicating that participants in health promotion activities tend to be those least in need of the program.

Unfortunately, most of these reports suffer from the same weaknesses which have been previously cited. These include poor or no controls, suspect record keeping, and an inability due to study design (or lack thereof) to make causal attributions to the health promotion activities themselves. The fact, for example, that program participants have lower turnover rates than nonparticipants may indicate nothing more than employees who are giving consideration to leaving the organization are less likely to involve themselves in a program spanning several weeks or months of time.

Morale and Attitude Improvement

Most reports of improved morale and employee attitudes stemming from health promotion programs are not research studies, but testimonials. Fielding (1982), Damberg (1984) and Feuer (1985), among others, cite reports of improvements in morale, organizational commitment, group spirit and other positive attitude changes. In some instances, as the authors themselves note, the evidence rests upon nothing more than second or third party perceptions and 'gut' feelings.

A few studies (as opposed to testimonials) have been reported. In a post-test-only design, Rhodes and Dunwoody (1980) found in a sample of exercise and fitness participants that 59 per cent had improved self-confidence and 51 per cent felt more positive about their jobs. In a pre- and post-test design, Cox, Shephard and Corey (1981) administered the Job Descriptive Index to employees in two similar companies, one with a health promotion program, and one without. No significant differences were found between the two companies pre- or post-health program, nor were there any differences between participants and non-participants. Thus, in one of the better studies of possible attitude change, no differences were found.

What conclusions can be drawn from the reports reviewed regarding the association of workplace health promotion activities with the four potential outcomes just examined? Considered in total, the reports are generally positive, indicating benefits of health promotion with respect to costs, performance, absenteeism/turnover, and job-related attitudes. The number of actual research studies which have investigated these variables, however, is extremely meager; moreover, most suffer from a lack of rigor and robustness. While it is gratifying that most results are supportive, it is disappointing that there are so few and that their findings must be treated with such caution.

We turn now to the second part of our discussion of organizational issues, and focus attention on confidentiality, ethical considerations, and unintended consequences.

Confidentiality

Confidentiality of health promotion information is clearly an ethical consideration and as such would logically be part of the discussion of ethics which follows. We feel however, that it is such an important and fundamental issue that it deserves the emphasis accorded by treating it as a distinct and separate issue. This is a health promotion issue over which their should be no equivocation. Simply put, all records of program utilization should be held in the strictest confidence, should be maintained separate and apart of an employee's personnel file, and should be released only with the express permission of the employee.

Clearly not all components of health promotion programs are equally sensitive. Records relating to participation in a smoking cessation program, for example, would ordinarily not be as sensitive as information identifying an employee as having enrolled in a drug rehabilitation program. None the less, confidentiality is important for humanitarian, legal, and program success reasons. Alderman (1984) points out that many programs with unusually high screening and compliance rates owe their success to steps taken to insure confidentiality and job security. Program components particularly affected by the confidentiality issue include substance abuse programs, stress management, and hypertension programs. Confidentiality does not relate just to release of information to management and supervisory personnel; it also includes behavioral science researchers as well.

Ethical Considerations

Ethical problems in worksite health promotion programs have been identified as representing an important new frontier (Roman and Blum, 1987). With respect to workplace programs, Bezold, Carlson and Peck (1986) identify three kinds of ethical concern. The first relates to confidentiality which we have already discussed. The second has to do with the questions about the compulsory or voluntary nature of such programs. If a particular program has been shown to have a significant risk reduction effect should participation be mandatory for all employees, or for all employees who are known to be at risk? This is very similar to the ethical dilemma identified by Stone (1984) which arises out of a conflict of two principles: the right of individuals to a free choice of actions, and the obligation to protect individuals who may be unable to do so themselves. The fact that the overwhelming majority of health promotion programs are currently voluntary does not change the importance of this issue. Compulsory participation may be a form of *health fascism* (Cataldo *et al.*, 1986) in which appropriate health behaviors and lifestyles are defined for other people by those with 'superior knowledge'.

The third set of ethical issues identified by Bezold *et al.* (1986) relates to scope and coverage of health promotion programs. For example, what justification is there for restricting participation to only those with certain job titles or responsibilities, or to those from whom the organization expects to receive the greatest payoff?

As an example of this kind of ethical consideration, consider the health promotion strategy known as *high-risk–high-yield* (Collings, 1982). This involves targeting programs for those who are most likely to have or develop a problem *and* who are most likely to benefit from the program. Consider hypertension as an example. If factors associated with the risk of developing high blood pressure can be identified, employees can be separated into high-risk (or high-need) and low-risk (or low-need) subgroups. By concentrating on the high-risk group, overall program costs can be reduced. The high-yield part of this strategy is based on recognition of the fact that all high-risk individuals are not as equally likely to respond successfully to interventions. If characteristics of individuals who are likely to be successful in lowering blood pressure can be specified in advance, first priority can be given to them, further increasing the probability of cost-effective and cost-beneficial programs. Such strategies involve important employee relations and ethical considerations.

Patton *et al.* (1986) suggest that health professionals need to address ethical concerns relating to proper assessment (the use of assessment devices with demonstrated reliability and validity); insuring that 'prescriptions' will do more good than harm (for example, participation in a rigorous exercise program may do more harm than good to individuals with unscreened pre-existing medical problems); and insuring that the participant be fully informed about the program and not coerced into participation. Related to these issues are questions regarding establishing criteria to determine when it is ethical to increase compliance of participants via behavioral, organizational and educational techniques (Sackett and Haynes, 1976).

Other ethical considerations which have been raised in regard to health promotion efforts include issues of paternalism, elitism, and subtle forms of coercion (Chadwick, 1982); conflicting loyalties and the dilemma of victim blaming (Allegrante, 1984; Winkler, 1987); and questions relating to whose interests are being served—employee or employer—and how a proper balance may be struck (Shain, Suurvali and Boutilier, 1986). Many of these ethical considerations are traditional in matters of health and medicine; others have been given birth by the advent of workplace health promotion. All, however, are important and must be considered and addressed by those involved, in whatever capacity, in health promotion activities. Included are industrial/organizational psychologists.

Unintended Consequences

Not all outcomes and consequences of workplace health promotion programs are intended or positive. Terborg (1986) identifies some possibilities: reduction of health care utilization may lead to higher unit cost for those employees who do use health and medical benefits; worker compensation costs may increase; participation in exercise and fitness programs may cause work scheduling disruptions and, particularly among those who are in poor physical condition to begin with, may increase fatigue, lower performance and increase accidents. Smoking restrictions may produce conflict between smokers and nonsmokers, contribute to negative attitudes among smokers, and reduce productivity as smokers are required to spend time away from work areas to smoke only in designated smoking areas (Walsh, 1984). Increased longevity of retirees may lead to increases in retirement program funding costs (Warner, 1987).

There is some indication that the diagnosis of a previously unknown risk factor may contribute to absenteeism. Suggestions that this may be true come from hypertension screening programs. Several studies have shown an annual increase in sick-day absences in the case of employees who previously did not know they had high blood pressure. Haynes *et al.* (1978) found annual before and after screening rates of 2.3 days compared to 8.8; Charlson, Alderman and Melcher (1982) reported 2.5 versus 4.5; and Alderman and Melcher (1983) found 2.7 versus 4.4 days of annual absences. Haynes *et al.* (1978) concluded that labeling people as hypertensive inadvertently encourages them to assume a 'sick' role.

Additionally, there may be legal consequences associated with health promotion efforts. Legal liability may extend to professional staff of the program, as well as to the sponsoring organization itself. Such liability can arise from acts of omission—failure to perform when performance could be reasonably expected—and acts of commission where an act is performed in a negligent manner (Herbert and Herbert, 1984). For example, ignoring an employee who had collapsed in an exercise facility may be an act of omission; on the other hand, dragging that same employee to the side of the room without first ascertaining if injuries had been sustained which might be aggravated by movement, might be an act of commission. Failure properly to maintain equipment which subsequently contributes to an injury may be a negligent act, leaving the organization open to civil action.

We have now examined several aspects of workplace health promotion programs. We have provided a brief historical perspective, identified several of the more popular program components, and examined some, but certainly not all, issues relating to these programs. Throughout, we have cited research which has been conducted relating to health promotion programs, finding much to criticize in published reports. The future growth and direction of health promotion depends on answers to numerous questions which can be addressed adequately only through rigorous and thoughtful research. It is to this topic that we now turn.

RESEARCH NEEDS

In spite of the great number of studies cited in this review, and the fact that the studies cited comprise only a fraction of the reports in the literature, not a great deal of research into workplace health promotion has been published. Much of the information which is available is anecdotal in nature and provides little or no information about organizational outcome variables such as changes in absenteeism and performance (Davis et al., 1984).

There are many reasons why relatively little research has been published. Some organizations simply believe in the value of health promotion efforts, and informal feedback to managerial personnel from participants regarding the value they place upon the program is sufficient. Xerox is an example (Wright, 1982). In many instances the company medical or personnel department responsible for the program has a vested interest in the program and is not overly enthusiastic about undertaking evaluation research which may end up to be nonsupportive of continuation. Still other organizations do not approach such programs systematically enough to have available the records necessary to conduct program research, nor are they sufficiently interested to expend the additional resources necessary to build and maintain adequate record systems. The fact that many outcome measures, such as a decrease in health care costs, a lowering of employee risk factors and the attendant effect on morbidity and mortality, may take several years to be measurable is another factor discouraging research.

Not only is there a need for more research, however, there is an equally powerful need for better research. The scope and rigor of health promotion program research can be significantly improved. Too much research lacks adequate controls, relies on single (many times, subjective) measures of outcomes, and there are too many correlational studies which may show associations or statistical relationships, but make no real contribution to demonstrating cause and effect. This is not to say there is nothing to be learned from uncontrolled, correlational studies utilizing subjective measures; clearly we can—and have—learned from such research. Just as clearly, however, industrial/ organizational psychologists, and other behavioral science researchers, must go beyond this if we hope to advance our understanding of health promotion programs and provide the empirical support which will be needed to insure that health promotion at the worksite gains a respectable, enduring place rather than joining the list of promising, but short-lived, organizational fads.

There are a number of areas in which health promotion research can be improved; some relate specifically to how the research is conducted while others relate to the scope of such research. We will briefly examine a very few of these needs in the remainder of this section.

Better Research Designs

The cry for the use of better, more rigorous designs is a frequent one in behavioral research; health promotion research is no exception to this time worn plea. A widely held, although not totally valid, belief is that laboratory research limits generalizability and non-experimental research limits our ability to make causal inferences. According to this view, to improve health promotion research we must concentrate on field experiments as opposed to field studies or laboratory experiments. While it is certainly true that a well-designed and executed field experiment is an elegant and powerful design, it is also true that, as a practical matter, very little evaluation research would ever be completed if we insisted on this design. Important contributions to our knowledge of health promotion program effectiveness can be made both through laboratory research and, particularly, non-experimental research.

We shall not discuss here the range of design options available for conducting health promotion research; that has been more than adequately addressed elsewhere (see, for example, Feldman, 1984). Rather, we shall comment on two aspects of design which are of particular importance in conducting health promotion research.

The first concerns control groups. While randomized controls are the ideal, practical considerations dictate that non-equivalent controls frequently be used; indeed, if everyone is to participate in the program, no separate control group exists. In these situations Komaki and Jensen (1986) recommend the use of within-group or single-case designs which are particularly useful in assessing changes introduced in applied settings (Barlow and Hersen, 1984). Such designs can effectively control for common validity threats such as history, maturation, and regression to the mean, that plague numerous studies. Komaki and Jensen (1986) discuss the use of two such designs, reversal and multiple-baseline, that are particularly appropriate for workplace health promotion research and the reader is referred to their discussion.

Where control groups are feasible, even if such controls are non-randomized, they must be used in a manner which will strengthen the research and help detect potential problems such as placebo effects. It is possible, for example for a program participation group to 'improve' on some outcome variable because they expected to improve, while a control group did not improve because they did not expect to. There is a need in health promotion research to cause our controls to expect to improve as well, and perhaps to have two control groups—one in which this expectation is created and one in which it is not.

The second aspect of design relates to the need for longitudinal research. Since health promotion and the behavioral and lifestyle changes it involves is an ongoing endeavor for most individuals, and since many of the outcome variables of interest may take months or years to manifest themselves, longitudinal research is a critical need in health promotion research. Among the many advantages of longitudinal designs are that they can contribute to attempts to establish causality and can help minimize the problems encountered when processes are inferred from cross-sectional data. To conclude on the basis of a single measurement taken at one point in time that a health promotion program is effective, while having no knowledge of its staying power, may lead to invalid and costly conclusions.

Better Measurement

Terborg (1986) makes the point that a great deal of work remains to be done in the development and validation of many outcome variables relevant to health promotion research. The use of self-report measures is common in assessing changes relating to satisfaction, health status, and lifestyle. Many measures used have been developed specifically for a particular setting or study and are of unknown reliability and validity. Frequently, research efforts would be improved by the use of widely available measures whose psychometric properties have been established over time. Use of standard measures would also greatly facilitate making comparisons across treatment, locations, populations and studies.

The use of multiple and repeated measures would also contribute to health promotion research. Even biomedical measures such as blood pressure readings and serum lipid measures are influenced by transitory factors such as time of day, prior activity, and even the equipment used (Fried, Rowland and Ferris, 1984). Repeated measurement can help reduce these problems. Similarly, the use of multiple measures can enhance research efforts. With some health promotion activities (stress management, for example) we must go beyond the simplistic notion of asking participants how they feel (more relaxed, less stressed, more energetic, more alert, etc.). Physiological, biochemical and performance measures can be used to tap more than a single dimension. A combination of historical, behavioral science and biomedical measures not only provides more information, but allows the researchers to exhibit a higher degree of confidence in research results as well. Health promotion has physiological, psychological and behavioral consequences; to adequately assess its consequences, we must be able to determine the extent to which it resulted in changes in any of these dimensions.

Better Cost-effectiveness/Cost-benefit Research

While certainly not the only consideration, costs and cost savings are an important item in health promotion programs. Decisions to initiate, continue and expand programs are more easily made (i.e. easier to justify) if it can be shown that results to date in current or similar programs demonstrate cost effectiveness and benefit. Once again, more and better research needs to be carried out in regard to these issues. Accomplishing this requires a clear and specific statement of program objectives.

Cost-effectiveness research helps answer the question of the extent to which program objectives are accomplished effectively with respect to costs; if program objectives are poorly formulated, this can not be done. For example, a smoking cessation program which attains a stated objective of achieving a quit rate of 50 per cent of the participants may be a rather ineffective one if only 5 per cent of smoking employees enter the program. Another program that achieves only a 25 per cent quit rate (assuming costs of the two programs are comparable) may be viewed as less effective unless we know that 30 per cent of smoking employees entered the program. Too often these kinds of data are not reported (and may in fact not be known), leading to inaccurate conclusions regarding program effectiveness.

Cost-benefit research aims at providing an indication, in dollar terms, of the ratio of program costs to program benefits. This is a particularly challenging exercise in that it is exceedingly difficult to assign monetary values to many of the outcomes. For example, how much is a 10 per cent increase in employee satisfaction worth, or a 3 per cent increase in energy level resulting from improved physical fitness? Significant improvements in cost-benefit research could be made simply by more clearing specifying what goes into determination of numerators and denominators of cost-benefit ratios. Although, as many have argued (see, for example, Hollander, Lengermann and DeMuth, 1985; DeMuth *et al.*, 1986), the specification of cost and benefit terms, and the relationships between and among those terms, is an exceedingly difficult and complex one, it is a challenge to which health promotion researchers must respond. Several cost-benefit analysis models are available (see, for example, Higgins, 1986) to assist the researcher in that response.

Participation and Attrition Rate

There are at least two research needs issues with regard to participation and attrition rates. One, to which we have previously alluded, concerns the need to improve program evaluation research by taking participation and attrition into account. To evaluate a weight loss program, for example, by saying that those completing the program average an 11 per cent weight loss, without considering how many participants dropped out or perhaps more importantly, how many in need of the program never participated at all, is likely to result in misleading, invalid and probably costly conclusions. Researchers must pay attention to participation and attrition rates in program evaluations.

The second need is for research into factors which shape both participation and attrition rates. Health promotion programs of whatever ilk will be successful only to the extent that those employees who will benefit the most become and remain involved. While participation rates vary widely, most fall into the 20–40 per cent range (Shephard, 1983; Fielding, 1984; Oldridge, 1984). Strategies designed to broaden participation and reduce attrition must be tested, along with research focused on increasing our understanding of organizational, demographic, psychosocial and behavioral factors associated with individual participation and adherence decisions.

Use of Incentives

Closely related to questions of participation and attrition is the use of employee incentives. Some organizations 'pay' employees who participate in health promotion activities, although most do not (see, for example, Shepard and Pearlman, 1985). Those who do generally reason that the employee is not really being paid to do something; rather, the company is sharing with the employee the 'profits' (through decreased health claims, decreased absenteeism, increased productivity) associated with having a healthier workforce.

The effects, or lack thereof, of incentive programs remains an under-researched area. Are incentives useful? Should they be individual- or group-based incentives? What form should incentives take (time-off, money, symbolic awards)? Are intra- and inter-organizational competitions effective? Are there undesireable consequences of such competitions? Should just participants be rewarded or should employees who already are at the desired end state be rewarded as well (non-smokers and non-overweight employees, for example). The use of incentives in workplace health promotion programs represents fertile research ground for industrial/organizational psychologists, likely to yield an abundant harvest of useful information.

Unintended Consequences

We have already raised the issue of unintended consequences of health promotion programs in an earlier section, citing such factors as negative social interactions, fatigue, increased retirement program costs, and possible legal liabilities. We identify this as an area requiring additional research to reinforce its importance. Workplace health promotion has a great deal of potential to yield significant individual and organizational payoffs; if that potential is to be realized however, we must minimize the probability that the 'cure' is more costly than the disease. This will require careful and thoughtful program planning and implementation which, in turn, must come from knowledge of program consequences that will come from additional research.

In discussing research needs we have repeatedly alluded to the need for more and better research. There is a positive side of the ledger, however. While it is true that there is a great deal which is yet to be learned about the effectiveness of health promotion programs through the use of more rigorous, better executed, and more creative research, it is also true that a great deal is known. Virtually all of the research, regardless of its limitations, can and has contributed. In some cases that contribution has taken the form of adding to the knowledge base regarding health promotion programs; in other cases, the contribution has been in increasing understanding of how to improve research designs in subsequent studies. The challenge facing industrial/organizational psychologists is to do better: to use more rigorous designs with better controls and more representative samples; to take the 'long view' offered by longitudinal research employing repeated measures; and to increase the number and types of measurements used to test hypotheses.

CONCLUSION

The growth of workplace health promotion programs has been extremely rapid over the last decade. A number of forces have aided and abetted that growth, including a growing tendency of national governments to concern themselves with issues of occupational health and safety, and the increase in public awareness of and interest in matters of health, fitness and overall quality of life. There is nothing in the literature reviewed here which suggests that the driving forces will diminish or that the growth will cease. The challenge is to insure that growth results in that maximization of individual, organizational and societal payoffs.

Bezold, Carlson and Peck (1986) suggest that in the future health promotion programs will no longer be seen merely as a fringe benefit, but will be acknowledged as an integral part of the work experience. They conclude that health promotion will 'become synonymous with productivity, performance, and with organizations that place a premium on their people' (p. 170). If this scenario is to come to fruition, industrial/organizational psychologists in corporate, governmental and academic settings will need to bring their interest and expertise to bear on an array of workplace health promotion issues. Health promotion program design, implementation and evaluation represent a potentially profound opportunity for I/O psychologists to make significant and visible contributions to individual and organizational health, effectiveness and well-being.

REFERENCES

Abrams, D. B. and Follick, M. J. (1983) Behavioral weight loss intervention at the worksite: feasibility and maintenance. *Journal of Consulting and Clinical Psychology*, 51, 226–233.

Alderman, M. H. (1984) Worksite treatment of hypertension. In J. D. Matarazzo *et al.* (eds) *Behavioral Health*. New York: John Wiley.

Alderman, M. H., Green, L. W. and Flynn, B. S. (1980) Hypertension control programs in occupational settings. *Public Health Reports*, 95, 158–163.

Alderman, M. H. and Melcher, L. A. (1983) Occupationally sponsored community provided hypertension control. *Journal of Occupational Medicine*, 25, 465–470.

Allegrante, J. (1984) Ethical dilemmas in workplace health promotion. *Health Promotion Technical Reports*, 1, 2.

Altman, D. G., Flora, J. A., Fortman, S. P. and Farquhar, J. W. (1987) The cost-effectiveness of three smoking cessation programs. *American Journal of Public Health*, 77, 162–165.

Baer, L, Parchment, Y. and Kneeshaw, M. (1981) Hypertension in health care providers: effectiveness of worksite treatment programs in a state mental health agency. *Journal of Public Health*, 71, 1261–1263.

Barlow, D. H. and Hersen, M. (1984) *Single-case Experimental Designs: Strategies for Studying Behavior Change*. New York: Pergamon.

Becker, M. H. (1986) The tyranny of health promotion. *Public Health Review*, 14, 15–25.

Beehr, T. A. and Bhagat, R. S. (1985) *Human Stress and Cognitions in Organization*. New York: John Wiley.

Bernacki, E. J. and Baun, W. B. (1984) The relationship of job performance to exercise adherence in a corporate fitness program. *Journal of Occupational Medicine*, 26, 529–531.

Bezold, C., Carlson, R. J. and Peck, J. C. (1986) *The Future of Work and Health*. Dover, Mass.: Auburn House.

Blair, S. N., Jacobs, D. R. and Powell, K. E. (1985) Relationships between exercise or physical activity and other health behaviors. *Public Health Reports*, 100, 172–180.

Brennan, A. J. J. (1983) Worksite health promotion can be cost-effective. *Personnel Administrator*, 28, 17–23.

Brennan, A. J. J. (1986) No smoking program proves cost-effective. *EAP Digest*, 6, 43–47.

Brown, B. (1984) Biofeedback for coping with organizational stress. In A. S. Sethi and

R. S. Schuler (eds) *Handbook of Organizational Stress Coping Strategies.* Cambridge, Mass.: Ballinger.

Browne, D. W., Russell, M. L., Morgan, J. L., Optenberg, S. A. and Clarke, A. E. (1984) Reduced disability and health care costs in an industrial fitness program. *Journal of Occupational Medicine*, **26**, 809–816.

Brownell, K. D., Cohen, R. Y., Stunkard, A. J., Felix, M. R. and Cooley, N. B. (1984) Weight loss competitions at the work site: impact on weight, morale, and cost-effectiveness. *American Journal of Public Health*, **74**, 1283–1285.

Brownstein, P. M. and Herd, J. A. (1986) Practical indicies of compliance in cardiovascular risk reduction programs. In M. F. Cataldo and T. J. Coates (eds) *Health and Industry*. New York: John Wiley.

Cady, L. D., Thomas, P. C. and Karweisky, R. J. (1985) Program for increasing health and physical fitness of fire fighters. *Journal of Occupational Medicine*, **7**, 110–114.

Cascio, W. F. (1982) *Costing Human Resources: The Financial Impact of Behavior in Organizations*. Boston: Kent.

Cataldo, M. F., Green, L. W., Herd, J. A., Parkinson, R. S. and Goldbeck, W. B. (1986) Preventive medicine and the corporate environment: challenge to behavioral medicine. In M. F. Cataldo and T. J. Coates (eds) *Health and Industry*. New York: John Wiley.

Chadwick, J. H. (1982) Health behavior change at the worksite: a problem-oriented analysis. In R. S. Parkinson and Associates (eds) *Managing Health Promotion in the Work-place*. Palo Alto, Calif.: Mayfield Publishing.

Charlson, M. E., Alderman, M. and Melcher, L. (1982) Absenteeism and labeling of hypertensive subjects. *American Journal of Medicine*, **24**, 511–514.

Cohen, W. S. (1985) Health promotion in the workplace. *American Psychologist*, **40**, 213–216.

Collings, G. H. (1982) Perspective of industry regarding health promotion. In R. S. Parkinson and Associates (eds) *Managing Health Promotion in the Workplace* Palo Alto, Calif.: Mayfield.

Cox, M., Shephard, R. J. and Corey, P. (1981) Influence of an employee fitness programme upon fitness, productivity, and absenteeism. *Ergonomics*, **24**, 795–806.

Cunningham, R. M. (1982) *Wellness at Work*. Chicago: Blue Cross Association.

Damberg, M. F. (1984) *Worksite Health Promotion: Examples of Programs that Work*. Washington, D.C.: US Department of Health and Human Services.

Danaher, B. G. (1980) Smoking cessation programs in occupational settings. *Public Health Reports*, **95**, 149–156.

Davis, M. F. (1980) Worksite health promotion. *Personnel Administrator*, **29**, 45–50.

Davis, M. F., Rosenberg, K., Iverson, D. C., Vernon, T. M. and Bauer, J. (1984) Worksite health promotion in Colorado. *Public Health Reports*, **99**, 538–543.

DeMuth, N. M., Fielding, J. E., Stunkard, A. J. and Hollander, R. B. (1986) Evaluation of industrial health promotion programs: return-on-investment and survival of the fittest. In M. F. Cataldo and T. J. Coates (eds) *Health and Industry*. New York: John Wiley.

Driver, R. W. and Ratliff, R. A. (1982) Employer's perceptions of benefits accrued from physical fitness programs. *Personnel Administrator*, **27**, 21–26.

DuPont, R. L. and Basen, M. M. (1982) Control of alcohol and drug abuse in industry: a literature review. In R. S. Parkinson and Associates (eds) *Managing Health Promotion in the Workplace*. Palo Alto, Calif.: Mayfield.

Elliot, G. R. and Eisdorfer, C. (eds) (1982) *Stress and Human Health*. New York: Springer.

Epstein, L. H., Wing, R. R., Thompson, J. K. and Griffin, W. (1980) Attendance and fitness in aerobics exercise: the effect of contract and lottery procedures. *Behavior Modification*, **4**, 465–479.

Everly, G. S. and Feldman, R. L. (1984) *Occupational Health Promotion.* New York: John Wiley.

Feldman, R. H. L. (1984) Evaluating health promotion in the workplace. In J. D. Matarazzo *et al.* (eds) *Behavioral Medicine.* New York: John Wiley.

Feuer, D. (1985) Wellness programs: how do they shape up? *Training*, **22**, 25–34.

Fielding, J. E. (1982) Effectiveness of employee health improvement programs. *Journal of Occupational Medicine*, **24**, 907–916.

Fielding, J. E. (1984) Health promotion and disease prevention at the worksite. *Annual Review of Public Health*, **5**, 237–265.

Fielding, J. E. (1986) Evaluations, results, and problems of worksite health promotion programs. In M.F. Cataldo and T. J. Coates (eds) *Health and Industry.* New York: John Wiley.

Fielding, J. E. and Breslow, L. (1983) Health promotion programs sponsored by California employers. *American Journal of Public Health*, **73**, 538–542.

Foote, A. and Eefurte, J. C. (1983) Hypertension control at the worksite. *New England Journal of Medicine*, **308**, 809–813.

Ford, J. D. and Ford, J. G. (1986) Health promotion: competitor or resource? *EAP Digest*, **6**, 23–28.

Foreyt, J. P., Scott, L. W. and Gotto, A. M. (1980) Weight control and nutrition education in the occupational settings. *Public Health Reports*, **95**, 127–136.

Fried, Y., Rowland, K. M. and Ferris, G. R. (1984) The physiological measurement of work stress: a critique. *Personnel Psychology*, **37**, 583–615.

Gibson, R. M. and Waldo, D. R. (1981) National health expenditures, 1980. *Health Care Financing Review*, **3**, 1–53.

Haskell, W. L. and Blair, S. N. (1982) The physical activity component of health promotion in occupational settings. In R. S. Parkinson and Associates (eds) *Managing Health Promotion in the Workplace.* Palo Alto, CA: Mayfield.

Haynes, R. B., Sackett, D. L., Taylor, D. W., Gibson, E. S. and Johnson, A. L. (1978) Increased absenteeism from work after detection and labelling of hypertensive patients. *New England Journal of Medicine*, **299**, 741–744.

Herbert, D. L. and Herbert, W. G. (1984) *Legal Aspects of Preventive and Rehabilitative Exercise Programs.* Canton, Ohio: Professional and Executive Reports and Publications.

Higgins, C. W. (1986) Evaluating Wellness Programs. *Health Values*, **10**, 44–51.

Hilkenberg, J. B. and Collins, F. L. (1982) A procedural analysis and review of relaxation training research. *Behaviour Research & Therapy*, **20**, 251–260.

Hollander, R. B., Lengermann, J. J. and DeMuth, N. M. (1985) Cost-effectiveness and cost-benefit analyses of occupational health promotion. In G. S. Everly and R. H. L. Feldman (eds) *Occupational Health Promotion: Health Behavior in the Workplace.* New York: John Wiley.

Howe, C. (1983) Establishing employee recreation programs. *Journal of Physical Education Recreation and Dance*, **54**, 34–52.

Ivancevich, J. M. and Matteson, M. T. (1980) *Stress and Work.* Glenview, Ill.: Scott, Foresman.

Jacobs, B. A. (1983) Sound minds, bodies... and savings. *Industry Week*, **216**, 67–68.

Kent, D. C. and Cenci, L. (1982) Smoking and the workplace: tobacco smoke hazards to the involuntary smoker. *Journal of Occupational Medicine*, **24**, 469–472.

Klesges, R. C. and Glasgow, R. E. (1986) Smoking modification in the worksite. In M. F. Cataldo and T. J. Coates (eds) *Health and Industry.* New York: John Wiley.

Komaki, J. L. and Jensen, M. (1986) Within-group designs: an alternative to traditional control-group designs. In M. F. Cataldo and T. J. Coates (eds) *Health and Industry.* New York: John Wiley.

Logan, A. G. (1981) Cost-effectiveness of a worksite hypertension treatment program. *Hypertension*, **3**, 211–218.

Matteson, M. T. and Ivancevich, J. M. (1987) *Controlling Work Stress*. San Francisco: Jossey-Bass.

McClellan, K. (1985) The changing nature of EAP practice. *Personnel Administrator*, **30**, 29–37.

Morris, J. N., Everitt, M. G., Pollard, R., Chave, S. P. W. and Semmence, D. M. (1980) Vigorous exercise in leisure-time: protection against coronary heart disease. *Lancet*, **2**, 1207–1210.

Muldoon, J. A. and Berdie, M. (1980) *Effective Employee Assistance*. Minneapolis: CompCare Publications.

Murphy, L. R. (1984) Occupational stress management: a review and appraisal. *Journal of Occupational Psychology*, **57**, 1–15.

Murphy, L. R. (1985) Evaluation of worksite stress management. *Corporate Commentary*, **1**, 24–32.

Naditch, M. P. (1986) STAYWELL: Evolution of a behavioral medicine program in industry. In M. F. Cataldo and T. J. Coates (eds) *Health and Industry*. New York: John Wiley.

Newman, J. E. and Beehr, T. A. (1979) Personal and organizational strategies for handling job stress: a review of research and opinion. *Personnel Psychology*, **32**, 1–43.

Numeroff, R. (1983) *Managing Stress*. Rockville, MD: Aspen Publications.

Oldridge, N. B. (1984) Adherence to adult exercise fitness programs. In J. D. Matarazzo et al. (eds) *Behavioral Health*. New York: John Wiley.

Parkinson, R. S. and Associates (1982) *Managing Health Promotion in the Workplace*. Palo Alto, Calif: Mayfield.

Patton, R. W., Corry, J. M., Gettman, L. R. and Graf, J. S. (1986) *Implementing Health/Fitness Programs*. Champaign, Ill.: Human Kinetics.

Pauly, J. T., Palmer, J. A., Wright, C. C. and Pfeiffer, G. J. (1982) The effect of a 14-month employee fitness program on selected physiological and psychological parameters. *Journal of Occupational Medicine*, **24**, 457–463.

Pelletier, K. R. (1984) *Healthy People in Unhealthy Places*. New York: Delacorte Press.

Popple, P. R. (1981) Social work practice in business and industry. *Social Service Review*, **6**, 257–269.

Preston, H. B. and Bierman, M. E. (1985) An insurance company's EAP produces results. *EAP Digest*, **5**, 21–28.

Renner, J. F. (1987) Wellness programs: an investment in cost containment. *EAP Digest*, **7**, 49–53.

Rhodes, E. C. and Dunwoody, D. (1980) Physiological and attitudinal changes in those involved in an employee fitness program. *Canadian Journal of Public Health*, **71**, 331–336.

Rittlemeyer, L. F. (1982) Minor tranquilizers: prescribing practices of primary physicians. *Psychosomatics*, **23**, 23–26.

Roman, P. M. and Blum, T. C. (1987) Ethics in worksite health programming: who is served? *Health Education Quarterly*, **14**, 57–70.

Rosen, R. H. (1985) Organizational mental health: a strategy planning issue. In C. L. Cooper (chair) *Stress Management Interventions: An Evaluation*. Symposium conducted at the 45th meeting of the Academy of Management, San Diego, August.

Rossi, P. H. and Freeman, H. E. (1982) *Evaluation: a Systematic Approach*, 2nd edition. Beverly Hills, Calif.: Sage.

Ruchlin, H. S. and Alderman, M. H. (1980) Cost of hypertension control at the workplace. *Journal of Occupational Medicine*, **22**, 795–800.

Sackett, D. and Haynes, R. (1976) *Compliance with Therapeutic Regimens*. Baltimore: Johns Hopkins University Press.

Salcedo, M. (1986) The 25 healthiest companies to work for. *EAP Digest*, **6**, 45–50.

Shain, M. and Groeneveld, J. (1980) *Employee Assistance Programs: Philosophy, Theory and Practice*. Lexington, Mass.: Lexington Books.

Shain, M., Suurvali, H. and Boutilier, M. (1986) *Healthier Workers*. Lexington, Mass.: Lexington Books.

Shepard, D. S. and Pearlman, L. A. (1985) Healthy habits that pay off. *Business and Health*, **2**, 37–41.

Shephard, R. J. (1983) Employee health and fitness: the state of the art. *Preventive Medicine*, **12**, 644–653.

Shephard, R. J., Corey, P., Renzland, P. and Cox, M. (1982) The influence of an employee fitness and lifestyle modification program upon medical care cost. *Canadian Journal of Public Health*, **73**, 259–263.

Shephard, R. J., Morgan, P., Finncane, R. and Schimmelfing, L. (1980) Factors influencing recruitment to an occupational fitness program. *Journal of Occupational Medicine*, **22**, 389–398.

Silverman, M. M., Eichler, A. E. and Williams, G. (1987) Self-reported stress: findings from the 1985 National Health Interview Survey. *Public Health Reports*, **102**, 47–52.

Singer, J. A., Neale, M. S., Schwartz, G. E. and Schwartz, J. (1986) Conflicting perspectives on stress reduction in occupational settings: a systems approach to their resolution. In M. F. Cataldo and T. J. Coates (eds) *Health and Industry*. New York: John Wiley.

Stacey, J. (1980) Business taking a new look at health care costs. *American Medical News*, **23**, 20.

Stachnik, T. and Stoffelmayr, B. (1983) Worksite smoking cessation programs: a potential for national impact. *American Journal of Public Health*, **73**, 1395–1396.

Stone, G. C. (1984) Overview: training for health promotion. In J. D. Matarazzo *et al.*(eds) *Behavioral Health*. New York: John Wiley.

Stunkard, A. J. and Brownell, K. D. (1980) Worksite treatment for obesity. *American Journal of Psychiatry*, **137**, 252–253.

Taylor, C. B., Agras, W. S. and Sevelius, G. (1986) Managing hypertension in the workplace. In M. F. Cataldo and T. J. Coates (eds) *Health and Industry*. New York: John Wiley.

Terborg, J. R. (1986) Health promotion at the worksite. In K. H. Rowland and G. R. Ferris (eds) *Research in Personnel and Human Resources Management*. Greenwich, CT: JAI Press.

Trice, H. M. and Beyer, J. M. (1984) Employee assistance programs: blending performance-oriented and humanitarian ideologies to assist emotionally disturbed employees. *Research in Community and Mental Health*, **4**, 245–297.

Waldo, D. R. (1982) National health expenditures and related measures. *Health Care Financing Trends*, **2**, 1–34.

Walsh, D. C. (1984) Corporate smoking practices. *Journal of Occupational Medicine*, **26**, 17–22.

Warner, K. E. (1987) Selling health promotion to corporate America: uses and abuses of the economic argument. *Health Education Quarterly*, **14**, 39–55.

Wasserman, B. P. (1982) The employee high blood pressure program of the National Institutes of Health. *Public Health Reports*, **97**, 122–126.

Wikler, D. (1987) Who should be blamed for being sick? *Health Education Quarterly*, **14**, 11–25.

Wright, C. C. (1982) Cost containment through health promotion. *Journal of Occupational Medicine*, **24**, 965–968.

Zimmerman, R. S., Safer, M. A., Leventhal, H. and Baumann, L. J. (1986) The effects of health screening in a worksite hypertension screening program. *Health Education Quarterly*, **13**, 261–280.

International Review of Industrial and Organizational Psychology 1988
Edited by C. L. Cooper and I. Robertson
© 1988 John Wiley & Sons Ltd

Chapter 10

RECENT DEVELOPMENTS IN THE STUDY OF PERSONALITY AND ORGANIZATIONAL BEHAVIOR

Seymour Adler
Stevens Institute of Technology
USA

and
Howard M. Weiss
Department of Psychological Sciences
Purdue University
USA

In a review of the literature on personality and organizational behavior that we conducted earlier this decade (Weiss and Adler, 1984), we noted the marginal status ascribed to personality in most theory and research in our field. Typical was a statement by Van Maanan and Schein (1979) in the first volume of *Research in Organizational Behavior*. There, in outlining their theory of organizational socialization, Van Maanan and Schein state as a basic assumption: 'We assume here that a theory of organizational socialization must not allow itself to be too preoccupied with individual characteristics, for example, age, background, personality characteristics' (p. 216).

One of the most widely cited appraisals of the potential contribution of personality in industrial/organizational psychology was one made by Mitchell (1979) in an *Annual Review of Psychology* chapter on organizational behavior. Mitchell writes:

> A review of personality research leaves one rather unsettled. The measures lack reliability and validity, the empirical results, while statistically significant, frequently lack practical significance... Much of the work seems to have relegated personality variables to the role of a moderator or a "fine tuned" variable... This secondary role seems justified and necessary... We will be better served by continuing in the direction we are headed. Personality variables probably control only a minor percentage of variance in behavior when compared to situational factors, and there is little

consistency over time or settings. . . . Thus the methodological and theoretical limitations of the use of personality variables is likely to limit their future importance (p. 247).

This low regard for personality constructs in mainstream I/O psychology is based on both conceptual and empirical grounds. On conceptual grounds, the use of personality constructs in organizational research has been criticized by both ends of the theoretical spectrum in our field. On the one hand, the radical humanists look at the use of personality dimensions in conceptual models and empirical research as reductionist, viewing trait-oriented research as somehow breaking apart the essential uniqueness of each individual. On the other end of the theoretical spectrum stand the radical behaviorists. Clearly, for the radical behaviorists, the study of personality constructs involves measuring variables that are not directly observable, constituting an intrusion into the 'black box' and hence falling out of the domain of scientific industrial/organizational psychology.

In fact, based on the empirical literature in area after area of I/O research, it is difficult to make the argument that personality variables have made a proven contribution to our understanding or work behavior. Positive findings, when they appear, are often of marginal significance and personality effects within a given research area are often inconsistent. For example, after reviewing the literature on individual differences and goal-setting, Locke *et al.* (1981) conclude that the only consistent trend in this area is the inconsistency of results.

An example of another trend in personality research—hope followed by disappointment—is evident in the work on cognitive complexity and perform-ance appraisal. Schneier's (1977) original article, which attracted much attention, demonstrated that error in performance ratings was a function of rater cognitive complexity. Schneier suggested that people who are less cognitively complex demonstrate greater error when providing performance ratings on more complex rating scales. However, subsequent research (e.g. Bernardin, Cardy and Carlyle, 1982) has failed to replicate Schneier's results and it is now assumed that cognitive complexity has no consistent, meaningful impact on rater accuracy.

These disappointing results reported in I/O psychology are, in fact, consistent with empirical findings in other areas of personality research. Best known is Mischel's (1968) famous critique of personality research in which he claimed, after reviewing the literature, that behavior is inconsistent across situations, and that rarely do personality variables account for more than 10 per cent of the variance in criterion behaviors of interest. Mischel argued that behavior is largely determined by situational factors.

I/O psychologists, following up on Mischel (1968), have made the same argument, that behavior in work organizations is largely situationally deter-mined. So, for example, the thrust of research on job enrichment, expectancy theory, work attitudes and many other areas has been along these lines. The approach recommended to organizations for creating a motivated workforce is not necessarily to hire people who are highly motivated personalities, but rather to change job conditions. After reviewing the limited literature on personality and performance rating accuracy—limited both in terms of number of studies and range of personality variables examined—Bernardin and Beatty (1984) similarly conclude: 'The research on individual-difference variables has not borne much fruit. Rating accuracy appears to be more related to situation-specific variables than to individual characteristics' (p. 246).

These critiques of the use of personality in I/O psychology have been so widely accepted that there are whole areas of personality research in I/O which were once productive and are now almost completely abandoned. The case of selection testing is illustrative. Over twenty years ago, Guion and Gottier (1965) wrote a review article on the role of personality in personnel selection. Their conclusion was very pessimistic: much of the literature was methodologically inadequate, atheoretorical, and often reported negative or inconsistent results. Recently, Guion (1987) wrote that he had abandoned an attempt to conduct a follow-up to Guion and Gottier (1965). There was simply too little published data over the last twenty years to justify another review article. Similarly, whereas in the past, trait-oriented studies of leader emergence were commonplace in our literature, a recent meta-analysis found not a single study published in this area since the mid-1970s (Lord, De Vader and Alliger, 1986). And Staw, Bell and Clausen (1986) have observed: 'The field has very nearly eliminated individual-level variables from the study of job attitudes. The field is no longer interested in what the individual brings to the work-setting in terms of behavioral tendencies, traits, and personality' (p. 57).

In the face of such neglect and negativity, we wish to state our position at the outset. Despite the apparently negligible support for personality constructs in I/O research thus far, we feel that there is, in fact, much for personality to contribute to theory and research. As we have stated before (Weiss and Adler, 1984), the potential for personality in our models, in our research, and in our practice, has scarcely been explored. In area after area, we note that research typically does not adequately test for personality effects. Often personality is of secondary interest to the researcher and is accordingly treated marginally, given little thought, often studied in inappropriate settings using inappropriate designs. In our evaluation, the most conservative conclusion is that the role of personality in organizational behavior has simply not yet been fully examined.

In this chapter, we want to discuss recent developments in theory and research that might contribute to a fuller examination of the role of personality in organizational behavior. Our discussion is not intended to be an exhaustive review of existing literature. Instead, we shall highlight issues related to three key elements that require careful consideration if we are to make our research in this area productive: the personality constructs to be studied, the criteria to be measured, and the context in which personality-criteria relationships are to be examined. In each area, we will review recent developments that we feel can contribute to the development of a more productive role for personality in I/O psychology.

PERSONALITY CONSTRUCTS

In our earlier review (Weiss and Adler, 1984), we found that I/O researchers often fail to consider the theoretical frameworks in which personality variables are embedded. In our view, however, it is difficult to defend the use of personality measures *without* adequate consideration of the underlying theory that gives these measures and relationships between measures meaning. We also noted the rather limited range of personality constructs considered in I/O research and the limited strategies employed to measure constructs of interest. It is to issues of underlying theory, construct selection and personality measurement that we shall first turn our attention.

Nomological Networks

Typically, I/O researchers have drawn on an existing personality measure and included this measure in studies of organizational behavior. Rarely have they examined in-depth the theory and empirical base from which the measure is drawn.

An illustrative example is achievement motivation. Most I/O researchers employing a measure of achievement motivation ignore the complex, interactive achievement theory network, a rich theoretical framework, that includes expectancies, task characteristics and fear of failure (Nygard, 1981). A more recent example is honesty testing. There is a large social psychological research base on the issue of honesty that even includes personality research. Cheating behavior has been related to such constructs as impulsiveness (Yates and Mischel, 1979) and Machiavellianism (see Snyder and Ickes, 1985, for a review). These constructs have well-developed nomological networks. Yet there is virtually no research relating honesty tests to fundamental personality constructs (Sackett and Harris, 1984).

There are some recent signs, though, that I/O researchers are beginning to draw on, and contribute to, more elaborate nomological networks in their personality research. For example, Brockner (1983; Brockner and Guare, 1983) has developed an interesting model of self-esteem and behavioral plasticity. Brockner looks at the susceptibility of people low in self-esteem to social influence and has systematically examined that influence before, during and after task performance, pinpointing differential effects for those high and low in self-esteem at various stages of task performance.

In the area of job enrichment, Graen, Scandura and Graen (1986) have recently re-examined the use of the growth need strength construct within the Hackman and Oldham (1980) Job Characteristics Model. They point out that the growth need strength construct has been inappropriately applied in job enrichment research. Growth need strength, if it has meaning at all, relates to growth *opportunities* on the job and hence is future-oriented. Drawing on these theoretical underpinnings, these authors hypothesized that people high in growth need strength should not necessarily react to *existing* levels of variety, identity, significance, autonomy and task feedback. Rather, they hypothesized, and found in a field experiment, that growth need strength interacts with future opportunities for growth on the job in determining productivity. Gardner (1986) has also broken away from the Job Characteristics Model to study personality and job design within an Activation-Arousal Theory perspective. Drawing on past work linking extraversion to stimulus sensitivity (Eysenk, 1981), he found that introverts and extraverts differed in their physiological reaction to stimulating and non-stimulating jobs.

Similarly, there are new developments in the leadership area in which nomological networks are being more productively utilized. For example, McClelland (1985a) has advanced a theory of leadership which defines a Leadership Motive Pattern. Instead of looking at bivariate relationships between motives and leadership, McClelland posits a network in which need power, activity inhibition, and need affiliation are examined together. According to this model, only those people who have high need power but also high activity inhibition will be sufficiently selfless to emerge as leaders, if they can also keep sufficient distance between themselves and their followers. Hence high-need power, high-activity inhibition and low-need affiliation comprise a Leadership Motive Pattern (LMP). McClelland points out, again in the context of a nomological network, that LMP will predict leader effectiveness only in non-technical environments, because in technical environments, technical expertise will to a large extent determine leader effectiveness. House and Singh (1987) have recently reviewed the evidence supporting the LMP construct.

We are beginning to see, then, research on personality and work behavior that is more commonly conducted within the context of a nomological network that includes a set of personality constructs, consideration of contextual variables and specification of criterion constructs that might relate to the personality variables of interest.

Research in other areas might be similarly advanced by consideration of underlying networks. In the goal-setting area, for instance, self-esteem has been found to have a marginal impact on goal setting variables of interest in previous research (Locke et al., 1981). Yet there are solid theoretical grounds for expecting a link between self-esteem and goal-setting behaviors (Campbell, 1982). Perhaps one explanation for earlier results lies in the type of task often used in goal setting studies. As Wood (1986) has pointed out, most research uses quite trivial tasks, alternate uses and anagram tasks being the most common. In a recent meta-analysis by Wood, Mento and Locke (1987), effects related to goal-setting conditions were found to be weaker in more complex tasks and stronger in simpler tasks. Task complexity, then, might be a worthwhile dimension to examine with respect to the potential effects of self-esteem or other personality constructs. The nomological network related to self-esteem would suggest that self-esteem is most likely to play a role in those task situations that are more complex, challenging and consequently self-relevant.

Two other emerging areas of research might also benefit from a more in-depth consideration of dispositional variables and their relationship to other elements in underlying theory. One is the study of charismatic leadership. Trice and Beyer (1986) emphasize environmental determinants of charisma, stressing the importance of situational factors (e.g. a crisis), and of follower perceptions of, and attributions about, leader behavior. Correspondingly, little attention has been given to leader dispositions in research on the transformational leadership construct (Bass, 1985; House and Singh, 1987). Yet, it seems reasonable to expect leader dispositions to play a critical role in charismatic or transformational leaderships, given that follower perception, and attributions are so often organized in trait-oriented cognitive categories (Lord *et al.*, 1986).

A more fully-developed role for personality could also benefit research in the study of job attitudes. Staw and Ross (1985) have taken a first step here by demonstrating significant consistency of job attitudes over relatively long periods of time (3–5 years), even when respondents change jobs and occupations. Costa, McCrae and Zonderman (1987) likewise found strong stability over a ten-year period for scores on a self-report measure of well-being, with this stability unaffected by changes in the employment or personal status of respondents over that period. Gerhart (1987), too, found job attitudes to be significantly consistent over a four-year period, although he emphasizes that changes in job complexity also had significant effects on attitudes.

Three brief comments on these initial studies are in order. First, the finding that job attitudes show significant stability over time and situations is *consistent with* a dispositional explanation, but in the absence of empirical linkages with specific dispositions, alternative explanations are possible. For example, as Gerhart (1987) suggests, attitudinal consistency might signify how relatively stable work environments are despite nominal changes in titles or organizational membership. Two, arguing for a dispositional explanation of attitudes on the basis of evidence that attitudes are stable implies that if attitudes were unstable, a dispositional explanation would not be viable. We think this reasoning is based on an excessively simplistic notion of dispositional causes. As Magnusson and Endler (1977) point out, personality factors may predict the *coherence* of attitudes across circumstances, rather than simple consistency. Both of the concerns we have raised here can be addressed by specifying underlying dispositional constructs and hypothesizing exactly how these constructs affect job attitudes. Our third point concerns the issue of whether dispositions account for more or less variance in job attitudes than do situational factors (Gerhart, 1987). As Sarason, Smith and Diener (1975) noted long ago, this is, on a theoretical level, a pseudo-issue in which this area would best avoid getting entangled.

Staw, Bell and Clausen (1986) have recently taken a second step toward developing a dispositional approach to the study of job attitudes. They have shown that general tendencies toward a positive or negative evaluation of life stimuli that are evidence earlier in life can predict specific job attitudes up to *almost 50 years later*. While these results are impressive, real progress in this area requires a better understanding of both the fundamental personality traits underlying affective disposition and the mechanisms whereby personality and attitudes are linked (Staw *et al.*, 1986). The agenda going forward in this area, then, is similar to that we have identified in other areas of I/O research: the need to develop theoretically meaningful and empirically testable nomological networks.

Type of Construct

Another construct-related issue we want to address is the issue of construct type. If one examines the use of personality constructs in I/O psychology, one will notice that most personality constructs historically have been motivational (Weiss and Adler, 1984), although in recent times there has been an upsurge in the use of cognitively-oriented constructs. Still, the types of personality factors we have examined in our work have been narrow, especially when we consider the wide range of variables we might be looking at. To illustrate this wide range, recently Buss and Finn (1987) developed a multidimensional taxonomy of personality constructs. They first distinguish three broad types: instrumental constructs, affective constructs and cognitive constructs. Within each, they then distinguish between those constructs related to the social environment and those that are nonsocial. Finally, each social trait category is further subdivided. They use their taxonomy to highlight which areas of personality research are relatively well explored and which are hardly explored at all. For instance, they find many instrumental–social traits (e.g. dominance, altruism) but relatively few affective–social traits (e.g. shyness). It might be worthwhile applying this or some other taxonomy to the types of variables that have been examined in I/O psychology. Such an examination might be a stimulus for more creative work.

Let us take one example just to illustrate this approach. Comer and Dubinsky (1985) conducted an exhaustive review on predictors of sales success. They found that virtually all personality research in this area looked either at sociability or forcefulness. Comer and Dubinsky (1985) find inconsistent results for these personality predictors of sales success. Recently, though, Seligman and Schulman (1986) used a cognitive, non-social disposition, explanatory style, as a predictor of the performance of life insurance sales agents. In two studies, one concurrent and the other predictive, insurance agents found to have a pessimistic explanatory style—i.e. a tendency to construe bad events as due to internal, stable, and global causes—performed more poorly and quit sooner than agents with a less pessimistic explanatory style. Perhaps research in this area would benefit from a further expansion in the range of personality predictors considered.

The variables we study have been limited in another way. In common with other areas, personality in I/O psychology has been generally thought of in terms of dimensions or continuous variables. However, Gangestad and Snyder (1985) have made an argument in favor of a more careful consideration of personality typologies or class variables. They point out that we have traditionally preferred continuous dimensions in part because they are amenable to correlation-based statistical techniques such as factor analysis. Treating personality as a dimension also fits a paradigm that we are accustomed to dealing with in psychology, namely ability factors. Gangestad and Snyder argue, however, that typologies are theoretically and philosophically defensible, empirically demonstrable and should be more seriously considered in personality research. They go on to present programmatic research findings which they interpret as supporting a particular personality typology, namely self-monitoring. The research they review suggests that high and low self-monitors are two different types of people rather than opposite ends of a single continuum. The most instructive element of this work in our view, though, is not about self-monitoring, but rather a point well stated by Gangestad and Snyder: 'In the case of self-monitoring, identification of a class variable *has led us to ask and pursue fundamentally different questions and research strategies*' (p. 344; emphasis added). If we begin thinking more creatively about the personality constructs we use in I/O research, then we might ask ourselves new kinds of research questions and find new kinds of settings to which personality would apply.

Measurement Strategies

The last issue we want to discuss with respect to constructs concerns the strategies used to measure our constructs. There are several new developments in this area.

To begin with the most traditional measurement strategy, the inventory. There are two new inventories that have been developed and validated on non-clinical populations and have been investigated in a number of recent studies. One of those inventories is the NEO Personality Inventory developed by McCrae and Costa (1984). This inventory has demonstrated not only validity but a high degree of stability over time, perhaps because it measures fewer, and more abstracted, personality dimensions than is typical in inventories. The key dimensions assessed by the NEO are neuroticism, extraversion and openness to experience. While neuroticism and extraversion have been extensively studied by Eysenck and others (e.g. Eysenck, 1981), the openness construct is relatively unexplored. In one study, Costa, McCrae and Holland (1984) found the three personality factors to be systematically related to vocational preferences. To date, though, application of the NEO to work contexts has been limited, although McCrae and Costa (1984) have outlined several promising avenues of organizationally-relevant research in this area. The openness construct in particular may be important in understanding the integration of, and adaptation to, change in today's dynamic organization environment.

The other relatively new inventory is the Hogan Personality Inventory (Hogan *et al.*, 1985). The measure is embedded in the context of a socioanalytic theory of personality (Hogan, 1982) which justifies the choice of constructs measured, provides conceptual definitions for those contructs, and explains the meaning of scores on the measure. Drawing on social cognition theory, Hogan (1982) argues that the Inventory evokes from respondents the same self-presentational strategies as do social situations generally. Those who can effectively present themselves on those key trait dimensions generally used by others to evaluate people, are likely to be successful in social settings. Accordingly, the Hogan Personality Inventory was specifically designed to evoke respondent self-presentation relative to six dimensions found to be common in the social effectiveness cognitive schema used by observers: intellectance, ambition, adjustment, sociability, likeability and prudence. Hogan *et al.* (1985) summarize a series of recent studies in which scores on the Inventory successfully predicted job performance, service orientation and other organizational criteria in samples of clerical employees, hospital workers, technicians and naval researchers. In addition, in a few of these studies, scores on the Inventory were as well-correlated with performance as aptitudes were, and personality added significantly to aptitude in the prediction of performance.

Another issue related to measurement strategy that concerns us is the scope of the construct measured. This issue is best described by the example of locus of control. Locus of control (LOC) is a measure of a person's generalized expectancy concerning the relationship between behaviors and outcomes. This construct has been found to relate moderately to a wide range of organizationally relevant criteria (Spector, 1982). In the hope of increasing the predictive power of LOC, researchers in this area have developed increasingly narrow measures of the construct. For example, Furnham (1986) reported on his development of a measure of economic locus of control beliefs. Montag and Comry (1987) have developed a measure of driving behavior locus of control and demonstrate that a driver's driving behavior internality–externality is a predictor of whether that driver is involved in a fatal car accident. Guion (1987) too notes this trend, stating that 'I perceive . . . a tendency to look at traits manifested explicitly at work more than to those shown in a broader array of situations' (p. 201). We believe that while this trend might indeed enhance prediction in specific individual contexts, the use of increasingly narrow measures in fact damages our hopes for the development of broad, generalizable theories of personality and work behavior.

One last issue related to measurement strategies concerns developments in the use of projective tests in I/O research. Cornelius (1983) has recently argued that projectives suffer from an unjustifiably poor reputation in our field. In reviewing previous research on projectives as predictors of job performance, Cornelius finds in fact that ten out of fourteen well-conducted, criterion-related studies actually report significant validities for the personality measures. Cornelius also points out that projectives measure different constructs than do self-report measures, and thus projective responses should not be seen as substitutes for self-reports. This argument is parallel to that made by McClelland (1985) comparing the TAT projective measure of need achievement and purportedly parallel self-report measures of need achievement. McClelland argued that the TAT measures achievement *motivation* or achievement *need*, whereas self-report instruments measure achievement *values*. Perhaps the most critical consequence of this distinction is that parallel projective and self-report measures may be weakly interrelated and predict different criteria.

Before we leave this area of projectives, it is worth noting two specific projective-type measures that have generated research interest in I/O psychology. One is the Miner Sentence Completion Scale (Miner, 1985). As far back as twenty years ago, Korman (1968) felt that the Miner Sentence Completion Scale (MSCS) was a promising instrument for use in the selection of managers. Miner (1985) has recently reviewed the literature on the MSCS and presents strong and consistent data supporting the test's validity for managerial jobs but only in bureaucratic organizations. These findings make sense in light of the role motivation theory underpinnings for the construct measured by the MSCS. The MSCS is designed to measure a construct Miner calls 'managerial motivation'. Managerial motivation is predicted to relate to managerial job performance, and performance in turn to relate to advancement, only in organizations that operate according to a merit system, as bureaucracies tend to do. These predictions for the managerial motivation cosntruct were confirmed once again in a recent study of managers at varying levels drawn from 68 different organizations (Berman and Miner, 1985).

A second promising new measure of personality employing a novel measurement strategy is Stahl's Job Choice Exercise (Stahl, 1983). This measure uses a policy capturing methodology to assess the three most frequently studied motives: power, affiliation and achievement. The Job Choice Exercise items present respondents with various jobs in which the characteristics of power, achievement and affiliation are orthogonally varied. The respondent reads the job description and indicates his or her preference for each job. A beta weight is then calculated for each one of the three motives reflecting the extent to which the respondent's preferences reflected the motive. In this way, a person's needs are unobtrusively captured through his or her preferences for jobs. In a concurrent study, Stahl (1983) found scores on need power and need achievement to correlate with both performance ratings and promotions. While the job choice exercise is not a projective measure as classically defined, it utilizes an unobtrusive approach that is a promising alternative to traditional self-report measures of personality.

CRITERIA

Long ago, Weitz (1961) identified three critical facets of criteria that he felt were likely to impact on predictor–criterion relationships. These facets are (a) criterion type, (b) criterion level, and (c) time of criterion measurement. Each of these criterion facets needs to be considered when we examine the relationship of personality to criteria of work behavior.

Type

Too often, there is little theoretical basis for expecting personality to relate to the type of criterion used in personality research in organizations. In part, this is the case because in much of our research, personality is of secondary interest to the researcher and is included merely for 'fine-tuning' or as a 'fishing expedition' for significant predictors beyond those of central concern (Mitchell, 1979). Even in those studies where personality is of central concern, the theoretical justification for expecting a relationship between the personality construct and the type of criterion measured is poorly articulated (Weiss and Adler, 1984). As an example, selection researchers rarely spell out precisely why a given personality dimension measured at time of hire should relate specifically to productivity or to turnover 24 months later. Perhaps that construct is more strongly linked to quality of performance or tardiness. Likewise, it is still not clear exactly *how* a leader's relationship–orientation impacts on leader effectiveness under situations of varying favorableness to the leader, as described in Fiedler's Contingency Model (House and Singh, 1987). Hence, it is unclear what *type* of effectiveness criterion—cohesiveness, output, group longevity, leader popularity, performance quality—is most suitable for evaluating the Contingency Model.

For our personality research to have theoretical and practical significance, then, the personality constructs we study have to be theoretically linked to the specific type of criterion of interest.

For example, certain leader personality traits, for example, dominance, might be totally unrelated to leader effectiveness, but might be theoretically related to leader *emergence*. A measure of the extent to which followers see that individual as a leader is a very distinct criterion from one which measures how effective that person is in guiding the group toward goal acccomplishment (Lord *et al.*, 1986).

Drawing on social cognition theory, Lord *et al.* (1986) develop a theoretical basis for expecting a link between an individual's personality and criteria of leader emergence. In a meta-analysis of past trait research, these authors find generalizable validity for several prototypical leadership traits: intelligence, masculinity, conservatism, adjustment, dominance and extraversion.

In the goal-setting area, a review of the literature reveals several studies that have looked at self-esteem in goal-setting situations where the design was such that there was no choice of goal level given to the subjects (Locke et al., 1981). As Campbell (1982) points out, there is little theoretical justification, under assigned goal conditions, for expecting a direct relationship between self-esteem and task performance. It is not surprising, then, that no consistent relationship has been found. Instead of looking at performance as a criterion for self-esteem in assigned goal conditions, perhaps a more suitable type of criterion is the subject's commitment to, or acceptance of, an assigned goal. Hopefully, recent interest in such goal-setting criterion variables as commitment, acceptance (Locke, Latham and Erez, 1986) and expectancies (Garland, 1984) will lead to more creative directions for personality research.

Along similar lines, Kane and Lawler (1979) have argued that we look not only at individual mean, total or typical job performance criteria but also at individual performance distributions. They suggest that it is important to consider variation in an individual's performance across tasks, situations or time. On a practical level, these distributional characteristics may have meaningful implications for the predictability or dependability of an individual's future work performance. More recently, Kane has developed a performance distribution assessment technique to index these distributional characteristics in the course of performance appraisal (Bernardin and Beatty, 1984). This work has clear implications for personality research in organizations: traits which have not demonstrated any link to criteria reflecting *typical* performance, may be linked to distribution-type performance criteria.

Level

Recent personality research has examined criteria at both more micro- and more macro-levels of analysis than has traditionally been the case. On the more micro-level, for example, Moran (1986) examined the relationship between personality and the effectiveness of apprentice electricians in diagnosing faults in electrical circuits. He found, as predicted, that those electricians who were classified as field independent were more effective than those classified as field dependent. Similarly, Seppala and Salvendy (1985) used personality to predict the length of time supervisors took to search for information on a computerized management information system database. They found that performance on this criterion was largely explained by scores on extraversion, neuroticism and field dependence. Along the same lines, Kagan and Douthat (1985) found that those more introverted and those closer to the type A personality profile were more adept at acquiring and utilizing the Fortran programming language. One positive feature of this more micro-analytic orientation is that researchers begin with a more thorough understanding of the criteria of interest upon which to base their personality predictions.

A few recent studies have examined the relationship between personality and macro-, organization-level criteria. Specifically, these studies look at whether the personality of the organization's leader influences organizational characteristics. Boyd (1984) studied a sample of 368 Chief Executive Officers (CEOs) of member organizations of a Small Business Association. Most of the sample were original founders of their organization. These CEOs completed the Jenkins Activity Survey and were classified in terms of fitting the Type A personality profile. Results showed a significant linear relationship between the extent to which the CEO fit a Type A personality profile and two criteria of organizational performance: profitability, as indexed by annual return on investment, and growth, as indexed by the average annual change in sales revenue.

In a more recent study, Miller and Droge (1986) examined the relationship between CEO personality and organizational structure, rather than performance. They hypothesized that CEO personality would have a stronger effect on organizational structure, the smaller and newer the organization, and the longer the tenure of the CEO. Drawing on need achievement theory, the authors expected CEOs high in need achievement to create more centralization, establish more individual organizational units so that concrete results could be more clearly monitored, and engage in more planning activity requiring integration across units. Data were collected at 93 firms in Quebec representing a variety of industries. Need achievement predicted all three criteria of organizational structure and this effect was stronger, as predicted, in smaller and newer firms. CEO tenure, however, did not moderate the effects of personality on structure. Importantly, when CEO personality and size were accounted for, the effects of more traditional predictors of organizational structure—technology and uncertainty—became nonsignificant. Here, then, is a good example of theory-based personality research—drawing on both personality theory and organization theory—that links an individual-level personality predictor with a macro-level organizational criterion.

Another criterion-relevant issue concerns not the level of analysis at which we measure criteria but rather the level at which we aggregate our criterion measures. In a series of influential papers, Epstein (e.g. Epstein and O'Brien, 1985) has argued that the low correlations typically found in personality research may be due to inadequacies in the behavioral criteria, rather than in the personality constructs used or their measures. The criteria used in personality studies are typically single measures of a behavior which, like single items on a test, are of low reliability and stability. Research by Epstein demonstrates how, when criteria measures are collected over several occasions and aggregated into composite scores, their stability increases and their correlations with personality predictors increase as well.

To test these notions, Adler and Weiss (in press) had subjects set goals for, and perform, four different tasks expressly chosen to represent different aptitude domains. Following Epstein, each task was presented over three trials. The personality variable chosen for this study, based on level of aspiration theory (Campbell, 1982), was self-esteem, as measured by the Rosenberg (1965) Self-esteem Scale.

Correlations between self-esteem on the one hand, and self-set goal difficulty level and task performance on a single trial of any particular task on the other, were typical of those found in the past. However, a meaningful increase in the predictive power of self-esteem occurred when criterion measures were aggregated across tasks and across trials.

These results are not cited to suggest that criterion aggregation be applied wholesale in personality research in organizations. First of all, in the study by Adler and Weiss (in press), aggregation made a meaningful difference only when some tasks were aggregated together but not others. Even from a practical perspective, then, the blind aggregation of criterion variables to form an overall composite may not necessarily enhance predictability. More critically, it should be theoretical interests that guide what is aggregated. As Schmidt and Kaplan (1971) pointed out long ago, wholesale aggregation of criteria into composites, even where predictability is enhanced, obscures our understanding of the behavioral phenomenon of interest. Typically, organizational researchers are most interested in single-act behavioral criteria measured over different occasions, for example speed of responsiveness of a service representative to customers of varying types with different requests. We are typically not interested in an aggregation of performance expectancies, goal acceptance, and outcome valences for assorted tasks. Furthermore, there are those criterion behaviors for which aggregation is simply inappropriate, as when behavior in one circumstance (e.g. performance in an emergency) cannot be compensated for by behavior in another, or when long-term trends are not of conceptual interest to the researcher. Where appropriate, however, measuring criteria at more aggregated levels appears a strategy that is likely to enhance the predictive power of personality in future research.

Time

In his paper on criteria for critera, Weitz (1961) first proposed that the effects of personality on job performance may vary in the course of time. More specifically, Weitz proposed and tested the hypothesis that basic ability factors account for much of the variance in performance early on, when the employee is learning the job, but that personality comes to play a significant role once this acquisition phase is over (Weitz, 1966). This notion was supported in a study of new managers by Dodd, Wollowick, and McIntyre (1970), using assessment center predictors. They showed that personality variables measured at the assessment center became increasingly important predictors of effectiveness over time.

More recently, Helmreich, Sawin and Carsrud (1986) have reported similar findings and have labelled the delayed impact of personality on job performance the 'honeymoon effect'. They examined the relationship between achievement motivation and interpersonal orientation on the one hand, and job performance on the other, in a sample of airline reservation agents. Correlations of the personality measures with performance over the first three months after the completion of training were nonsignificant. The personality predictors were significant, however, when correlated with reservationists' performance as measured after six months and eight months on the job.

Really what we are looking at here is a special case of what we commonly refer to in I/O psychology as 'dynamic criteria'; the differential weights of those skills, abilities and personality dispositions that impact on performance change over time. Correspondingly, Katz (1980) has described how various motivational dispositions change in relative influence on work-related attitudes and behavior as a person enters and becomes socialized into a new job. In a comment made about selection research that would be equally applicable to most other areas of research in our field, Helmreich *et al.* (1986) raise the 'disturbing possibility that personality has been dismissed as a predictor only because of the timing used for criterion measurement in past predictive validation research' (p. 187).

The real challenge for our field going forward, however, is to develop *a priori* hypotheses about the time frames during which personality should or should not affect work behavior. McGrath and Kelly (1986) note the lack of attention that temporal issues have received throughout psychology. If we took a closer look at temporal aspects of work behavior, we would find many important issues (e.g. the nature of temporal patterns in organizational life; overlapping individual, work group, organizational, economic cycles) to which personality constructs are likely to contribute. Our major problem here, both for understanding temporal issues in past research and for advancing hypotheses in future research, is the absence of theory. Helmreich *et al.* (1986) cannot justify the choice of six or eight months as the critical time for measurement of reservationists' performance. Nor can we predict whether personality effects will continue to be significant after eight months. It is especially crucial in personality research, as McGrath and Kelly (1986) state, 'that we begin to specify much more carefully not only the time order but also the time intervals between our putative causes and their alleged effects. Time intervals between cause and effect should be a matter of theory rather than experimental convenience' (p. 164).

CONTEXT

Of course, any discussion of developments in personality research in I/O psychology has to go beyond consideration of personality constructs and criteria to address the context in which personality criteria relationships are examined.

Situational Strength

One new development that concerns research context is increased awareness of the concept of situational strength. Most recently, for example, Mitchell and Larson (1987) have argued that serious consideration to the situational strength concept could help revitalize the study of personality and work behavior. According to Mischel (1977), strong situations are those which provide salient cues, have a high degree of structure, induce uniform expectancies, require skills that are generally possessed, constrain behavior, and have a strong incentive for performance of a particular response pattern. Strong situations, then, are those that minimize individual differences. Weak situations are ambiguous, low in structure, and allow for a wide range of behaviors. It is in weak situations, according to Mischel, that we are most likely to find personality making a difference. In our earlier review, we found that most research in I/O psychology is conducted in situations that are strong (Weiss and Adler, 1984). It is usually the situational manipulation that is of primary interest to the researcher, norms or expectancies are fairly clear, and hence it is not at all surprising that personality is found to be of trivial importance.

However, before we start looking for weak situations in order to find more powerful personality effects, there are several fundamental questions that need to be resolved. One, how do we specify at a theoretical level what the characteristics of strong situations are? Mischel's (1977) definition of strong situations is grounded in the cognitions and perceptions of those in the situation. But as researchers, what we need are a set of objective situational characteristics that define strength so that we can design situations *a priori* that are strong or weak and not be dependent on determining *post hoc* whether they were strong- or weak-based on the perceptions of people in those situations.

Secondly, what are situations? As in the case of time, we do not have an adequate theory of situations, or even a comprehensive list of dimensions with which to describe situations. There are many ways that situations have been conceptualized in our field. For instance, among contingency theories of leadership, Fiedler's theory (1967) takes a very broad view of situations. The leader's situation in this theory is not bounded by either time or space. When we assess situational favorability we only have to do it once and, while it can of course change, witness Leader Match, the leader's situation is singular and broad in scope. In contrast, in their model, Vroom and Yetton (1971) recognize that the leader may encounter multiple 'situations' during the day. Each situation has its own characteristics and demands a different behavioral response. The conception of situations in the Vroom and Yetton model is more defined and limited in time.

Vroom and Yetton's approach would appear to be the more useful one for identifying situations for assessing situational strength. That is, we need to focus on definable situations of smaller scale and duration. During an eight-hour work day a person might have only three hours of situations, the rest being transition time. This conception of situations is very much like the concept of social interaction episodes which Forgas (1982) has discussed, well-structured common patterns of social interactions, which generally have well-accepted rules of conduct. He too observes that the episodes we encounter can vary in their prototypicality and therefore, presumably, vary in their behavioral uniformity.

Finally, there is the question of how to scale situational strength. Price and Bufford (1974), for example, have suggested that subjects be presented with a matrix of situations and behaviors and asked to scale the appropriateness of each behavior for each situation. Then averages or standard deviations can be calculated across behaviors for each situation as measures of situational strength. The situation is strong when few behaviors are seen as appropriate. A situation is weak when a wide range of behaviors is considered appropriate in that situation.

One relatively unstructured context in which researchers lately have shown a renewed interest in personality is negotiation behavior. Huber and Neale (1986), for instance, predicted that Machiavellians would perform more effectively in a novel bargaining situation and, based on past success in such situations, would also set higher goals relative to non-Machiavellians. Indeed, in testing a well-articulated path model, these researchers found that Machiavellianism had the predicted direct and indirect effects on goals and performance. In another study, Greenhalgh, Neslin and Gilkey (1985) predicted that negotiator personality would both directly and indirectly affect the outcome of negotiations. They looked at a broad array of personality variables, measured through self-reports, interviewer evaluation and projective instruments. They, too, found an overall effect for personality in an unstructured negotiation context. However, no specific justification was provided for the 31 personality predictors included in this study, and the study was further limited by the small sample size relative to the size of the predictor set.

Similar to researchers studying negotiation contexts, Kabanoff (1987) also has examined the effect of personality on conflict-resolution behaviors. Although none of these researchers have explicitly scaled situational strength, it does appear that the negotiation context is one in which strength is low and personality is likely to contribute.

Suitable Contexts

Situational strength is a general structural feature of the research context in which the relationship between personality and behavior is being examined. As such, strong situations attenuate these relationships, irrespective of the particular personality or criterion variables of interest. Our concern in this section is with the identification, on a theoretical basis, of those contextual variables that influence the magnitude and direction of a *particular* personality-criterion relationship. Serious consideration to such contextual factors can illuminate creative new directions for research, as two recent examples will illustrate.

Researchers have long presumed a positive relationship between self-esteem and task performance (Korman, 1970). Based on an earlier study by Weiss and Knight (1980), Knight and Nadel (1986) suggested that in certain situational contexts, 'humility has utility', and consequently the relationship between self-esteem and performance would actually be negative. Specifically, subjects were placed in a computerized business game, where each subject managed a company over a simulated 24-week period. Each week the subject could, at some cost, request feedback on the effectiveness of past policy and could opt to continue or change policy. Feedback was always negative. Placed in such a situation, those high in self-confidence requested feedback less often, and adhered to failing policies longer than those low in self-confidence. As in the earlier Weiss and Knight (1980) study, the lack of confidence in their own judgement evidenced by those low in self-esteem, and their search for extensive external corroboration before acting, was, in such contexts, facilitative of effective performance.

These results converge with recent findings by Ackes, Dawes and Christensen (1986) on a construct they refer to as 'cognitive conceit', general competence in one aspect of a subject area which leads people to perceive themselves as possessing expertise in all topics within that subject area. In their study, subjects were given a prediction task and provided with a decision rule that yielded a correct prediction in 75 per cent of the cases. Those competent in one aspect of the subject area—an aspect not directly relevant to the task at hand—tended not to rely on the decision rule and consequently were less effective on the task. Those less competent in that other aspect of the subject area relied more often on the decision rule with which they were provided and were, as a result, more effective on the task.

Another illustration comes from the field of group dynamics. Past research has consistently found Field Independent individuals to be instrumentally-oriented and more effective in group tasks than the Field Dependent people. Gruenfeld and Lin (1984) suggested that the direction of the field articulation–effectiveness relationship may be dependent on contextual factors. Past research consistently employed structured tasks in a mechanistic group environment. Using an unstructured task in an organic T-group type setting, Gruenfeld and Lin found that the Field Dependents were actually more task-oriented and effective than Field Independents. The researchers went beyond merely examining the overall relationship between personality and criteria to analyse group process using the SYMLOG technique (Bales and Cohen, 1979). They found that those who were Field Independent demonstrated frequent self-direction and self-control behavior during group meetings, in the process putting psychological distance between themselves and other group members and minimizing their contributions to group progress.

By analysing critical contextual factors and developing a clear, theory-guided understanding of how linkages between personality and behavior are affected by these contextual factors, these researchers have arrived at creative hypotheses and significant findings. Personality research in I/O psychology is likely to become productive if this approach is more often imitated.

Interactionism

The implications of interactional psychology for the study of organizational behavior has recently been reviewed by Schneider (1983). Here we wish to highlight just one aspect of interactionism, the study of dynamic interactions. Magnusson and Endler (1977), in developing their interactional psychology, contrast mechanistic and dynamic interactionism. The mechanistic interactionism approach typically treats personality as a component of an interaction term within the traditional ANOVA model. Dynamic interactionism, in part, examines the reciprocal effects of personality and situational variables. In organizational behavior, this dynamic approach is probably best exemplified by the longitudinal research of Kohn and Schooler (1982) who looked at how personality affects the type of job that people hold and how the job, in turn, shapes personality over time. Using sophisticated analytical techniques, these authors were able to identify contemporaneous and lagged interrelations of job conditions (e.g. variety) and personality (e.g. intellectual flexibity) over a ten-year period.

A number of other recent studies illustrate the value of examining such dynamic relationships between personality and situations. Wolfle and Robert-shaw (1982), for instance, measured the locus of control of a sample of high school seniors along with a number of ability and background factors. The authors subsequently readministered the locus of control measure to this same sample four years later. They found that subsequent locus of control correlated with whether or not the subject had attended college during the intervening four years. Using LISREL, Wolfle and Robertshaw (1982) were able to demonstrate that the relationship between college attendance and locus of control is primarily due to the influence of initial locus of control and scholastic ability on both college attendance and subsequent locus of control.

In a similar study, Tiggeman and Winefield (1984) measured the self-esteem and locus of control in a sample of Australian high school students. They then readministered these measures one year later to those who were no longer in school, some of whom were employed, others of whom were unemployed. They found a general increase in self-esteem over time among those women who found jobs, but a decrease among those women who did not; no similar trend was found for men. In general, self-esteem predicted employment among males, self-esteem was a consequence of employment among females. In following up on a sample of workers who had lost their jobs due to a plant closing, Kinicki (1985) found that Protestant ethic beliefs did not predict how quickly workers found new employment, but did predict coping behaviors designed to minimize the impact of the prolonged lay-off.

Now there are two clear implications of dynamic interactionism for research in I/O psychology. First, that personality might very well be an interesting *dependent* variable in I/O research. To give an example from goal-setting research, performance feedback at a given level, when people are operating under specific daily goals, may have a stronger effect on chronic self-esteem or self-efficacy than when people perform at that level in the absence of specific goals. Or, following Mossholder (1980) and Manderlink and Harackiewicz (1984), operating in a job that is characterized by frequent, assigned, proximal (or short-term) goals may have the effect of decreasing employee internal locus of control. We are talking, then, about theory-guided research that explicitly examines the manner in which work experiences shape and modify dispositional characteristics.

A second implication of dynamic interactionism is that more longitudinal research is needed in the area of personality and work behavior. Not only would longer-term research be more reflective of real-world settings but also, the reciprocal effects of organizational conditions on personality are likely to occur only with long-term exposure, such as the ten-year timespan in Kohn and Schooler's (1982) work.

Of course, the issue of studying dynamic relationships of personality and situational factors once again raises questions about appropriate time frames. Without theories that attach hypothesized time frames to hypothesized causal sequences (McGrath and Kelly, 1986), our measurement interventions are shots in the dark which may or may not be close to the target.

CONCLUSIONS

Our intention in this chapter was to review recent literature in I/O psychology that relates to a more productive role for personality constructs. We detect an emerging change in attitude on the part of theoreticians and researchers in I/O psychology toward personality. Reflective is a recent statement by Mitchell and

Larson (1987) that stands in dramatic contrast to Mitchell's (1979) pessimistic assessment of personality quoted at the beginning of this chapter:

It may be time to take a second, closer look at the role that personality plays in determining organizational behavior. It seems unlikely that personality will ever become *the* predominant variable explaining all, or even most, behavior in organizations. But if we start taking account of factors such as situational strength and self-monitoring tendencies, it is quite possible that new organizational circumstances can be discovered in which personality does play a vital role. This would seem to be an important direction for future research. (p. 108)

This change of attitude is not unique to Mitchell. Since publication of an earlier review (Weiss and Adler, 1984), a major new book entitled *Personality Assessment in Organizations* (Bernardin and Bownas, 1985) has been published, the most recent chapter on Organizational Behavior in the *Annual Review of Psychology* (House and Singh, 1987) dedicated considerable space to the power motive and other personality-related issues, and sessions on personality have become a standard part of convention programs.

This emerging trend has its roots, we believe, in both theoretical and practical developments within I/O psychology. On the theoretical side, there is increasing awareness of developments in personality research (e.g. aggregation, situational strength) that have clear implications for the study of personality in organizations. Also, the social cognition prospective that has, for the past decade, influenced so much of our research in I/O, has also become increasingly sensitive to individual differences. I/O psychologists are beginning to notice social cognition research that considers cognitive complexity, self-monitoring, locus of control, and field articulation and are beginning to incorporate these variables in I/O research.

On the practical side, recent meta-analytic studies have repeatedly demonstrated in area after area that negative and inconsistent findings in past personality research were due, in large part, to artifactual rather than substantive sources. Thus, in the selection context, Hunter and Hunter (1984) find generalizable validity for several personality predictors; Loher *et al.* (1985) find that growth need strength does moderate the relationship of job scope to job attitudes; Lord *et al.* (1986) find that personality traits do in fact predict leadership. Corresponding to these meta-analytic findings are recent reports of significant predictive validities for personality measures in several large sample, long-time frame studies. These include work over a twenty-year period at Sears (Bentz, 1985) and Exxon (Sparks, 1985) as well as more recent research conducted as part of the US Military's Project A (e.g. Hough, 1987).

Beyond empirical findings, other practical developments have created an atmosphere that may be more conducive to personality research in the future. For now, at least, there appears to be less of a concern with the invasive nature of personality testing that was frequently a concern in the 1950s and 1960s. Correspondingly, there appears to be an increased belief on the part of the public that personality factors play a critical role in the performance of certain sensitive and visible jobs, such as air traffic controller and police. Furthermore, the availability and operational ease of inexpensive computer systems for administering, scoring and interpreting personality instruments (see Vale, Keller and Bentz, 1986, for a recent example), enhances the utility of such instruments for both application and research. These practical factors suggest that personality will play an increasingly prominent role in both the theory and practice of I/O psychology.

As we have seen so often in the past, *more* research and application does not necessarily mean *better* research and application. We close, then, by appealing once more for more systematic, theory-guided thought in the selection of personality constructs, in the specification of links between personality and criteria of interest, and in the identification of settings within which to study the relationship of personality and work behavior.

REFERENCES

Ackes, H. R., Dawes, R. M. and Christensen, C. (1986) Factors influencing the use of a decision rule in a probabilistic task. *Organizational Behavior and Human Decision Processes*, **37**, 93–110.

Adler, S. and Weiss, H. M. (in press) Criterion aggregation in personality research: A demonstration looking at self-esteem and goal setting. *Human Performance*.

Bales, R. F. and Cohen, S. P. (1979) *SYMLOG: A System for the Multiple Level Observation of Groups*. New York: Free Press.

Bass, B. M. (1985) *Leadership and Performance Beyond Expectations*. New York: Free Press.

Bentz, V. J. (1985) Research findings from personality assessment of executives. In H. J. Bernardin and D. A. Bownas (eds) *Personality Assessment in Organizations*. New York: Praeger, 82–144.

Berman, F. E. and Miner, J. B. (1985) Motivation to manage at the executive level: A test of the hierarchic role-motivation theory. *Personnel Psychology*, **38**, 377–391.

Bernardin, H. J. and Beatty, R. W. (1984) *Performance Appraisal: Assessing Human Behavior at Work*. Boston: Kent.

Bernardin, H. J. and Bownas, D. A. (eds) (1985) *Personality Assessment in Organizations*. New York: Praeger.

Bernardin, H. J., Cardy, R. L. and Carlyle, J. J. (1982) Cognitive complexity and appraisal effectiveness: Back to the drawing board? *Journal of Applied Psychology*, **67**, 151–160.

Boyd, D. P. (1984) Type A behaviour, financial performance, and organizational growth in small business firms. *Journal of Occupational Psychology*, **57**, 137–140.

Brockner, J. (1983) Low self-esteem and behavioral plasticity. In L. Wheeler and P. Shaver (eds) *Review of Personality and Social Psychology*, Vol. 4. Beverly Hills, CA: Sage.

Brockner, J. and Guare, J. (1983) Improving the performance of low self-esteem individuals: An attributional approach. *Academy of Management Journal*, 26, 642–656.

Caldwell, D. F. and O'Reilly, C. A. (1982) Boundary spanning and individual performance. The impact of self-monitoring. *Journal of Applied Psychology*, **67**, 124–127.

Campbell, D. J. (1982) Determinants of choice of goal difficulty level: A review of situational and personality influences, *Journal of Occupational Psychology*, **55**, 75–95.

Comer, J. M. and Dubinsky, A. J. (1985) *Managing the Successful Sales Force*. Lexington, Mass.: Lexington Books.

Cornelius, E. T. (1983) The use of projective techniques in personnel selection. In K. M. Rowland and G. D. Ferris (eds) *Research in Personnel and Human Resources Management*. Greenwich, CT: JAI Press.

Costa, P. J., McCrae, R. R. and Zonderman, A. B. (1987) Environmental and dispositional influences on well-being: Longitudinal follow-up of an American national sample. *British Journal of Psychology*, **78**.

Dodd, W. E., Wollowick, H. B. and McNamara, W. J. (1970) Task difficulty as a moderator of long-range prediction. *Journal of Applied Psychology*, **54**, 265–270.

Epstein, S. and O'Brien, E. (1985) The person-situation debate in historical and current perspective. *Psychological Bulletin*, **98**, 513–537.

Eysenck, H. J. (1981) *A Model for Personality*. New York: Springer-Verlag.

Fiedler, F. E. (1967) *A Theory of Leadership Effectiveness*. New York: McGraw-Hill.

Funder, D. C. and Ozer, D. J. (1983) Behavior as a function of the situation. *Journal of Personality and Social Psychology*, **44**, 107–112.

Funrham, A. (1986) Economic locus of control. *Human Relations*, **39**, 29–43.

Gangestad, S. and Snyder, M. (1985) To carve nature at its joints: On the existence of discrete classes in personality. *Psychological Review*, **92**, 317–349.

Gardner, D. G. (1986) Activation theory and task design: An empirical test of several new predictions. *Journal of Applied Psychology*, **71**, 411–418.

Garland, H. (1984) Relation of effort–performance expectancy to performance in goal-setting experiments. *Journal of Applied Psychology*, **69**, 79–84.

Gerhart, B. (1987) How important are dispositional factors as determinants of job satisfaction: Implications for job design and other personnel programs. *Journal of Applied Psychology*, **72**, 366–373.

Graen, G. B., Scandura, T. A. and Graen, M. R. (1986) A field experimental test of the moderating effects of growth need strength on productivity. *Journal of Applied Psychology*, **71**, 484–491.

Greenhalgh, L., Neslin, S. A. and Gilkey, R. W. (1985) The effects of negotiator preferences, situational power, and negotiator personality on outcomes of business negotiations. *Academy of Management Journal*, **28**, 9–33.

Gruenfeld, L. W. and Lin, T. R. (1984) Social behavior of Field Independents and Dependents in an organic group. *Human Relations*, **37**, 721–742.

Guion, R. M. and Gottier, G. F. (1965) Validity of personality measures in personnel selection. *Personnel Psychology*, **18**, 135–164.

Guion, R. M. (1987) Changing views for personnel selection research. *Personnel Psychology*, **40**, 199–214.

Hackman, J. R. and Oldham, G. R. (1980) *Work Redesign*. Reading, Mass.: Addison-Wesley.

Helmreich, R. L., Sawin, L. L. and Carsrud, A. L. (1986) The honeymoon effect in job performance: Temporal increases in the predictive power of achievement motivation. *Journal of Applied Psychology*, **71**, 185–188.

Hogan, R. (1982) A socioanalytic theory of personality. In M. Page and R. Dienstbier (eds) *Nebraska Symposium on Motivation*. Lincoln, NE: University of Nebraska Press, 55–89.

Hogan, R., Carpenter, B. N., Briggs, S. R. and Hansson, R. O. (1985) Personality assessment and personnel selection. In H. J. Bernardin and D. A. Bownas (eds) *Personality Assessment in Organizations*. New York: Praeger, 21–51.

Hough, L. M. (1987) Overcoming objections to use of temperament variables in selection: Demonstrating their usefulness. Paper presented at the American Psychological Association Convention, New York.

House, R. J. and Singh, J. V. (1987) Organizational Behavior. *Annual Review of Psychology*, **38**.

Huber, V. L. and Neale, M. A. (1986) Effects of cognitive heuristics and goals on negotiator performance and subsequent goal setting. *Organizational Behavior and Human Decision Processes*, **38**, 342–365.

Hunter, J. E. and Hunter, R. F. (1984) Validity and utility of alternative predictors of job performance. *Psychological Bulletin*, **96**, 72–98.

Kabanoff, B. (1987) Predictive validity of the MODE conflict instrument. *Journal of Applied Psychology*, **72**, 160–163.

Kane, J. S. and Lawler, E. E. (1979) Performance appraisal effectiveness: Its assessment and determinants. In B. M. Staw (Ed.) *Research n Organizational Behavior*, Vol. 1. Greenwich, CT: JAI Press.

Katz, R. (1980) Time and work: Toward an integrative perspective. In B. M. Staw and L. L. Cummings (eds) *Research in Organizational Behavior*, Vol. 2. Greenwich, CT: JAI Press.

Kinicki, A. J. (1985) Personal consequences of plant closings: A model and preliminary test. *Human Relations*, **38**, 197–212.

Knight, P. A. and Nadel, J. I. (1986) Humility revisited: Self-esteem, information search, and policy consistency. *Organizational Behavior and Human Decision Progress*, **38**, 196–206.

Kohn, M. L. and Schooler, C. (1982) Job conditions and personality: A longitudinal assessment of their reciprocal effects. *American Journal of Sociology*, **87**, 1257–1286.

Korman, A. K. (1968) The prediction of managerial performance: A review. *Personnel Psychology*, **21**, 295–322.

Korman, A. K. (1970) Toward a hypothesis of work behavior. *Journal of Applied Psychology*, **54**, 31–41.

Locke, E. A., Shaw, K. N., Saari, L. M. and Latham, G. P. (1981) Goal setting and task performance: 1969–1980. *Psychological Bulletin*, **90**, 125–152.

Locke, E. A., Latham, G. P. and Erez, M. (1986) The determinants of goal commitment. Unpublished manuscript.

Loher, B. T., Noe, R. A., Moeller, N. L. and Fitzgerald, M. P. (1985) A meta-analysis of the relation of the job characteristics to job satisfaction. *Journal of Applied Psychology*, **70**, 280–289.

Lord, R. G., DeVader, C. L. and Alliger, G. M. (1986) A meta-analysis of the relationship between personality traits and leadership perceptions: An application of validity generalization procedures. *Journal of Applied Psychology*, **71**, 402–410.

Magnusson, D. and Endler, N. S. (1977) Interactional psychology: Present status and future prospects. In D. Magnusson and N. S. Endler (eds) *Personality at the Crossroads: Current Issues in Interactional Psychology*. Hillsdale, N.J.: Lawrence Erlbaum.

Manderlink, G. and Harackiewicz, J. (1984) Proximal versus distal goal setting and intrinsic motivation. *Journal of Personality and Social Psychology*, **47**, 918–928.

McClelland, D. C. (1985b) How motives, skills and values determine what people do. *American Psychologist*, **40**, 812–825.

McClelland, D. C. (1985a) *Human Motivation*. Glenview, Ill.: Scott Foresman.

McCrae, R. R. and Costa, P. T. (1984) *Emerging Lives, Enduring Dispositions: Personality in Adulthood*. Boston: Little, Brown.

McGrath, J. E. and Kelly, J. R. (1986) *Time and Human Interaction*. New York: Guilford.

McRae, R. R. and Costa, P. J. (1986) Openness to experience. *Perspectives in Personality*, **1**, 145–172.

Miller, D. and Droge, C. (1986) Psychological and traditional determinants of structure. *Administrative Science Quarterly*, **31**, 539–560.

Miner, J. B. (1985) Sentence completion measures in personnel research: The development and validation of the Miner Sentence Completion Scales. In H. J. Bernardin and D. A. Bownas (eds) *Personality Assessment in Organizations*. New York: Praeger, 145–176.

Mischel, W. (1968) *Personality and Assessment*. New York: John Wiley.

Mischel, W. (1977) The interaction of person and situation. In D. Magnussen and N. S. Endler (eds) *Personality at the Crossroads: Current Issues in Interactional Psychology*. Hillsdale, N.J.: Lawrence Erlbaum.

Mitchell, T. R. and Larson, J. R. (1987) *People in Organizations: Third Edition*. New York: McGraw-Hill.

Montag, I. and Comrey, A. L. (1987) Internality and externality as correlates of involvement in fatal driving accidents. *Journal of Applied Psychology*, 72, 339–343.

Mossholder, K. W. (1980) Effects of externally mediated goal setting on intrinsic motivation: A laboratory experiment. *Journal of Applied Psychology*, 65, 202–210.

Nygard, R. (1981) Toward interaction psychology: Models from achievement research. *Journal of Personality*, 49, 363–387.

Rosenberg, M. (1965) *Society and the Adolescent Self-image*. Princeton, N.J.: Princeton University Press.

Sackett, P. and Harris, M. (1984) Honesty testing for personnel selection: A review and critique. *Personnel Psychology*, 37, 222–246.

Sarason, I. G., Smith, R. E. and Diener, E. (1975) Personality research: Components of variance attributed to the person and the situation. *Journal of Personality and Social Psychology*, 32, 199–204.

Schmidt, F. R. and Kaplan, L. B. (1971) Composite versus multiple criteria: A review and resolution of the controversy. *Personnel Psychology*, 24, 419–434.

Schneider, B. (1983) Interactional psychology and organizational behavior. In L. L. Cummings and B. M. Staw (eds) *Research in Organizational Behavior*. Vol. 5. Greenwich, CT: JAI Press, 1–31.

Schneier, C. E. (1977) The operational utility and psychometric characteristics of behavioral expectation scales: A cognitive reinterpretation. *Journal of Applied Psychology*, 62, 541–548.

Seligman, M. E. P. and Schulman, P. (1986) Explanatory style as a predictor of productivity and quitting among life insurance sales agents. *Journal of Personality and Social Psychology*, 50, 832–838.

Snyder, M. and Ickes, W. (1985) Personality and social behavior. In G. Lindzey and E. Aronson (eds) *Handbook of Social Psychology*, 3rd edition, New York: Random House, 883–948.

Sparks C. P. (1983) Paper and pencil measures of potential. In G. F. Dreher and P. R. Sackett (eds) *Perspectives on Employee Staffing and Selection*. Homewood, Ill.: Irwin.

Spector, P. E. (1982) Behavior in organizations as a function of an employee's locus of control. *Psychological Bulletin*, 91, 482–497.

Staw, B. M., Bell, N. E. and Clausen, J. A. (1986) The dispositional approach to job attitudes: A lifetime longitudinal test. *Administrative Science Quarterly*, 31, 56–77.

Stahl, M. J. (1983) Achievement, power and managerial motivation: selecting managerial talent with the job choice exercise. *Personnel Psychology*, 36, 775–789.

Staw, B. M. and Ross, J. (1985) Stability in the midst of change: a dispositional approach to job attitudes. *Journal of Applied Psychology*, 70, 469–480.

Tiggerman, M. and Winefield, A. H. (1984) The effects of unemployment on the mood, self-esteem, locus of control, and depressive affect of school leavers. *Journal of Occupational Psychology*, 57, 33–42.

Trice, H. M. and Beyer, J. M. (1986) Charisma and its routinization in two social movement organizations. In B. M. Staw and L. L. Cummings (eds) *Research in Organizational Behavior*. Vol. 8. Greenwich, CT: JAI Press.

Vale, C. D., Keller, L. S. and Bentz, V. J. (1986) Development and validation of a computerized interpretation system for personnel tests. *Personnel Psychology*, **39**, 525–542.

Vroom, V. H. and Yetton, P. W. (1973) *Leadership and Decision-Making*. Pittsburgh: University of Pittsburgh Press.

Weiss, H. M. and Adler, S. (1984) Personality and organizational behavior. In B. M. Staw and L. L. Cummings (eds) *Research in Organizational Behavior*, Vol. 6. Greenwich, CT: JAI Press, 1–50.

Weiss, H. M. and Knight, P. A. (1980) The utility of humility: self-esteem, information search and problem solving efficiency. *Organizational Behavior and Human Performance*, **25**, 216–223.

Weitz, J. (1966) Criteria and transfer of training. *Psychological Reports*, **19**, 195–210.

Weitz, J. (1961) Criteria for criteria. *American Psychologist*, **16**, 228–231.

Wolfle, L. M. and Robertshaw, D. (1982) Effects of college attendance on locus of control. *Journal of Personality and Social Psychology*, **43**, 802–810.

Wood, R. E., Mento, A. J. and Locke, E. A. (1987) Task complexity as a moderator of goal effects: a meta-analysis. *Journal of Applied Psychology*, **72**, 416–425.

Wood, R. (1986) Task complexity: definition of the construct. *Organizational Behavior and Human Decision Process*, **38**, 60–82.

Yates, B. T. and Mischel, W. (1979) Young children's preferred attentional strategies for delaying gratification. *Journal of Personality and Social Psychology*, **37**, 286–300.

INDEX

ETS (Educational Testing Service), 218
Exercise programs, 287–8, 293–5
Expatriate careers
  assessing managers for, 193–4
  success factors in, 263

Fair employment practices, 63
Fiedler's Contingency Model, 54, 316, 321
Fitness programs, 287–8, 291
FJA (Functional Job Analysis), 219
Fluid intelligence, 77
Focused sampling
  and theory building, 115–16

GATB (General Aptitude Test Battery), 219–20
General systems philosophy
  and training, 45–50
Generalizability theory, 221–2
Goal-setting behaviour
  and personality, 311, 317
GRIP (Graphic Information Processing Tests), 223

HCU (hard-core unemployed)
  training for, 60, 65
Health promotion, 279–301
  definition and history of, 280–1
  organizational issues of, 290–6
  program components, 282–90
  reasons for, 281–2
  and research needs, 296–300
  unintended consequences of, 295–6, 300
Hogan Personality Inventory, 314
Holland congruence model, 253, 255, 258, 265–6
Honesty testing, 310
Hypertension screening and control, 284–5
  and absenteeism, 295
  costs of, 290, 294

Identity, personal
  and group relations, 6–8
Identity, racial and ethnic
  rejection of, 9–10
Identity groups, 13–14
Identity types, in Marcia
  and career choice, 252–3, 257

Incentives, use of
  in health promotion programs, 299–300
Individuals
  in racial and ethnic studies, 2–13
Induction
  and theory building, 113–25
Industrial Betterment Movement, 280
Insider knowledge
  in racial and ethnic studies, 24–5
Instrumental personality constructs, 313
Integration of vocational concept, 257
Integration versus differentiation
  in racial and ethnic studies, 25–6
Intelligence
  and ability, 218
  and career choice, 255
  and leadership, 76–7, 78, 87
    theory building in, 104
  see also Cognitive ability testing
Interactionism
  and personality research, 323–4
Interest inventories and tests
  and managerial selection, 175–6
Interests
  and career choice, 253–4, 265–6
International (cross-cultural) training, 61–3
Interviews
  candidates' reactions to, 194–5
  and managerial selection, 177–9
  in racial and ethnic studies, 21–3
  situational, 187–8, 189
  and theory building, 116, 124
Intrapreneurialism
  assessing managers for, 191
IRT (Item Response Theory), 220–2
Italian-Americans
  racial and ethnic studies of, 12–13, 15

Jenkins Activity Survey, 318
Job analysis, 49
  and assessment centres, 182, 185
  and career management, 268
  and management selection, 163–4, 189
  methods, 46–7
Job attitudes
  and personality, 312
Job characteristics model, 310

Transactional theories of leadership, 73–4
Transformational leadership
and personality, 311
theories of, 78–82, 87–8
Transitory career concept, 247, 249, 250
and career anchors, 251
and career indecision, 259

United States
assessment centres in, 182
and fair employment practices, 63
health care programs, 281–2
presidents
as leaders, 75, 79, 79–80
racial and ethnic studies in, 10–13, 26–35
testing for licensing and certification, 233–4

Validity generalization
and ability measurement, 216–24
VCM tests, 228

Verbal-work samples, 229
Vertical Dyad Theory, 73, 80
Vocational maturity, 255–6

Weight control programs, 286–7
Witkin's field independence model, 256
Women
black, 32, 173, 183
and careers, 251, 253, 259, 261, 262
as entrepreneurs, 191
in management, 65, 66
and management selection, 173, 183
interviews, 177–8
self-esteem, and employment, 324
and training programs, 44, 65, 66
working mothers, 248–9, 261
Wonderlic Personnel Test, 224
Work
and non-work, 246, 248–9
and socialization, 260–1
Work values, 250–1
Work-sample testing, 229–30
and managerial selection, 180–1, 197, 198

*International Review of Industrial
and Organizational Psychology
1986*

CONTENTS

International Review of Industrial
and Organizational Psychology
1987

CONTENTS